Biblical Philosophy

In *Biblical Philosophy*, Dru Johnson examines how the texts of Christian Scripture argue philosophically with ancient and modern readers alike. He demonstrates how biblical literature bears the distinct markers of a philosophical style in its use of literary and philosophical strategies to reason about the nature of reality and our place within it. Johnson questions traditional definitions of philosophy and compares the Hebraic style of philosophy with the intellectual projects of ancient Egypt, Mesopotamia, and Hellenism. Identifying the genetic features of the Hebraic philosophical style, Johnson traces its development from its hybridization in Hellenistic Judaism to its retrieval by the New Testament authors. He also shows how the Gospels and letters of Paul exhibit the same genetic markers, modes of argument, particular argument forms, and philosophical convictions that define the Hebraic style, while they engaged with Hellenistic rhetoric. His volume offers a model for thinking about philosophical styles in comparative philosophical discussions.

Dru Johnson directs the Center for Hebraic Thought and is an associate professor of biblical studies at The King's College, New York City. He has authored five books on the intellectual world of the Bible, including *Epistemology and Biblical Theology* (2018), *Knowledge by Ritual* (2016), and *Biblical Knowing* (2013).

Biblical Philosophy

A Hebraic Approach to the Old and New Testaments

DRU JOHNSON
The King's College, New York City

CAMBRIDGE
UNIVERSITY PRESS

University Printing House, Cambridge CB2 8BS, United Kingdom

One Liberty Plaza, 20th Floor, New York, NY 10006, USA

477 Williamstown Road, Port Melbourne, VIC 3207, Australia

314–321, 3rd Floor, Plot 3, Splendor Forum, Jasola District Centre, New Delhi – 110025, India

79 Anson Road, #06–04/06, Singapore 079906

Cambridge University Press is part of the University of Cambridge.

It furthers the University's mission by disseminating knowledge in the pursuit of education, learning, and research at the highest international levels of excellence.

www.cambridge.org
Information on this title: www.cambridge.org/9781108831307

DOI: 10.1017/9781108924030

First published 2021

A catalogue record for this publication is available from the British Library.

Library of Congress Cataloging-in-Publication Data
NAMES: Johnson, Dru, author.
TITLE: Biblical philosophy : a Hebraic approach to the Old and New Testaments / Dru Johnson, King's College, New York City.
DESCRIPTION: Cambridge, United Kingdom ; New York : Cambridge University Press, 2021. | Includes bibliographical references and index.
IDENTIFIERS: LCCN 2020041953 (print) | LCCN 2020041954 (ebook) | ISBN 9781108831307 (hardback) | ISBN 9781108932691 (paperback) | ISBN 9781108924030 (epub)
SUBJECTS: LCSH: Bible–Criticism, interpretation, etc. | Jewish philosophy.
CLASSIFICATION: LCC BS511.3 .J637 2021 (print) | LCC BS511.3 (ebook) | DDC 220.6–dc23
LC record available at https://lccn.loc.gov/2020041953
LC ebook record available at https://lccn.loc.gov/2020041954

ISBN 978-1-108-83130-7 Hardback
ISBN 978-1-108-93269-1 Paperback

ליורם חזוני

(To Yoram Hazony)

Contents

Figures

Tables

Acknowledgments

For both his comradery over the last decade and his insistence that I write this book, my gratitude for Yoram Hazony pervades me like gravity. Alongside Yoram comes Joshua Weinstein and all the good folks who have participated in the Herzl "Philosophical Investigations of the Hebrew Scriptures, Mishnah, and Talmud" conferences over the last decade. Jaco Gericke has also been a constant companion in this quest and I am profoundly grateful for both his scholarship and friendship.

I wrote this book mostly while on research leave at the Logos Institute for Analytical and Exegetical Theology (University of St. Andrews, 2017–18). That community vibrated ideally with critiques and encouragements for this project. I was especially helped by conversations with Alan Torrance, Andrew Torrance, Tom "N. T." Wright, T. J. Lang, Madavi Nevader, Bill Tooman, Joshua Cockayne, and the postgraduate gang: Kimberley Kroll, Christa L. McKirland, Stephanie Nordby, Jeremy Rios, Jonathan Rutledge, Taylor Telford, Koert Verhagen, and the rest. As well, I thank the Evangelical Philosophical Society / American Academy of Religion (Joseph Gorra) panel members and Henry Center Symposium respondents on my paper "A Biblical Nota Bene on Philosophical Inquiry": Oliver Crisp, Kevin Vanhoozer, Joshua Blander, and J. T. Turner, along with the editors Geoffrey Fulkerson and Joel Chopp.

Michael Rhodes bravely trudged through every last page and commented on earlier drafts. Robbie Griggs, Jonathan Pennington, and Ben White helped me to formulate a clearer NT picture of Hebraic philosophy. Many thanks to those who read or commented on the drafts and ideas that fomented into this book: Billy Abraham, Harry Bleattler, Jim

Diamond, James Duguid, Jim Hoffmeier, Samuel Lebens, and Jeremiah Unterman. The Cambridge University Press reviewers were especially encouraging and helpful in their critiques and Beatrice Rehl was an ideal editor in the process.

I would like to offer my most measured thanks to Robert Nicholson for his principled support and cheerleading of this project. Also Abby Smith, the first administrative director of the Center for Hebraic Thought (CHT), was a constant interlocutor while reforming many of these ideas. I am deeply thankful for all of my students, but especially for those who suffered through the spring 2019 seminar on Hebraic Philosophy at The King's College along with Josh Blander who helped shape those discussions. Heather Ohaneson earned crowns for her gracious help in workshopping the opening chapters with me in this book's earliest form. Matt Lynch has been a steady and helpful discussion partner. Drew Hepler's keen eye helped to clean up rough drafts. Micah Long tackled my onerous footnotes and bibliography. Celina Durgin, the second administrative director of the CHT, was magisterial in editing later drafts to make them consistent and coherent. If the reader enjoys anything in this work, it is most likely her fault.

Additionally, the "Second Order Thinking in the Ancient Fertile Crescent" workshop organized by Jan Dietrich, Jaco Gericke, and Marc Van De Mieroop added rich context to the landscape of ancient intellectualism. The "Wrestling with Life: Analytic Theology and Biblical Narratives" workshop organized by Godehard Brüntrup, Moshe Halbertal, David Shatz, and Eleonore Stump helped me to translate some of these ideas for philosophers (though I surely haven't done enough on that front).

Finally, Stephanie, Benjamin, Claudia, Olivia, and Luisa Johnson have all conspired to help in this project, encouraging and supporting me with the whole of their lives. Moving between continents solely for my research pursuits creates no small burden on a family and ours grew in love and admiration of each other. Oh, how much I have learned from my son and daughters, how much more so the wisdom that has poured like a river from my wife to me!

A Case for Retrieving Hebraic Philosophy

The biblical tradition is an intellectual tradition. That is the bold thesis of this book. Seeking to understand the biblical texts is its own enterprise. But that is not the task here. The texts and the communities that practiced their directives handed down an intellectually rigorous tradition uniquely capable of shaping an entire people into a shrewd and discerning lot. And so, it was passed down as texts, rituals, and community – philosophy as a way of being a people.[1]

Scholars of the ancient Near East have generally held this truism close to their collective vests for two generations or more: the Hebrew Bible/ Old Testament contains its own distinct philosophical style in league with the philosophies of Greece and Rome. More recently, a cadre of scholars have become convinced of the intellectual prowess of Hebrew Scriptures, hosting conferences and publishing a growing core of books. But for some reason of academic sociology, many biblical scholars never knew that the ancient Near East scholars felt this way. Hence, it would not be a surprise if many of them would deem the above statement about the biblical texts to be an overreach.

Just the idea of a Hebraic philosophical style simultaneously breaks several widely trusted paradigms about:

1. what counts as philosophy
2. the nature and purpose of the biblical literature
3. how societies have argued for abstract notions of reality

[1] Like many before me, I realize that people generally skip anything titled "Introduction." This chapter is, in fact, the introduction, and thus, has been named otherwise.

I will illustrate and argue in the coming pages that all three of these paradigms have suffered from a lack of contact with wider philosophical history. One of those paradigms – what counts as philosophy – broke, for me, while reading Greek philosophy.

Studying philosophy proper, students are required to read a story about a crotchety old man who wandered the streets of an ancient city disturbing the peace of its most noble residents. His target was one's degree of certainty, and at the false peace of men's souls the old man aimed. Goading them with questions, he teased out their intellectual securities and dizzied them. Like birds to a snare or an ox to the slaughter, their sense of justice, knowledge, and other sundry ideals dissembled at the old man's relentless prodding. Proffering no scheme in its place, he often left them confused and now knowing only that they no longer know.

After reading a few of these stories about this old man – the troubler of Athens – students begin to realize that the author was not merely relaying a story about a troublesome sage. The serpentine dialogues ambled down paths too complex to hold in their heads. As they follow these tales, trusting those who recommended them as "classic philosophical literature," they will eventually come to realize that the author was *not merely* telling them a story about a crotchety old man. The anonymous author was reaching through these narratives to argue with them!

He was using the old man, in stories spanning a diverse corpus, to prod their assumptions about what they think they know. *He was attempting to reason with them*, to get them to give up what they thought they knew in favor of a different method for knowing. Plato was doing philosophy through Socrates with them – reasoning with them about the nature of reality, justice, knowledge, ethics, politics, and more.

As they begin to read other literature, they will realize that not all ancient texts are up to this task. Not all stories are attempting to reason with an audience in this way. There was something about the systematicity, the rigor, the confidence in an undergirding matrix of understanding that enabled this sort of storytelling to work as a form of philosophizing.

Surveying other more ancient literature from Mesopotamia, Egypt, and Israel, we might also conclude that the Hebrew Bible stands out as another such example of philosophical literature. At some point, the systematicity and prescriptive guidance of the biblical texts seems less like mere storytelling and more like reasoning with us about the nature of reality, justice, knowledge, politics, and ethics – at the least.

Upon further investigation, we would find that we would not be the only ones to notice. As far back as the 1940s, ancient Near Eastern scholars were noting the unique intellectual world cast in the biblical literature. Presumably, that same realization is what led the ancient Near Eastern scholar Henri Frankfort to claim, "[the people of Israel were] without peer in the power and scope of their critical intellectualism."[2] For him, the Hebrew Scriptures were not merely telling stories, but were also intellectually engaging readers through story, poetry, law, and more.

Remarkably, the intellectual world of the Hebrew Bible has been rather obvious to ancient Near Eastern scholars, yet this perspective has not been generally appropriated by all biblical scholars. It has been one of the better-kept secrets of ancient Near Eastern scholarship.

Until recently, discussions of the "critical intellectualism" of the Hebrew Bible have been scarce and isolated (though that is changing).[3] If they have even heard of such a proposition, the notion of biblical philosophy amongst both philosophers and biblical scholars elicits cautious optimism at best, and specious rejection at worst. Jaco Gericke was not exaggerating when he claims, "Those familiar with the stories of 20th century biblical theologies ... will know that many leading OT theologians claim to hate philosophical principles and abstractions."[4]

[2] Henri Frankfort et al., *The Intellectual Adventure of Ancient Man: An Essay on Speculative Thought in the Ancient Near East* (Chicago: University of Chicago Press, 1946), 234. Although there has been a revision of the field recently and some critique of this original work, that critique has focused largely on the school of religion and progressivist assumptions of the authors. I have seen little to no critique of their evaluative claims I am invoking here. For such a critique, see Francesca Rochberg's summary of Frankfort et al.'s progressivism and evolutionism, "A Critique of the Cognitive-Historical Thesis of the Intellectual Adventure," in *The Adventure of the Human Intellect: Self, Society, and the Divine in Ancient World Cultures*, ed. Kurt A. Raaflaub (Ancient World: Comparative Histories; Hoboken, NJ: Wiley-Blackwell, 2016), 16–28.

[3] E.g., Yoram Hazony, *The Philosophy of Hebrew Scripture* (New York: Cambridge University Press, 2012); Jaco Gericke, *The Hebrew Bible and Philosophy of Religion* (Society of Biblical Literature Resources for Biblical Study 70; Atlanta: Society of Biblical Literature Press, 2013); Arthur Gibson, *Biblical Semantic Logic: A Preliminary Analysis* (Oxford: Basil Blackwell, 1981); Joshua A. Berman, *Created Equal: How the Bible Broke with Ancient Political Thought* (New York: Oxford University Press, 2011); Jeremiah Unterman, *Justice for All: How the Jewish Bible Revolutionized Ethics* (Philadelphia: Jewish Publication Society, 2017).

[4] Jaco Gericke, *A Philosophical Theology of the Old Testament: A Historical, Experimental, Comparative and Analytic Perspective* (Routledge Interdisciplinary Perspectives on Biblical Criticism; New York: Routledge, 2020), 29. Gericke has explored the many and complex reasons why biblical scholarship has hesitated in asserting a philosophical world within Scripture in his commendable and witty volume, especially chs. 1–2.

We must ask: Why is a wing of scholarship literate in the ancient Near Eastern libraries and familiar with the Greco-Roman literature so out of joint with some biblical scholars and philosophers/theologians on the question of philosophy in Hebrew Scripture? I will explore that divergence more closely in the chapter "What Counts as Philosophy?" Beyond the Hebrew Bible, how do the texts of Hellenistic Judaism, especially the New Testament (NT), compare on this front? It is enough for now to notice that an intriguing disparity exists and that one's predisposition toward the biblical texts, not necessarily the content of the texts, funds it.

Aims

This book is not an attempt to pronounce *the* only philosophy of Christian Scripture. Rather, I suggest that the biblical literature might represent an entire, distinct, and coherent philosophical style.[5] And this Hebraic style has often gone unnoticed by modern comparative philosophers and my fellow religionists for reasons that I could only suppose and sociologists might be able to enumerate.

I will argue why the Hebrew Bible and New Testament betray a philosophical impulse akin to that found in Hellenism, but not in Egypt or Mesopotamia, carried out with a discrete philosophical method for its own goals. In the coming chapters, I will survey the speculative worlds of Israel's neighbors, Mesopotamia and Egypt, which will clarify why scholars of the ancient Near East have generally thought of Israel as more of a philosophical peer to Greece and *not* the Near East.

I intend to show how Hellenism's influence on Judaism might have bent this Hebraic philosophical style to the point of breaking, had not the New Testament authors recovered it in a robust *ad fontes* retrieval movement. In the end, Paul – yes, even Paul – might be leaning into his Hebraic philosophical heritage while merely dressed in the loose-fitting garb of Roman rhetoric and Hellenistic philosophy. Finally, I will give examples of how various philosophical topics might be broached, developed, and advocated within and across the many genres of biblical literature.

5 By "biblical literature," I am referring to the Hebrew Bible/Old Testament and New Testament as usually construed, though this will also include parts of the Apocrypha in the sweep of the thesis. All biblical quotations herein will be the author's adaption from the NRSV or quotes from the Masoretic Text of the *Biblia Hebraica Stuttengartensia* and the Nestle-Aland *Novum Testamentum Graece*, 27th ed.

Many biblical authors seemed to write as if there is a complex and invisible second-order *something* to be reasoned out. By second-order something, I mean the nature of something as such and apart from any particular historical instance of it – justice apart from any particular trial, knowing apart from any discrete experiment, etc. This central feature of systemic abstraction locates biblical discourse in the realm of philosophy. The biblical authors believe in second-order *somethings*, where the embodied and historical entailments need to be understood in relation to the abstraction. The philosophical approach they advocate spans various pieces of literature and genres and might have more purchase on human understanding than a linear-deductive approach aimed at mere mental reasoning.

If a philosophical style exists in the biblical texts themselves, then my task is to trace the genetic markers of that style and define what is distinguishable about it. I will eventually argue that a Hebraic philosophical style and supporting convictions distinguish this philosophy from Israel's neighboring speculative worlds of Egypt, Mesopotamia, Greece, and Rome, neighbors from which Israel could have easily borrowed.

My method for discerning a philosophical style will be laid out in full in Chapter 3. In brief, I will be asking of the biblical texts three questions:

1. Is there a matter of second-order understanding presently, persistently, and relevantly pursued in the text?
2. Is a method of reasoning about that second-order issue advocated by the text itself?
3. What style of philosophy is employed?

I am making an admittedly "big claim" in this book. None is more aware than I of the largess of this claim. But I am not spelling out the philosophy of Scripture. Rather, I hope to fire up the scholarly imagination, to build a satisfactory heuristic for discerning something called "Hebraic philosophy," which colleagues can then begin to test and try out for fit.

In some ways, I want to tap into the energy of a parallel movement in the literary style of Hebrew Scripture. Robert Alter, Meir Sternberg, and others have made a case that the literary savvy of the Hebraic style of poetics and narrative has been overlooked. They claim that our contemporary stylistic preferences have run interference. Our proper literary style today cannot tolerate the incessant repetition of vocabulary and parataxis (e.g., repetitive "and" conjunctions) that the Hebrew style relished.

And so, we translate away these stylistic choices valued by the biblical authors in what Alter calls our "rage to explain."[6]

Alter and others appreciate the native Hebraic style of narration and poetry, a style comfortable with shaping and reshaping a notion by repeatedly using a particular verb over differing situations. But the authors' desired literary effect can vanish in translations that shake up the repetitious use of verbs, for example, with English synonyms. Alter hoped to show the literary savvy of the Hebrew authors to a world of readers often numb to such literary devices.

Similarly, I hope to cultivate an appreciation of the philosophical savvy of the biblical authors, using techniques that might seem initially foreign to those of us ensconced in the footnotes of philosophy ensuing Plato.[7] The Hebraic philosophical style, like the Hebraic literary style, cuts across aspects of human thinking and action that heirs of European philosophies have not usually considered "philosophical." Hebraic philosophical style is, after all, an Asian philosophical tradition. Despite its antiquity and estrangement, I will illustrate why this philosophical style closely resembles our scientific enterprise, maybe even more than the intellectual world of Hellenism does.

Age of Methodology

Many scholars have tried to outline the thought-world within ancient texts. In biblical studies, the domain of intellectualism has typically consisted of the so-called wisdom literature.[8] Whybray's *The Intellectual Tradition in the Old Testament* is one shrewd example, categorizing and synthesizing the wide array of intellectual language across the traditional genre of wisdom literature.[9] But merely analyzing the linguistic stock does not guarantee an apt inroad into the biblical thought world.

[6] Robert Alter, *The Art of Bible Translation* (Princeton, NJ: Princeton University Press, 2018), 6.

[7] Alfred North Whitehead famously said, "The safest general characterization of the European philosophical tradition is that it consists of a series of footnotes to Plato." *Process and Reality* (New York: The Free Press, 1978), 39.

[8] I take Kynes's corrective to be accurate, that limiting "wisdom" to the wisdom literature becomes defeatist in light of the larger theological project of Israel. Will Kynes, *An Obituary for "Wisdom Literature": The Birth, Death, and Intertextual Reintegration of a Biblical Corpus* (New York: Oxford University Press, 2019).

[9] Roger N. Whybray, *The Intellectual Tradition in the Old Testament* (Beiheft zur Zeitschrift für die alttestamentliche Wissenschaft 135; Berlin: De Gruyter, 1974).

James Barr's renowned critique looms over this current project, as it should. Barr leveled his aim at those projects seeking to identify singular concepts behind words or word-roots across the canon – a goal he argued to be infeasible, and for good reason.[10] This volume hopes to avoid the word-root trap about which Barr is concerned.[11] But I will also push beyond Barr's limits to include the human and social body in reason.

Why this examination of a Hebraic philosophy now? Aside from Yoram Hazony's book – *Philosophy of the Hebrew Scripture* – which I discuss later, scholarship appears to be an age of methodology on this front, ready to "have the discussion." Several works come to mind that challenge our assumed meanings from the thought-world of the biblical authors but do so by carefully setting current theological assumptions aside, as best they can, and looking afresh at the biblical texts.

David Lambert's *How Repentance Became Biblical* argues that contrition has been overread into the words associated with repentance (e.g., *šûb*, *strephō*, *metanoeō*).[12] This importation of contrition distorts our understanding of behaviors such as the ritualization of fasting for seeking God's mercy. Thus, the "turning," the goal of "fasting," and the physicality of "return" in the conceptual ether of the Hebrew Bible, Hellenistic Jewish texts, and the New Testament can all be lost on us.

Matthew Bates argues similarly regarding the epistemic term "faith" (*pistis*) in the New Testament.[13] For Bates, the connotation of political

[10] Barr tackles the debate between Thomas F. Torrance and Arthur G. Hebert on their claim that there is a "fundamental meaning" of a Hebrew word root (e.g., אמן), for instance. The problem for Barr is that they both neglect word formation. This is symptomatic of the myopia concentrated on what he later terms the "lexical stock" of Scripture. Focusing on individual terms and their meaning leads to a theologizing from this "lexical stock" scattered across the canon. But how can one guarantee that they are discerning a pattern inherent to the biblical literature itself? James Barr, *The Semantics of Biblical Language* (Eugene, OR: Wipf & Stock, 1961), 161–287. See also: Arthur G. Hebert, "'Faithfulness' and 'Faith,'" *Reformed Theological Review* 14, no. 2 (June 1955): 33–40; Thomas F. Torrance, "One Aspect of the Biblical Conception of Faith," *Expository Times* 68, no. 4 (1957): 111–14.

[11] David Lambert has suggested that scholars should retrieve much of Barr's philological suggestions and cited my work on epistemology in *Biblical Knowing* as example of someone who "represents an advance forward." That gave me no small amount of unearned confidence. David A. Lambert, "Refreshing Philology: James Barr, Supersessionism, and the State of Biblical Words," *Biblical Interpretation* 24, no. 3 (2016): 332–56.

[12] David A. Lambert, *How Repentance Became Biblical: Judaism, Christianity, and the Interpretation of Scripture* (New York: Oxford University Press, 2016).

[13] Matthew W. Bates, *Salvation by Allegiance Alone: Rethinking Faith, Works, and the Gospel of Jesus the King* (Grand Rapids, MI: Baker Academic, 2017).

fealty has been overlooked by the broad-brush translation of *pistis* into "faith" – a word that in modern English has sometimes assumed the exact opposite meaning of its Greek original. "Allegiance" might be a more apt translation for many, but not all, instances of *pistis*. That single interpretive move entails a reorientation toward the role of fiduciary and political commitment across the New Testament.

Additionally, a recent spate of scholars has made compelling cases for the unique contributions of political and ethical philosophy from the Hebrew Bible to Western thought. Joshua Berman's *Created Equal* and Jeremiah Unterman's *Justice for All* both demonstrate remarkably the Hebrew Bible's discrete philosophical shifts away from ancient Near Eastern thought (and Greek thought) to impact much of Western history: the labor-rest cycles, human equality, consent of the people, care for the marginalized, immigration rights, and more.[14]

In *The Hebrew Bible and Philosophy of Religion*, Jaco Gericke offers the first rigorous attempt to examine, categorize, and catalog the various kinds of philosophical content across the Hebrew Bible.[15] Gericke takes an all-encompassing approach to what he calls the "folk philosophy" of Yahwism in the Hebrew Bible. By "folk philosophy," he only means to describe the philosophical assumptions behind the texts even if the texts do not offer a treatise on epistemology, logic, metaphysics, etc. He espouses a rigorous method to analyze how the biblical authors used concepts and language to build both logically fuzzy[16] and coherent philosophical ideas about metaphysics, ontology, epistemology, and ethics.

Gericke constructs a case for "philosophical criticism" as a new form of biblical criticism. Though Gericke openly affirms that the Hebrew Bible is not a "textbook in the philosophy of religion," he finds the anti-philosophical bent in much of biblical studies unhelpful.[17] He contends instead that ancient Hebrews did have some sort of folk metaphysics, folk epistemologies, etc., and, because they had beliefs about philosophical topics, they must be expressed in the Hebrew Bible. His methodology

[14] See Berman, *Created Equal*; Unterman, *Justice for All*.

[15] Gericke, *The Hebrew Bible and Philosophy of Religion*. This summary of Gericke's work is adapted from my review: Dru Johnson, review of *The Hebrew Bible and Philosophy of Religion* by Jaco Gericke, *Journal of Analytic Theology* 4 (2016): 428–33.

[16] Gericke cites Peter Hajek's use of the term "fuzzy logic" in Hajek, "Fuzzy Logic," *The Stanford Encyclopedia of Philosophy*, Summer 2010 ed., ed. Edward N. Zalta, http://plato.stanford.edu/archives/fall2010/entries/logic-fuzzy/.

[17] Gericke, *The Hebrew Bible and Philosophy of Religion*, 9.

then adopts a conceptual analysis that explores the texts through the tools of biblical criticism.

In arguing for philosophical criticism, Gericke must make the case that the Hebrew Bible is capable of making philosophical arguments. Just as Plato selected prose in Book 1 of *The Republic* to depict a philosophically principled city-state, so too can the Hebrew Bible use narrative to argue.[18] Hence, it is not a matter of whether narrative and poetry contain philosophy; rather, how do we grasp the philosophy of ancient Semites through their texts without merely importing all of our notions, folk or otherwise?

Gericke's new interpretive methodology aims to be both philosophical and historical, providing a hermeneutically legitimate way of involving the philosophy of religion in the reading of ancient texts without distorting their contents.[19] Because Gericke has the clarification of textual meaning as his focus, he does not need to make historical claims about the texts or religious prescriptions for the faithful.

The Hebrew Bible and Philosophy of Religion genuinely cracks the door open for biblical scholars in a significant way different from other such attempts. Gericke's more recent volume, *A Philosophical Theology of the Old Testament*, serves up a roaring survey of the Old Testament guild's reticence to analyze abstraction in the biblical literature. He shows how OT theologians can commit to specious forms of philosophical analysis while simultaneously devaluing the idea that Hebrews abstracted or philosophized.[20] And so Gericke's systematic, linguistic, and historically sensitive approach shows what it could look like to put modern analytic philosophy in conversation with the Hebrew Bible while letting the Hebrew Bible speak for itself, as it were.

Because of works like these and others, the time is right to think yet again about the Hebrew Bible as offering a philosophical tradition, among other things. But in this volume, I want to push even further to suggest that some Second Temple Jewish authors reappropriated this Hebraic philosophy in a Jewish literary world steeped in Hellenistic philosophical styles. If any of this rings true, even if it cannot be exhibited exceptionally well here, then the implications for theology, biblical studies, and comparative philosophy become pointedly manifest.

[18] Gericke, *The Hebrew Bible and Philosophy of Religion*, 176.

[19] Gericke, *The Hebrew Bible and Philosophy of Religion*, 199.

[20] Gericke, *A Philosophical Theology of the Old Testament*, 1–21.

Companionship and Divergence: Hazony's *The Philosophy of Hebrew Scripture*

Yoram Hazony's landmark book *The Philosophy of Hebrew Scripture* set off a wide-ranging discussion amongst philosophers and biblical/religious scholars about the philosophical nature of the biblical texts.[21] The assumption that the bible is a work of revelation alone has unhelpfully stifled the exploration of its philosophically robust content. As evidence, the study of philosophy in Hindu and Buddhist texts has exploded in the last two decades in the West. Yet, virtually no major work, outside of the odd monograph, tackles the biblical literature on its own philosophical terms.

Hazony's work was pivotal in starting the conversation from a Jewish perspective and correspondingly restricted to the Hebrew Bible. Reviewers often shared a common concern for Hazony's generalizing, admittedly a feature of all books making large and general claims. Even if those critiques were fair, I want to highlight methodologically what Hazony was doing in that book to reveal the need for it. Whether readers believe he delivered enough evidence to demonstrate the claims is a secondary issue for me.

Companionship

Despite differences in scope and structure, Hazony's work creates the context for this current book. By "going big" with his thesis, Hazony was able to give scholars from various disciplines onramps and offramps to the concept, but all promoted his basic thesis: that the Hebrew Bible has philosophical impulses that should no longer be ignored.

First, Hazony threw down the gauntlet against the naïve assumption that the Hebrew Bible is a work of revelation. The thinking goes like this: because philosophers tacitly regard biblical texts as divine oracles, we cannot, therefore, analyze them as a work of reason – as we would the Socratic dialogues or Aquinas' Summa, for example. Socrates and Aquinas reflected on the nature of the universe and human knowledge as such without claiming to be divine messengers.

[21] Two journal symposia were dedicated to responding to Yoram Hazony's work: *Journal of Analytic Theology* 2 (2014) and *Perspectives on Political Science* 45 (2016). Additionally, the book won an award in the category of theology/religion from the American Association of Publishers.

But Hazony points out both that the biblical authors did not always claim divine authorship and shows that the Greek philosophers admitted to a divine origin behind some of their thoughts. In the Hebrew Bible, Genesis through Kings include words reported to be from God, but the texts themselves are anonymously authored and contain clear signs of authorial savvy in the handling of abstract topics.

Hazony then goes on to show how the story of Cain and Abel, if not viewed merely as a divinely revealed fratricide of old, initiates a steady trope of political philosophy in the Hebrew Bible that persists up through the period of the kings.[22] In so many words, he intends to point out that the annexation of the Hebrew Bible from amongst ancient philosophical texts appears to practice disparate treatment at best and uncharitable ignorance at worst.

The details of Hazony's argument are less important here, and I might come to different conclusions than him at points. However, the method of seeing narratives as carefully constructed advocacy for how to think about the nature of political authority, for example, cannot be missed. And indeed, such philosophical narration has not been missed when it came to the Socratic dialogues: dialogue-narratives containing and advocating philosophical content. Hazony calls for parity.

To reiterate: At some point while reading a Socratic dialogue, we realize that Socrates' questions are not just the interrogations of an unusually curious old man. We realize that Socrates' use of story within the dialogue is never for mere entertainment. We read this literature knowing that the author expects the reader to pick up on what is going on. This is a narrative style, among other literary styles, of portraying and prescribing philosophy. And so it goes for the Hebrew Bible and the New Testament. This kind of agenda is explicitly flagged up near the end of John's Gospel: "Now Jesus did many other signs in the presence of his disciples, which are not written in this book. But these are written so that you may come to trust that Jesus is the Messiah" (John 20:30–31).

Second, I share Hazony's vehemence about maintaining the Scripture's philosophical language and constructs as primary for our thinking about philosophy. Although I want to translate philosophical concepts from Christian Scripture into the contemporary discussions, I do not presume that our current philosophical schemes or methods are sufficient or

[22] James A. Diamond's recent work also launches the human philosophical impulse as a moral duty from the Cain and Abel story. *Jewish Theology Unbound* (New York: Oxford University Press, 2018), 31–34.

superior. For example, I will argue in Chapter 9 that the biblical scheme for truth and its epistemic effects better describes the realities of knowing today and more aptly fits with modern scientific epistemology than the Platonic view or the so-called Standard View of knowing today.

Thus, I do not intend to presume a progressivist or evolutionist view of philosophy. For this account, then, we are not ape-philosophers becoming über-philosophers. While we can speak of development in thought – e.g., sophistication in logic or empirically driven neuro-philosophy – I do not tacitly accept the idea that we philosophize in a qualitatively superior way today compared to the ancients. I presume that second-order reasoning has been ever-present in human history, and certainly in human literary history. Any appearance of progressivism in this volume is therefore unintentional.

Divergence

When I first read Hazony's *The Philosophy of Hebrew Scripture*, I quickly saw the bounty of benefits, but also the deficits of his work from a Christian perspective. Though Hazony fired up a much-needed paradigm shift regarding Hebraic philosophy, I do not think that *The Philosophy of Hebrew Scripture* has sufficiently:

1. represented the philosophy of the Torah or New Testament with enough detail
2. presented the actual picture of philosophy in the New Testament texts apart from considering them as having radically divergent aims from the Hebrew Bible
3. proposed a clear and rigorous method that holds scholars accountable to the biblical texts

Admittedly, he and I will disagree on the fundamental nature of the New Testament texts, and my third point about a clear and rigorous method was never his aim.[23] These need not occupy any further discussion. But the nature of the Hebrew Bible's philosophical advocacy and its relationship to the New Testament authors requires clarification up front, as it defines the very reason for this book.

Hazony's depiction of the New Testament portrays it as juridical in nature, premised upon the witness of and theology flowing from a

[23] Hazony, *The Philosophy of Hebrew Scripture*, 265.

punctiliar event: Jesus' resurrection. He rightly notes that the language of "witnessing" strewn throughout the NT "relies on metaphors drawn from a court of law ... The juridic metaphor is central, indeed paradigmatic, to the self-presentation of the Christian texts."[24] He goes on to cite the revelation of mystery in this singular historical nonrepeating event called "the Incarnation" as more evidence of its report-like tone.

Hazony sees the eyewitness conviction of Peter and Paul, who name themselves and tell you that they saw these things with their own eyes, as sharply contrasted with the anonymous historical texts of the Hebrew Bible that theologically stylize the report of history.[25] Several things can be said in response to this.

First, the primary record of the Incarnation event is neither Paul nor Peter, but the anonymously authored Gospels, the stories to which Paul and Peter refer and to which they connect themselves. Hazony mistakenly cites the Epistle to the Hebrews as Pauline, which itself is an anonymously authored text to a Jewish audience.[26]

Second, by ignoring genre, any statement about the "purpose of" a text will inevitably falter. Hazony quotes epistles, which are personal letters written to particular groups of people in specific cities at a precise time. No matter what view of sources one takes on the historical narrative of the Hebrew Bible, they have no such audience in mind. Hence, the special pleading of witnessing such events has to do with the authority of the epistolary content and author, not the event referenced.

Beyond genre confusion, the timeframe of writing and cultures throughout the Mediterranean Basin will dictate the tone and mode as well. It is not my intent to go point for point here, but this general notion of equivalency in texts leads to erroneous assumptions about the New Testament texts, most of which were written by first-century Jews. I will further examine this "encyclopedist" approach to the texts in Chapter 6.

Third, Hazony fails to see that the Jewish authors of the NT texts saw themselves in radical continuity with the Hebrew Bible. Though they freely quote from the Septuagint (the Greek translation of the Hebrew Bible), those are merely the overt points of continuity. Specifically, the gospels:

1. broadly affirm the Torah
2. affirm the practice of the Torah in the land of Israel

[24] Hazony, *The Philosophy of Hebrew Scripture*, 51.

[25] Hazony, *The Philosophy of Hebrew Scripture*, 55.

[26] Hazony, *The Philosophy of Hebrew Scripture*, 55. Because I commented on drafts of the book and failed to note this, the error is as much mine as anyone else's.

3. require knowledge acquired by practicing Torah
4. ritualize the historic events of the Passion Week as the Torah did the exodus
5. reify tropes of Hebraic discourse found from the Torah to the prophets

Demonstration will follow in the coming chapters, but this to say that no New Testament scholar sensitive to the same literary analyses that Hazony prescribes for the Hebrew Bible fails to see these intensive and nuanced employments of Hebrew biblical concepts and texts throughout the NT.

Fourth, the Torah's witness to history itself centers upon a series of historically unique and punctiliar moments that are then ritualized for the sake of Israel's understanding. Creation, the flood, the exodus, and entry into Canaan all form the core of the Torah's history. The historical and communal memory of covenants and these unrepeatable events are then ritualized into the lives of Israel according to her calendar.

So too, the unrepeatable events of the New Testament are ritualized through baptism and communion by Jesus acting as the arch-prophet of Israel.[27] Both Communion and baptism represent ritualizations of first-century Jewish rituals stemming from the Torah's Levitical cleansings and Passover, at the least, but more likely from the entire ritual world of Israel.[28] Again, the content of the New Testament texts aims at continuity. I will demonstrate the details of this further in Chapters 5–7.

[27] Wright has convincingly demonstrated throughout Part II of *Jesus and the Victory of God*: "The best initial model for understanding this praxis is that of a prophet; more specifically, that of a prophet bearing an urgent eschatological and indeed apocalyptic, message for Israel." And, "All the evidence so far displayed suggests that he [Jesus] was perceived as a prophet." N. T. Wright, *Jesus and the Victory of God* (Christian Origins and the Question of God 2; Minneapolis: Fortress Press, 1996), 150, 196. Leonhard Goppelt had also made the same claim in *Typos: The Typological Interpretation of the Old Testament in the New*, trans. Donald H. Madvig (Grand Rapids, MI: Eerdmans, 1982), 61–77. "It is true that from the historian's point of view the working concept which guided Jesus in the task of his ministry was that of 'prophet'": David Hill, *New Testament Prophecy* (Marshalls Theological Library; London: Marshall, Morgan & Scott, 1979), 68. "On balance the Jesus of Mark's Gospel appears as one who in his teaching supersedes and transcends Scripture more than as one who makes the Scripture point to himself as its fulfillment," and, regarding Jesus' lack of Scripture citation, "This may well have contributed to the impression of authority which distinguished his preaching from that of the scribes": Hugh Anderson, "The Old Testament in Mark's Gospel," in *The Use of the Old Testament in the New and Other Essays: Studies in Honor of William Franklin Stinespring*, ed. James M. Efird (Durham, NC: Duke University Press, 1972), 304.

[28] Dru Johnson, *Knowledge by Ritual: A Biblical Prolegomenon to Sacramental Theology* (Winona Lake, IN: Eisenbrauns/Penn State University Press, 2016), 256–60.

Fifth, the matter of the afterlife in the New Testament seems out of joint with the Hebrew Bible according to Hazony. Many scholars have argued that, like the Hebrew Bible, the New Testament authors are not that interested in the afterlife.[29]

Reiterating the teaching of the Hebrew Bible, at death, humans go to *Sheol* (Hebrew: *šĕʾōl*; Greek: *hadēs*). After the resurrection, all are judged and either enter into the second death (metaphorized sometimes as *Gehenna* in the NT) or enter the new earth and heavens. One does not even need the New Testament texts to deduce these basic points of eschatology from the Hebrew Scriptures repeated by the NT authors.[30] Hazony appears to have later Christian apologists in mind on this matter (Clement, Origen, Augustine, etc.).

Sixth, and finally, Hazony thinks that the revelation of secrets and mystery does not fit with the history or prophets of the Hebrew Bible. But this mystery-talk in the NT derives uniquely from Deuteronomy, among other places. Regarding Hazony's concern, he slips away from the larger question of the revelation of mystery and secrets within the Torah.

The inaugural event in Israel's national history is Sinai, which creates a bold instance of the Hebraic notion of revelation: God revealing previously unknown things to Israel alone. Deuteronomy 29 returns to the problem at Sinai, which was posed as an epistemological mystery: You saw everything God did with your own eyes (juridical language), *yet you didn't see it* (Deut 29:2–3; 29:1–2 Hebrew Bible).

How could they have eyes and yet not see? The answer comes immediately: "To this day, Yahweh has not given you a heart to know, eyes to see, or ears to hear" (Deut 29:4). This section of Deuteronomy closes with an enigmatic saying, "Hidden things to Yahweh, revealed things to us and our children forever, that we may do all the things of this *torah*" (Deut 29:29 [28]).

In other words, the Sinai event was about who could know what and how. The "hidden things" – *krypta* in the LXX – revealed at Sinai are to be performed throughout the generations by Israel. The *how* is Yahweh's revealing act to them alone, not merely seeing it with one's own eyes – a

[29] E.g., Joel B. Green, *Body, Soul, and Human Life: The Nature of Humanity in the Bible* (Grand Rapids, MI: Baker, 2008); N. T. Wright, *The Resurrection of the Son of God* (Christian Origins and the Question of God 3; Minneapolis: Fortress Press, 2003).

[30] Jon D. Levenson has argued persuasively that resurrection is conceptually present early on in the Torah, rather than being a later development in Second Temple Judaism: *Resurrection and the Restoration of Israel: The Ultimate Victory of the God of Life* (New Haven, CT: Yale University Press, 2006).

theme that will be put to regular use in the prophets and in the Gospels. Indeed, the earliest gospel begins Jesus' instruction to the disciples by reemploying these exact words and concepts from Deuteronomy 29 combined with Isaiah's twist on the theme (cf. Isa 6:9–10; Mark 4:10–12).[31] The stated purpose is to reveal to the disciples the mysteries of the kingdom of God. Like the Torah, Jesus will also take his disciples up on a mountaintop where Jesus will be highlighted above Moses and Elijah (Matt 17:2; Mark 9:2–3; Luke 9:28–36). The New Testament authors take themselves to be describing a renewed covenant (Jer 31) and renewed Torah (Matt 5) with reritualized rituals, a practice found within the Hebrew Bible as well.[32]

To Hazony's contention, none of the anonymously authored gospels emphasize the role of disciples as eyewitnesses, but rather, they portray the event as formative for the people leading this new covenant kingdom of God. By using the language of mystery, I have shown elsewhere that this term means nothing less than the enigmatic description of Israel's inability to see, a concept intentionally derived from Deuteronomy 29.[33] The use of secret (*mystērion*) in coordination with Deuteronomy 29 should tip off the reader that mystery is being employed in a particular construct. Hence, the NT's concept behind its employment of the word *mystērion* is not new; it is taken from the theological headquarters of the Torah: Deuteronomy.

Hazony demonstrably understands the historical event that holds the New Testament texts together. And he is correct to note that something significant has happened, which these texts portray and affirm *as witnessed* (more on this in Chapters 5–7). The problem with Hazony's brief analysis concerns its focus on superficial features of language and its insensitivity to genre, rather than the deeper conceptual, lexical, and thematic structures. If we asked the same questions in a slightly different way, as I have sketched out briefly above, we see the intentional continuity of the New Testament's Jewish and Gentile authors with the Hebrew Bible.

New Testament scholarship has demonstrably leaned in favor of continuity of the New Testament with the Hebrew Bible, even though dispensationalist theology of discontinuity has reigned in popular American Christianity over the last century. Similarly, naïve supersessionism has remained a consistent threat to claims of continuity. The more that New

[31] I examine this extensively in *Epistemology and Biblical Theology: From the Pentateuch to Mark's Gospel* (Routledge Interdisciplinary Perspectives in Biblical Criticism 4; New York: Routledge, 2018), 110–47.

[32] E.g., Elisha takes ritual cleansing for leprosy (Lev 14) and ritualized it for Naaman the Syrian (2 Kgs 5:1–14). Cf. Johnson, *Knowledge by Ritual*, 181–205.

[33] Johnson, *Epistemology and Biblical Theology*, 101–2.

Testament scholarship has developed in its literary approach, a method with which Hazony would be sympathetic, the deeper the Hebrew Bible's language and constructs seem to penetrate the thought world of New Testament authors.

What Is the Point of Hebraic Philosophy?

Dressing philosophical prescriptions in descriptive accounts, the biblical authors carried out discernible and consonant advocacy for abstract reasoning. With consistent savvy, they wrote extended discourses through poetry that compiles *genus/differentia* reasoning, through legal reasoning from principle to incident, and with the logic of signs and wonders as epistemic justification. Like much of Greek philosophy, the Hebraic philosophical style can only be practiced as a way of communal life. The remainder of this book will be dedicated to filling out that proposal and will show examples of how it faithfully represents the intellectual world of the Hebrew Bible and the New Testament.[34]

Interdisciplinary Dangers

In Orkney I'm English;
in England I'm Scottish;
in Scotland, Orcadian.[35]

In the following pages, I want to demonstrate sufficiently but not conclusively that there is such a thing as a Hebraic style of philosophy that extends from the Hebrew Bible into the New Testament. I want to backlight this Hebraic style with the philosophies of neighboring cultures – Mesopotamian, Egyptian, Greek, and Roman philosophies *du jour* – with which biblical authors engage in various modes.

34 NB: When discussing philosophical enterprises or "knowledge" in the biblical texts, most people assume that means "philosophizing about God" or "knowledge of God." While inherent to the task of biblical philosophy, just as it was in much of Greek philosophy, I am usually *not* referring to either of these in this present work. The goal of the second-order thinking advocated across Christian Scripture is to foster a discerning community with reference to the so-called natural world, political affairs, mathematical operations, human sociology, and so on. These texts appear to presume that, through discerning nuances in such affairs, knowledge of God comes along (though not to be confused with second-person knowledge of God).

35 Thanks to Steve Holmes for tipping me off to this poem. Harry Giles, "Visa Wedding," *Tonguit* (Glasgow: Freight Books, 2016).

Demonstrating that there is such a thing as a Hebraic philosophical style requires that I step on the toes of my colleagues in biblical studies, ancient Near East studies, philosophy, and theology. This would presumably require a certain competence (or insanity) on my part and charity on the reader's part.

Like the Orcadian poet cited above, raised in the Orkney Islands but now living in Edinburgh: amongst philosophers, this looks like biblical scholarship; amongst theologians, philosophy; amongst biblical scholars, theology. Never belonging fully to one guild, this project shows why interdisciplinary endeavors such as this are vital to understanding the Hebraic intellectual world and even our world today.

The goal is to create a vigorous discussion that I believe is a long time coming – to propose and sufficiently demonstrate a robust view of Hebraic philosophy spanning what we now call Christian Scripture. This includes the Hellenistic Jewish texts within and apart from the Apocrypha, but I will show why they play an oddly significant contrasting role to the Hebraic philosophical style of the New Testament.

This is an audacious task, one that requires a coherent and sustained argument, but one that I cannot possibly get entirely right on the first try. *Is there a Hebraic philosophy of Christian Scripture?* I think so and it is fairly obvious to me. *Can I sketch out a skeletal case for how Hebraic philosophy drives the rhetorical and communitarian aims of the New Testament authors?* I think so, but I can only sketch the contours and fill in a few areas.

What is my burden? To describe enough of this thesis, with enough examples from the biblical texts, to fire up the philosophical and exegetical imaginations of these guilds so that they can assess the claims in areas of Scripture and philosophy that I cannot address here. That conversation with scholars more expert than me in all of these areas is desperately needed, if for no other reason than parity with parallel claims in Egyptology, Assyriology, and Central/East Asian philosophy.

Non-Western philosophies have now reentered the fray with the Hellenist and the Enlightenment traditions in the formal study of philosophy. Hebraic philosophy remains notably absent from this current ecumenical trend. Some might cite its absence from the philosophical canons *du jour* as evidence for the lack of philosophical content in the Hebrew Bible. If that is an informed and reasoned view, then so be it. Yet, uncritical dismissal of the claim of Hebraic philosophy can only serve to reinforce a naïve view of biblical literature.

In order to make this claim, I will first require some flexibility with the terms currently used in philosophy. What I term "epistemological," "metaphysical," or "ethical" might not immediately strike us as fitting neatly into current buckets for such concepts, if the current categories even have clear and accepted definitions (and, they do not.). However, this terminological conflict has more to do with what has traditionally counted as philosophy in the Anglo-American world over the past centuries. I will address the question – what counts as philosophy? – in the next chapter. In the meantime, I ask for leeway in using these terms to describe what is going on in the biblical texts, which can be assessed for accuracy and fit with current philosophical coinage after the case has been heard.

Second, this book already takes part in a conversation formally begun by Yoram Hazony's *The Philosophy of Hebrew Scripture*, among others. In many ways, I am working in partnership with many of his suggestions in that volume. However, this present work is also a response to Hazony, as will become clear.

Third, if a Hebraic tradition of philosophy exists in the Hebrew Bible, then I must consider the employment or neglect of that tradition in Hellenistic Judaism and the New Testament. Second Temple Jews either ignored, mixed, or extended Hebraic philosophy into their texts, and my task here is to show signs of mixture and extension.

PART I

PHILOSOPHICAL STYLES

1

What Counts as Philosophy?

In 2007, I gave a paper at Oxford University at the British Society for the Philosophy of Religion titled "Why God Might be Poly-present, not Omnipresent." It was not a well-crafted essay. Regardless, I argued that the Christian Scriptures consistently present God – Father, Son, and Holy Spirit – in particular spatial locations, not ubiquitously present everywhere that there is a where. Taoism, on the other hand, has something akin to a coherent model of omnipresence, but the biblical literature seems uninterested in such a view of God. I am still debating whether or not that particular argument is a good one, but that is beside the point.

In the questions that followed the paper, I realized that something was wrong. The first question got straight to the point: "Why are you here?" I sputtered in response, stunned by the question. The philosopher continued, "I mean: Why are you at a philosophy conference making arguments from the Bible?" He meant it as a constructive question, and it was a fair point. After all, it was not a Christian philosophy conference and I was making arguments directly from the Protestant canon.

But still, his simple question gathered up many of my conversations with Christian philosophers at various conferences into one particularly pointed objection. In these conversations, Christian philosophers were often perplexed at my repeated attempts to find philosophically rigorous thought in the Scriptures themselves. I was equally perplexed as to why they did not see the biblical literature as a resource rich in philosophical thought.

I think it is fair to say that all of our combined perplexities have come a long way over the last decades.[1] For our part, scholars of biblical literature have learned how to better say what we mean. I have written several monographs to demonstrate what a "biblical philosophy" could look like, including this one. Christian philosophers have proved to be more willing to engage Scripture's speculative thought in sophisticated ways.

Skepticism toward the premise alone – that the Bible contains philosophy – has been the most prominent and recurring stumbling block in these conversations. Two Jewish philosophers, Shalom Carmy and David Shatz, encapsulate the sentiment well: "Much of what the Bible has to say about subjects of manifest philosophical importance seems primitive to later philosophical sensibilities."[2] Philosophers might be skeptical for good reason: They need to see for themselves the rigorously philosophical content demonstrated in Scripture.

I will advocate a three-part distinction in literary traditions that could help us clarify why literary works like Seneca's and Deuteronomy are philosophical and not merely speculative or scholarly texts. We can detect a philosophical style by their use of logic, rigor, second-order reasoning, and advocating such reasoning. Not all scholarly writing in antiquity explores second-order notions and not all reasoning advocates a particular style of thinking. On this account, if Hellenistic thinkers like Seneca fit the bill for philosophy – so too does Deuteronomy.

But there might also be some hypocrisy in our fondness for the Hellenist's style of discourse. Though I would not appropriate his revelation–reason dichotomy in all its details, Yoram Hazony argues that only in our intellectual myopia can we ignore the divine-revelatory aspects of Greek and Roman philosophies. Hazony shows with a minimum of examples that divine revelation undergirds the Hellenistic philosophical tradition, even if we choose to look past it. Citing passages from Parmenides, Empedocles, Heraclitus, and Socrates, he reminds us that they all attribute portions of their thought and reason to divine revelation. His summary startles us from our general perception of Greek philosophy as solely based on reason:

[1] Jaco Gericke places this shift at the year 2000. "When Historical Minimalism Becomes Philosophical Maximalism," *Old Testament Essays* 27, no. 2 (2014): 412–27.

[2] Shalom Carmy and David Shatz, "The Bible as a Source for Philosophical Reflection," in *History of Jewish Philosophy*, ed. Daniel H. Frank and Oliver Leaman (New York: Routledge, 1997), 14.

What these texts suggest is the following: During the two hundred years between Jeremiah [the biblical prophet] and Plato, there flourished a philosophical tradition – the very tradition that gave birth to Western philosophy – in which the ability to conduct philosophical inquiry was frequently seen as partially or wholly dependent on revelation or some other form of assistance from a god.[3]

And though this divinity-to-philosopher influence is neither new nor revelatory, Hazony notes that Bertrand Russell flags it without exploration in his history of philosophy.[4] A more recent and focused monograph by Shaul Tor – *Mortal and Divine in Early Greek Epistemology* – reaches a similar conclusion: "There exists an artificial schism in the scholarship between conceptions of the early Greek philosophers as systematic, relational thinkers and as poets, mystics and religious figures."[5]

At one time, I might have tacitly presumed that rigorous reasoning funds and pervades all Greek philosophy, which would seem to exclude Christian Scripture as a source of philosophical thinking.[6] But Hazony effectively dissolves the sharp reason–revelation dichotomy by merely acknowledging what is obvious: both Greek and Hebrew literature incorporate reason and revelation as we commonly understand them today.

Pierre Hadot has argued that Hellenist philosophy primarily concerned itself with the practice of the lived life honed through "spiritual exercises."[7] Philosophy was not merely the definitions, arguments, and discourses that we have come to regard as characterizing Greek philosophy. Hence, the thin paradigm of reason-against-revelation has to be rejected or repaired, if only in the assumptions we bring to these texts.

3 Yoram Hazony, *The Philosophy of Hebrew Scripture* (New York: Cambridge University Press, 2012), 9.

4 Hazony, *The Philosophy of Hebrew Scripture*, 9–10.

5 Shaul Tor, *Mortal and Divine in Early Greek Epistemology: A Study of Hesiod, Xenophanes, and Parmenides* (Cambridge Classical Studies; New York: Cambridge University Press, 2017), 7. Or, as one reviewer put it, "For Tor, early Greek epistemology can be both rational – that is, logical and systematic – and still profoundly religious and even theological." Hilary Bouxsein, review of *Mortal and Divine in Early Greek Epistemology: A Study of Hesiod, Xenophanes, and Parmenides* by Shaul Tor, *Bryn Mawr Classical Review*, April 8, 2020, https://bmcr.brynmawr.edu/2020/2020.04.08/.

6 Hazony, *The Philosophy of Hebrew Scripture*, 1–27. *The Journal of Analytic Theology* dedicated four essays in response to Hazony's book. *The Journal of Analytic Theology* 2 (2014): 238–81.

7 Pierre Hadot, *What Is Ancient Philosophy?*, trans. Michael Chase (Cambridge, MA: Harvard University Press, 2002); *Philosophy as a Way of Life: Spiritual Exercises from Socrates to Foucault*, trans. Michael Chase (Oxford: Blackwell, 1995).

For those who take the biblical literature to be a revelation from God through the prophets, that does not exclude the possibility that these prophets reasoned with the reader through story, poetry, law, and more. Even more striking, prophets required their audiences to bring reason to revelation for it to be understood – though the Hebraic epistemology quickly complicates this.

Biblical scholars have noticed the literary savvy that created these texts in their final forms, texts which interweave complex themes and detailed arguments masterfully. Once scholars returned to literarily sensitive readings of the biblical texts, the question eventually and repeatedly surfaced: What did those ancient Hebrew authors and editors think they were doing by crafting these texts in these particular ways? They seem to think that they were shaping something within their audience's conceptual world, but what?

In other words, the writing craft behind the text evinced a sense of purpose, and I want to propose that one of the purposes of the biblical literature is to prescribe a ritualized method for thinking about the world in both its historical and its abstract-transcendent granularities. Throughout, a discrete epistemological method is prescribed, developed, and presented again and again in its *genus* form (proper knowing) and *differentia* (erroneous knowing). That proper epistemic method features as primary as it determines proper formation and boundaries of Israel's ontological, metaphysical, ethical, and political philosophy.

What Has Counted as Philosophy?

Rome || Greece || **Israel** || Mesopotamia || Egypt

If we asked most scholars to group the intellectual worlds of the above cultures according to affinity, we could probably guess the answers in advance. Most biblical scholars and philosophers/theologians will inevitably chunk Greece and Rome together intellectually, and then Israel/ Egypt/Mesopotamia together as a distinct group almost in opposition to Hellenism, like so:

Rome, Greece |- -| **Israel**, Mesopotamia, Egypt

Interestingly, ancient Near Eastern scholars put the Hebrews with the Greeks (and the Romans in tow) as intellectual innovators in the Fertile Crescent, freed from the Egyptians and Babylonians, like so:

Rome, Greece, **Israel** |- - - - - - - - - - - - - - - - - - - -| Mesopotamia, Egypt

In other words, those who study the intellectual worlds of the ancient Fertile Crescent place the thought-world of the Hebrew Bible in the camp of Hellenism. Note Frankfort's reactions to abstract thought found across the Hebrew Bible:

> This [Hebrew] conception of God represents so high a degree of abstraction that, in reaching it, the Hebrews seem to have left the realm of mythopoeic thought . . . . The Old Testament is remarkably poor in mythology of the type we encountered in Egypt and Mesopotamia.[8]

> It is possible to detect the reflection of Egyptian and Mesopotamian beliefs in many episodes of the Old Testament; but the overwhelming impression left by that document is one, not of derivation, but of originality.[9]

> It remained for the Greeks [following the Hebrews] . . . to discover a speculative thought in which myth was entirely overcome.[10]

There has been some recent pushback on the scholars who held these views. However, that criticism has not focused on their observations of the Hebraic texts in their contexts, but on the more general theories of progressivism that informed their views of advances in thought.[11] Their conclusions about the distinctions between these intellectual worlds remain to be evaluated.

And despite these rather evocative conclusions proposed amongst Assyriologists and Egyptologists alike, anecdotal evidence suggests that most Christian philosophers and theologians today (along with many biblical scholars!) would place the intellectualism of the Hebrew Bible alongside Babylon and Luxor *as opposed to* the thought-world of ancient Athens.

Scholars fluent in the philosophy of Hellenism also see the affinities between the distinct "Christian" philosophical style (i.e., its Hebraic

[8] Henri Frankfort et al., *The Intellectual Adventure of Ancient Man: An Essay on Speculative Thought in the Ancient Near East* (Chicago: University of Chicago Press, 1946), 367.

[9] Frankfort et al., *The Intellectual Adventure of Ancient Man*, 367.

[10] Frankfort et al., *The Intellectual Adventure of Ancient Man*, 373.

[11] "The result was a work both of great originality, but also of no small allegiance to progressivism, according to which cultural, intellectual, and cognitive history is viewed as one of inexorable advancement and sees culture (the arts, technology, and science) as establishing control, knowledge, and ever greater distance from nature over the course of history." Francesca Rochberg, "A Critique of the Cognitive-Historical Thesis of the Intellectual Adventure," in *The Adventure of the Human Intellect: Self, Society, and the Divine in Ancient World Cultures*, ed. Kurt A. Raaflaub (Ancient World: Comparative Histories; Hoboken, NJ: Wiley-Blackwell, 2016), 16–28.

roots) and Hellenism.[12] Some have a sharper critique of Hellenism, suggesting that the heights of its philosophical naturalism still never broke from mythology: "To the effect that Aristotle's conception of motion is effectively a transmuted animism, shows again how far less successful the Greeks were than the Hebrews in demythologising the ancient creation myths."[13]

Given the reflections above, we might even include the Hebrew Bible as affirming what Greeks would later recognize as a philosophy: a particular way of life reckoned to abstract thinking about physics and ethics.

We will return to these reflections in later chapters. But for now, we must ask ourselves: Why does the idea of an implicit philosophical style in the biblical texts sound exotic to everyone except those who are expert in ancient philosophies of Hellenism and the Fertile Crescent?

Some might object that the genres within the biblical literature do not lend to philosophizing. This objection seems to have in mind that biblical literature mainly consists of narrative, law, poetry, genealogy, parable, aphorism, and more. However, diversity of literary genres has never excluded written works from being considered philosophy in modern philosophy departments.

Even though the question of what counts as proper philosophy has not garnered consensus amongst today's philosophers, it has recently been a topic of interest.[14] Consider the wide spectrum of literature within the Christian Bible, and then note that philosophers have always engaged with and advocated critical second-order thinking derived from a breadth

[12] At its origins, Christianity . . . announced the imminent end of the world and the coming of the Kingdom of God. Such a message was completely foreign to the Greek mentality and to the perspectives of philosophy; rather, it was *inscribed within the intellectual universe of Judaism*, which Christianity overthrew, *but not without preserving some of its fundamental notions.* Nothing, it seems, could have predicted that a century after the death of Christ some Christians would present Christianity not only as a philosophy – that is, a Greek cultural phenomenon – but even as the sole and eternal philosophy.

(Italics mine. Hadot, *What Is Ancient Philosophy?, 238)*

[13] Colin E. Gunton, *The Triune Creator: A Historical and Systematic Study* (Grand Rapids, MI: Eerdmans, 1998), 31.

[14] E.g., Justin Weinberg, "What Kinds of Things Count as Philosophy?" *Daily Nous* (Blog), June 11, 2015, http://dailynous.com/2015/06/11/what-kinds-of-things-count-as-philosophy/; Eric Schwitzgebel, "What Philosophical Work Could Be," *The Splintered Mind* (Blog), June 11, 2015, http://schwitzsplinters.blogspot.co.uk/2015/06/what-philosophical-work-could-be.html.

of literary milieux. Reviewing the breadth of literary forms commonly associated with the most influential philosophers taught in Anglo-American academia today, the objection to a particular genre or form makes less sense. Consider what Gericke calls the "varieties of philosophical exegesis":[15]

Dialogue with an embedded story (Socrates)
Manual (Epictetus)
Allegory (Plato; Gettier; Frank Jackson, e.g., "What Mary Didn't Know")
Sentences (Peter of Abelard)
Disputations (Aquinas)
Meditation entries (Descartes)
Pseudonymous postscript (Kierkegaard)
Treatises (Locke, Hume)
Journal entries (Marcus Aurelius)
Personal reflections (Camus)
Aphorisms (Cicero, Nietzsche)
Essay (Montaigne)
Novella (Nietzsche)

This list reveals what is obvious: Anglo-American philosophers require literacy in a wide breadth of literary genres from their colleagues and students. Additionally, they appear to take a fairly inclusive stance – literarily speaking – on what counts as philosophy. To wit, a forthcoming anthology – *Philosophy through Science Fiction Stories* – collects over twenty newly written science fiction essays aimed at philosophical exploration through fiction.[16]

Outside of the odd inclusion of Ecclesiastes (Qohelet) into existentialism or meaning of life philosophy courses, the Christian Scriptures simply have not *counted* as philosophy to most philosophers today. Apart from anecdotes and intuitions, it is difficult to ascertain why this is the case (if it is indeed still the case). In charity, one must assume that the primary reason for this exclusion, especially amid a philosophical culture of such literary inclusion, must pertain to either the lack of philosophical content within the biblical literature or the lack of understanding about how that literature carries out philosophy. I believe the latter to be the case.

15 Jaco Gericke, *The Hebrew Bible and Philosophy of Religion* (Society of Biblical Literature Resources for Biblical Study 70; Atlanta: Society of Biblical Literature, 2012), 43.

16 Helen De Cruz, Johan De Smedt, and Eric Schwitzgebel, eds., *Philosophy through Science Fiction Stories* (New York: Bloomsbury, 2021).

Comparative Philosophy: Including Hebraic Philosophy in the Fold

Enough scholarly monographs now dot the academic landscape for us to take seriously the claims that the Indians, Chinese, Babylonians, Egyptians, and Hebrews were all civilizations that thought and wrote philosophically.[17] Philosophy departments in the West undervalue or ignore comparative philosophy in favor of identifying themselves in a particular trope, most often analytic or continental. In style and content, "Hellenist-inspired and ancestrally European" would not be an unfair caricature of most. And so, in our traditions of thinking and speaking, the name – *philosophia* – says it all. Philosophy is Greek![18]

Richard King opens his book on Indian philosophy feeling that he must defensively attack the neglect of comparative philosophy in Western academia: "The main motivation behind this work then is to challenge the parochialism of 'western philosophy' and to contribute to the growth of a relatively new, and much-maligned, field known as 'comparative philosophy'."[19] King wrote these words in 1999, and it is now the case that Chinese and Indian philosophies are indeed on the menu of courses taught by philosophy departments in the West, and no longer relegated to religion departments only. Yet, the philosophy of the biblical literature remains almost, perhaps entirely, nonexistent in these same departments.

Dismay over Western parochialism also presumably led to a recent *New York Times* opinion piece titled: "If Philosophy Won't Diversify, Let's Call It What It Really Is," which later became the book *Taking Back Philosophy*.[20] The authors' suggestion was to rename most philosophy departments "Department of European and American Philosophy"

[17] For Babylonian literature and practice as philosophy, see: Marc Van De Mieroop, *Philosophy before the Greeks: The Pursuit of Truth in Ancient Babylonia* (Princeton, NJ: Princeton University Press, 2016). Hebrew literature as philosophy: Gericke, *The Hebrew Bible and Philosophy of Religion*; Michael Carasik, *Theologies of the Mind in Biblical Israel* (Studies in Biblical Literature 85; Oxford: Peter Lang, 2005); Hazony, *The Philosophy of Hebrew Scripture*; Dru Johnson, *Epistemology and Biblical Theology: From the Pentateuch to Mark's Gospel* (Routledge Interdisciplinary Perspectives on Biblical Criticism 4; New York: Routledge, 2018); etc.

[18] For an adept survey of ancient and modern world philosophies in reference to the current thesis, see Jaco Gericke, "Possible Analogies for a Philosophy of Ancient Israelite Religion," in *The Hebrew Bible and Philosophy of Religion*, 155–98.

[19] Richard King, *Indian Philosophy: An Introduction to Hindu and Buddhist Thought* (Washington, DC: Georgetown University Press, 1999), xiii.

[20] Jay L. Garfield and Bryan W. Van Norden, "If Philosophy Won't Diversify, Let's Call It What It Really Is," *The New York Times* (*Opinion Pages*), May 11, 2016, www.nytimes.com/2016/05/11/opinion/if-philosophy-wont-diversify-lets-call-it-what-it-really-is.html.

because of the obvious lack of diversity. The book generated from the overwhelmingly positive response to the opinion piece and tackled what the author saw as "pseudo-argumentation that is typically used to dismiss philosophy that is outside the Anglo-American canon."[21] Other indigenous philosophers have lodged similar complaints.[22]

Yet, even the *Oxford Handbook on World Philosophy* – an entire volume dedicated to non-Western philosophy – covers Chinese, Islamic, and Indian philosophies, but no ancient Near Eastern thought.[23]

Costica Bradatan has recently connected the Western bias in philosophy with the problem of defining the field of philosophy itself:

> A lively conversation has been taking place lately on mainstream philosophy in the West today and the way it treats non-Western traditions of thought as insufficiently philosophical. Such bias, though serious, is only a symptom – one among many – of parochial, purist philosophy's misunderstanding of itself. Not only are other philosophical traditions easily dismissed, but within the Western tradition itself important genres, thinkers, bodies of work are rejected just as arrogantly.[24]

The citation of national newspaper articles here is intentional. How we define what counts as philosophy is of public interest and consideration. The task of this present book is to push the discussion, even amongst our philosophically ecumenical colleagues, across their pencil-drawn borders to consider the inclusion of Near Eastern thought – and in this case: Hebraic thought.

Beyond a lack of diversity of perspectives taught within English-speaking philosophy departments, the Bible faces a historical and lingering threat to exploring its philosophical content. A long-debunked claim persists that ancient Semites were incapable of the kind of objective and abstract thinking required to do philosophy.

[21] Bryan W. Van Norden, *Taking Back Philosophy: A Multicultural Manifesto* (New York: Columbia University Press, 2017), 16.

[22] Cf. Aboriginal philosophy in Australia: "Aboriginal knowledge is inseparable from questions of who gets to be educated, how the custodians of knowledge are treated in modern Australia, why such knowing is marginalised, and how it might be vital at a time when civilisation teeters on the edge of a precipice." David Rutledge, host, "Thinking the Country," *The Philosopher's Zone*, July 7, 2019, www.abc.net.au/radionational/programs/philosopherszone/thinking-the-country/11278558. See also: Arindam Chakrabarti and Ralph Weber, eds., *Comparative Philosophy without Borders* (New York: Bloomsbury, 2016).

[23] Jay L. Garfield and William Edelglass, eds., *The Oxford Handbook of World Philosophy* (New York: Oxford University Press, 2013).

[24] Costica Bradatan, "Philosophy Needs a New Definition," *Los Angeles Review of Books*, December 17, 2017, https://lareviewofbooks.org/article/philosophy-needs-a-new-definition/.

With modernist progressivism and evolutionism in hand, scholars such as Johannes Pedersen and Thorleif Boman speculated about ancient intellectual trends – from the supposed non-abstract writings of ancient Semites to the transcendent ideas of the Greeks upon whom the dawn of philosophical light supposedly shone.[25] The biblical writings themselves testified to the progression, which even spawned an evolutionary neurological approach to the biblical texts.[26]

Some of their descriptive insights, especially those in Boman, took seriously a nativist approach to Hebraic thought and should not be dismissed out of hand. On the other hand, these scholars overclaimed that Israelites did not perform abstract thought according to the early writings in the Hebrew Bible itself. Despite the debate and definitive disapproval of their claim in the scholarly consensus, these progressivist and evolutionist ideas about ancient philosophy took root and occasionally surface overtly and covertly in academic discourse today.

[25] Though Boman and Pedersen (and Tresmontant following them) made observations that had depth and precision about aspects of cognition on display in the Hebrew texts, their grander claims about the dichotomy between Hebrew and Greek mentalities were dismissed by most. James Barr's unfavorable appraisal of these two-mind critiques was definitive. For Barr, these Hebrew-Greek dichotomy theories were predicated upon the nature of language – the philology of mind in the extant texts of the Hebrew Bible. Barr's basic rejoinder aims at the faulty claim of two mentalities as expressed by the languages of the people represented. First, if Hebrew represents the "verb" mentality and Greek the "noun," does that dichotomy reflect their mentality per se or the nature of the texts? Barr argues for the latter, pointing out the phenomenological aspect of the extant texts: "The typical vehicle of Hebrew thinking is the historical narrative or the future prediction, both forms of literature in which the verb is likely to be of great significance." James Barr, *The Semantics of Biblical Language* (Eugene, OR: Wipf and Stock, 1961), 15.

His second major critique points to the vague nature of the comparison itself. Boman et al. have constructed a theory of mind that includes their own European mentality and Indo-European language group as contrasted to Hebrew mentality and the Semitic language group. This creates an ineffectual comparison to which Barr raises one penetrating implication: "[I]f the Greek language can be somehow correlated with certain abstract or static features of Greek thought, how is (say) the Albanian language, which is also Indo-European, related with these features?" Barr, *Semantics*, 18.

Cf. Thorleif Boman, *Hebrew Thought Compared with Greek*, trans. Jules L. Moreau (Library of History and Doctrine 1; London: SCM, 1960); Johannes Pedersen, *Israel, Its Life and Culture* (2 vols.; Oxford: Geoffrey Cumberlege, 1959); Claude Tresmontant, *A Study of Hebrew Thought*, trans. Michael Francis Gibson (New York: Desclee, 1960). For a fuller analysis of the Greek-Hebrew mind debate, see Carasik, *Theologies of the Mind in Biblical Israel*, 1–11; Dru Johnson, *Knowledge by Ritual: A Biblical Prolegomenon to Sacramental Theology* (Winona Lake, IN: Eisenbrauns/PennState Press, 2016), 96–99.

[26] Julian Jaynes, *The Origin of Consciousness in the Breakdown of the Bicameral Mind* (Toronto: University of Toronto Press, 1976).

If we have dismissed the idea of Hebraic philosophy out of hand, then it is not that Scripture does not contain philosophy or a philosophical style. Rather, we have not yet approached the Christian Scriptures systematically with that question in order to assess: Is there a philosophy to be traced across Christian Scripture?

Complicating Factors

First, does Scripture have philosophical content? To put it another way, does the biblical literature have a coherent, sustained, and discernible thread of second-order thinking? By "second-order thinking," I only mean something like demonstrable "thinking about thinking" or "thinking about the nature of things as such."[27] (I will clarify later by distinguishing *scholarly* and *speculative* works from *philosophy* itself.)

As Marc Van De Mieroop has recently argued in his book *Philosophy before the Greeks*, if we define philosophy by the stylistically distinct discourses of Hellenism, then only the Greeks and their direct intellectual/literary descendants can *do philosophy*.[28]

However, if *speculative* thinking is that which entails rigorous and sustained second-order reasoning, then Scripture certainly contains philosophical speculation.[29] A recent research workgroup (Second Order Thinking in the Ancient Fertile Crescent, University of Aarhus)[30] formed to make the case that the Hellenist tradition of philosophy emerges in an already existent field of more ancient lines of intellectual traditions, going back a thousand years before Socrates *and including the Hebraic biblical tradition*.

Second, how does one aptly discover what Scripture has to say about the nature of metaphysical relations, epistemological states, meta-ethics,

[27] David Edmonds and Nigel Warburton, hosts, "What Is Philosophy?," *Philosophy Bites*, November 14, 2010, http://philosophybites.com/2010/11/what-is-philosophy.html.

[28] Van De Mieroop, *Philosophy Before the Greeks*, 1–12.

[29] For a brief example of this, see my essay "A Biblical Nota Bene on Philosophical Inquiry," *Philosophia Christi* (Blog), Evangelical Philosophical Society Symposium, www.epsociety.org/library/articles.asp?pid=238.

[30] This research unit included scholars from Columbia University (New York), Aarhus University (Denmark), and North-West University (South Africa), http://pure.au.dk/portal/en/projects/the-origins-of-second-order-thinking(4a620d0e-ab46-4659-ab58-38ffb4d63198).html.

logic, and more?[31] Let us be brutally honest on this point. Some in Christian philosophy and theology fund their ideas primarily from the discourses of their traditions and then secondarily find Scriptures that seem to support them. Most of us will catch ourselves doing this at points. However, we might consider this particular methodology to be *the lowest form of philosophy that engages Christian Scripture*: baptizing our contemporary ideas with proof-texts.

Equally problematic, resorting to word searches – "know" for epistemology or "time" for metaphysics – provides shoddy lenses for investigating Scripture and often distorts our understanding of the biblical thinking on such topics. I will examine the biblical vocabulary most central to epistemology in Chapters 8–10. Surprisingly, the most obvious epistemological keyword, "know" (Hebrew: *yāda'*; Greek: *ginōskō*/*eidon*), is an inadequate term for understanding the breadth of biblical epistemology. Hence, methodology, which I will address in Chapter 4, is crucial to how such a project should proceed.

Hebraic philosophy should be examined and expounded on its own terms within comparative philosophy. The Hebraic intellectual world is not dependent on it "being like" other forms of philosophy. This should also serve to reinforce the fact that Greek philosophy is *not* the standard by which all other traditions are measured.

Third, how should the philosophical content of Scripture relate to our philosophical method and thinking? This question is difficult because so few people publish works that directly deal with Scripture's philosophical style. Hence, several scholars have had to carve out a tenuous path while simultaneously walking it – learning to assess how Scripture should shape our philosophy and theology. Certainly, there have been guiding influences, yet sadly, those were almost entirely biblical theologians and rarely philosophers.

Because few scholars work on the philosophical world of the biblical literature itself, our methodologies had to crystalize through a process of stumbling forward. We had to craft methodologies that gave us confidence in its results as scholars.

[31] Similar methodological questions have been posed in non-Western philosophies, but the question might already presume the superiority of Western philosophy. Disparate texts and genres of writing have never slowed Western scholars from presuming philosophical content in poetry, meditations, reflections, narratives, and more. Comparative philosophy continues in non-Western contexts with the presumption that those disparate texts and genres might also contain philosophical content. See also John S. Mbiti, *African Religions and Philosophy* (London: Heinemann, 1969).

Of course, there must be some value for methodological pluralism in such pursuits. Various and mutually enriching methods can help us collectively move toward a shared end. More biblical scholars and philosophers publishing in this area could certainly create a welcomed methodological pluralism.[32] But it is currently the case, as far as I know, that Jewish and atheist scholars are taking the biblical literature more seriously, philosophically speaking, than Christian philosophers and theologians. Such pluralism will inevitably stem from the diversity of commitments from scholars as well.

Definitions of Philosophy

To maintain modest consistency in comparative philosophy, I divide ancient sources into three categories: scholarship, speculation, and philosophy. Defining "philosophy" generates thorny forests of notions from philosophers themselves. The typical dissection of the Greek term *phileō* (love) and *sophia* (wisdom) will not suffice. As Colin McGuinn recently argued in *The New York Times*, little evidence for love of wisdom exists across the work of professional philosophers today. Since passionately seeking wisdom is not what philosophers actually do, he then suggests truth in advertising:

> I have a bold proposal: Let us drop the name "philosophy" for the discipline so called and replace it with a new one. The present name is obsolete, misleading and harmful – long past its expiration date. ... To load the dice, we might also wish to describe ourselves as doing "ontical science," at least until our affinity with the sciences sinks in – then we might abbreviate to "ontics."[33]

His diagnosis and solution might err on the side of the dour, but the point is taken. "Philosophy" as a title for the profession is a misnomer for most professional philosophers today.

Diverse answers to the question "what is philosophy?" abound amongst philosophers. The *Philosophy Bites* podcast dedicated an entire 27-minute episode to seeking a definition of philosophy from professional

32 For instance, myself (Christian), Yoram Hazony (Jewish), Seizo Sekine (a Japanese scholar), and Jaco Gericke (atheist) have all worked on philosophical constructs in the Hebrew Bible, but from different methodologies and faith commitments. I do not think all approaches are equally fruitful. For my assessment of these approaches, see my comparative review of Sekine and Gericke in *Journal of Analytic Theology* 4 (2016).

33 Colin McGuinn, "Philosophy by Any Other Name," *The New York Times* (*The Opinion Pages*), March 4, 2012, https://opinionator.blogs.nytimes.com/2012/03/04/philosophy-by-another-name/.

philosophers. Over a dozen philosophers gave widely varying definitions, some qualifying as interpretations, but it became obvious that professional philosophers have very different views from each other about the nature of their task.

These examples suggest that it would be futile to demand that we inaugurate this present venture by defining philosophy once and for all. However, outside of the Hellenist pedigree, there must be a rubric for delineating what counts as philosophy when the ancient texts follow neither the style nor substance of the tacitly accepted styles of European philosophy of Greek lineage.

Hence, I do not wish to define philosophy per se but to distinguish philosophical styles from other intellectual and literary traditions for the sake of examining the various texts and genres within the biblical literature, and the texts of Israel's neighbors. The three-part distinction – scholarship, speculation, and philosophy – will act as a rubric for this task of distinguishing different types of literature or discourses in the ancient Near East. Namely, the qualitative difference focuses upon systematicity and rigor as indicative of scholarly texts, the use of second-order thinking as indicative of speculative texts, and advocating a particular method of second-order thought as indicative of philosophy texts. The term "philosophy," here, designates a philosophical style as a sociohistorical tradition, not the nature of philosophy itself. Hence, I will distinguish the three types of works produced in the ancient intellectual worlds of the Mediterranean and Near East accordingly:

1. *scholarly* texts (rigorous/systematized)
2. *speculative* texts (displays second-order thinking)
3. *philosophy* texts (advocates a method/s of shaping second-order thought)

These are not inherently inclusive or exclusive from one another and do not necessarily progress from 1 to 3. Scholarly or speculative discussions can be advocated, but only speculative discussions become philosophy when they are methodologically advocated. Hence, I can differentiate ancient works in Greece like the epigrammarian poems of Simmias of Rhodes as scholarly but not speculative.[34]

By scholarly I mean that there is a clear and logically worked out system of relationships within or between texts. The Babylonian

[34] Simmias both wrote on grammar and practiced textual play, creating poems physically shaped on the page according to the content of the poem.

divination texts might be good candidates for scholarly thinking exhibited in texts. These omen lists systematically develop *modus ponens* (If P, then Q) relationships over myriad observable phenomena. I will further discuss their logic and systematicity in Chapter 2. Whatever else they may be, they meet the standard of scholarship at the least.

To take a contemporary example, meteorologists today participate in a scholarly enterprise – observing, recording, and calculating. And because of this rigor, a meteorologist can make measured judgments about the future. Likewise, in the Hebrew Bible, the census lists of Ezra (e.g., 2:1–70) might count as a scholarly activity: rigorous, logical, and ordered according to patrilineal connections, but not meant to display or advocate second-order reasoning.

By speculative, I mean writing that demonstrates second-order thinking, which is generally construed to be thinking about thinking or thinking about the nature of reality apart from any individual instance of it. Van De Mieroop argues that the scribal innovations within the exhaustive Mesopotamian word lists – maintained in two languages simultaneously – goes beyond mere wordplay and evinces a type of speculative thinking.[35] I will say more about this in the next chapter, but observing scribes at play in their speculative thought puts Van De Mieroop's thesis at the level of speculative, but not necessarily philosophy.

By philosophy, I am not including merely rigorous second-order thinking, but prescriptive second-order thinking regarding the usual field of suspects: political thought, epistemology, metaphysics, ethics, and more. For instance, when Hugh Benson argues that there exists a distinct Socratic method in the Socratic dialogues, he sees advocacy of method as a formal indicator of Socratic philosophy and eventually causing Socrates' death sentence.[36] Treating advocacy as distinctive of a philosophical tradition might seem initially odd until we consider that advocating a method for second-order reasoning has a reputable pedigree in the history of philosophy.

Distinguishing philosophical traditions by their advocated method offers two advantages. First, the personal force behind the philosophical style means that it held some value in its own context. For instance, Van De Mieroop has shown a style of second-order thought

[35] Van De Mieroop, *Philosophy before the Greeks*, 59–84.

[36] Hugh H. Benson, "Socratic Method," in *The Cambridge Companion to Socrates*, ed. Donald R. Morrison (Cambridge Companions to Philosophy; Cambridge: Cambridge University Press, 2010), 179–200.

at work amongst Babylonian scribes in the way they speculatively played with the language and omens. However, how could one discern whether that was a normative style of reasoning or if the scribes believed this to be a discrete method for understanding their world? The possibility that Babylonian intellectualism is speculation does not exclude it from being philosophy in the way I have differentiated it here, only that advocacy for the style of abstract thinking has yet to be demonstrated.

The Babylonian compendia of texts and skills displayed an astonishing array of magisterial knowledge, later marveled at by the Greeks. When Diodorus of Sicily visits Mesopotamia, the question pregnant in his description of Babylonian (Chaldean) divination is: How do they manage these encyclopediæ of details? He answers that divination is a family office, and so children train in this mode of thought since childhood. (He notes the distinct advantage of the father as the teacher who does not, therefore, have to suffer from challenging students.[37]) Handing down a scholarly tradition is certainly a form of advocacy; however, it is unclear that the texts themselves advance such advocacy and the texts make no demands for an exclusively speculative method.

Second, advocacy allows us to see the style as necessarily including methodological elements in philosophizing while also excluding others. Contrast the speculations of Babylonian scribes with the Socratic dialogues. In Socrates' teaching, it becomes clear that the author himself wants readers to understand that Socrates has a particular method he is advancing and practicing to understand the world more truly – even if that method is primarily aimed at disrupting the knower. Later, Plato will eventually defame other philosophers because of their fruitless methods.[38] Though Plato is skeptical about students who want to turn his teaching into a unified system, his writings advocate a discrete philosophical style of abstract reasoning about thinking and the nature of reality.[39]

More will be said in Chapter 2 about scholarly, speculative, and philosophical traditions across various literary genres and texts in the Christian Scriptures and the ancient Near East. For now, these categories

[37] Diodorus Siculus, *Library of History*, Vol. 1, trans. C. H. Oldfather (Cambridge, MA: Loeb Classical Library, 1933), 447.

[38] Apparently put off by Diogenes' deformed practice of Socratic method, Plato describes Diogenes the cynic as "a Socrates gone mad." *Diogenes Laertius*, Book 6, Chapter 54. NB, this letter has disputed authorship. Unless otherwise stated, all references to classical Greek sources outside of the New Testament are from the Loeb Classical Library.

[39] Plato, *Epistle* VII.

give us a way of thinking about texts that were more focused on people's interactions with gods than directing people about how they think about the nature of reality itself. However, in the Hebrew Bible and New Testament texts we find sustained advocacy for an epistemological process that entails metaphysical commitments.

Like Plato's purported convictions about his teaching that could not summed in a book, the biblical focus on philosophical method requires seeing something new in the same old reality, imbued in the community as a way of life. Like Plato's vision of the forms, the end goal of Hebraic philosophy cannot be truths written and passed along to the next student.

Although I will discuss speculative movements in the ancient Near East and Hellenism more generally, this will not be a work of comparative philosophy. I will not define Hebraic philosophy by flatly comparing it to Greek, Egyptian, or Babylonian thought. Comparisons will be helpful in many places as points of reference and unavoidable when discussing Hellenistic Judaism and the New Testament. But in general, the Hebraic style of advocating a way of reasoning through philosophical problems should speak for itself.

The Philosophical Style of Hellenism

The basic philosophical questions have varied little through the millennia, yet there exists in Christian Scripture a Hebraic style of raising abstract questions, reasoning through them, and offering distinct answers to those questions. The most striking feature of Hebraic philosophy is not its use of diverse literary genres (e.g., narrative, law, poetry, etc.), but the accumulation of instances in patterned usages that point to an abstract principle.

To illustrate it philosophically, by telling and retelling historical accounts of *chairs* in covenant relationship to Yahweh, *chair-ness* and its philosophical significance would be pointed up to the reader. Instances *of*, rhetorical structure *about*, a logical structure *within* narratives, and more may be like invisible arrows through them that make the instances of chairs – as it were – across Scripture more than philosophical objects to be studied, but philosophical vectors that become coherent only upon integration into the whole. This is not always the case, but it is often how abstract ideas are worked out in the Hebrew Bible, reflecting ancient Near Eastern modes of reasoning over the later typically linear Greek modes.

At one point in Greece's history, philosophizing resembled this inductive/abductive style. Nietzsche's first work, *Birth of Tragedy*, argued that

Greek tragedy was the most poignant form of epistemology.[40] Or one might say on Nietzsche's behalf: If we want to profoundly help someone else to understand something, do not deductively walk them through premises toward a conclusion. Rather, create theater to engage the whole individual within the community.

In the revolutionary new literature of Plato, one could argue that Socratic philosophy also worked in such a non-linear way, where example after example meant to disrupt and distract the man who thinks he understands something as simple as justice. However, a clear linear trace of that disruption can be made in the Socratic dialogues, revealing that the method only seems to be haphazardly exemplarist. In hindsight, it appears to follow a scripted path to a particular end. The end game, for Socrates, does not appear to be a delineated definition, but a new disposition of the knower – an existential shift.

Taking these two different aspects of Hellenism on board – theatrical engagement and linear argument – the term "Hellenism" will serve here *only* as a caricature of the intellectual world and traditions that ensued and reacted to Socrates. As employed here, "Hellenism" will ignore Nietzsche's idealized abductive view of epistemology prized in Greece's intellectual traditions of theater.

Moreover, literary styles varied significantly across Hellenism's intellectual history. In Hellenism, we rifle through fables, theater, dialogues, narratives, treatises/essays, and more, most of which employ both linear arguments and patterned examples piled up to form an argument. Hence, any caricature of Hellenism's philosophy will always fail to do justice to such a rich tradition, but some general features can be outlined.

I seek here to sketch a philosophical style from Socrates onward to the Roman expressions of the tradition. By "style," I mean that texts collectively reveal a general mode of argument and a set of convictions that enable the particular forms of argument to function.

The style metaphor tugs on a set of convictions and expectations by those who are literate in the tradition, which allows for a particular end. In the Hellenistic philosophical style, for instance, linear discourse was not an end, but an instrument to the practice of justice.[41]

40 Friedrich Nietzsche, *The Birth of Tragedy and Other Writings*, ed. Raymond Geuss and Ronald Speirs; trans. Ronald Speirs (Cambridge Texts in the History of Philosophy; New York: Cambridge University Press, 1999).

41 "[D]iscourse was philosophical only if it was transformed into a way of life." Hadot, *What Is Ancient Philosophy?*, 173.

If the philosophical style is the overarching collective of traits, then I would divide the "style" of Greek philosophy into two categories: (1) its *mode* of argument (not to be confused with the particular form of argument, such as syllogism, enthymeme, *maieutic* questioning, etc.) and (2) its *convictions* about the extent and task of inquiry, including the requisite views of the psychology and sociology involved in intellectual grasping.

Philosophical Modes

First, Hellenism generally favored a *linear mode of* argument, traceable in form and autonomous in function. Hellenistic schools of philosophy sometimes ordered this linearity into formal logic, but the kernel of linearity is clear in early Greek philosophy. Of course, notable exceptions to the linear style exist. Hellenistic Stoics such as Epictetus and Marcus Aurelius certainly departed from a linear style in some of their written works. But that is precisely the point: We think of a loose collection of journal entries – à la Aurelius' *Meditations* – as departing from some basic standard in the Greek philosophical style.

By *traceable* in form, I mean that the argument takes a distinctly deductive path, even if inductive arguments are employed along the way. As in Socratic dialogue and Aristotle's description of forms, readers can directly trace the single flow of the argument backward from conclusion to premises. Even when Socrates' goal is only to show the person that they do not know what they think they know, the row of arguments guides the participant down a path. And, like both metaphors, "row" and "path," they are typically linear.

Significant exceptions to the linear style exist, namely the later Roman Stoics who, notably, have been paired with Paul's epistles. Again, Marcus Aurelius' *Meditations* cannot be accused of employing a linear style of argument. Likewise, Seneca emphasizes the non-linear lived life of the philosophers above the words of their discourses: "Plato, Aristotle, and the whole throng of sages who were destined to go each his different way, derived more benefit from the character than from the words of Socrates. It was not the classroom of Epicurus, but living together under the same roof, that made great men of Metrodorus, Hermarchus, and Polyaenus."[42]

[42] Seneca, *Epistle* VI.

I want to be careful to note that, despite these exceptions, the overall caricature of Greek thought, in its literature, favors the linear argument.

By *autonomous* in function, I mean that each stage of the argument must stand on its own. Inductions, empirical evidence, and deductions are employed as stand-alone units toward a grander argument. Though each step of the argument may be historically or literarily contextualized for greater understanding, the arguments do not rely on such contexts for validity – to be deductively efficacious.[43]

Philosophical Convictions

Hellenism's philosophical style carries a set of convictions. The term "convictions" may sound like we have left the world of philosophy and entered some moralistic sphere. However, even in the most cutting analytic endeavors, Gary Gutting has demonstrated that even today, deductively linear arguments do not determine the favorable receptions of philosophical ideas amongst analytic philosophers. Some of the most famous twentieth-century analytic critiques do not contain deductively sound argumentation, even if they are linear in approach. He cites the favorable reception of Quine's "Two Dogmas of Empiricism" – a renowned essay from a premier logician – as a prime example: "Even more than the critique of the second dogma, this final statement of Quine's holistic vision of knowledge and reality is strikingly unargued. ... Quine's holism ... seems supported by nothing more than persuasive rhetoric. His presentation is impressive as a philosophical manifest or program, but not as a cogent argument for a conclusion."[44]

Gutting goes on to show that philosophers, like scientists, often accept linear arguments not based on their autonomously logical and deductive functions, but largely on intuitions and convictions imbued in them through their traditions.[45] Taken together, Gutting's case studies reveal that convictions are central to the philosophical community and play an outsized role in their judgments of new arguments. Hence, we ought to consider the role of the following four convictions soberly.

[43] E.g., the role of argument in Plato's *Euthyphro*, Epictetus' *Enchiridion*, etc.

[44] Gary Gutting, *What Philosophers Know: Case Studies in Recent Analytic Philosophy* (New York: Cambridge University Press, 2009), 30.

[45] Gutting, *What Philosophers Know*, 91–101, 121.

First, there appears what I would call a *domesticationist* bent to Hellenist philosophical inquiry: that most or all of the true nature of reality can be deduced by the power of reason, even if that entails the "spiritual exercises" of the particular school of philosophy (Stoic, Skeptic, Plato, etc.). Like a farmer bringing an unbroken horse into the corral, the philosopher wrestles and breaks down wily and deceitful appearances of the world into the understandable realm of the spirit. And indeed, that sums up the task of human inquiry. For example, Epictetus echoes this sentiment in relating the task of philosophy to domains of control: "Philosophy does not claim to secure for us anything outside of our control. Otherwise, it would be taking on matters that do not concern it" (*Discourses* I, 15).[46]

Though Socrates surely has a mysterionist bent to his inquisitions, the ensuing schools of philosophy have less of one. For him, we are historically bound creatures and so the nature of our inquiry cannot be anchored solely in our historically contingent understanding. As Epictetus later says, "if we haven't fully grasped and refined the instrument [i.e., logic] by which we analyse other things, how can we hope to understand [those other things] with any precision?"[47] Part of the goal, then, aims at an individual's ability to transcend the historical instances, to abstract free from our mediated experience.

Second, various schools took differing *abstractionist* routes, but all assumed the power of the mind to transcend, claiming that abstraction offers the true form of the reality under consideration. Reality, when studied apart from history, yields up proper order and tranquility of the soul. Plato uses one such exercise of contemplating everything, literally *everything*, to assess one's own value. "Do you think that a mind habituated to thoughts of grandeur and the contemplation of all time and all existence can deem this life of man a thing of great concern?"[48] The problem of a boundless mind in an all-too-bounded body evinces this kind of domesticationist conviction that dreams, "If only we were unbound, then we could know."

It is the philosophical sage who then has found such freedom of mind, which yields a totality of understanding to him alone *in abstraction*: "The consciousness he has of the world is something particular to the sage.

46 Epictetus, *Discourses and Selected Writings*, trans. Robert Dobbin (New York: Penguin Books, 2008).

47 Epictetus, *Discourses*, I, 17.

48 Plato, *Republic*, 486a.

Only the sage never ceases to have the whole constantly present to his mind."[49]

Third, the psychology of Hellenism's philosophical style proposes a strongly *mentalist* model of understanding: "The beginnings of philosophical ambition during this period involved the desire to achieve *via rational inquiry a deeper understanding of the nature and workings* of the world and thereby of our place in it."[50] Though ritualism plays a heavy-handed role in both Greek and Roman "religion" and education, Hellenism's philosophical inquiry emphasized that which happens in the mind – the "equanimity of the soul."[51] What we might now call "mental events" act as the primary and target site of philosophical practices.

We might be tempted to characterize Socrates' famous *maieutic* procedure as itself an embodied ritual. After all, a man taking time to verbally prod another man with questions meant to birth knowledge embedded in the mind is, by most definitions, an embodied rite. But embodiment is an epistemically complicating factor for Socrates and those who ensued him, the body often acting as the source of deception. In the end, for any ritual required for the spiritual practice of Hellenistic philosophy, the goal of that rite was individual transformation of the mind/soul. Hence, Hellenism relies upon a *mentalist* conviction in its philosophical style.

Fourth, the sociology that proceeds from this *mentalist* psychology and anthropology also sometimes establishes a *classist* conviction within Hellenism. The *classist* bent means that only some can understand by means of philosophical inquiry, while others will be unable by dint of their constitution. For Plato, the split fell along sociocultural boundaries, which are reified by the advocated division of the soul:

> Reason equates to statesmen/philosophers.
> The spirit/passions equate to guardians.
> Appetite equates to craftsmen and farmers.[52]

In most schools of philosophy – excepting Plato's desire to see women as guardians in *Republic* V – women and the working class were cut out of the philosophical method. Such classism was often associated with Stoicism – "this notion of a sage superior to humanity,

[49] Bernhard Groethuysen quoted in Hadot, *What Is Ancient Philosophy?*, 229.

[50] Italics mine. James Warren, "The World of Early Greek Philosophy," in *The Routledge Companion to Ancient Philosophy*, ed. James Warren and Frisbee Sheffield (New York: Routledge, 2014), 5.

[51] Hadot, *What Is Ancient Philosophy?*, 221.

[52] Plato, *Republic*, Book IX.

exempt from faults and misfortunes ... was a concept common to all the schools."[53] This classism was said to increase in the Roman schools due to the textualizing of philosophers and the requisite knowledge to enter the debates. James Warren sets the scene: "It remained at this period to a large extent the business of a close community of intellectuals who were well-informed about one another's views and, in all likelihood, engaged in close and detailed, probably face-to-face, debate with one another."[54]

The above cannot serve as *the* definition of Hellenism's philosophical style, but rather, a collection of genetic markers accurate enough for us to make distinctions between Hellenism and other ancient styles of philosophizing (e.g., Egyptian, Mesopotamian, and Israelite).

As I depict the philosophical style of the Scriptures in the coming chapters, similarities to Hellenism in emphasis and practice have already been noticed. Pierre Hadot's *What Is Ancient Philosophy?* makes this claim most dramatically, demonstrating that Greek philosophy did not solely huddle around the fire of rational discourse. Rather, Hellenistic philosophy took torches out into the body politic and adjacent spheres of culture. Philosophy was *practiced* alongside discourse, not merely *discussed*.

In this sense, there is a ritualist bent to Greek philosophy "as a way of life," even if the rites ultimately focused on the mentalist conviction aimed at an individual's spiritual formation. Recent suggestions have been made that the current analytic tradition of theology could pattern itself as a "way of life" in this same way and for similar reasons.[55]

Greek philosophy typically demonstrated understanding through life practices. For instance, when Hippias turns the question back on Socrates about the meaning of justice, Socrates refers to his life:

> "Indeed, Hippias! Haven't you noticed that I never cease to declare my notions of what is just?"
>
> "And how can you call that an account?"
>
> "I declare them by my deeds, anyhow, if not by my words. Don't you think that deeds are better evidence than words?"

53 Émile Bréhier, *Chrysippe*, quoted in Hadot, *What Is Ancient Philosophy?*, 232.

54 James Warren, "Hellenistic Philosophy: Places, Institutions, Character," in *The Routledge Companion to Ancient Philosophy*, ed. James Warren and Frisbee Sheffield (New York: Routledge, 2014), 394.

55 William Wood, "Analytic Theology as a Way of Life," *Journal of Analytic Theology* 2 (May 2014): 43–60.

"Yes, much better, of course; for many say what is just and do what is unjust; but no one who does what is just can be unjust."[56]

And hence the embodied practice is the philosophy, "that it is the just person's life and existence which best determines what justice is."[57]

Turning to early Christianity, Hadot notes a similar emphasis on life practice as forming the soul. Largely ignoring the biblical texts, he jumps to Hellenistic Christian writings of Clement, Origen, Augustine, and the like. He quite rightly observes in their texts: "Like Greek philosophy, Christian philosophy presented itself both as a discourse and as a way of life."[58]

But Hadot skips, almost entirely, over the philosophical style of the New Testament, not to mention the Hebrew Bible. This omission is one gap I aim to patch in part. The low hanging fruit of synthetic Hellenist-Christian apologetics in the early church certainly imbibed in the "vocabulary and concepts of secular philosophy."[59] The question I will try to answer in this book is: Does the Christian Scripture, consisting of the Hebrew Bible and New Testament, maintain a stable and discernible philosophical style despite the employment of philosophical vocabulary and constructs from surrounding cultures?

Why "Hebraic" Philosophy?

I use the term "Hebraic philosophy" to refer to the philosophical style of the Torah that carries forward into the rest of the Hebrew Bible and the New Testament. Surely the biblical scholars will ask: Why not call this "Semitic philosophy," or use some other term such as "Israelite," "Jewish," or "Judahite" to modify philosophy?

The term "Hebraic" only refers to the language and people from whom the Hebrew Bible descends. Of course, those texts come to us early in Greek (i.e., the LXX), just as early as the Hebrew. But, more importantly, the Hebrew biblical texts have no traces of Hellenism in content. I could have chosen "Israelite philosophy" or "Jewish philosophy," which flags up the problem with any term I use. Every term carries historical assumptions and complexities that are sometimes perpendicular to what I am arguing for here.

56 Plato, *Xenophon Memorabilia*, 4.4:10–11.
57 Hadot, *What Is Ancient Philosophy?*, 31.
58 Hadot, *What Is Ancient Philosophy?*, 239.
59 Hadot, *What Is Ancient Philosophy?*, 249.

The term Hebraic, with the questions it raises and problems implicit to it, gives me a suitable designation for a philosophical style antecedent to Hellenism and distinct from other speculative schools in the ancient Near East. This style does not necessarily belong to the Judahite returnees; though one could make the case that they had their finalizing editorial hands on these texts.

Maybe we could deem it Jewish philosophy in that sense. But the Judaism that grows out of the Second Temple Period as a sibling religion alongside Christianity makes the term "Jewish" entirely too complicated for my purposes. "Israelite philosophy" seems to miss the Judahite provenance of these texts. "Semitic" bears too much breadth to be useful, as it would effectively include Arab, Assyrian, and more.

And so, the term "Hebraic philosophy" will have to do. "Hebraic" offers, at the least, a way to minimally bind the extant collection of texts with the language going back to the tenth century BCE and the general people group associated with both.

What Distinguishes Hebraic Philosophy?

The Hebraic philosophical style will be explored more fully in Chapter 3. For now, an abbreviated list can sufficiently sketch out the distinctive style and forms of Hebraic arguments that persist into the New Testament.

The Hebrew perception of the cosmos creates the conditions from which they can conceptualize it. I mean that, for example, if we view the cosmos as having a strict cause and effect on relationships based on what we now call "the laws of physics," then our examinations of and conclusions about the operations of the world will follow suit. What aspects of the cosmos acted as the primary referents for Hebraic intellectualism?

1. Hebrew creation accounts set out a discrete metaphysical structure to the cosmos with primacy placed upon personal relations between God and all objects in the universe. God regulates and orders all movements and objects of the cosmos.
2. The first story (Gen 2–3) centers upon establishing an epistemological structure for critically exploring the cosmos.[60]

60 Johnson, *Epistemology and Biblical Theology*, 17–55.

3. Truth and justification entail personal agency and not brute appeals to logical necessity. Deductively logical arguments are secure on the basis of the persons involved, not merely the internal coherence of deductions.
4. A critically engaged community, or not, reflecting upon historically divine acts features as the style of second-order explorations of natures and relations in reality.
5. This Hebraic style of philosophy is reified in the speech and acts of the authorized prophet Jesus of Nazareth.
6. In the Apostles' speeches and the epistles, reflection on the speech and acts of Jesus attains a status equivalent to divine speech and acts in the Hebrew Bible.

This minimal collection, which could be easily expanded, frames the conditions under which Israel thinks abstractly about the world around her.

For example, something as religiously loaded as "fear of Yahweh" acts philosophically in the Hebrew Bible. The fear of Yahweh, including the discernment that develops from that fear, is intellectually formative. According to Proverbs, there is something about trusting that "Yahweh is the creator" that will change the way you think about justice and political structures and ethics and knowledge itself: "Wisdom [based in "fear of Yahweh"] discerns the whole in relation to its individual parts ... based on the recognition that even exhaustive data is inadequate, for it is the relationships between the things that make knowledge most useful."[61]

Unless such concepts are revered as intellectually formative, these can also distance modern Western thinkers from an insider understanding of the second-order topics explored within the biblical literature.

As for the style of Hebraic philosophy, from the Hebrew Bible into the New Testament, argumentation comes in both familiar and alien packages. I will demonstrate in Part II of this book that the Hebraic style of philosophy places primacy on narrative and instruction texts in training a philosophical community of disciples, all of which is aimed at discernment. The Hebraic philosophy is an epistemically-centered tradition: who knows what and how.

The style of philosophy then refers to those elements that frame and compel the modes of argument according to the required convictions. In

[61] Ryan P. O'Dowd, *Proverbs* (The Story of God Bible Commentary; Grand Rapids, MI: Zondervan, 2017), 34–35.

Chapter 3, I discuss the two modes (pixelated, networked) and four convictions (ritualist, transdemographic, mysterionist, creationist) central to the Hebraic style of philosophy.

The specific forms of philosophical argument are the literary methods adequate to explore topics according to the style. Biblical authors employ all or some of the following forms of reasoning to accomplish this goal:

1. Narratives as argument
2. Definition by *genus* and *differentia*
3. Analogical reasoning
4. Lists and taxonomical thinking
5. Pre-Aristotelian logic with non-binary truth[62]
6. Discernible cause and effect relationships

Much more will be said about each of these in the coming chapters, but this list already reveals philosophical methods both familiar and foreign to the style most commonly practiced in the West today.

Conclusions

Now that the possibility that Christian Scripture might count as philosophy has been established, we can proceed. In this book, I will explore the live question: Is there a biblical philosophy of Christian Scripture? By putting the variegated texts of the Christian canon alongside its peer intellectual worlds, I hope to show that not only does Christian Scripture advocate a discrete form of philosophical insight, but that our intellectual world today shares more in common with the conceptual world of the Christian Scriptures than the Greeks, Egyptians, or Mesopotamians. In this sense, its prescriptive reach might still extend to us.

[62] By pre-Aristotelian logic, I only mean that the most basic rules of *modus ponens* and *modus tollens* appear to operate in judgments. Giving primacy to a non-binary view of truth does not exclude true/false predications from a Hebraic view of logic, rather, it makes true/false determinations secondary issues. Susanne Bobzien, "Ancient Logic," *Stanford Encyclopedia of Philosophy*, Summer 2020 ed., ed. Edward N. Zalta, https://plato.stanford.edu/archives/sum2020/entries/logic-ancient/.

2

Philosophy before the Greeks

The Ancient Near Eastern Intellectual Context

Before diving into the philosophical content of Christian Scripture, it is important to understand that the biblical authors are always at once engaging and critiquing the philosophies and practices that surround them. Nowhere in the Christian Scriptures can one claim that authors merely recite Babylonian myth, Egyptian folklore, or tenets of Middle Platonism. These all make their appearances in the biblical texts, but most often as a foil, a part of a grander argument to affirm what is laudable, or a reorientation away from erroneous thinking.

To continue in distinguishing Hebraic philosophy from other styles, the ancient Near Eastern context will aid us in seeing Israel's discrete philosophical trajectory, quite distinct from its peer literary traditions. Scholars such as Peter Machinist have considered the theologically distinctive nature of Israel based primarily on her relationship to Yahweh, Yahweh's proximity, and more.[1] Yet, the pronounced rhetorical style of Israel has received less examination.[2]

In this chapter, I focus on theology, metaphysics, epistemology, and ethics, grossly summarizing what ancient Near East scholars have concluded about these empires and populations that rooted themselves in Mesopotamia, the Levant, and Egypt. Though this summary will be

[1] Peter Machinist, "The Question of Distinctiveness in Ancient Israel: An Essay," in *Ah Assyria ...: Studies in Assyrian History and Ancient Near Eastern Historiography Presented to Hayim Tadmor*, ed. Mordechai Cogan and Israel Eph'al (Scripta Hierosolymitana 33; Jerusalem: Magnes Press, 1991), 196–212.

[2] The obvious examinations of Israel's philosophical rhetoric would be the work of Thorleif Boman, Michael Carasik, Yoram Hazony, Henri Frankfort, Jaco Gericke, etc.

necessarily sweeping and incomplete, I intend for it to give a sufficient description for thinking about how Hebrews appropriate and critique the intellectual world of the ancient Near East from within their independent writing tradition.

The Intellectual Adventure of Ancient Man

In 1946, Henri Frankfort first published a collection of essays on ancient intellectualism titled *The Intellectual Adventure of Ancient Man: An Essay on Speculative Thought in the Ancient Near East.*[3] The essays were produced as lectures initially with his colleagues at the University of Chicago's prestigious Oriental Institute: Thorkild Jacobsen, William A. Irwin, and John A. Wilson. Frankfort's synthesis of the philosophical potential of all three regions – Egypt, Mesopotamia, and Israel – bookends the volume, a summary to which I will return. The book has been widely read in ancient Near Eastern studies, but much less so in biblical scholarship.

One common mid-twentieth-century bias is worth noting up front: the authors share a progressivist bent and overtly argue for the ability to transcend myth as the hallmark of fully philosophical literature. This kind of progressivism *du jour* was to be expected in the age of positivism. Per Frankfort et al., the Egyptians and Babylonians were prescientific – fastidious in recording the world around them, but without a theoretical analysis to tie the data together. Conversely, the Greeks abstracted objects like *ideas* and *forms* to speculatively ground their empirical observations of the heavens and earth a millennium later. Frankfort's volume wants to explain the gulf between the prescientism of the Babylonians from the full-orbed conceptually abstracted world of the Greeks.

Representative of her guild, Assyriologist Francesca Rochberg believes that Frankfort's progressivist critique is no longer sustainable in light of the past decades of research. Frankfort's *Intellectual Adventure*, Sir James Frazer's *The Golden Bough*, and Johannes Pedersen's *Early Physics and Astronomy* all marvel at the mathematical complexity of Mesopotamian astrology yet lament that it cannot be "scientific" because it was aimed at

[3] Henri Frankfort et al., *The Intellectual Adventure of Ancient Man: An Essay on Speculative Thought in the Ancient Near East* (Chicago: University of Chicago Press, 1946), 37.

omenology: the study of predicting historical events coordinated with omens.[4]

Rochberg laments what these works collectively overlooked: Mesopotamian astrology does indeed have a theoretical basis, it was mathematically predictive, and "the demarcation criteria formerly used to justify a rigorous separation of science from other forms of knowledge and practice were found to be neither necessary nor sufficient for a universal definition of science."[5]

More simply, if we define "science" as "what the Greeks did," then the outcomes follow quite predictably. A parallel and equally problematic definition of philosophy seems to follow the same trend (see Chapter 1). Rochberg and others suggest that by surveying the logical structure, the inner workings of the Babylonian astrology, and the predictive prowess of their astrological skill, the prescientific/scientific boundary is no longer helpful.

Revisiting a point from early chapters, it would surprise many to find that when *The Intellectual Adventure of Ancient Man* surveys the scholarly achievements of Egypt, Mesopotamia, and the Hebrews, Frankfort et al. separate the Hebraic intellectual tradition for acclaim. Specifically, it was the Hebrews alone, according to Frankfort and Irwin, who transcended the concrete instances of history in order to abstract from the world around them. Though Frankfort and his colleagues still believe the Hebrew Bible to be stuck in myth, as required for structuring their thought, these scholars marvel at the intellectual achievement of the biblical texts. For them, Hebrew thought exhibits a different order and degree of intellectualism.

These Assyriologists and Hebraists celebrate the Hebrews above other ancient Near Eastern literature in a manner rarely witnessed in the world of biblical scholarship. "[The Hebrews] propounded, not speculative theory, but revolutionary and dynamic teaching."[6] Frankfort singles out the intellectual inertia of monotheism for what now seems to be commonplace assumptions: "This conception of God represents so high a degree of abstraction that, in reaching it, the

[4] Francesca Rochberg, *The Heavenly Writing: Divination, Horoscopy, and Astronomy in Mesopotamian Culture* (New York: Cambridge University Press, 2004), 30–43. See also Eric Voegelin, *Order and History: Israel and Revelation*, ed. Maurice P. Hogan (The Collected Works of Eric Voegelin; Columbia, MO: University of Missouri Press, 2001), 93–94.

[5] Rochberg, *The Heavenly Writing*, 288.

[6] Frankfort et al., *The Intellectual Adventure of Ancient Man*, 373.

Hebrews seem to have left the realm of mythopoeic thought."[7] Perceptively, Frankfort notices that the rampant parallelomania – finding literary parallels between the Hebrew Bible and Mesopotamian texts – needs calibration in the Hebrew texts, which have innovations not found elsewhere: "It is possible to detect the reflection of Egyptian and Mesopotamian beliefs in many episodes of the Old Testament; but the overwhelming impression left by that document is one, not of derivation, but of originality."[8] Most extraordinary for many of us, he sees the philosophical roots of modern Western Civilization *not in the Greco-Roman world* but growing out of the Hebrew Bible. His wonderment deserves our attention, as this basic premise has resurfaced in recent Jewish scholarship, notably in the works of David Novak, Yoram Hazony, Joshua Berman, and Jeremiah Unterman:[9]

> The boundary between the ancient world and the modern is to be traced, *not in the Aegean or the middle Mediterranean, but in the pages of the Old Testament*, where we find revealed Israel's attainments in the realms of thought, her facility in literary expression, her profound religious insights, and her standards of individual and social ethics.[10]

I want to affirm many of the insights offered by Frankfort et al., most of which remain underappreciated in biblical studies. I cannot, however, propagate their bias that myth is an incapable form of speculation in a philosophical system. The myth of "intellectually-vapid religious myths" has some purchase in assessing the coherence of a system of thought. However, religious myth cannot automatically count against a system of thought in all cases, such as when a creation narrative is integral to understanding the philosophy of the whole system. If it did, then, current scientific cosmogonies based on the Big Bang Theory would not pass Frankfort's standard of transcending myth. According to one British philosopher's account, evolution would not make the cut

7 Frankfort et al., *The Intellectual Adventure of Ancient Man*, 369.

8 Frankfort et al., *The Intellectual Adventure of Ancient Man*, 367.

9 David Novak, *Jewish Social Ethics* (New York: Oxford University Press, 1992); *Athens and Jerusalem: God, Humans, and Nature* (The Gifford Lectures 2017; Toronto: University of Toronto Press, 1992); Yoram Hazony, *The Philosophy of Hebrew Scripture* (New York: Cambridge University Press, 2012); Joshua A. Berman, *Created Equal: How the Bible Broke with Ancient Political Thought* (New York: Oxford University Press, 2011); *Ani Maamin: Biblical Criticism, Historical Truth, and the Thirteen Principles of Faith* (Jerusalem: Magid, 2020); Jeremiah Unterman, *Justice for All: How the Jewish Bible Revolutionized Ethics* (Philadelphia: Jewish Publication Society, 2017).

10 Italics mine. Frankfort et al., *The Intellectual Adventure of Ancient Man*, 224.

either.[11] As a matter of history, scientists today are often fastidiously unaware of the theoretical underpinnings of their work. Ignorance of the philosophy of science and scientific epistemology, in particular, has been anecdotally reported across the academy. And yet, despite this ignorance, we do not therefore assume their scholarship to be fruitless.

With this all-too-brief history of intellectualism studies of the ancient Near East in hand, I now turn to the thought-worlds of Egypt and then Mesopotamia. In the writing traditions of these two civilizations, if we can pare them down to two, a philosophical style is discernible but thinner than what we will find in the Hebrew Bible and NT.

Egypt

Uniformity of cult, art, and language remained unusually stable over three thousand years of Egyptian history. Despite the complexity of the Egyptian pantheon and theology, the evolution into monotheism and out again,[12] and the competing political theologies of creation, the radical continuity of Egyptian culture surpasses anything known in the ancient or modern world. That continuity emerging alongside a society crowded into a long and lean strip of land hemming the Nile River partially explains the conceptual girth that both enables and impedes development in the Egyptian intellectual world. What was at once conceptually wondrous, ultimately proved inflexible.

Jan Assmann makes this unwavering uniformity poignant in his fictional depiction of a man visiting a memorial. He ponders what the notion of "history" would mean to a Roman Egyptian (ca. 125 CE) reading the hieroglyphed walls of a monument inscribed in the fourth millennium BCE. Because of the impossibility of us empathizing with such a circumstance, it is worth reading (and visualizing!) in full:

> Let us imagine for a moment the case of an educated Egyptian living in the period of the Roman Empire – under Hadrian [ca. 125 CE], say – and visiting the remains of the mortuary cult of Djoser from the Third Dynasty [ca. 3000 BCE]. This man would be able to read not only the inscriptions left during an epoch dating back over two thousand eight hundred years ... but also the hieratic graffiti of other visitors before him – fifteen hundred years before! He would contemplate the monument with the awareness of belonging to the same culture; his cultural

[11] Mary Midgley, *Evolution as a Religion: Strange Hopes and Strange Fears*, revised ed. (New York: Routledge, 2002).

[12] I.e., the Amarna Period of the eighteenth dynasty.

identification thus would extend back over thousands of years, and would result not from an exceptional personal education or "sense of history" but from his present cultural parameters, which ensure that the old is so well preserved in the new as to make identification with it possible. In Egypt, the old remained present; it never became alien in the sense of representing something left definitively behind, something unrecoverable or irretrievable.[13]

It would be a forced gesture to say that Egypt had a discernible philosophy, but it certainly had a robust intellectual world with complex metaphysical relations and a functional epistemology centered upon analogical reasoning. Egyptians' metaphysics and epistemology were both grounded in creation narratives, which shifted and conflicted over time. Like Israel, Egypt's creation narratives shaped how Egyptians understood themselves, which is presumably why later Memphite Theology conscientiously renarrated Egypt's creation story to justify Memphis as the regional power, for instance.[14] Unlike Israel's scriptures, Egypt's creation narratives originated in Egyptian locales and different accounts involved different gods, often revealing political maneuvering.

In the waning years, when deteriorating pyramids reminded Egyptians of a former and glorious age of permanence, the promise of eternal political power through the god-kings of Egypt also flagged, producing existential speculations on the worth of man and political power.[15]

The success or failure of kingship produced literary reactions as well. Hymns serenaded the golden age of pyramids. Centuries later, dirges lamented the hard times in an age of wind-whipped monuments that now stood as megalithic evidence of deteriorating confidence in the god-kings.[16] So Voegelin sums it, "When the symbols of eternity [stone monuments] were themselves passing away, the attempt to build eternity materially into this world must have appeared convincingly futile."[17] Those so-called Times of Trouble have been diagnosed through archaeology, but mostly through the writings that question the worth of the dynastic project.

Egyptians, living in a quirky land, spoke of themselves as outsiders to the rest of the world. John Wilson called it the "green gash" that is Egypt, a fertile stripe extending from the banks of the Nile, rimmed by cliffs and

13 Jan Assmann, *The Mind of Egypt: History and Meaning in the Time of the Pharaohs*, trans. Andrew Jenkins (New York: Metropolitan Books, 1996), 20.

14 Voegelin, *Order and History*, 98.

15 I am thinking here of the "Song of the Harper," Voegelin, *Order and History*, 97.

16 Frankfort et al., *The Intellectual Adventure of Ancient Man*, 71, 80.

17 Voegelin, *Order and History*, 133.

gutting the open desert from the Mediterranean southward.[18] A singular highway could bring news and commerce along that fertile rut from Lower to Upper Egypt.

I want to briefly discuss central and stable principles that contributed to the intellectual world of Egypt. Though these are terse treatments, I aim at bringing the reader into the world of the biblical literature and its natural interlocutors of a period spanning from the late Bronze to the Iron Age (1200–400 BCE). The Egyptian literature goes back much further (ca. 3000 BCE), but these points of philosophical interest will help us to understand the overt philosophical thought in the Hebrew Bible as compared to Egypt.

To understand their cosmos, we can consider that any intellectual system in Egypt depends upon deference to the following aspects of its thought-world:

- Water-based creation of the cosmos: Egypt was founded during the creation of the cosmos where the universe began as a "primordial mound" rising *out of the water*.
- Egyptians analogically reasoned from experience with their peculiar physical locale along the Nile.
- Though not peculiar to Egypt, Egyptian thought about the cosmos covaried with the contemporary political structure.
- Egyptian god-kings ruled within a metaphysically rooted political philosophy.
- Egyptian literature gives only hints at its epistemological anthropology.

Because these aspects of Egyptian thought unfold, interweave, and morph over millennia, I will pare them down to these three themes: creation cosmology, epistemology, and the metaphysics of political philosophy, to give a taste of their speculative world.

Creation

It was this verdant highway of a nation called "Egypt" with its seasonal floods that gave rise, quite literally, to creation's story. Any description of Egyptian creation can be footnoted by later versions of the account. The characters and locations of creation will change over time, and even a supplementary story will emerge to explain how humans are formed and breathed to life.

[18] Wilson in Frankfort et al., *The Intellectual Adventure of Ancient Man*, 31.

In some ways, Egypt's collection of creation accounts resembles the Hebrew Bible's dual account: two creations side by side, but from different perspectives. They hold on to these two accounts, not in tension, but as complementary. Primeval creation of the world happens at the behest of a chief god, but humans are handcrafted on the potter's wheel of Khnum. Unlike Egypt's account, however, no hint of a theogony of god exists in the Hebrew Bible.[19]

Gods and humans are created in different accounts in Egypt. The theogenic account begins with the first god Atum sneezing (or ejaculating) the first collection of eight gods.[20] The anthropogenic account depicts the god Khnum (not one of the eight original gods) crafting little humans from the Nile's silt and the goddess Heket giving them the "breath of life" before setting them on their way.[21]

Though several iterations of cosmogony populate Egyptian literature, their basic agreement centers on a primordial hill rising from the primordial waters of chaos (the Nile) and springing forth life. This reportedly mirrored a local phenomenon of Nile flooding that, when receding, revealed muddy hillocks that quickly sprung to life with plants. Creation was a process of divine animation of nature establishing Egyptian supremacy.

All versions of the creation story include the gods being assigned to and animating the elements of what we would call "the natural world." Egyptian theology assigned gods to the earth (Geb), wind (Amun), sun (Ra), atmosphere (Shu), and lion (Sekhmet), and even the pharaonic king himself becomes deified by a god. Gods were colocated with natural phenomena, though it is indiscernible whether Egyptians thought the gods existed ubiquitously across natural phenomena or locally. For instance, it is unclear whether *Sekhmet* is present in all individual lions, in the species as a whole, or manifested in particular lions under discrete circumstances.

[19] James K. Hoffmeier, "Some Thoughts on Genesis 1 & 2 and Egyptian Cosmology," *Journal of the Ancient Near Eastern Society* 15 (1983): 39–49. See also: Tony L. Shetter, "Genesis 1–2 in Light of Ancient Egyptian Creation Myths," April 22, 2005 (https://bible.org/article/genesis-1-2-light-ancient-egyptian-creation-myths), which summarizes part of his dissertation: Tony L. Shetter, "The Implications of Egyptian Cosmology for the Genesis Creation Accounts" (PhD diss., Asbury Theological Seminary, 2005).

[20] Referring to the Hymn to Ptah: Frankfort et al., *The Intellectual Adventure of Ancient Man*, 51–60.

[21] Henri Frankfort, *Ancient Egyptian Religion: An Interpretation* (New York: Columbia University Press, 1948), 20–21.

They projected their understanding of the world *Egyptian-ly*, or, one could say they conceptually *Egyptianized* everywhere that was not Egypt.[22] Notably, these creation accounts happen *in Egypt*. Egypt is the center of the universe so much so that Egyptians depicted other "miserable Asiatic" regions in terms of their Nile-centric experience. They described other countries, where it rains, as having their Nile in the sky.

In their thinking, Egypt itself was the norming norm of the cosmos – from its river that flowed north to its seasonal flooding. The centrality of Egypt in their own thought-world extended beyond the creation accounts into their vocabulary. For instance, though many societies made rigid insider-outsider distinctions (Israelite/Gentile, Greek/Barbarian, etc.), the Egyptian term itself for "human" referred exclusively to Egyptians. Foreigners were, quite literally, not humans in their lexica. The word for "land" referred to the land *of Egypt*. As John Wilson put it, "Egyptians were self-centered and had their own satisfied kind of isolationism."[23] (These factors – isolationism and Egypt's sense of superiority – make the biblical account of Queen Sheba's comments about Solomon in 1 Kings 10 almost inconceivable.)

Their isolationism maintained a both broad and lengthy uniformity over millennia of dynasties. But Egypt's cultural force might have been what also restrained transcendent sensibilities in their thought. So, Jan Assmann believes, "The more compact and undiversified a culture is, the less able it is to engage in self-criticism and change."[24] In contrast to the self-critical and dynamic aspects of Hebraic thought, Egypt's rigid thought-world was both its enduring legacy and possibly its philosophical debility.

The Egyptian creation story was central in Egyptians' speculative-world. The same is true for the Hebrew Bible and the New Testament, where the twin creation accounts, their rhetorical force, and the conceptual spheres they broach will also shape Hebrew thought. The Hebrew god creates and eventually commissions one family so that "all the families of the earth shall be blessed" (Gen 12:3). This family left Mesopotamia and sojourned among the Hittites, then down through Canaan and with the Egyptians. Possibly, it was the cosmopolitan and critically engaged nature of the Hebrew creation accounts, or their

[22] Frankfort et al., *The Intellectual Adventure of Ancient Man*, 37–38.

[23] Wilson in Frankfort et al., *The Intellectual Adventure of Ancient Man*, 37.

[24] Assmann, *The Mind of Egypt*, 16.

connective tissues into the formation of Israel as a nomadic nation, that explains the lack of any such Hebrew isolationism.

Epistemology

Ancient Egypt does not appear to advocate a particular view of knowledge in her writings.[25] However, this has not restrained scholars from waxing widely about the concepts constructed by their phenomenal experience of the land. This kind of experienced-based reasoning has been termed "analogical reasoning" and has proven fruitful for explaining the network of models and metaphors that proliferate in our most technical descriptions of reality today, including conceptual models in scientific epistemology.[26]

Permit me a brief aside on analogical reasoning to clarify some of the discussion surrounding Egyptian speculative thought (cf. Chapter 9 for a fuller discussion of analogical reasoning). Analogical reasoning attempts to describe how we use concepts derived from embodied understanding or analogies to examine or rationalize an idea. For instance, if I claim, "Divorcing ethics from medical practice will bear unimaginable consequences," I am using something more than a metaphor to make the idea comprehensible. In this example, I draw upon the reader's knowledge of "divorce" as a regrettable separation of two things intended to be united. It is a strong analogy because divorce is usually *wrapped* in intense emotions, a *breakdown* of relationships, and can psychologically *injure* the spouses and their children. (Notice that "wrapped," "breakdown," and "injure" are all metaphorically *deployed* descriptors, as is "deployed.") Not to mention the other analogy being used to conceptualize the problem of the divorce: it cannot happen without "unimaginable consequences."

George Lakoff and Mark Johnson *launched* an all-out *assault* in the 1980s on naïve literalism with their book *Metaphors We Live By*. They

[25] In a working group with Jan Assmann and Amr El-Hawary, among others (Second Order Thinking in the Ancient Fertile Crescent Conference, Aarhus, Denmark, 2017), we discussed the idea of an ancient Egyptian epistemology and El-Hawary presented a compelling paper on a possible epistemic playground created by the so-called crossword stela (Amr El-Hawary, "New Platonic, Post-Structuralistic – Except Modern: Ancient Egyptian Representations of Pre-modern Dynamic Thinking"). However, it is difficult to know if this artifact presents a broadly held epistemological text or if a one-off piece.

[26] Mary Hesse, *Revolutions and Reconstructions in the Philosophy of Science* (Brighton: The Harvester Press, 1980); *The Structure of Scientific Inference* (London: Macmillan Press, 1974).

argued that almost every way we *frame* reality with words requires *deeply embedded* metaphors.[27] In later works, Lakoff and Johnson each *build* on their metaphor theory to suggest that our conceptual *structures* themselves *spring* from our embodied experience and our ability to imaginatively *employ* analogies.[28]

For example, because we experience cause and effect by pushing or pulling a physical object with our bodies (e.g., pushing a shopping cart), we conceptualize these as different forms of COMPULSION, which we can then *extend* into our abstract reasoning. In math and deductive logic, we can think of the example of logical necessity. The square root of 961 ($\sqrt{961}$) must necessarily equal 31, and it could not be any other answer. Why could it not be otherwise? Thirty-one (31) is required by the logical necessity of mathematics – it deductively must be the case. How do we *arrive* at this abstract sense of "it must be the case" and not just "it ought to be the case"? Notice that we do not try to logically justify the necessity of the logical conclusion. After all, what argument could we possibly *deploy* in its favor?

Alfred Whitehead and Bertrand Russell's *Principia Mathematica* (Volume 1) is one such attempt. Over the course of a 700-page book, they attempt to deductively justify that $1 + 1 = 2$.[29] Alas, Whitehead and Russell were not ultimately successful. But even if they were successful, most people do not appeal to the *Principia Mathematica* to justify the logical necessity of "the square root of 961 must necessarily equal 31." Lakoff and Johnson argued that instead we use our conceptualized analog of COMPULSION – learned only through our body – and analogically *map* that sense of COMPULSION onto the idea (the conviction, actually) of logical necessity. Mathematical solutions are compellingly true, like pushing a wheelbarrow is compelling it forward. Without *dropping* into the *deep end* of metalogical problems in the twentieth century, we can simply note that analogical concepts are useful for thinking about Egypt and other cultures (including the modern West).

[27] George Lakoff and Mark Johnson, *Metaphors We Live By* (Chicago: University of Chicago Press, 1980); see Johnson's further development: Mark Johnson, *The Body in the Mind: The Bodily Basis of Meaning, Imagination, and Reason* (Chicago: University of Chicago Press, 1987). For precise examples from mathematics, see George Lakoff, *Women, Fire, and Dangerous Things: What Categories Reveal about the Mind* (Chicago: University of Chicago Press, 1989), 353–69.

[28] Johnson, *The Body in the Mind*; Lakoff, *Women, Fire, and Dangerous Things*.

[29] Alfred North Whitehead and Bertrand Russell, *Principia Mathematica*, Vol. 1, 2nd ed. (New York: Cambridge University Press, 1963).

Returning to the intellectualism of Egypt, scholars claim that their conceptual world was *awash*[30] in such analogical conceptions. Three facile examples and one more complex notion demonstrate this kind of conceptualization at work: (1) the god of wind, (2) the course of the sun as death–rebirth, (3) binary categories conceptualized from topography, and (4) the eternal permanence of the king through god-king manifestation.

First, and most simply, the god Amun (who eventually merged with Ra to become Amun-Ra) is the god of wind, but also a god who remains hidden. The word itself *amun* means "hidden" or "invisible." Hymns to Amun muse about this play on words: "He who hides, his name is Amun."[31] Most basically, the experience of wind as an invisible yet powerful force is deified in the god Amun, one of the supreme gods in later Egyptian theology. The concept-to-experience relation is strong in this example.

Second, humans do not have raw experience of reality, but we presumably interpret our direct observation of daily events through rubrics, narratives, and schemas. Hence, ancient conceptual structures built off of daily observations differ from how we might conceptualize the same events today. For instance, the modern narrative of a rotating earth in reference to the sun will affect the concepts we analogize from our experience. It makes perfect sense to us if we analogically reason about the odds of winning the lottery by saying, "The sun is always shining on someone" – even if the logic of this statement is statistically specious.[32] That statement would be incoherent in ancient Egypt for reasons I will discuss. Conversely, it would not make sense to us from our interpreted experience of the sun if we said, "The sun teaches us that you have to die, then battle to be reborn every day."

For ancient Egyptians, the sun proceeds across the sky every day in the boat of Ra, who is portrayed in later texts as the creator god. Because the cosmos is a flat disc, the sun's disappearance at the end of Ra's course means it has been swallowed by darkness. Dead, it then battles in the

30 From this point onward, I will not italicize metaphors and analogies.

31 Jan Assmann, *God and Gods: Egypt, Israel, and the Rise of Monotheism* (Madison: The University of Wisconsin Press, 2008), 64.

32 Carl Gustav Hempel famously demonstrated through logical equivalence that a statement such as "all ravens are black" could be logically confirmed by observing any instance of a nonblack object that is also not a raven, for instance. This paradox remains a difficulty for the basic logic of confirmation to this day. "Studies in the Logic of Confirmation (I)," *Mind* 54 (1945): 1–26.

underworld through the night with a serpent and is then reborn every day to sail the sky in Ra's ship once again. Thus, Egyptians carried in them a basic death–battle–rebirth pattern of analogical thought and employed it conceptually to reason about their cosmos. Notice that the narrative or schema one brings to the experience of a sunrise determines what kind of analogical reasoning is conceptually possible.

Darkness represents the trepidation over whether Ra can win and deliver the sun in the morning – in both senses of "deliver."[33] This fear of darkness goes beyond the generic fear that we all must conquer in ourselves. Taking Hume's arguments about inductive inferences to their fullest and most terrifying conclusion, each night's darkness is ultimately uncertainty about the fate of Ra. (Now we can appreciate how pointedly Exodus' penultimate plague of darkness was meant to terrorize Egypt.)

The daily construct of death–battle–rebirth also describes the Nile's annual journey from recession to flood. Through creation narratives, Egyptians saw something different than what we see in the sky: a drama between a powerful god and an uncertain night journey. The conceptual output of the sun's night journey becomes death–battle–rebirth – a concept they then freely applied to the annual flooding of the river. It is a concept that cannot be built today out of our solar-system model with a rotating earth.

Third, although scholars debate the source of the dualism, a clear sense of balanced binaries frequently occurs in Egyptian texts and art. This is not the kind of oppositional dualism found in later Persian Zoroastrianism.[34] This binary or symmetrical dualism posits every sphere of life dualistically. In the cosmos, we find the expected opposites of heaven/earth, north/south, etc. And, in the political realm, kings are both gracious and terrifying.[35]

Much like the dualism in the Hebrew Bible (e.g., heaven/earth, blessing/curse, good/evil, etc.), the terms of Egyptian dualism seem to point to epistemic categories that help to carve up the universe more than to ontological claims on reality. Unlike our contemporary binary concepts in absolute opposition (e.g., on/off), these pairs express balance and symmetry, which does not necessarily entail opposition (possibly reflecting the Egyptian principle of order: *ma'at*).

33 Frankfort et al., *The Intellectual Adventure of Ancient Man*, 48.

34 Frankfort et al., *The Intellectual Adventure of Ancient Man*, 41; Voegelin, *Order and History*, 106.

35 Frankfort et al., *The Intellectual Adventure of Ancient Man*, 71.

Fourth, a complex concept of the state's permanence is analogically worked out in various forms. Stone monuments exude the analogy of the eternal state. Massive and steady, these onerously built monuments dotted the Nile valley. Their uniform presence from generation to generation made for ready analogs of the gods' eternal favor upon Egypt. Even more, writing and art found in those monuments bespeak the millennia-long uniformity noted above (e.g., Assmann's Egyptian Roman at the tomb) and made ancient history immediately present.

An intricate version of state-permanence can be seen in the presence of gods in animals.[36] Gods were somehow present in a species, though again, it is unclear to what degree and extent.[37] Despite the ambiguity, Frankfort observes that the divine manifestations in animals might have also contributed to an average Egyptian's trust in an eternal state. How so? "The animals never change [generation to generation], and in this respect especially they would appear to share – in a degree unknown to man – the fundamental nature of creation."[38] Just as the pyramids might have provided analogs of stability unknown among humans – who each look, speak, and behave differently – sheep do not appear to change generationally.

Eric Voegelin believes the analogical train of thought runs from species to individual animal, and then from animal to king.[39] If gods manifested themselves across a species, then the community is greater than the individual, because "the animal species, outlasting the existence of individual man, approaches the lasting of the world and the gods."[40] The creator god also manifests himself in the king (hence the term "god-king" that I have used throughout). Voegelin then clarifies how a god manifests to the whole society: "The god, therefore, can manifest himself not in any

36 Henri Frankfort, *Kingship and Gods: A Study of Ancient Near Eastern Religion as the Integration of Society and Nature* (Chicago: University of Chicago Press, 1948), 16.

37 Pharaoh is Horus, and of this god little enough is known. His symbol is the falcon, but we do not know whether the bird was thought in some way to be merely the god's manifestation; whether the god was embodied, temporarily or permanently, in a single bird or in the species as a whole; or whether the falcon was used as a sign referring to a much more intangible divinity. The latter possibility does not exclude the others, and modern parallels suggest, as we shall see, that we must not expect a rigid doctrine on matters of this type but rather a fluid belief of interrelationship which may assume almost any specific form.

(Frankfort, *Kingship and Gods*, 37)

38 Frankfort, *Ancient Egyptian Religion*, 13.

39 Voegelin, *Order and History*, 112–13.

40 Voegelin, *Order and History*, 113.

random man as representative of the species but only in the ruler as representative of society."[41]

The metaphysics of the god-king relation will come up again, but it is worth noticing these narratives and schemas that might have analogically conveyed difficult metaphysical constructs through one's embodied experience of Egyptian life. Whether this was the intent of the literature or a consequence of Egypt's theology of deification cannot be determined. The permanence and the presence of the god with the people strikes the ancient Egyptian's lived experience at several angles, but always reinforcing the eternal state through a succession of pharaohs as god-kings.

Alongside analogical reasoning, I would be remiss if I leave aside what some might politely call complementary reasoning. Frankfort calls this phenomenon a "multiplicity of approaches," where, "side by side certain *limited* insights ... were held to be *simultaneously* valid, each in its own proper context."[42] Unless this is a form of metaphysical speculation, this complementary view of counterfactuals might leave many of us in knots. And it is not clear what underlies the ability to simultaneously believe multiple statements about the nature of reality that do not seem compatible to us today.

For instance, regarding the physics of the sky dome and how it was supported above the earth, Wilson speculates, "We should want to know in our picture whether the sky was supported on posts or was held up by a god; the Egyptian would answer: 'Yes, it is supported by posts or held up by a god – or it rests on walls, or it is a cow, or it is a goddess whose arms and feet touch the earth.'"[43] This kind of talk about the cosmos might show a deference to tradition above all else, and so I cannot make much more of it as epistemologically significant.

To be fair, many Christians might make similar claims about the nature of God, especially in Trinitarian theology. But such theological statements would most likely defer to Trinitarian traditions more than reveal the speakers' own thoughts on the ontology of the Trinity. Similarly, claims about the sky dome might not represent the claims of work-a-day Egyptians, but of their literary tradition.

Finally, hints at the anthropology of Egyptian epistemology can be found in the inner/outer model of human thought. Early Memphite Theology refashioned the creation narrative to center on the god Ptah and establish Memphis as the capital of creation and Egypt. Concerning

[41] Voegelin, *Order and History*, 113.
[42] Frankfort, *Ancient Egyptian Religion*, 4.
[43] Wilson in Frankfort et al., *The Intellectual Adventure of Ancient Man*, 45.

how one knows, it describes Ptah's decrees of creation as sensory input. These sensoria come into his heart. But thoughts originating from the heart are then spoken by the tongue:

> [Ptah prevails] by thinking [as heart] and commanding [as tongue] everything that he wishes.
>
> The sight of the eyes, the hearing of the ears, the air-breathing of the nose they report to the heart.
>
> It [the heart] causes every thought to come forth, and the tongue announces what the heart thinks.[44]

Again, it is not clear how representative this would be of a widely accepted epistemic anthropology. But the heart as the seat of logic and volition comports generally with the Hebraic notion of epistemic organs: heart, eyes, and ears. This connection between the heart and tongue might also betray what every Egyptian feared most: the tongue revealing deeds that the heart remembers in the judgment after death, thus rendering one unfit beyond the tomb.

Metaphysics of Political Philosophy

Akin to their religious cult, the metaphysical constructs of ancient Egypt changed little over time. I would like to mention only a few topics that will best situate us for later exploring the Hebrew Bible and NT: consubstantiality, principled justice (*ma'at*), and dual constructions of time.

First, as hinted at above, the rise of pharaonic kingship eventually led to the view of god-kings. The pharaoh him or herself was not ontologically a god; rather, the god manifested in the pharaoh and to Egypt through the pharaoh. In this sense, gods were *consubstantial* with the king, and with him only. This is not a monophysite god–man relation, but a man *as the king* in whom the god manifests himself while remaining distinct from the king. The god is present amongst Egypt as a whole insofar as the god is present in the king who rules over Egypt, maintaining the god's distinctly divine person and power (as the Christian creedal formulas might call them), without confusion.

Unlike a god-creature manifestation in animal species, the god-king relationship was metaphysically unique and shored up questions about

[44] Quoted in Voegelin, *Order and History*, 92–93. See also Miriam Lichtheim, *Ancient Egyptian Literature: The Old and Middle Kingdoms* (Berkeley: University of California Press, 1973), 50–54.

the stability of the eternal state among a succession of human rulers. Upon death, the kings went to be with the gods, which gave his or her rule in this life durative effect beyond death.

Second, the closest thing to an abstract and pervasive substance in ancient Egypt is that of *ma'at*. Unlike the Torah, Egypt maintained a sharp distinction between justice (*ma'at*) and formal religion. Justice for the vulnerable was under the aegis of the king; justice that ordered things properly against chaos (*isfet*) was controlled in the cultic sphere. In the Egyptian cult, *ma'at* was focused not on justice for the poor as in the Hebrew Bible, but on order and balance between gods and humans.[45] Kingship was a political office established in creation, and so the metaphysical ordering of justice includes the political rule of the king against chaos in the kingdom.[46] The term itself derives analogically from its more pedestrian meaning "levelness, evenness, straightness," rising almost to the status of the metaphysical principle of "righteousness."[47] The closest parallel to *ma'at* in Greek culture would be something like *logos* – conforming to the rational order of things.

Third, having referred to the permanence of the eternal state above, the nature of time can be viewed both politically and more generally. Like most cultures today, Egyptian culture treated time as both cyclical and linear. Assmann cannot summon a contemporary notion of linear time familiar to us that would have a direct counterpart in Egypt. He divides their two ideas of time by the language of "becoming" (*neheh*) and "being" (*djet*):

> Neheh, or cyclical time, is the never-ending recurrence of the same; it is generated by the movement of the heavenly bodies and hence determined by the sun. ... Cycles come and go, and what takes shape in the individual cycles disappears again in the hope of renewed becoming.[48]

Djet is about both time and stability, and thus will connect intimately with ideas about the state, but not necessarily contribute to an idea of history where there is a schema of a beginning, middle, and end:

> *Djet* is associated with the concept of stability, of remaining, lasting, being permanent; its sign is that of the earth, its symbols are stone and mummy, its god Osiris, who guards the realm of the dead. *Djet* is a sacred dimension of

45 Assmann, *God and Gods*, 11.
46 Frankfort, *Ancient Egyptian Religion*, 54.
47 Frankfort et al., *The Intellectual Adventure of Ancient Man*, 108.
48 Assmann, *The Mind of Egypt*, 18.

everness, where that which has become – which has ripened to its final form and is to that extent perfect – is preserved in immutable permanence. This is precisely the meaning of the name borne by Osiris as lord of *djet:* "Wennefer" means "he who lasts in perfection." Hence *djet* is not a linear concept of time, but rather the suspension of time.

Recalling that fictional Roman Egyptian reading the millennia-old hieroglyphs in a tomb, we can appreciate why a linear notion of time does not do as much conceptual work for the Egyptian as for us today. The vast uniformity of societal structures made the ancient past present to him in an isolated culture that materially locked itself into an Egyptianized cosmos and afterlife – an afterlife that continued directly on from this life.

In contrast to the Hebrew Bible's journey to death, the descent into Sheol followed by resurrection offers a remarkably linear and punctuated sense of history.[49] We swim today in those Hebraic waters of history, isolating us from the Egyptian sense of time regulated by life-giving cycles and an enduring political structure proceeding into and beyond death.[50]

From this all-too-brief sketch, it is now obvious that we cannot affirm that the Egyptians were advocating speculation about metaphysics. However, they certainly constructed and thought with thick metaphysical concepts. These constructs usually connected to the livelihood of the state, and thus the livelihood of the society.

In the end, it is difficult to describe a particular style of philosophical method advocated across the literature of Egypt. Their analogical concepts of gods, time, political duration, animals, humanity, cosmological structure, and more can be philosophically explored, but Egyptian authors do not appear to be disposed to that task. For this reason, we can affirm the intellectual world of the Egyptians as *scholarly* and possibly *speculative*, but not *philosophy*.[51]

49 Jon D. Levenson has argued persuasively that resurrection is conceptually present early on in the Torah, rather than being a later development in Second Temple Judaism: *Resurrection and the Restoration of Israel: The Ultimate Victory of the God of Life* (New Haven, CT: Yale University Press, 2006).

50 Even if one affirms Assmann's assertion that the "counterworld" of the dead was an Egyptian rebellion against death in the form of a religion, the point of continuity remains. Jan Assmann, *Death and Salvation in Ancient Egypt*, trans. David Lorton (Ithaca, NY: Cornell University Press, 2005), 15–19.

51 As a caveat to this summary, I am not a primary reader of Egyptian texts and have had to rely heavily on the best Egyptologists for this summary. Hence, it could be the case that the philosophy of Egyptian literature has yet to be demonstrably worked out. I would happily amend my conclusions here if that were to be the case.

Mesopotamian Philosophy

Like Egypt, the various regional powers between the Tigris and Euphrates also spanned millennia, but with considerably less cultural homogeneity. I will speak about "Mesopotamian philosophy," but this generic term encompasses texts and traditions from the libraries of Sumer, Akkad, Assyria, and Babylon spanning three millennia.

Though the gods and cultures of these empires varied, the archaic language of Sumerian was maintained with a peculiar constancy in parallel to Akkadian up to the end of the final Babylonian empire. Historically speaking, Babylonian texts were often the final interpreters of more ancient traditions in the region, and so, the term "Mesopotamian philosophy" will often stand in for Babylonian philosophy.

Before examining the Babylonian style of philosophical thinking, I first want to think through a few centralizing themes and peculiarities of Babylonian literature. As in Egypt, the narratives of Babylon framed the concepts they build from lived experience. Unlike Egypt, Babylon had multiple languages, a highly disparate climate and terrain, political factions, and shifting gods and imperial capitals, all of which created a robust conceptual world. This might help to explain why scholars believe the conceptual world peculiar to Mesopotamia became instantiated in the written language more than other ancient Near Eastern cultures. To understand the speculative texts, we need to grasp the power and influence of her written languages.

First, as unbelievable as this may seem to us, Mesopotamian empires maintained the Sumerian picture-based (logographic) language in cuneiform script in parallel to Akkadian, the syllabic language of the people. For most of Babylon's history, Sumerian was an unspoken language, akin to the Latin of Babylon, known only to her scholars. Divination and omen texts were written mostly in the spoken language of Akkadian, but lexical lists maintained the Sumerian parallels.[52] Even more remarkably, and unlike anything today, Babylonians "treated Sumerian and Akkadian as parallel languages that worked in harmony," and "considered the languages to be inherently tied together."[53] The way they translated the picture-based words of the then-extinct Sumerian into the syllable-based words of Akkadian reveals how they thought about the objects being translated.

[52] Marc Van De Mieroop, *Philosophy before the Greeks: The Pursuit of Truth in Ancient Babylonia* (Princeton, NJ: Princeton University Press, 2017), 7.

[53] Van De Mieroop, *Philosophy before the Greeks*, 7.

Creation stories again emerge as central to establishing the intellectual world of the culture. Regarding the final two hundred lines of the Marduk creation narrative in the *Enūma Eliš*, Assyriologist Marc Van De Mieroop notes that the naming sequence is not merely an addendum: "Every aspect of civilization came into being at the time of creation through this naming process."[54]

Creation guaranteed knowledge of the real world because the gods had ordered it: "Everything was made according to divine plan." Additionally, Van De Mieroop believes that the extended list of Marduk's attributes in that addendum to the creation account generated a textual circumstance that justified knowledge but required a high degree of skilled literacy in both Sumerian and Akkadian: "In order to understand even a single name [of the god Marduk] or a word the reader had to know the rules of interpretation in full."[55] The creation of the cosmos and polyglottal textual understanding are thus inseparable mates in Babylonia's speculative enterprise.

Second, creation stories, lexical lists, and omens functioned as forms of speculative exploration. In much of twentieth-century scholarship, evolutionary and progressivist assumptions ruled mythology out of the rational world of philosophy a priori. Scholars predicated this on the axial age belief that rational speculative thought arose by intellectuals breaking their bonds with more ancient mythic traditions (à la Frankfort et al.) – as they presume the Greeks did. Only then could ancients set aside their myths methodologically for the sake of philosophical examination. These same scholars were then only left to ponder how a civilization could be so systematically genius in its intellectual prowess and simultaneously hold to fanciful stories about reality that ultimately hindered them from transcending the immediately real world before them.

Mary Douglas has critiqued the progressivist assumptions, arguing that analogical and rational-instrumental thought represent two different philosophical styles of broaching and evaluating the nature of something. Rational-instrumental reasoning, which identifies the mode often associated with the modern West, exhibits a certain direction and flow from universals to particulars:[56]

54 Van De Mieroop, *Philosophy before the Greeks*, 9.

55 Van De Mieroop, *Philosophy before the Greeks*, 10.

56 Thanks to Eric Smith for pointing this conversation out to me. "The Sumerian Mythographic Tradition and Its Implications for Genesis 1–11" (PhD diss., University of Bristol, 2012).

> Our logic is based on part-whole relations, the theory of types, causal implications and logical entailments. It organizes experience in theoretical terms. Rational construction based upon it always goes in a direction away from the concrete particular towards the universal. . . . Most important of all, the rational ordering which we employ presupposes a unique structure or pattern, complete, comprehensive, and closed.[57]

Texts provide particular instances presumed to require abstraction, which demands an inductively logical focus. Leaning on Hall and Ames's explanations of scholarly literature in Han Dynasty China, Douglas believes that analogical reasoning differs in that it posits concrete examples without a linear structure of reasoning. Rather, these examples are given in a scheme of "correlative" and "suggestive" relationships.[58]

So, too, Van De Mieroop describes this same style of scholarly thinking in Babylon, "cumulatively exploring issues case by case."[59] These tediously long descriptions of the king at the end of the creation saga "were not word games, but analyses that aimed to reveal truth. Babylonian scholars grasped reality through its written form. Their readings were thus exercises in epistemology."[60]

In myth, depicting a battle to tame chaotic waters and bring order might be a way of analogically reasoning. If we only had one creation myth, then not much more could be said outside of analyzing its narrative structure. However, Assyriologists have myriad omen tablets, lexical lists, and mythologies of theogony, cosmogony, and anthropogenesis.

Third, learned Babylonian culture held a high view of the gods' abilities to inscribe messages in the heavens and earth. I will discuss this more below (see "Divination"), but this creates a unique lens through which to view the cosmos. The universe is, quite literally, textualized: the heavenly bodies and their movements, the paths of animals as they walk, the height of doorways, and the livers of animals can all be "read" by the literate few. The gods may have retreated from the realm of humans, but they can and have tipped off humanity to future events, and it was only through the rigorously maintained omen lists and skilled learning of generations of scholars that allowed them to read these divine texts scratched into the cosmos.

[57] Mary Douglas, *Leviticus as Literature* (New York: Oxford University Press, 1999), 15.

[58] David L. Hall and Roger T. Ames, *Thinking through Confucius* (Albany, NY: State University of New York Press, 1987).

[59] Van De Mieroop, *Philosophy before the Greeks*, 30.

[60] Van De Mieroop, *Philosophy before the Greeks*, 9.

Epistemology

Assyriologists argue that two forms of scholarly activities demonstrate philosophical thought: omenology and lexical lists. Both of these enterprises hail from massive libraries of texts and interpretive techniques required to be mastered by ancient scholars. Both collections of tablets show textual play, where scribes and diviners freely included impossible omens (e.g., lunar eclipses at sunset) and neologisms (e.g., inventing new words in a more ancient and then-dead language of Sumerian). Noticing that these lists do something more speculative than merely *list* things, scholars designated these types of lists *Listenwissenschaft* (the science of lists).

The two questions pertinent to this current work are: How do these two genres – lexical and omen lists – seek to transcend the individual instances of word play or omens in order to explore the general nature of something? And, by doing so, are they advocating an exclusive methodology for philosophical thinking? Ultimately, these complex scholarly projects reveal epistemic tendencies more than epistemology – a worked-out notion of who can know what and how. They are speculative, but not demonstrably philosophy.

Two general features of the Mesopotamian intellectual world act as cardinal points of entry into their scholarly projects: the gods spoke by textualizing all of reality and the scholars maintained a diglot ledger of the omens and words required to "read" the textually inscribed world.

Divination. Because the gods inscribed all of reality with portents, divination and omenology enabled reality to be read by those trained in the craft. Late evidence suggests that the skills were transmitted as a family trade.[61] Babylonian scholars collected their skilled knowledge of how to interpret the textualized world in vast libraries of tablets. They discerned these signs through logical analysis and practice.

[61] During the first millennium, authoritative knowledge was located in traditional texts, which were carefully transmitted from one generation to another – at least in theory. Such an immutable concept of knowledge and authority is a valuable tool for collecting libraries, for foundational narratives, or for displaying universal knowledge through intertextual references. When it comes to practical application, however, knowledge from before the flood is a burden more than an asset.
(Niek Veldhuis, "The Theory of Knowledge and the Practice of Celestial Divination," in *Divination and Interpretation of Signs in the Ancient World*, ed. Amar Annus [Oriental Institute Seminars 6; Chicago: University of Chicago Press, 2010], 87)

A cloud formation, a cat crossing one's path, a lunar eclipse, the liver of a sacrificial sheep, and anything else could be the tablet upon which the gods wrote their messages. Hence, ancient scholars recorded in detail their empirical studies of reality to figure out what the gods were saying – haphazard as the skill often was.

Nevertheless, Van De Mieroop reminds us that theirs was not merely an empirical sport: "The Babylonian theory of knowledge was to an extent empirical – observation was crucial. It was also fundamentally rooted in a rationality that depended on informed reading. Reality had to be read and interpreted as if it were a text."[62] The same case has been made of the Copernican Revolution in the history of science. By seeing all cosmic events as quantifiable, they could be recorded and analyzed. In other words, our cosmos could finally be read.[63]

The analysis of language and the divine signs relied upon secret knowledge which was also passed down from the gods in creation, survived the flood, and was maintained by the scholarly class.[64] Babylonians sometimes viewed these as judgments passed down from the courtroom of the gods. Their task was direct, if not inordinately complex:

> Babylonian divination is based on a very simple proposition: Things in the Universe relate to one another. Any event, however small, has one or more correlates somewhere else in the world. This was revealed to us in [preflood] days of yore by the gods, and our task is to refine and expand that body of knowledge.[65]

[62] Van De Mieroop, *Philosophy before the Greeks*, 10.

[63] Michael Polanyi, *Personal Knowledge: Towards a Post-Critical Philosophy* (Chicago: University of Chicago Press, 1962), 3–4.

[64] "The worldview represented by the omen series is not irrevocable determinism, in the sense that every event is causally determined by an unbroken chain of prior occurrences. The omens revealed a conditional future, best described as a judicial decision of the gods." Amar Annus, "On the Beginnings and Continuities of Omen Sciences in the Ancient World," in *Divination and Interpretation of Signs in the Ancient World*, ed. Amar Annus (Oriental Institute Seminars 6; Chicago: University of Chicago Press, 2010), 2. The valuation of knowledge as secret tends to place it in a system of knowledge exclusively held by the gods and passed through a tight successive chain. See Alan Lenzi, *Secrecy and the Gods: Secret Knowledge in Ancient Mesopotamia and Biblical Israel* (State Archives of Assyria Studies XIX; Helsinki: Neo-Assyrian Text Corpus Project, 2008), 45–64. "All the important knowledge was revealed by the gods before the time of the flood and the scholars and kings of the present day owe their knowledge, directly, to primordial sages." First millennium versions of Gilgamesh make, "Gilgameš into a *literate* hero, one who wrote down his adventures and thus allowed later generations to profit from the lessons that he learned." Veldhuis, "The Theory of Knowledge," 77, 78.

[65] Ulla Koch-Westenholz, *Mesopotamian Astrology: An Introduction to Babylonian and Assyrian Celestial Divination* (Carsten Niebuhr Institute Publication 19; Copenhagen: Museum Tusculanum Press, 1995), 18–19.

Omenology and provoked divination – such as asking a god to impress a sign into a sheep's liver or rising smoke – relied on long lists of conditionals that strictly followed the *modus ponens* structure: If *P*, then *Q*. If the diviner sees a signaling event (the protasis), and especially if that sign coordinates with other known omens (protases), then the outcome (apodosis) follows inevitably.

This simple construct appears to have created a rigorous methodological framework far more than it provided a predictive science. As Francesca Rochberg puts it, "Anchored by its tight logical structure, the lists of conditionals 'if P, then Q' proved to be an effective instrument for making connections, *and also served as a systematizing device*."[66] The great matter of concern, for us, though not for the Babylonians, was the frequency with which signaling event (protasis) actually corresponded to the outcome (apodosis). At the very least, a high correspondence existed between interpreting these omens and the anxiety of the one seeking to know the outcome, often a king. In this sense, many Assyriologists have noted that divination was much less about future events and more about present royal anxieties.

By what authority did they interpret the textualized world? The authorization and skill underpinning the scholarly trade-craft were generationally transmitted, going back to the founding of the world. Benjamin Foster sums this knowledge-lineage from Gilgamesh: "According to the Epic of Gilgamesh, the alpha and omega of knowledge was understanding what transpired before the flood, which was seen as the beginning of empirical time."[67]

The prominence of the written word as a central feature to the enterprise appears again with all variations of divination and omen reading. Divination became "a systematized science, covering nearly all observable phenomena and permitting detailed predictions of unanticipated events ... The technological advance that made the development possible was writing – only writing could store the immense amount of data."[68]

Without the textualization of the observed omens and related outcomes, the scholarly enterprise would not exist, though some folk form of it would likely persist. Textualization, recording vast amounts of

66 Italics mine. Francesca Rochberg, "'If P, then Q': Form and Reasoning in Babylonian Divination," in *Divination and Interpretation of Signs in the Ancient World*, ed. Amar Annus (Oriental Institute Seminars 6; Chicago: University of Chicago Press, 2010), 25.

67 Benjamin R. Foster, "Transmission of Knowledge," in *A Companion to the Ancient Near East*, ed. Daniel C. Snell (New York: Wiley-Blackwell, 2004), 247.

68 Koch-Westenholz, *Mesopotamian Astrology*, 14–15.

events, enabled a textualized science of reading the cosmos as a text. However, over centuries of practice, the chase overshadowed the catch, "divination was nothing more and nothing less than a means to predict the future – not very reliable, perhaps, but the best they had."[69]

Subsequently, the practice of divination as understood through these texts is best represented as a science rather than an epistemology. Yet, many of us cannot set ancient divination and modern genetic sciences, for instance, on the same continuum. In her deft critique of anachronistic attempts to discredit Babylon's divination as science, Rochberg makes the modest appeal:

> But as science . . . [divination] reveals what for a particular community constitutes knowledge, skill in reasoning, and, in some relative way, truth – specifically, truth derived from such reasoning – the thousands of conditional statements compiled in omen series are of the essence for understanding how Babylonian and Assyrian scribes perceived and conceived the world in which they functioned, how they thought about what connected or related the propositions comprising conditionals, and, consequently, what for them constituted knowledge, skill in reasoning, and even truth.[70]

Van De Mieroop maintains that this describes an epistemology, where theories are not front and center; rather the principle of theorization lies in the cumulative effect of learning to understand the logic of the texts and events they describe: "They do not state theories but develop examples on the basis of underlying principles. Their reasoning is pointillistic, cumulatively exploring issues case by case. . . . They disclose what Babylonians thought about reality; they reveal a Babylonian epistemology."[71] Not all agree, and some scholars do not hide their skepticism. For them, the collection of Mesopotamian divination texts is nothing more than a concatenation of "observational sciences, common-sense attitudes, and religious beliefs."[72]

Lexicography. Not only did they attempt to understand a divinely textualized world, but the Babylonians also worked in two languages side by side: unspoken Sumerian known only to scholars and Akkadian. To these ancient scholars, the two languages were bilateral, meaning corresponded identically from one language into the other. These took the form of lexica, lists of words translated between Sumerian and Akkadian.

69 Koch-Westenholz, *Mesopotamian Astrology*, 18.
70 Rochberg, "If P, then Q," 25.
71 Van De Mieroop, *Philosophy before the Greeks*, 30–31.
72 Annus, "On the Beginnings and Continuities of Omen Sciences in the Ancient World," 13.

These lists were sometimes over ten thousand terms long and go back as early as the third millennium BCE.

This bilateralism between the languages strikes Assyriologists as remarkable considering dissimilarities between the two languages. Sumerian uses a logogram (picture/character) script rendered in cuneiform while Akkadian uses a syllabic script, analogous to Latin's syllabized diphthongs æ or œ, also rendered in cuneiform. To the untrained eye, the languages might look quite similar on the clay tablet.

As a crude analogy of this peculiar lexical system, this would be comparable to the United States Library of Congress maintaining a parallel copy of English-language books in ASCII or emoticons – "side by side in parallel columns" on the page (e.g., « – « ¬ || ||).[73]

This bilateral use of extinct and living languages provides Van De Mieroop enough examples to claim something more than translation in these lists. By noticing how the Babylonian scholars translated and invented terms in the dead Sumerian column, we can see how they thought about the objects of study in their word lists.

Even the skeptical Amar Annus admits that the hypothetical "encyclopaedic curiosity" of scribes demands explanation as it "comfortably steps over the boundary of the observable."[74] The lexicographic lists, thousands of words long in Sumerian-Akkadian columns, is precisely where modern scholars find lexical play and hypothesis. Just as they invented hypothetical omens to play out the logic of some divination trope interesting to them, they also might have played with Sumerian characters, inventing words to describe and fill out what might be missing in the other column of understanding. Van De Mieroop regards it as speculation, "They made up fantasy words that never appeared outside this type of text and had no practical use at all."[75]

So, Van De Mieroop homes in on lexicography as the evidence of epistemology, by which he seems to mean "how they thought," and not "how they thought about thought." His metaphor of their scribal practices of scattering a concept across a corpus, what he calls "pointillism," deserves our attention:

> The Babylonians listed cases in which they were applied, progressing systematically through what can seem endless minor variants that, like a pointillist painting,

[73] To clarify, « – « ¬ || || was my feeble attempt to depict logographically "side by side in two parallel columns" in ASCII script.

[74] Annus, "On the Beginnings and Continuities of Omen Sciences," 2.

[75] Van De Mieroop, *Philosophy before the Greeks*, 37.

> end up providing a clear picture. Each statement had meaning only within the overall context. … The logic of lexicography was imprinted upon the minds of anyone who engaged with written scholarship from the first moment of learning.[76]

But the "logic of lexicography" describes a tradition that advocates a methodological inroad required for one's insight, which hints at it being a philosophical style and not just speculation.

Conclusions on Mesopotamian Philosophy

No overt advocacy for a method or methods appears in the divination or lexical texts. Nothing moves them from speculation to philosophy. Though certainly involved with a systematized epistemic realm, lack of method keeps me from labeling this endeavor an epistemology proper, as I have construed it in this present work.

What Babylonian scholars practiced over the centuries might be called epistemology in the barest sense diagnosable: traditions that were advocated through familial instruction that formed the textualized thought-world of the community. Some "logic of lexicography" must have existed, which in itself betrays some aspect of methodological strictures. Considering these, I am inclined to agree with Rochberg and say that the waxing elements of scientific community appear present, and to agree with Van De Mieroop that some epistemology ought to have existed, traces of which the texts only hint at. Less apparent is the role of critical feedback and connections to cause-and-effect in the real world (i.e., statistical analysis of predictions), making Babylon's intellectual world a clear case of speculation and scientistic, but a borderline case of philosophy. Ulla Koch-Westenholz also wonders about this lacuna and hints at their lack of follow-through in analyzing the celestial reality above: "With the rise of mathematical astronomy in the fifth century B.C., by which it became possible to calculate the movements of the planets and predict eclipses, it is hard to understand how such events could be seen as portentous accidents or willed communications from the gods."[77]

Indeed, it is difficult to comprehend how Babylon's mathematically predictive prowess and divinely appointed signs metaphysically fit together. As we leave this period and culture, we recognize a perplexing mixture of reasoning that is logical and empirical but presented in

[76] Van De Mieroop, *Philosophy before the Greeks*, 187.
[77] Koch-Westenholz, *Mesopotamian Astrology*, 22.

pointillist style (what I will refer to as "pixelated") with haphazard divination, and both alongside an emerging ability to predict celestial movement. As Amar Annus concluded on these perplexities, "Even if not all Babylonian theories of signs make sense to a modern mind 'etically,' it may not be wrong to assume that they certainly did 'emically' to the participants of that culture."[78]

Conclusions (and a Note on "Axial Age" Theory)

My aim here focused on explaining and exploring the intellectual context in which the Hebrew Bible appeared. From my straw poll, most biblical scholars and theologians – much less, philosophers – seem unaware of such studies, lumping Hebrew Scripture together with a pile of antiquated religionist traditions that spoke and thought solely about religion. Not so for the so-called orientalists who praised the intellectual achievements of the Hebrew Bible as compared with Egyptian and Mesopotamian thought-worlds. Indeed, they put the Hebraic thought-world in league with Hellenism, which brings axial age thinking to bear on the Hebrew Bible.

The axial age stands out as a theory central to all discussions of ancient intellectual worlds. Most simply, it posits that there was a time when second-order thinking was not. Through some concatenation of cultural and political forces, philosophy sprung forth in a cluster of civilizations, even when those peoples did not seem to influence one another. Specifically, the axial age ties into a culture's persistence in breaking *out of* established mythology as an explanation of the operations of the cosmos and *into* abstracted thought: thinking about thinking itself and thinking about the nature of a chair outside of the chair under me right now.

Yehuda Elkanna defines the axial turn as any attempt to have "images of knowledge": "The conscious resolve to demystify the world is not only about the world; it is also an effort to guide one's thoughts: it is thinking about thinking . . . as long as it consists of thoughts *about the world*, [it] is not second-order thinking."[79]

78 Annus, "On the Beginnings and Continuities of Omen Sciences," 13.

79 Yehuda Elkanna, "The Emergence of Second-Order Thinking in Classical Greece," in *The Origins and Diversity of Axial Age Civilizations*, ed. Shmuel Noah Eisenstadt (Albany: State University of New York Press, 1986), 40.

Egyptologist Jan Assmann opens the definition further to include a culture's skepticism toward the intellectual status quo "in light of new 'transcendental' concepts of truth and order."[80] Assmann prefers to see a cascade of transcendent truths that emerged in Egypt over centuries rather than a singular turn to second-order thought.

The ensuing discussion about the Hebraic philosophical style of the Christian Scripture will complicate the picture of innovation created by axial age theory. I will later argue why the Hebrew Bible shows "images of knowledge" as central to its task, but for now, I want to leave the axial age conversation to the side, as its success does not determine the course of my task here.

[80] Assmann, *God and Gods*, 76.

PART II

HEBRAIC PHILOSOPHY

3

The Hebraic Philosophical Style

> [The Hebrews were] without peer in the power and scope of their critical intellectualism.[1]

> It was only by virtue of their skeptical mood that the Hebrew thinkers were able to attain a view of the world that still shapes our outlook.[2]

Henri Frankfort wrote these words, reflecting upon hundreds of pages of his colleagues' summaries of intellectualism in Egypt, Israel, and Mesopotamia. When the Hebrew Scriptures were examined side by side with the literature of surrounding empires spanning millennia, it was the Hebrew literature that stood out, only rivaled by the later Greek tradition. In its own time, Israel was "without peer." Some Christian theologians and philosophers might find Frankfort's awe to be itself shocking. What did he see in these biblical texts that made him think of them as exhibiting such "power and scope" in a "skeptical mood"?

Frankfort saw a Hebrew "critical intellectualism" that allowed it to transcend concepts imprisoning neighboring empires despite the brilliance of their intellectual capacities. I want to home in on Frankfort's phrase "critical intellectualism," because in using this description he calls attention to what distinguishes Hebraic philosophy from its peer intellectual traditions: argumentation and critical feedback.

To make the case for the philosophical thinking advocated in central biblical texts, I will differentiate between style, modes, and convictions.

[1] Henri Frankfort et al., *The Intellectual Adventure of Ancient Man: An Essay on Speculative Thought in the Ancient Near East* (Chicago: University of Chicago Press, 1946), 234.

[2] Italics mine. Frankfort et al., *The Intellectual Adventure of Ancient Man*, 234.

The modes and convictions of the philosophical style refer to the collection of features, conditions, and predispositions that allow the forms of reasoning to work. Form refers to particular kinds of logic, argument, and justification used within the style. Hence, a Roman philosopher and a Hellenistic Jewish thinker might employ story or deductive form of argument for different reasons and toward different stylistic ends.

The Style of Hebraic Philosophy

In arguing for an essentially Socratic philosophical style, Hugh Benson observes a form, strategy, and epistemological presupposition found across the Socratic dialogues.[3] The form consists of interrogating the supposedly "wise," and when their answers are found wanting, advocating another way of thinking. The strategy "requires . . . that the interlocutor recognize or is aware of his [own] doxastic commitment," to show its ultimate incoherence.[4] The presupposition is that a "robust conception of knowledge or wisdom" entails doxastic coherence.

Similarly, I propose that the Hebraic style consists of modes of raising philosophical problems, often in contraposition to the wisdom of Israel's neighbors, and asking the reader to think through the doxastic commitments required by them. As with discerning a "Socratic method" in the disparate texts depicting Socrates, a particular set of dispositions and commitments is required to see this philosophical style in the Christian Scriptures.

Alongside a proper epistemology advocated in the text, a steady beat of depictions *of* and indictments *against* erroneous and incoherent understanding pulses across Scripture. From the Torah to the prophets to the Gospels, hard-heartedness and "having eyes yet not seeing" are but two such indictments. This includes a series of episodes in which biblical characters endure tests or create them to confidently know, on a good day (e.g., Num 5:11–31), or die in their error on a not-so-good day (e.g., Num 16:1–35).

I do not wish to suggest that the Hebraic style is in any way Socratic. I only want to highlight the commonality: being able to discern a coherent

[3] Hugh H. Benson, "Socratic Method," in *The Cambridge Companion to Socrates*, ed. Donald R. Morrison (Cambridge Companions to Philosophy; Cambridge: Cambridge University Press, 2010), 179–200.

[4] Benson, "Socratic Method," 193.

style of philosophy across ancient texts with second-order thinking depicted throughout them.

Peter Machinist's article "The Question of Distinctiveness in Ancient Israel" throws cold water on the "trait list" approach to such tasks.[5] I want to demonstrate that the Hebraic philosophical style is distinct and distinguishable from peer traditions. However, the genetic markers that I will proffer do not fall prey to the concern of developing a "trait list." First, Machinist is worried about scholars overextending their analysis of Hebrew thought beyond the curated and redacted texts of the Hebrew Bible. Second, thin notions like "monotheism as belief in one god" are not distinguishable from subtle forms of henotheism, for instance. Hence, a simple list of traits in comparison to other cultures could not genuinely clarify differences significant enough to withstand scrutiny.

I propose that the biblical literature functions as a collected and curated philosophical tradition, and the genetic markers of its style are nuanced enough to detect unique philosophical movements in the texts. These genetic markers are not merely traits but form an organic unity within the style. This organic unity will then create difficulties for the later hybridization of the Hebraic style in Hellenistic Judaism. I will demonstrate that the New Testament authors (examined in this work) exhibit an originalist bent, seeking to maintain the Hebraic organic unity.

The philosophical style I want to demonstrate features this cluster of attributes: *pixelated*, *networked*, *ritualist*, *transdemographic*, *mysterionist*, and *creationist* (Table 1). I can only offer brief examples of each from across the Christian Scriptures and these will leave us wanting. I intend these to be illustrations of the style with its modes and convictions rather than examples of philosophy itself.

In brief: the Hebraic philosophical style consists of (1) modes of argument and (2) convictions.

Most basically, the philosophical style of Hebraic philosophy:

1. presents exemplars that are systematically arranged (pixelated)
2. is intertextually developed from the Torah and prophets into the gospels and beyond (networked)
3. regularly acknowledges the logical inability to exhaustively understand the nature of reality *in se* (mysterionist)

[5] Peter Machinist, "The Question of Distinctiveness in Ancient Israel: An Essay," in *Ah, Assyria ...: Studies in Assyrian History and Ancient Near Eastern Historiography Presented to Hayim Tadmor*, ed. Mordechai Cogan and Israel Eph'al (Jerusalem: Magnes Press, 1991), 196–212.

TABLE 1 *Hebraic and Hellenist philosophical styles*

	Hebrew Bible	Hellenist Tradition
Philosophical Style	**Modes of Argument:** 1. Pixelated (structure) 2. Networked (literary) **Convictions:** 3. Mysterionist 4. Creationist 5. Transdemographic 6. Ritualist	**Modes of Argument:** 1. Linear 2. Autonomist **Convictions:** 3. Domesticationist 4. Abstractionist 5. Classist 6. Mentalist

4. is grounded in the notion of Yahweh as creator and present-day sustainer (creationist)
5. is to be understood through a matrix of ritual participation (ritualist)
6. aims to develop expertise across Israel's social positions (transdemographic)

Caveat lector: I am aware that philosophers will bring to this book a specific set of questions traditioned into them from their various boutiques of philosophy. The goal of this book is primarily to describe accurately the indigenous philosophy of the Christian Scriptures. Only once we have grasped something central to Hebraic philosophy can we begin to put its questions and insights into conversation with other philosophies.

Pixelated

By "pixelated," I mean that biblical authors define the contours of a second-order abstraction with pictures *of* and episodes *about* a concept through iterations and reiterations across narrative, law, and poetry.[6] Just as one pixel participates in assembling the image being displayed on a screen, the arguments of Scripture are broached and reified in various locations across Scripture. To see the second-order pattern emerge, one must step back and take in the whole image, which necessarily includes each discrete pixel.

Or as Benjamin Sommer describes it, "They speak in the concrete terms that typify most ancient Near Eastern speculative thought, employing *a*

[6] This concept is borrowed from Assyriologist Marc Van De Mieroop, who used the "pointillist" metaphor in his claims about Mesopotamian epistemology.

rhetoric that is nonsystematic though self-consistent."[7] Any story, set of related laws, or aphorisms assume that the reader will inductively reach the principle from those depictions, stepping back to induce their connections.

As an example, to which I will return in Chapter 10, no discussion of epistemic justification can be found in the Christian Scriptures. There are episodes – pixels of epistemic justification – that appear to play out a theme with variation. Across these instances, a consistent pattern of what counted as epistemic justification emerges where the stakes were high. Like the pointillist paintings of Georges Seurat (e.g., "A Sunday on La Grande Jatte – 1884"), the dot or pixel itself only becomes meaningful within the aggregate.

For comparison, scholars have made a similar observation about the difference between what I am calling "pixelated" on the one hand and "linear" on the other in the field of logic. Susanne K. Langer (a student of Alfred North Whitehead!) coined the dichotomy as "presentational" forms of reasoning versus "discursive":

> Presentational symbolism as a normal and prevalent vehicle of meaning widens our conception of rationality far beyond the traditional boundaries, yet never breaks faith with logic in the strictest sense.[8]

She contrasts presentational symbolism with discursiveness:

> This property of verbal symbolism is known as *discursiveness;* by reason of it, only thoughts which can be arranged in this peculiar order can be spoken at all; any idea which does not lend itself to this "projection" is ineffable, incommunicable by means of words. That is why the laws of reasoning, our clearest formulation of exact expression, are sometimes known as the "laws of discursive thought."[9]

Anthropologist Mary Douglas will later associate Langer's dichotomy of reason with her own formulation of it. Presentational reason becomes "analogical ordering" for Douglas, and discursive reasoning becomes "rational-instrumental reasoning."[10] If there is a generalizable idea that spans Van De Mieroop (pointillism), Langer (representational), and

[7] Italics mine. It should be noted that Sommer would cite diverse sources in the unified texts (i.e., Documentary Hypothesis) as one reason for this. Benjamin D. Sommer, *Revelation and Authority: Sinai in Jewish Scripture and Tradition* (New Haven, CT: Yale University Press, 2015), 24.

[8] Susanne K. Langer, *Philosophy in a New Key: A Study in the Symbolism of Reason, Rite, and Art* (New York: New American Library, 1948), 79.

[9] Italics original. Langer, *Philosophy in a New Key*, 66.

[10] Mary Douglas, *Leviticus as Literature* (New York: Oxford University Press, 1999), 15–29.

Douglas (analogical), that is all that I mean by pixelated: many variegated instances presented to discern their coherence.

The proliferating array of metaphors for God – a shepherd, mother hen, warrior, potter, father, husband, king, etc. – betray the pixelation impulse of biblical authors to let a fuller picture of God emerge from a well-dotted canvas.

As a working example of an epistemological problem, the opening story of Genesis already requires a critically engaged reader, and by "critically engaged" I am including criticism of every character's words, actions, and motives, including God's. In this example, the question is who can guide the man and woman in Eden to better knowing? The answer most of us bring to the text is surprisingly absent from the story. The author does not tell us to whom the couple of Eden should listen; rather, the author shows us, but not inside this story itself.

In brief, a singular creator-god makes things and puts them in their places. He makes a man and commissions him with the simplest instructions imaginable: eat from every tree but one. Then he leads the man to discover the woman built by the creator-god. Everything seems normal until a serpent starts talking, sows dubious seeds in the woman's understanding (with the man attending silently), and contradicts the creator-god's words, "Dyingly you will not die! For God knows that when you eat of it your eyes will be opened and you will be like God knowing good and evil" (Gen 3:4–5).

The narrator is at pains to show that every single thing the serpent says comes true. They did not die on that day (cf. Gen 2:17; 3:4). In fact, according to the author, the man did not die until over 300,000 days later (Gen 5:5), if the numbers are read flatly. Their eyes were opened, knowing good and evil, just as the serpent had said (cf. Gen 3:5, 7). And according to God, they had "become like one of us, knowing good and evil" (cf. Gen 3:5, 22).

All of this to say, the text itself opens with a story that demands the reader to be skeptical of the creator-god and possibly trust in a specious species. The biblical narrative demands a critical reading, and readers must traipse through quite a bit of the story before they can affirm that the man was wrong to reject the instruction of the creator-god. Not until we compare the retelling of the event in Genesis 16 – another woman "taking" and "giving" things to a man – alongside Genesis 27 – a woman seeking to obtain a blessing – can we see a pattern emerge that would make us dubious of Eve's decision to listen to the serpent within Genesis. Not until the final phase of Genesis do we encounter the first man – Joseph – who would “not listen” to the voice of a woman with a skewed desire, Potiphar’s wife. Finishing the text of Genesis, we have now inductively collected a potential *genus* and *species* of erroneous practices through similar narrative structures and concepts carefully tied together with a formulaic use of language.[11]

Once we arrive at yet another need for divine feeding, this time in the wilderness, God instructs the people to eat their fill, just as in Eden. And like the instructions to the man, the prophet Moses propagates the most basic condition for gathering food imaginable: do not collect on the Sabbath (Exod 16). We know the setup – eat your fill, with one condition – and the outcome ensues predictably. The goal of this divine feeding is also given in epistemological terms. God sends manna “that I may test them” in order to know “whether they will walk in my *torah* or not” (Exod 16:4). And for the people, God gives them meat and bread so that “you all shall know that it was Yahweh who brought you out of the land of Egypt” (Exod 16:6).

Who knows what and how features as the central conflict to resolve both in Eden and here again in the manna feeding during the exodus. These two stories share the particular language of Eden and the conceptual structures of the story. In one set of stories, Eve, Sarai, Rebekah, and Potiphar’s wife all demand that their men listen to their voice while they make their plans. In three cases – those of Eve, Sarai, and Potiphar’s wife – the wrong kind of knowing is at stake: knowledge of good and evil and inappropriate sexual knowing. “To know” and “to have sex” are used interchangeably in the Hebrew Bible, though “knowing” (*yādaʿ*) as sex is rarer, but some conceptual tie is operative here.[12] Similarly, Eden and the giving of manna are parallel stories with knowing as the natural outcome of the test, both for God and for the Israelites.

In short, though nothing internal to the logic of Genesis 3 helps answer whether the couple should have listened to the serpent and embodied his prescribed ritual of eating, the pixelated totality of retellings of this story

[11] The linguistic construction that unites these instances involves a female “taking” and “giving” something to the male with the comment or command “listen to her/my voice.” Dru Johnson, *Epistemology and Biblical Theology: From the Pentateuch to Mark’s Gospel* (Routledge Interdisciplinary Perspectives on Biblical Criticism 4; New York: Routledge, 2018), 41–55.

[12] There are only a handful of instances out of 174 in the Pentateuch where “know” (*yādaʿ*) is employed to mean “sexual intimacy.” Although rare, sexual intimacy is part of the semantic range of the term.

in theme and variation outline the contours of an answer – yielding *genus* and *differentia* of knowing gone rightly and wrongly.[13]

The mere presence of narratives without linear reasoning does not entail the kind of pixelated reading that I am suggesting as distinctively Hebraic. In the Hebraic style, the exemplars gain complexity and variegation when further unveiled. And this seems reasonable. If the goal is to develop nuanced discernment, then texts profuse with complexity offer the best proving grounds for testing the development of such second-order thinking.

For instance, the narratives of Abram's challenge to Yahweh about his promised land (Gen 15:8) and questioning of Yahweh about the destruction of Sodom (Gen 18:22–32) create a rich background conflict in the story of the binding of Isaac (Gen 22:1). How so? Abraham, who misunderstood God's promises of a nation and prostituted his wife twice (Gen 12, 20), takes his son to Mount Moriah without protest (Gen 22). Whatever explanation we might develop about the metaethical principles that would guide one in that situation, the complexity of Abraham's character provides the waypoints for thinking about what undergirds such contrasting scenes of skepticism and fealty in the texts. Levitical laws about child sacrifice and marrying one's half-sister then provide further conversation partners to this ethically complex tapestry being woven in Genesis 22 (cf. Lev 18).[14]

Remarkably, no biblical authors attempt to underwrite these ethical principles with thin ethical notions such as "Abraham's righteousness," despite that notion being readily available in Genesis. Instead, the rash and weak fortitude of Abraham is on full display alongside his credited righteousness with regards to Yahweh. The reader or hearer has to work across these pixelated stories and laws to see what, if anything, binds them together. Such a pixelated style of abstract reasoning appears endemic to the intellectualist project of Christian Scripture, and it is flagged up by the pixelated reuse of language, concepts, and storylines.

[13] This brief scrape over the biblical accounts requires a comprehensive examination that can justify these connections. For a detailed exegetical analysis of the Torah's epistemology, see Johnson, *Epistemology and Biblical Theology*.

[14] See Shira Weiss's work on the philosophical utility of ethically ambiguous character development in the biblical narratives: *Ethical Ambiguity in the Hebrew Bible: Philosophical Analysis of Scriptural Narrative* (New York: Cambridge University Press, 2018).

Networked

The *networked* structural style refers to the literary practice of intra- and intertextual reliance upon ideas developed in coordination *with* (intra) or meaning derived *from* (inter) other texts. In other words, the reasoning itself requires the reader to transume or contextualize material from elsewhere in the imagined corpus, but it alerts the reader to this demand by establishing clear literary networks to that other material.

Obvious to any reader of the Christian Scriptures, biblical authors do not blatantly define their terms or the concepts to which they allude. Indeed, definition-seeking may violate the very point of the philosophy being advocated. Rather, instances are made coherent by understanding their network within the whole. We might consider literary networking to be good interpretive practice, and it is, but the networking I refer to here also includes the author's expectations of readers.

For instance: In Luke's gospel (Luke 20:27–39), Sadducees approach Jesus to define the nature of resurrection concerning marital relationships here and now. The narrator flatly introduces the characters as "some Sadducees, those who say there is no resurrection ..." (Luke 20:27). Borrowing a scenario from the apocryphal book of Tobit, they ask Jesus: If a woman is married and widowed seven times, whose wife is she in the resurrection? They seem to presume that all the normal marital relations apply.

Jesus' answer seems to abolish the marital relationship in the age of resurrection: "The sons of this age *marry and are given in marriage* (*gamousin kai gamiskontai*), but those who are considered worthy to attain that age and to the resurrection from the dead *neither marry nor are given in marriage* (*oute gamousin oute gamizontai*)" (Luke 20:35).

Many have taken this response to these resurrection-deniers as Jesus' definitive annihilation of the institution of marriage, a kinship relation founded in creation itself. Yet, to the reader of Luke's networked literature, that phrase "marrying and giving in marriage" should pique her interest. For one, "marrying and giving in marriage" appears in precisely one other place in Luke's gospel, which also happens to address the eschaton: Jesus' teaching on his return and judgment of humankind (Luke 17:27).[15] In that context, Jesus describes the unaware people in

[15] Parallels are networked to Matt 22:30; 24:38; Mark 12:25.

the days of Noah and the destruction of Sodom and Gomorrah. What were they doing to deserve wholesale annihilation?

[People in the days of Noah] were:

eating and drinking, marrying and being given in marriage (*egamoun egamizonto*),

[People in Sodom and Gomorrah] were:

eating and drinking, buying and selling, planting and building

Considering what we know about Sodom and Gomorrah from Genesis, we might have been surprised to find that the crimes Jesus listed were not crimes at all. Though not linguistically parallel to the Greek version, Jeremiah once advised the exiles in Babylon to do *these same things* almost six centuries prior: build, plant, marry and give in marriage (Jer 29:5–7, MT; Jer 36:1–7 LXX) (Figure 1).

In Luke's literary network, the phrase "marrying and giving in marriage" cannot mean in Luke what it plainly might otherwise mean. The same holds true if we extend the analysis into the networked parallels in Matthew and Mark (Matt 22:30; 24:38; Mark 12:25). For Luke's Jesus, this phrase did not refer to marriage in the resurrection; rather, *it appears to address the mentality of those who are blind to the coming judgment*, or something to that effect.

Earlier in Luke, this kind of blindness appears as a running critique from Jesus (cf. Luke 12:54–56). This explains the cutting question latent in what Jesus describes as persons who are ready for resurrection. He calls them "those who are worthy to attain that age," intimating that the Sadducees are not worthy. What begins as a lesson in the metaphysics of marriage ends with a rebuke. The particular language of that rebuke across the Lukan and Synoptic Gospel literary networks equated the Sadducees with the people who died in the flood and in Sodom and Gomorrah for not paying attention.

Luke's Jesus has already prepared us for the schismatic epistemology of the Sadducees. Earlier, Jesus castigates Galilean farmers as "hypocrites" because they can interpret meteorology to their own benefit but cannot apply the same skill of interpretation to "this present time" (Luke 12:54–56). They can "see" the invisible implications of a cloud rising (i.e., the possibility of rain) or shifting winds (i.e., scorching heat), but, hypocritically, they do not "interpret the present time." Luke develops a fairly robust view of epistemological blind spots due to bad habits and obstinacy. As strange as it may strike the unacculturated ear, "marrying

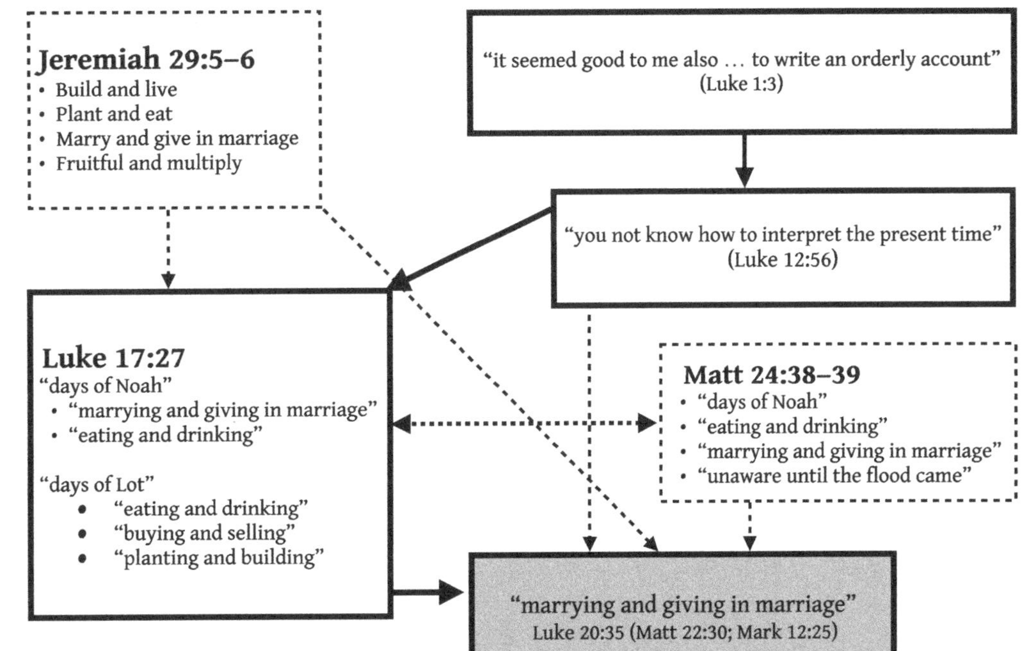

FIGURE 1 "Marrying and given in marriage" network
Source: Created by Dru Johnson

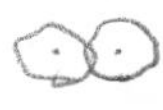

and giving in marriage" operates in a matrix of metaphors that depict a lackadaisical status quo focused on present economies and a habituated unawareness of impending divine judgment.

Not only is the Hebraic philosophy pixelated, but the pictures of philosophical interest in the biblical texts become coherent when networked within Luke, then among the gospels, and then within biblical texts more broadly. In this instance, the rhetoric of judgment across the Synoptic Gospels properly networks the ethical metaphysics of resurrection more than the literal words of the dialogue itself do. Metaphysical relations among persons after the resurrection are left to the side while Jesus homes in on the ethical preparation required for the age to come, emphasizing its judgment in both texts with the peculiar phrase "marrying and giving in marriage."

Examples easily multiply with what John Hollander, and later Michael Fishbane and Richard Hays, identify as metalepsis, allusion, and echo.[16] This kind of networking is required within genres (Synoptic Gospels, wisdom, legal code, etc.) as well as across them. At times, legal codes network with narrative and vice versa, a practice I will examine in the coming chapter. I will also spell out my method for assuring integrity and consistency across a diverse compilation of literature in the coming chapter, including the ability to discern *genus* and *differentia* from such examples.

Mysterionist

By mysterionist, I mean that if there is a closed causal system for the ancient Hebrew, we do not have access to its inner workings or holistic structures. This mysterionist bent might be similar to Colin McGinn's mysterianism concerning mind–body consciousness: structured and real, but ultimately not able to be holistically understood.[17] The Hebraic philosophical style advocates a mysterionist conviction but without loss of a creationist metanarrative.

Despite the common assumption, mystery does not entail illogical structures and secret knowledge. W. V. O. Quine made a similar

[16] John Hollander, *The Figure of Echo: A Mode of Allusion in Milton and After* (Berkeley: University of California, 1981); Michael A. Fishbane, *Biblical Interpretation in Ancient Israel* (Oxford: Clarendon, 1985); *Biblical Myth and Rabbinic Mythmaking* (New York: Oxford University Press, 2003); Richard Hays, *Echoes of Scripture in the Letters of Paul* (New Haven, CT: Yale University Press, 1989).

[17] Colin McGinn, *The Problem of Consciousness* (Oxford: Blackwell, 1991).

argument against the reductionistic physicalism and logical positivist movements of his day.[18] These movements sought a scientifically reduced description of phenomena in a closed physical and causal system of relationships. If the cosmos is chemicals in a closed system, then eventually, physics ought to be able to reduce and describe any event, be it psychiatric, chemical, or engineering. The tree of knowledge that scientists and logicians coproduced would be rooted in uncontroversially true axioms where inductively gathered scientific data can be grafted in and thus deductively grounded.

Employing the help of Nelson Goodman, Carl Hempel, and Kurt Gödel, Quine showed that such a logically connected system of truths and relations turns out to be logically impossible to complete – where all truths are provable without appeals to truths outside the system. It simply could never be a closed system that we can comprehensively justify to ourselves. Prior to the mathematical spadework of Quine's conclusions, the biblical authors spoke out against the logical positivism in their day.

Qohelet (Ecclesiastes), the narrator, attempts to exhaustively map out the closed system of relationships constituting the cosmos. Though he has all means to knowledge available, he ends by acknowledging that God is the creator and that only the creator can comprehend the created system:

> When I applied my mind to know wisdom, and to see the business that is done on earth, how one's eyes see sleep neither day nor night, then I saw all the work of God, that no one can find out what is happening under the sun. However much they may toil in seeking, they will not find it out; even though those who are wise claim to know, they cannot find it out.
>
> (8:16–17)

> Just as you do not know how the breath comes to the bones in the mother's womb, so you do not know the work of God, who makes everything.
>
> (11:5)

Man's only proper response in light of such ignorance focuses on God as creator, ritual participation in the community, and seeking wisdom from experts within the community. The "preacher" (*qōhelet*) makes a reckoning of what can be known and draws a line that should not and cannot be epistemically crossed. Hence, mysterionist framing is just that,

[18] W. V. O. Quine, "Epistemology Naturalized," in *Naturalizing Epistemology*, 2nd ed., ed. Hilary Kornblith (Cambridge, MA: MIT Press, 1997), 15–32; "Natural Kinds," in *Ontological Relativity and Other Essays* (New York: Columbia University Press, 1969), 114–38.

offering a frame and method with natural boundaries to be discerned through training:

> Remember your creator in the days of your youth, before the days of trouble come . . .
>
> (12:1)

> *My son, beware of anything beyond these.* Of making many books there is no end, and much study is a weariness of the flesh. The end of the matter; all has been heard. Fear God, and keep his commandments; for that is the whole duty of everyone. For God will bring every deed into judgment, including every secret thing, whether good or evil.
>
> (12:12–14)

Similarly, when Job and his friends attempt to pull back the curtain to understand the cosmic machinery, Job is confronted not by a god, but by the creator of the cosmos (Job 38).

We should not confuse this kind of mysterionist line with the use of the term "mystery" (*mystērion*) in the New Testament. As I argued in the introduction chapter, this NT use of hiddenness places mystery in a process of revelation and blocks off areas that are not profitable for speculation (cf. Deut 29:29/Mark 4:10).

Akin to the goal of Socrates' questioning, the Hebraic philosophical style entails a generalized agnosticism: because we know that we don't fully grasp X, then we probably should attenuate how we speak about Y.

Some have suggested this kind of mysterionism in the bible emphasizes awe and wonder. The fact that awe is central to how we think about the nature of the divine, for instance, also indicates this mysterionist conviction.[19]

Creationist

By creationist, I refer to the conviction of Hebraic philosophy to found its metaphysics, ethics, epistemology, and more in the creation event of Genesis 1–3 that flows historically into an Israelite's present history. The creationist disposition presumes contiguity with a particular

[19] Ohaneson traces this language of "awe" and "wonder" throughout the Hebrew Bible and reflects on its implications for prescriptive limits to Perfect Being Theology. Heather C. Ohaneson, "Turning from the Perfection of God to the Wondrousness of God: Redirecting Philosophical-Theological Attention in Order to Preserve Humility," in *The Question of God's Perfection: Jewish and Christian Essays on the God of the Bible and Talmud*, ed. Yoram Hazony and Dru Johnson (Philosophy of Religion – World Religions 8; Leiden: Brill, 2018), 211–30.

cosmological and genealogical narrative. Like Egypt and Mesopotamia, a return to creation narratives, creation themes, and creation language runs throughout the philosophical thinking of the Christian Scriptures.

Most biblical texts overtly or covertly presume a creational metaphysical structure, where Yahweh arranges and orders the cosmos as a field of objects separate from him and each other. Nothing akin to Brahminist oneness, pantheism, or panentheism stems from the biblical texts.

Yahweh's forming and commissioning of humankind, the guided discovery of the woman, and the unity of the biologically sexed pair is hardly ever referred to directly after Genesis 4. However, we see the presumption of it almost everywhere in the biblical literature.

For example, Leviticus details most but not all unsuitable sexual relationships under the general principle of "close relative" (Lev 18:6). Not every sexual combination that humans will eventually think up makes the list of specific relations to avoid (Lev 18:6–23; 20:10–21). Leviticus even addresses inappropriate sexual contact between a husband and wife during menstruation (Lev 18:18). In all the thoroughgoing instruction about sexual contact, not once do the biblical texts ever patently prescribe what a proper sexual relationship might look like. They merely presume that Genesis 2 covers that ground as the *genus*, and the proliferating dangers of other sexual contacts are taxonomically listed out as the *differentia* (see discussion in the "Definition by Genus/Differentia" section below).

In a question about marital corruption (the *differentia*), Jesus assumes that the network extends back to the *genus* of Genesis 2 as the normative relationship (Matt 19:4–6). In this, he reifies that the normative has been given in the description of creation, and Jesus expected his audience to also share his presumption. The normative was, for Jesus, to be found in the metaethically descriptive account of creation.

I am attempting to draw attention to the tendency of biblical authors to focus on history and place.[20] Because Yahweh created this universe and emplaced humanity on the map in Mesopotamia, all Hebraic philosophy has to refer in some meaningful way to history commenced in and networked from creation. In defining the metaphysical contours of marriage, Jesus roots his thinking in the creation and expects that his hearers should have as well.

[20] Craig Bartholomew's work on role of *place* in the Christian canon makes for an exemplary model. *Where Mortals Dwell: A Christian View of Place for Today* (Grand Rapids, MI: Baker Academic, 2012).

Transdemographic

> As far as Jeremiah is concerned, no individual is exempt from this requirement of independent investigation .... Here, as elsewhere in Scripture, wisdom is to be found in the streets – a metaphor that refers to those experiences in the daily life of a people that are public and accessible to everyone.[21]

Though Hazony derives the point in Jeremiah, the commitment to reason that is both available to and required of all is both unique and striking in ancient literature. By "transdemographic," I mean that the goal of the philosophical enterprise in the Christian Scriptures aims at fostering a discerning social body with diverse but mutually enriching perspectives on reality. No one person can be "the Hebraic philosopher." Neither Moses nor Jesus relied alone on being the singular philosopher; rather, they were both depicted as experts in a community who could properly lead others to see that which was there before them.

Transdemographic epistemology focuses on know-how: socially distributed discernment in order to properly understand facts and states of affairs (know-that). This acknowledges that the individual body always practices philosophical thinking within the social body, trained from youth by specialists. Moses was formed to lead the Israelites and taught the plans for the tabernacle, but it was two other experts who were able to actualize the plan (Exod 36:1). Diverse streams of knowing create strength in transdemographic culture, just as we view the scientific enterprise or liberal arts today.[22]

Transdemographic convictions do not allow for naïve inclusivism, but instead, a dispersion of expertise. Disparate forms of participation included everyone who joined themselves to Israel. The high priest, prophets, priests, kings, fathers, children, mothers, lepers, émigré, judges, and elders all had different access and discernment that they brought to the community. The Torah and later Jesus and his apostles expected that the community would employ these disparate types of know-how in order to intellectually grasp second-order notions. Transdemography emerges

[21] Yoram Hazony, *The Philosophy of Hebrew Scripture* (New York: Cambridge University Press, 2012), 165–66.

[22] Comparing the Hebrew Bible's view of training to Mesopotamia, Shawn Flynn says, "This [Hebrew] religious instruction idealizes a particular type of specialist religious instruction and encourages it for every household." *Children in Ancient Israel: The Hebrew Bible and Mesopotamia in Comparative Perspective* (New York: Oxford University Press, 2018).

most pointedly in Deuteronomy, where the goal of God's instruction aimed at "a wise and discerning people" (4:6). The many voices of their shared expertise were accessible and distributed across their discerning community, as in the scientific community, which is precisely what makes the enterprise robust and discerning.

Returning to Luke 12, Jesus articulates the transdemographic expectation most poignantly when he chastises farming communities for not seeing what was plainly in front of them. We see the sharp edge of his disappointment when he calls them "hypocrites" (12:54–56):

> He also said to the crowds, "When you see a cloud rising in the west, you immediately say, 'It is going to rain'; and so it happens. And when you see the south wind blowing, you say, 'There will be scorching heat,' and it happens. You hypocrites! You know how to interpret the appearance of earth and sky, but why do you not know how to interpret the present time?"

Jesus notices that they can see the invisible implications of weather patterns, a jab that pokes directly at their trust in God's provision of water while living in a parched land devoid of large regulated rivers. When they look at a small cloud, they see rain. Notice, though, that the small cloud is not the rain. Instead, they could discern that the small cloud is an indicator of future rain to come and currently invisible to the eye. Conversely, when they see the invisible wind blowing from the south (i.e., from Egypt), they discern scorching winds coming, both of which will affect their crops.

But why does Jesus call them "hypocrites," a term usually reserved for people deeply concerned with looking righteous?[23] Given their ability to expertly discern meteorological conditions, especially when directly connected to their livelihoods, Jesus' ire targets their failure to employ *that same discernment* to the present circumstance of his teaching and wonders. Hence, having eyes, they did not see the invisible yet discernible empire of God coming.

Jesus expected that even predictive meteorology could develop a transdemographic community that provides tools for seeing these Jesus-events differently, grasping the invisible implications that must flow from them. They are hypocrites, within the logic of the story, because they apply their discernment in one facet of life's immediate concerns, but not in the realm of the historic "empire of God" event being revealed to them.

[23] Jonathan T. Pennington, *The Sermon on the Mount and Human Flourishing: A Theological Commentary* (Grand Rapids, MI: Baker Academic, 2017), 91–92.

The epistemologically centric focus of Hebraic philosophy aims at honing discernment in the community. In the coming chapters, I intend to show how prophetic appeals utilize classical logic, how the prophets revisit the Torah from various perspectives in theme and variation, and the acknowledgment of a base mysterionist conviction that rebuffs both reductionism and attempts at an exhaustive understanding of the cosmos. But all of these reifications, appeals, interpretations, and more require the wisdom of the community of diverse expertise. Their wisdom tradition, unlike all other ancient civilizations, was expected to spread to all: women, men, children, elderly, foreigners, and natives alike.

Ritualist

Unique to the Hebrew Bible amongst its peers, rituals are designated for epistemological effect and shaping the community. I have argued elsewhere that all pedagogical and cognitive activities are inherently ritualistic and embodied.[24] However, by "ritualist," I mean that the biblical authors are openly aware of the epistemic function of rituals and unashamedly employ them for the sake of accurate knowing. Not just knowing, but Israel is to become a particular kind of community, which includes but is not limited to their intellectual world shared between them.[25]

In the Torah, Moses instructs the Hebrews to perform rites in order to know. The kind of knowing that issues from a ritual performance is a type of discernment. Leviticus 23 provides the clearest example of this, though the Hebrew Bible and New Testament are rife with epistemologically focused rituals.[26] For the week-long Feast of Booths (*sukkōt*), the instructions are terse but direct. Israelites are to build shelters and live in them with their families for seven days. The author of Leviticus goes on to state the reason for the week-long incursion into the normalities of life: "that your generations might know that I made the people of Israel live in booths (*sukkōt*) when I brought them out of the land of Egypt: I am Yahweh your all's God" (Lev 23:43).

This epistemic purpose reveals much about the use of rituals, memorials, tests, and ceremonies in Israel. Notice that Sukkot narrows upon a

[24] Dru Johnson, *Knowledge by Ritual: A Biblical Prolegomenon to Sacramental Theology* (Journal of Theological Interpretation Supplements 13; Winona Lake, IN: Eisenbrauns/PennState Press, 2016).

[25] Thanks to Michael Rhodes for making me say what I actually meant here.

[26] I address ritual epistemology across the Christian Scriptures in detail in my monograph *Knowledge by Ritual.*

historical fact to be known (what some philosophers call knowing-that knowledge): "that I made the people of Israel live in booths when I brought them out of the land of Egypt." But whatever Leviticus intends to be known, it cannot be properly known apart from the community and ritual by which it is to be understood (i.e., "You all shall live in shelters for seven days," Lev 23:42). Or, in the language of contemporary epistemology, they practiced rites in order to know-how, in order to properly know-that.

Ritualization becomes the *modus operandi* of Hebraic philosophy, much as embodied *peripatetic* walking rituals enabled Socrates' *maieutic* birthing technique for recalling knowledge. The Torah promotes no single ritual as paradigmatic or sufficient for understanding but choreographs a calendar and matrix of rites interwoven with ethical behaviors that prepared the rites to be accepted by their god. This prescription of a ritualized life will surface again in the New Testament where rituals of the Torah and culturally improvised rites of Second Temple Judaism will be reritualized for the new covenant Christian community. In this present work, communities stratified by rituals of discernment will come to the fore in my discussion of the philosophy of science in Chapter 8.

Summary

These two structural elements (pixelated, networked) and four convictions (mysterionist, creationist, transdemographic, and ritualist) form the genetic markers of the Hebraic philosophical style. When they are present, I will argue that we see a discrete style of philosophy being practiced, distinct from Israel's neighbors in the ancient Fertile Crescent and later northern Mediterranean conquerors. Additionally, these aspects of the Hebraic style will be distinguished from the particular modes of philosophical discourse.

The Forms of Hebraic Argument

In constructing a Hebraic philosophical style, the biblical texts deploy various literary instruments: story, stylized speech, poetry, law, compiled aphorisms, and other verbal forms and genres. How do they advocate through story or poem, for instance? We see advocacy not just in the content of a story or poem, but by asking why it is written in this form, for what purpose, and to what end. Of similar ilk, newspapers and scientists tell stories about the cosmos, but savvy readers also understand that they are always advocating something. I will address the mechanics of how texts reason with us in Chapter 4.

Because of the diversity of texts, we cannot rely upon word studies that naïvely attempt to span the Christian Scriptures. Authors have their ways of telling the story and advocating, which means that epistemology cannot be found out merely by studying the use of the word *yāda*ʿ (Hebrew: "know") or *ginōskō* (Greek: "know"). For instance, the Hebrew word *yāda*ʿ is used across the Hebrew Bible to describe discerning (Gen 3:22), trusting belief (Gen 15:8, 13), marital sex (Gen 4:1), rape (Gen 19:6), and confirmation (Gen 18:21; 22:12). All of these uses are in Genesis alone. Yet other concepts and language are intimately connected with knowing in Genesis and beyond, namely, the relationship of "listening" (*šāma*ʿ) to "seeing" (*rāʾâ*). As Owen Barfield once framed it: "To anyone attempting to construct a metaphysic in strict accordance with the canons and categories of formal logic, the fact that the meanings of words change, not only from age to age but from context to context, is certainly interesting; but it is interesting solely because it is a nuisance."[27] Paramount to my task, we must understand how biblical authors utilize disparate language to refer to deeper conceptual structures. However, just as is the case in philosophy today, each author and editor will have preferred ways of talking about the same conceptual structures.

What, then, are the core forms of argument used within the Hebraic philosophical style? I offer the following forms of exploring and advocating a methodology of abstract reasoning, or, second-order reasoning. More may be present, but these create the essential toolbox for many biblical authors to advocate philosophical methodology:

1. narratives as an argument; discursive and presentational
2. definition by *genus* and *differentia*
3. analogical reasoning and metaphor
4. ritualized learning environments
5. taxonomical paradigm creation
6. pre-Aristotelian logic not restricted to a binary notion of truth
7. presumption of discernible cause and effect relationships

Narratives as Argument

In Chapter 4, I examine in more detail how to map arguments from narratives. But first, it is worth considering the basic proposal that

[27] Owen Barfield, *Poetic Diction: A Study in Meaning* (Middletown, CT: Wesleyan University Press, 1974), 61.

narratives can be a form of argument.[28] The fact that the Christian Scriptures are roughly structured as a grand narrative in a poetic collection corresponds with the networked mode and creationist conviction. Some have suggested that only in the Hebrew Bible do we find a programmatic intellectual effort ever self-aware of its unfolding story with a beginning, middle, and end. That claim to exclusivity might be too strong, but the insight is correct. Story matters because the biblical authors consistently employ their philosophical work in the story. This entails an author's ever-present awareness of the role of oracle, law, or story in the metanarrative, even if you want to conceive of the whole collection of texts as a work of poetics.

How does a story function as an argument? As philosophers have found, story can be a way to bring someone into a rigorous and complex philosophical topic and say something about it using the persuasive force of the narrative.

But first, we ought to recognize the persuasive role of story in contemporary philosophy and science because scholars do not typically associate stories with a rigorous analytical explanation.

Consider the arguments of chemists and philosophers trying to advocate a particular explanation within their fields. A standard approach to explaining why an electron stays in the orbit of the nucleus of an atom employs a story. We know that electrons are not in "orbit," and picturing them as such might inject a distorting metaphor when thinking about the location of an electron with respect to the nucleus. Here is how one scientific explainer dealt with it (I have noted the setting, characterization, conflict, plot tensioning, and resolution):

> [**Conflict**] There is a problem with thinking of electrons as little chunks of matter orbiting a bigger chunk of matter. They don't actually behave that way.
>
> [**Characterization**] An electron can't be thought of as a planet, and must instead be thought of as a kind of cloud of probability .... To understand the electron's behavior, we have to think about where that cloud will be the most dense, or where there is the greatest probability of an electron, or where there is the maximum negative charge.

[28] Without having to agree with every detail, philosophers are making fine-tuned arguments about the narrative's philosophical power in fiction, history, and journalism, but also in the history of philosophy. Cf. Peter Kivy, *Once upon a Time: Essays in the Philosophy of Literature* (New York: Rowman and Littlefield, 2019); Garry L. Hagberg (ed.), *Fictional Characters, Real Problems: The Search for Ethical Content in Literature* (New York: Oxford University Press, 2016); John Woods, *Truth in Fiction: Rethinking Its Logic* (New York: Springer, 2018).

[Plot tensioning] Let's picture the journey towards the proton-hydrogen nucleus again.

[Setting] [E]xcept picture it as you would if you were measuring each tiny volume of space with a probabilitometer. Far away from the nucleus, the probabilitometer would register virtually no probability of negative charge. As you slowly move closer, the meter would go up and up, until it registered highest probability at the nucleus . . .. The trick here is understanding that a tiny volume of space on a line a certain distance from the nucleus is not the best way of measuring the probability of an electron being in any particular volume of space. We're not puzzled about whether the electron is above, below, to the left, or to the right of the nucleus. We just want it a certain distance away. Meaning it could be anywhere on a spherical "shell" around the nucleus . . . the farther we go away from the nucleus of the atom, the less likely that atom's electron is to be found.

[Climax] So the highest probability of finding the electron is going to be the "sweet spot" radius where the volume of the shell is big enough that the probability is high, but the distance from the nucleus isn't too large for the probability to be low.

[Resolution] Graph that and you find that the electron's highest probability is close to the center of the atom, but not inside it.[29]

In this standard mode of scientific explanation, there are characters and setting (electron, protons, nucleus, etc.), a clear conflict, and a plot that increases tension by offering various explanations, one of which heightens the plot to its climax and provides its resolution. *It is a reasoned explanation as emplotment.*

Philosophical arguments often take a similar narrative approach. The conflict can be stated as naïve intuitions, deep intuitions, old arguments, "we used to think . . ." and more. For example, a recent public philosophy event constructed this narrative explanation for the metaphysical view that "time actually exists," presented by three speakers. I summarize their presentation here:

Setting/characters: they explain concepts of time, our time measurements, our variable sense of time, etc.

Conflict: they open by stating some intuitions about time or what traditions have taught us (e.g., "we have lots of intuitions about time, such as: the present is more real than the past or future").

Tensioning: they offer various approaches to time (e.g., presentism, eternalism, and growing block theories), but these all have problems that make them inconclusive.

[29] Esther Inglis-Arkell, "Why Don't Electrons Just Fall into the Nucleus of an Atom?," *io9/ Gizmodo* (Blog), http://io9.gizmodo.com/why-dont-electrons-just-fall-into-the-nucleus-of-an-ato-1597851164/.

Climax: they say that the physics of time under relativity theory and the unidirectional flow of entropy make compelling cases for time existing.

Resolution: they conclude that the time capsule view of time best accounts for both the physics and our intuitions about time.[30]

The constituent parts of a story, what makes the story flow and work, are all present in this argument about whether time exists. The narrative is played out in the hearer. We, the audience, enter the story, with our vague notions of time, perplexities, dissatisfactions, and ultimately our relief at finding some logical resolution. The basic logic of the narrative approach to scientific and philosophical argument is not classical or propositional logic per se. In other words, why not just offer a propositionally stated and deductively valid argument? We could have just said:

P1: IF all intuitions about time yield sufficient epistemic warrant,
AND IF time is an adequate concept for something that exists,
THEN some theories adequately conceptualize our intuitions by adequately mapping onto actual time,
IF AND ONLY IF our notions of actual time and time itself refer to the same ontological object, namely time.
P2: Presentism is a theory of time that has features X, Y, and Z.
P3: Presentism has difficulty explaining phenomena A, B, and C.
P4: Eternalism is another theory of time that has features M, N, O, and P.
P5: Eternalism might explain A, B, and C, which Presentism cannot.
P6: Growing Block theory has features D, E, and F.
... and so on.

This formalization of an argument about time will proliferate well beyond the point I am making here. The complex series of premises can eventually be put into symbolic logic to make deductively valid arguments on an ever-growing list of premises that might feature in some conclusion drawn from the above.

Why not just use formal arguments, the kind we were taught in logic? Several reasons will be offered in the coming chapters. But most basically, we cannot simultaneously hold all of the hidden and articulated premises in our conceptual space needed to do the calculations of formalized

[30] This is my summary of a recent argument concerning the reality of time presented by Elay Shech (Auburn University) and Jonathan Tallant (University of Nottingham), David Rutledge, host, "Three Things You Should Know about Time," *The Philosopher's Zone*, August 27, 2017, www.abc.net.au/radionational/programs/philosopherszone/the-three-things-you-should-know-about-time/8817626/.

propositional arguments. Yet, somehow, when the same argument is put into a narrative structure, we can grasp it.

Why use a story arc to argue at all? I propose that the deductive argument has the same basic features that make story such a persuasive form of argument: *epistemic relief*. When a conflict formally kicks off a narrative, we the hearers feel tension about the unresolved state of the conflict. When resolved appropriately, we feel satisfied, as if the knot is now untangled. If taken seriously, this points to an uncomfortable aspect of logic, whether narratological or symbolic: *logical necessity always has an emotional-cognitive component*. It must relieve *the emotional tensions within us* in order to logically satisfy us. This does not reduce logical necessity to emotional "relief," but acknowledges our emotions are engaged by any abstract function of necessity, including mathematical operations.

And today, some philosophers argue that not even philosophers themselves accept arguments based on their deductive force or the evidence offered, but on the plausibility that creates a condition in which they are ready to accept the argument.[31] This sentiment flirts with emotional and narratological preparation for hearing arguments.

In mathematical thinking, emotions play a significant role in our analysis. In his book *How Humans Learn Mathematically*, David Tall summarizes the empirical research on acquiring and facilitating mathematical skills:

> In this way there is an intimate relationship between emotion and progress in mathematical thinking. If, at any stage, the learner encounters a new situation that is problematic, the confident learner, who has a previous record of making sense, is more likely to see the new problem as a challenge to be conquered, whereas the learner who is already feeling the strain may feel alienated and become increasingly disaffected.[32]

This emotive reasoning might also explain the high volume of poetry in the Hebrew Bible and New Testament, where prophets deliver the most crucial messages in a distinct poetic logic. For us post-Romantics, poetry has been associated with a logically thin and metaphor-heavy sentiment. However, throughout much of literary history, poetry functioned as shrewd critique precisely because of its implicative reach. Robert Alter

[31] As William G. Lycan has recently and boldly argued: "No philosopher has ever proportioned her/his belief to the evidence." *On Evidence in Philosophy* (New York: Oxford University Press, 2019), 67.

[32] David Tall, *How Humans Learn to Think Mathematically: Exploring the Three Worlds of Mathematics* (New York: Cambridge University Press, 2013), 26.

suggests the power of poetry, like narrative and logic, derives precisely from its implications, direct vocative address, and cognitive-emotional elements: "The poetic instrument of conveyance, however, generated powers of signification that pressed beyond the immediate occasion; and the imaginative authority with which history was turned into a theater of timeless hopes and fears explains why these poems still address us so powerfully today."[33]

The same could be said of deductive problem sets. They can present a conflict, even in the most rudimentary form of a syllogism. The premises create a tension to be resolved and we believe that the resolution must flow by the necessity of logic. I have alluded to the conceptual girth of that concept "logical necessity" in Chapter 2, but one thing is plain: *completed logic problems offer the person who completes them epistemic relief.* Neither the nature nor source of that relief can be plumbed here, *but neither can that epistemic relief be an entirely objective attribute of the logic problem itself.*

Philosophers, scientists, and biblical authors, among others, employ narratological description as a logical mode of both *engaging in* and *advocating* abstract reasoning. In Chapter 4, I will address the inner workings of narratological argument and how we can discern premises that logically belong to the conclusions.

Definition by Genus/Differentia

Because the style of Hebraic philosophy prefers pixelated demonstration, it would be insufficient to call it philosophy unless those pixelated instances differentiated concrete examples of a principle from those examples that do not fit. Aristotle's observation suffices here: that definition must identify the properties that distinguish something, and how to differentiate things that merely share superficial resemblances. The biblical authors pursue the same what-it-is (*genus*)/what-it-is-not (*differentia*) line of demonstration.[34] This effectively moves the Hebraic intellectual world from *speculative* toward advocating *philosophy*, directing how one should think about an abstract topic and also what is out of bounds.

33 Robert Alter, *The Art of Biblical Poetry*, new and revised ed. (Edinburgh: T&T Clark, 2011), 162.

34 *Genus/differentia* are the Latin equivalents to the Greek: γενος/διαφορα. See Aristotle, *Posterior Analytics* II:13.

For instance, the opening story of humanity – the man's aloneness in Eden – plays out an episode of *genus/differentia* discernment. The man is alone and that is "not good" (Gen 2:18). Then the man is put on a trajectory meant to end in his discovery of his proper mate. Notably, the path to discovery of the *genus* – "At last, bone of my bones" – goes through the naming of animals among which, "he could not find for himself a fit helper" (Gen 2:20).[35] Somehow, the *differentia* of the animals leads the man to discover – at first sight – his suitable mate. Instances of such *genus/differentia* distinctions abound as we explore the Hebraic philosophical style.

Analogical Reasoning and Metaphor

Analogical reasoning is the form of reasoning that requires our concepts, formed through and in our bodies, for certain ideas to be made logical to us. For instance, if we hear that "Judy's career path is taking off," then we know that this is a good thing, in general. However, any grammatical analysis of that sentence would be forced to reckon with its incoherence. How can we make any sense of this sentence at all?

The phrase "career path" and "taking off" both require schemas and concepts to mediate the meaning to us. To be more specific, there is no world where a career can be on a path, much less take off, in the plain meaning of the terms, or by scrutiny of the grammar and syntax. Particularly, we would need to understand what a path is, which we only know because we have physically vectored from one place to another, point A to point B. Since we can only conceptualize from our physical experience with a "path," we can analogically employ the concept of "path" and apply it to other things that go forward in time, like a career. But even here, "career" is a collection of events deemed significant and tracked over time.

Notice that there are also embodied notions of time and progress embedded in the term "career path." The same goes for "taking off," which makes for a decidedly different analog after the space race than prior to it. "Taking off" could mean leaving, as in "Joey is taking off," or as in "leaving the earth's atmosphere." For most of us, "taking off" probably tugs on our experience of something that has been stagnant

[35] Umberto Cassuto argues that *māṣā'* (Gen 2:20) must be interpreted as reflexive for the man: "he did not find for himself." Umberto Cassuto, *A Commentary on the Book of Genesis* (Jerusalem: Magnes Press, 1961), 133.

for a long time and then suddenly moves in a progressively positive direction (i.e., a rocket launch).

All of these meanings *require* an embodied experience, in person or imagined, that provides conceptual parallels for the meaning and maps the analog to the current statement in order to make that sentence comprehensible.

The metaphors and analogs are not decorative to the task, but function cognitively in a way that supposedly "literal" discourse cannot.[36] Metaphors and mental modeling appear in close kinship to analogical reasoning. Because metaphors cannot be translated into propositions without loss, their ability to provoke reasoning in us makes them adept philosophical tools. Erin Heim describes the unique cognitive-linguistic function of metaphors that are new to us: "[Metaphors] are capable of shaping how a person conceives of reality; a truly creative metaphor communicates truths which have no literal paraphrase."[37] And when metaphors employ a model, such as a scientific construct, "these models create new connections and knowledge for their hearers/readers, knowledge that is only accessible through these particular metaphors."[38]

Indeed, when we hear novel metaphors, we cognitively simulate aspects of the metaphor in order to reason through the relationships. Some researchers in the cognitive sciences believe this means that metaphors can generate new abstract concepts.[39] Hearing "China is a paper tiger" may be a dead metaphor to some, where the meaning is known and can be applied directly to China. Yet, if we have not heard this metaphor, then we are visually simulating a paper tiger in our brains and attempting to figure out the meaning of the object "paper tiger" itself, and then its relationship to China. Because that phrase carries emotional overtones and can signal in-group people (i.e., those who already understand the "paper tiger" metaphor), it is not translatable as a solo utterance. It does

[36] See Heim for a disputation of the false dichotomy: literal versus figurative. Erin M. Heim, *Adoption in Galatians and Romans: Contemporary Metaphor Theories and the Pauline Huiothesia Metaphors* (Biblical Interpretation Series 153; Leiden: Brill, 2017), 69–71.

[37] Heim, *Adoption in Galatians and Romans*, 70.

[38] Heim, *Adoption in Galatians and Romans*, 71.

[39] Anja Jamrozik et al., "Metaphor: Bridging Embodiment to Abstraction," *Psychonomic Bulletin and Review* 23, no. 4 (2016): 1080–89; Raymond W. Gibbs, Jr. and Teenie Matlock, "Metaphor, Imagination, and Simulation: Psycholinguistic Evidence," in *The Cambridge Handbook of Metaphor and Thought*, ed. Raymond W. Gibbs, Jr., 161–76 (New York: Cambridge University Press, 2008); "Metaphor Interpretation as Embodied Simulation," *Mind & Language* 21 (2006): 434–58.

more than so-called literal language can do while it builds a visual model in us and prods us to understand the new relations it is making.

The biblical literature *teems* with such *nondecorative* reasoning, both analogical and metaphorical. So does the previous sentence. The seemingly garden-variety phrase "listen to the voice" gains technical status as a metaphor for obedience throughout the Hebrew Bible and into the NT. No distinct word for "obey" exists in Hebrew or NT Greek. Rather, the term "listen/hear" (Hebrew: *šāmaʿ* / Greek: *akouō*) becomes a metaphor for submitting to someone's authority. In fact, the phrase "obey the voice" attempts to translate the metaphor being employed. But obviously, one cannot obey a "voice." The phrase tugs on social power structures, indicates internal states, and in the biblical epistemology, determines what can be "seen" (i.e., known) in the objectively real world. More on this in Chapters 8–10.

Reading the repeated uses of "listen to the voice" without translating them into "obey the voice" not only creates an image – a voice proceeding from one person to another – but also invokes a power dynamic between the two and heightens tension: How will they respond? Will they listen?

In the NT, Jesus' teaching proliferates with overlapping metaphors explicitly intended to be visually simulated in order to understand an abstract concept. Luke's gospel even shows Jesus verbally wrestling with the appropriateness of the overlapping metaphors – seed and leaven:

> He said therefore, "What is the kingdom of God like? And to what shall I compare it? It is like a grain of mustard seed that a man took and sowed in his garden, and it grew and became a tree, and the birds of the air made nests in its branches." And again he said, "To what shall I compare the kingdom of God? It is like leaven that a woman took and hid in three measures of flour, until it was all leavened."
>
> (Luke 13:18–20)

Jesus *shelved* linear discourse for the sake of pixelated *overlapping* metaphors, *steeped* in visual imagery, to *fabricate* concepts otherwise difficult to translate. Paul liberally *peppers* his *linear* discourses with *rich* metaphors from *realms* as diverse as sports (1 Cor 9:24), legal settings (Rom 3:4), adoption (Gal 4:5), feces (Phil 3:8), parenting (1 Cor 3:2), and every *corner* of lived life to *create* and *convey* the abstract notions which he was trying to get them to *grasp*.[40]

[40] The pervasiveness of metaphors backlighting our vocabulary is highlighted here. By italicizing the metaphors in this last paragraph, you can see my use of them to analogically reason with you. See further: George Lakoff and Mark Johnson, *Metaphors We Live By* (Chicago: University of Chicago Press, 1980); Mark Johnson, *The Body in the Mind: The Bodily Basis of Meaning, Imagination, and Reason* (Chicago: University of Chicago Press,

Though not unique to the biblical literature, one must stay alert to the pervasive use of analogical reason and metaphor to grasp how the Hebraic philosophical style itself functions. If we declare metaphor to be merely illustrative or philosophically inferior, without demonstration, then we cut off a vital inroad to understanding Hebraic thought, but also our own thinking too.

Ritualized Learning Environment

I have argued in *Knowledge by Ritual* that rites of the Hebrew Bible and New Testament have an implicit and sometimes explicit epistemological goal.[41] In other words, Israel is to practice the rituals in order to know what God is showing her – to see the same thing with new insight. Rituals are scripted to bring about knowledge, often necessary for survival. In this view, rituals are typically normal practices strategically reoriented toward a new end, namely skilled understanding.

What, precisely, an Israelite came to know through practicing these rites is a separate matter. That the rituals were inherently epistemological speaks to the matter of methodological advocacy – a philosophical style. Israel must perform rites to know – to become a wise and discerning people. Her target knowledge is ritualized in form and discerning in function.

Lists and Taxonomical Thinking

Lists of objects, actions, and rites can be a way of generating paradigms and the conditions for reasoning through the nature of the items listed. By urging a hierarchical *genus/differentia* process, the inexhaustive lists of the biblical literature create categories and conditions – a conceptual paradigm for the reader to apply to the world of *things not on the list*. The technical name for this style of second-order thinking is *Listenwissenschaft* – "science of lists" – first noted in Assyriology and Egyptology. Anthropologists today are revisiting this ancient form of list-intellectualism to proffer "that lists can be considered as genuine research technologies."[42]

1987). For precise examples from mathematics, see: George Lakoff, *Women, Fire, and Dangerous Things: What Categories Reveal about the Mind* (Chicago: University of Chicago Press, 1989), 353–69.

41 Johnson, *Knowledge by Ritual.*

42 Staffan Müller-Wille and Isabelle Charmantier, "Lists as Research Technologies," *Isis* 103, no. 4 (2012): 743.

The use of lists varies within the Hebrew Bible and the New Testament. Though we typically think of genealogies, legal codes, and the like as lists, Michael V. Fox proposes that the long lists of aphorisms in Proverbs follow the genre of *Listenwissenschaft* to produce "Israelite didactic wisdom."[43] Jacob Neusner describes the epistemic effect of lists this way: "That mode of thought defines ways of proving propositions through classification, so establishing a set of shared traits that form a rule that compels us to reach a given conclusion."[44]

Thus, lists of this sort exemplify the pixelated style most directly. Again, Leviticus outlines forbidden sexual partnerships (Lev 18:1–18) and then sexual behaviors that are forbidden within permissible and impermissible relationships (Lev 18:19–23). Each account lists propositions about sexual relationships under the principled description: "None of you shall approach any one of his close relatives to uncover nakedness" (Lev 18:6). The paradigm being conceptualized is something like "genetic and nongenetic relationships between close relatives." The ensuing list then outlines some sexual behaviors not permitted within and without legitimate sexual relationships: with one's spouse (18:19), with another's spouse (18:20), with the same sex (18:22), and with an animal (18:23), with the prohibition of child sacrifice injected between these prohibitions (18:21).

Neither list in Leviticus 18 nor 20 exhausts the possibilities. We can easily generate people and scenarios not on the list. Depending on the concept of law one brings to these texts, the list defining "close relatives" does not prohibit sex with one's grandmother. In the second list of prohibited sexual behaviors, there is no mention of having sex with a stranger's wife, a woman who is not married, a dead body, etc. Yet, we still presume that these would have been included on a more exhaustive list.

Remarkably, this seemingly comprehensive list is radically silent on saying what a *proper* sexual relationship is (*genus*), and it does not address several sexual acts that it would seem to condemn. However, if the point is to establish a set of shared traits that form a paradigm that compels us to reach a given conclusion, then the list is comprehensive in shaping a sufficient paradigm that can extend into novel circumstances. Thus, a paradigm-shaping list engages the second-order reasoning of its

43 Michael V. Fox, "Egyptian Onomastica and Biblical Wisdom," *Vetus Testamentum* 36, no. 3 (1986): 302.

44 Jacob Neusner, "The Mishnah's Generative Mode of Thought: *Listenwissenschaft* and Analogical Contrastive Reasoning," *Journal of the American Oriental Society* 110, no. 2 (1990): 317.

audience. It explains why a list so concerned with sexual activity (but not desire or attraction) does not just say what kind of sexual relationship is required, which may be presumed by network extension to Genesis 2.

Likewise, Paul's epistles practice this distinct form of reasoning. A principled paradigm is stated and then conceptualized with the ensuing list often strategically redeployed from lists known in Roman culture. For example, Romans 1 ends with a paradigm of people who "did not see fit to acknowledge God" and were therefore given over to a "debased mind and to things that should not be done" (Rom 1:28). Like Leviticus 18, he includes lists within lists where a principle is stated, and then concrete instances are given to thicken the concept (Rom 1:29–31):

> Filled with every kind of wickedness, evil, covetousness, malice.
>
> Full of envy, murder, strife, deceit, craftiness,
>
> They are gossips, slanderers, God-haters, insolent, haughty, boastful, inventors of evil, rebellious toward parents, foolish, faithless, heartless, ruthless.

Paul's use of the list forces us to find the common concepts (*genus*) without having an equally terse and instructive *differentia*. Like Leviticus 18 on the matter of sexuality, this passage gives no quick positive example of those who "acknowledge God" and "do what ought to be done."

Listenwissenschaft reasons with the reader, forcing her to conceive of what ties these things together. It guides her to think about sexuality, or acknowledging God, apart from the particular historical acts of sex or righteous behaviors listed. The exact paradigm of sexuality Leviticus constructs for the reader here is a separate concern from mine. Demonstrating that Leviticus and Paul seek to reason with the audience about the nature of sexuality and God-fearing *as such* is my primary objective here.

Are all lists philosophical in the Christian Scriptures? No, and conversely, some biblical scholars have only observed the scholarly function of lists to create logical relationships.

Listenwissenschaft can imbue taxonomical thinking as a form of reasoning, even taxonomies on mundane topics. Lists of nations and animals use abstract categories that reveal something about that which coheres the individual members together. "Amorites" is a generic term used to refer to a specific cluster of nationalities and ethnicities. So too with "donkey," a *genus* category that inevitably included various species, but also criteria that were definitive for what a donkey is not (*differentia*). How Israelites carved up their universe by lists reveals ontological categories.

Reflecting on two aspects of scientific thought in the biblical languages and taxonomical lists in the Hebrew Bible, Rolf Knierim's framing identifies these lists as *scholarly*, but not necessarily treaties of second-order abstraction:

> These languages [Hebrew, Aramaic, Greek] are clearly and logically structured, and the texts based on them are for the most part the result of intensive intellectual activity: conceptualized thought, disciplined composition, and rational argumentation as in *the ancient science of rhetoric*. They are anything but impressionistic, in both their poetry and their prose. … They [taxonomies] are the products of organized efforts to comprehend individually distinguishable identities as belonging together in conceptualized groups, to order their listing according to certain systematized principles.[45]

And yet, any time we see ancient taxonomies or calendars, we see people moving away from the realm of concrete historical instances and toward abstracted thought. For instance, modern calendars do not schedulize a "March 29," but instead, categorize a day according to solar, lunar, or calendar adjustment criteria to count as "March 29." Likewise, taxonomic lists do not refer to discrete historical instances of a particular rock badger. Rather, they refer to a suite of criteria commonly known to describe a species: a class with many possible members and presumed criteria to discern what is and is not rock-badger-esque.

Evidence of abstraction meets only one aspect of *philosophical* thinking. Hence, everything that Knierim cites as "scientific thinking" falls into the *speculative* category because, for him, it reveals rigorous and logically applied systematicity that requires speculation about "certain systematized principles." Similarly in Babylon, Van De Mieroop argues for an inherent speculative use of lexical lists and omens. Hence, we ought to consider taxonomical lists of all varieties as candidates for second-order speculation, but not necessarily philosophy apart from some form of advocacy. The fact that many lists are used across the Christian Scriptures for advocating how Israel and the church ought to live and think, suggests philosophy.

Pre-Aristotelian Logic Not Restricted to a Binary Notion of Truth

By using "pre-Aristotelian" to modify "logic," I am only flagging up our sense of logic in the broadest sense possible. "It follows that …" or "thus it was …" conjunctions highlight logical connections between events as interpreted by narrators and authors. Other logical features of poetry and

[45] Italics original. Rolf Knierim, "Science in the Bible," *Word and World* 13, no. 3 (1993): 245.

narrative will be mapped out more specifically in the coming chapters, but for now, "logical" just means that there is some entailment involved in all meaning-making, and that the biblical authors are fully engaged in demonstrating such logic in their stories, law, and poetry.

First, basic logical relationships, best described as pre-Aristotelian, appear to factor in all judgments. The biblical texts exhibit *modus ponens* (If P, then Q) and *modus tollens* (If not Q, then not P) rationality throughout, and sometimes explicitly (e.g., Gideon's fleece, Judg 6:36–40). The logic of justification within narratives and rituals offers our best glimpse into the rationality schemes at work in Scripture.

Second, the biblical language itself regarding notions of truth reveals a different construct than is often supposed by our contemporary truth-talk. Specifically, truth or *true-ness* does not appear in contraposition to false-ness, but rather, truth operates on a continuum with false. In the Hebrew Bible, Greek Septuagint, and the New Testament, "true" more closely refers to fidelity, which creates a different discourse on the function and meaning of what we might call "truth claims," "absolute truths," or the definite noun, "the truth." Thus, biblical and contemporary notions of truth might be commensurable with each other, but they cannot be construed as univocal.

I will examine the operative use of logic and truth as epistemic frameworks in Chapter 9.

Discernible Cause and Effect Relationships

Creation sets out a metaphysic of the cosmos with personal relations between God and all objects in the universe. Biblical authors, from all appearances, deem cause and effect relationships to be discernible and presumed throughout the cosmos. By cause and effect, I only mean a view where *A causes B* or more complex versions such as $A+A_1$ *cause B*, $A+A_1+A_2$ *cause B*, and any other concatenations. This view includes God as a primary causal force, double causation, and also God permitting secondary causes.

Some cause/effect relationships must be learned, where characters in the biblical narratives did not discern a relationship between two events. But the overarching view of the Torah, the prophets, Jesus, and the apostles is that the universe is "lawful" because of a king-creator who reigns over the cosmos and orders it so. Even this lawfulness (e.g., the law of gravity, as it is commonly called today) derives from the royal metaphor taught in Scripture. The "laws of physics" metaphor originally entailed the notion of a king and law-giver to whom the physical universe was subject.

This to say, we do not encounter a bizarre world of cause and effect in Israel's literary works, but one akin to how we might think of our world today.

Hebraic Philosophy in the Context of the Ancient Near East

Finally, having surveyed the intellectual worlds of Egypt and Mesopotamia in the prior chapter, the differences between the Hebraic philosophical style and the others should now appear striking. As far as similarities go, *pixelation* can certainly be attributed to both Mesopotamian and Hebraic speculation in their texts, if not Egypt as well. The *creationist* conviction that primeval history acts as a primary referent carries across the thought-world of the ancient Fertile Crescent. But this is where the similarities fade.

The ritualist conviction takes center stage in all ancient (and modern) cultures, but only in the Hebraic style do rituals themselves function overtly within an epistemology that seeks to develop *transdemographic* wisdom.

A brief note regarding divination and prophecy: the style of Hebraic philosophy includes the use of ouija technology such as casting priestly lots (i.e., *ʾûrîm* and *tummîm*). However, this practice as recorded in both the Hebrew Bible and New Testament contrasts with the divination practiced in Egypt and Mesopotamia. Appropriately practiced in times of needing assistance, casting lots was God's response to seemingly faithful servants who could not discern how to proceed (cf. 1 Sam 23:1–3; Acts 1:23–26).

What Hebraic ouija is not: There is little evidence of sign/omen reading in the Christian Scriptures; rather we see personally guided understanding wrought through authorized agents, usually prophets. Unlike Mesopotamia, Israel's God did not textually inscribe the universe in order for it to be read by an elite class of diviners. Though Joseph and Daniel will reason with kings within such cultures of divination, for their part, Hebrew prophets are not an elite class. Prophets arrive on the scene with varying backgrounds – from Egyptian-royalty-turned-shepherds (e.g., Moses) to resistant locals called to the office (e.g., Jeremiah, Amos).

And in the metaphysics of kingship, Hebrew kings could not have been more different in mode and means from Egyptian pharaohs. By law, Israelite kings were supposed to hail from the people (Deut 17:14–20).

The first messianic king (i.e., a Yahweh-chosen prophetically anointed king) even came from the specious tribe of Benjamin (e.g., Saul), a tribe nearly annihilated for their Sodom-like atrocities (Judg 19). God's presence does not indwell the king, but instead takes up physical residence in the cultic headquarters of the Tabernacle and later Temple.

Unlike the Babylonians, the Torah does not textualize the cosmos or explore it through the playful use of lexica, but rather uses persons authorized and textually instantiated to instruct Hebrews back to the embodied and ritualized life for the sake of understanding their world.

This genuinely novel philosophical style, distinct from Israel's peers and later Hellenist philosophical styles, shares deep affinities with contemporary views of ethics, polity, and our practice of the scientific enterprise today.

Conclusions

Does the Hebrew biblical tradition advocate a particular method for second-order thinking? Advocacy ties directly into the epistemic nature of Hebraic ritual itself. If knowing is a process of authorities prescribing embodied practices to dispose knowers toward insight, then the explicitly commanded ritual participation of Israel also functions as her advocated epistemology.

If one has to "do this" in order to "know that," then we see Israel's philosophical style of knowledge actively advocated in the text where authorities are authenticated to Israel specifically for the sake of commanding Israelites to "do this" and sometimes more specifically, "do this in order to know that" (e.g., Gen 15:7–21; Lev 23:42).

Rising above the level of scholarly texts, the biblical authors intentionally pursue a philosophical discourse through various forms of argument. What Israelites and non-Israelites can come to know depends entirely upon heeding the prophets that Yahweh authenticates to them, and then embodying the ritualed life prescribed by those prophets in order to see what the prophets are showing them. But because Yahweh *commands this discrete epistemological structure*, giving sufficient historical and rational reasons to trust it, I suggest that this method of thought in the Hebrew Bible moves beyond scholarly speculation and clearly into the realm of advocated philosophy.

4

Mapping Philosophy in Narrative, Law, and Poetry

> The very formula, "Naus means a ship," is wrong. *Naus* and ship both mean a thing, they do not mean one another.[1]

Mapping out a Hebraic philosophical style risks a litany of errors. We must span centuries, languages, technological shifts, and empires, and all among many unnamed authors and editors. The metaphor of "mapping" reveals the connective lines that spread tree-like from the core narratives of the biblical literature.[2] The map metaphor means that we are tracing what is presumably already indigenously there in the text at some point in the text's history.

This literary investigation requires sensitivities to the intertextual networks between passages, final texts, corpii, and codex. As C. S. Lewis lamented about the philological naïveté in his day that could reduce two languages to equivalent meanings (e.g., *naus* = ship), so too I worry about how to philosophically navigate the variegated texts of the Christian Scriptures.

Though compilation and editing rendered these texts into their present states, the specificity with which some biblical scholars mark out their sources appear underdetermined by the biblical data and historical sources.

The literary focus of this study raises all sorts of source-critical issues that I would like to quell (or, set aside). Editorial remarks and narratorial

[1] C. S. Lewis, *Surprised by Joy: The Shape of My Early Life* (San Francisco: HarperOne, 2017), 140.

[2] I borrowed this "arborescent" analogy from Marc Van De Mieroop, *Philosophy before the Greeks* (Princeton, NJ: Princeton University Press, 2017).

voice guide this task, but I do not claim any particular hypothetical source arrangement regarding the divisions *within a text*.

A Hebraic philosophy, therefore, is not a Yahwistic or Deuteronomistic philosophical style (though such projects will certainly correspond to my work).[3] My task is to discern a tradition-historical philosophy with literary sensibilities to the Hebrew Bible and later Jewish texts of Christian Scripture. Jaco Gericke's work maps out philosophical notions based on Yahwism in his 2012 SBL book *The Hebrew Bible and Philosophy of Religion*.[4] I have argued for a methodological pluralism to Gericke's method of *philosophical criticism* in my recent volume *Epistemology and Biblical Theology*.[5] We see philosophical criticism as a form of biblical criticism, but the selection of texts for examination is not endemic to the form of criticism.

Hence, diversity in philosophical criticism could include examinations of the later forms of texts or Yahwist, Priestly, Elohimist, or Deuteronomist constructions alone – though difficulties arise no matter which collection of texts and sources one examines.

Being conservative, I could choose an uncontroversially minimalistic collection of Priestly texts to examine or I could examine the widest physically intact curated collection – as Assyriologist and Dead Sea Scroll scholars typically do. I lean toward the latter, but with a view that it could be put in conversation with the former.

Specifically, then, my project to map out *Hebraic philosophy* refers to the ancient Hebrews' advocacy of a particular style of second-order thinking as traced through the biblical literature that has borne uncontroversial provenance *over the last twenty-three centuries or more*.

If we take the Hebrew Bible and New Testament texts in their rough final forms, though no absolute final form seems plausible, how can we be true to texts that have been interpreted so variously and with diverse agendas and ideologies?

3 Some have argued that these hypothetical source divisions themselves represent principled arguments between ancient Hebrew and Jewish authors and editors. See Benjamin D. Sommer, *Revelation and Authority: Sinai in Jewish Scripture and Tradition* (New Haven, CT: Yale University Press, 2015).

4 Yahwism, not to be confused here with Yahwistic texts of the Documentary Hypothesis. Jaco Gericke, *The Hebrew Bible and Philosophy of Religion* (Society of Biblical Literature Resources for Biblical Study 70; Atlanta: Society of Biblical Literature Press, 2012).

5 Dru Johnson, *Epistemology and Biblical Theology: From the Pentateuch to Mark's Gospel* (Routledge Interdisciplinary Perspectives on Biblical Criticism 4; New York: Routledge, 2018), 1–16.

I suggest that we treat the text like a game, such as Monopoly or billiards. The rules for these games are sufficiently complex and ambiguous so that they always accrue "house rules" wherever played. These local variants of the game are negotiated beforehand to set proper expectations for playing. Though they may vary from house to house, these "house rules" also have boundaries that, if crossed, would violate the nature of the game itself.

For instance, if a "house rule" for a billiard game permitted using any ball as the cue ball, that would distort the material nature of the game (i.e., why only one ball is completely white) but does not seem to *violate* it. Maybe this is how some play with children or those with dementia who are not skilled enough to use the cue ball every time. However, if the "house rule" removed the pool cues or the billiard balls or the slate entirely, that would be a different game altogether. So too, if we removed the dice or property cards from Monopoly, then we might have violated the material structure of the game.[6] Something about the play of the game manifests discernibly from the materials included in the box. Everything in the box is intended to be used in play.

How do we know the intention of the game? I only want to argue that interpretation needs to respect the basic structures of the texts in the same way that we would the material structures of Monopoly. Everything that comes in the box, as it were, has an intentional function. The language, genre, history, and literary structures are like the board, game pieces, money, little plastic houses, and so on. I will not ignore or throw out the structural pieces of the biblical literature; neither will I rearrange the pieces to make them suit my thesis, hopefully. I address this concern in this chapter as the *persistence* and *relevance* criteria for discerning structural philosophical elements in the biblical literature.

The "house rules" can vary from one tradition of biblical scholarship to the next. Some "house rules" examine texts for theological content or silenced voices from the margins. As for me and my house, our focus will be on philosophical developments as presented in the structures of the biblical texts. These philosophical elements, in the box, are as demonstrable as economic discourse discernible in the material structure of the Monopoly game – though they are rarely overt philosophical discourses in the ways we have come to expect in the West.

[6] Thanks to Stephanie Johnson for giving me this apt game and "house rules" analogy.

Methodological Convictions

How does one discern philosophical content from the biblical texts? Surely the reader is experiencing a growing concern about methodology. And even then, how will we check for commensurability within and across texts written centuries apart. I too share this concern. The briefest way to allay some of their methodological wariness is to say that my process will:

1. assess the literary forms of texts on their own as texts – not assuming that Genesis will examine a topic similarly to Exodus, for example
2. seek formal, lexical, and conceptual parity – going beyond mere word studies to understand how a text may explore topics without naming them in a particular vernacular (though some terms and phrases do indeed become formulaic)
3. work within the logic of literary formal structures; parables will not be treated as narratives, nor poetry as prose
4. maintain a methodological rubric for determining which texts adequately represent the Hebraic philosophy under consideration

Regarding that final point, the question of a Hebraic philosophical style turns on which texts one explores and how they develop their exegesis within those texts. Hence, I want to spell out the criteria employed here to determine suitable networks and passages for philosophical examination.

Signal Detection Theory (SDT) offers a categorical structure similar to what I want to accomplish. SDT breaks down an incoming stream of data according to the desired signal into four possible cases: hits, misses, false positives, and correct rejections. For our purposes, the desired signal is some concatenation of the style of *philosophy* and not merely *scholarly* or *speculative* texts. Accordingly, the thesis of this book attunes us to which category biblical passages should fall under:

Hits: advocated second-order thinking with a demonstrable style (*genus*)
Misses: advocated second-order thinking that went unnoticed
False Positives: passages that superficially appeared to be advocated second-order thought, and were mistakenly classified as a "hit"
Correct Rejections: passages that superficially appeared to be advocated second-order thought, but on closer inspection were not (*differentia*)

I aim to develop the maximum number of "hits" and "correct rejections" with the minimum number of "false positives" and "misses." However, I fully expect there to be many more "misses" than "hits" because my task cannot exhaust the possible instances of "hits" in the Christian Scriptures. Rather, I intend to demonstrate reasons for asserting the Hebraic style of philosophy that persists into the New Testament that will then become a lens for the eyes of anyone else who looks.

In this volume, we are looking for stories, poems, laws, and more, that demonstrably and structurally exhibit the Hebraic style of philosophy. Essentially, what counts as Hebraic philosophy is signaled in various ways across disparate texts of the Christian Scriptures. My use of SDT's categories only provides a way of conceptualizing the task in Bayesian terms of confidence. However, the question remains regarding how I justify a "hit" or "correct rejection."

Literary Rubric for Discerning "Hits"

To this end, I will follow a rubric summarized under three principles: *presence*, *persistence*, and *relevance*.[7] First, the *presence* of advocated philosophical content will be considered when it appears both lexically and conceptually or in the formal structure of a text (the resolution, the narrative's central conflict, etc.).

Second, beyond conceptual/lexical presence in a text, the biblical author must *persistently* pursue the topic. By this, I mean that the author appears to intentionally develop the topic and not as a one-off idiosyncratic instance. Persistence entails that this topic represents a concern within the author's rhetorical strategy.

Third, the philosophical content must have *relevance* to the central story being told or the instruction at hand. Merely seeing a character in a narrative figure something out as a positive move in the narrative's rhetoric does not qualify it for investigation. However, when a passage or network of pixelated passages meets all three requirements of *presence*, *persistence*, and *relevance*, then it crosses the threshold for further analysis to reveal a possible instance of Hebraic philosophy.

The Normative Dressed as Descriptive

John's Gospel, though written in a vulgar dialect of Koine Greek, makes sophisticated rhetorical moves at key junctures in the story. He moves from third-person narrative to second-person prescription in a seamless

[7] This section (Literary Rubric for Discerning "Hits") has been adapted from its original form as it appeared in Johnson, *Epistemology and Biblical Theology*, 7.

feat not encountered anywhere else in the New Testament, or possibly any other ancient literature.

Regarding Thomas' untrusting reaction to the disciples' good news of the resurrection, John paints the story with a vivid focus on Thomas' lack of trust in his colleagues (John 20:19–29). Mark's long ending paints the picture similarly: "And he upbraided them for their lack of faith and stubbornness, *because they had not believed those who saw him after he had risen*" (Mark 16:14). This scene supposes that the one person not present to see the resurrected Jesus also refuses to trust his peer's reports about the resurrection. So John uses and reuses the language of trust (*pistis*) to depict Thomas' stubbornness: "Unless I place my hand … I will never trust [you all]" (John 20:25). The resurrected Jesus then appears and chastises Thomas for not trusting his peers: "Do not be untrusting [of them], but trust [them]" (John 20:27).

Now for the remarkably subtle tie-in, where John takes a story about an event and breaks the fourth wall with the reader, speaking to her in direct address on the matter of trusting a disciple's report of that which the hearer/reader herself has not seen. In other words, the reader has become Thomas (20:29–31):

> Jesus said … "Blessed are those who have not seen and yet have trusted [the disciples' report]."
>
> Now Jesus performed many other signs that are not written in this book, but these are written *so that you* [the hearer/reader] *may trust* [the narrator] that Jesus is the Christ ….

In one quick train of phrases, the narrator binds up the story and the reader. Beginning with description, he then pivots effortlessly into the normative. The question now pregnant in this rhetorical move is: How much of John's gospel was meant to function similarly as the "normative disguised as descriptive"? In this epilogue, John includes his entire gospel "written in this book" as normatively descriptive; so too does Luke in his prologue (Luke 1:1–4). It's difficult to resist seeing the same rhetorical force behind Matthew and Mark, or Genesis through Kings.

Gordon Wenham has argued for something similar in the narrative portions of the Pentateuch.[8] By carefully identifying authorial perspective and ideal readers, the author's rhetorical purposes emerge – stronger in

[8] Gordon J. Wenham, *Story as Torah: Reading Old Testament Narrative Ethically* (Grand Rapids, MI: Baker Academic, 2000). See also John Barton, *Ethics in Ancient Israel* (New York: Oxford University Press, 2017).

some cases than others. In Genesis' local creation account, Wenham goes further to assert a second-order universal inference from the descriptions of the "leaving and cleaving" directive (2:24): "The writer also makes it quite plain at the end of the chapter that the story has universal relevance, for he appeals to it to explain a general principle."[9]

I suggest with Wenham and others that these are no mere stories, whatever genre we cast them in. They are extended arguments meant to persuade the hearer to trust or to reify the reasons for their trust in the theo-political movement of the Way. In the case of John's ending, the narrator brings attention to the fact that *the gospel itself was intended to take part in a pixelated argument*. More instances could be added, but this collection of instances in narrative format was meant to persuade you, the hearer/reader.

The descriptive narratives and poetry of Scripture signal their prescriptions through various means. For instance, the cold telling of a story without commentary can serve as the *differentia*, the opposite of the principle being advocated. But clearly, negative consequences could indicate the purpose of the story and implied prescriptions. The same can be true for stylized dialogue (e.g., Gen 22:1–14; 1 Sam 15:13–25; Mark 4), parables without interpretation (Luke 16:19–31), retelling stories using the same form and language but different setting/characters (cf. Gen 19; Judg 19; or Gen 1:28–30; Gen 9:1–10), and reification of a theme with variation (e.g., Prov 10:11; 12:10; 13:5).[10] Marc Arvan, a scholar of Buddhism, illustrates it simply: "I am well aware of how the normative is often disguised as descriptive. 'It is seven o'clock' says the mother, but what she means is rather 'Get up! You have to go to school.'"[11] So, too, do the biblical authors.

Narratological Argument

Like many ancient philosophical traditions, the Hebrew tradition created didactic stories for several purposes, one of which is philosophical instruction. It is not controversial to say that over the last three centuries the European philosophical and scientific traditions have effectively outshone

[9] Wenham, *Story as Torah*, 30.

[10] By my count, there are twenty-six righteous/wicked contrasting parallelisms spread across Proverbs chapters 10–26. These represent a literary collection that both exhibit the pixelated style and the *genus/differentia* mode.

[11] Marc Arvan, "What Counts as Philosophy? On the Normative Disguised as Descriptive," *The Philosophers Cocoon*, http://philosopherscocoon.typepad.com.

the biblical narrative – I'm thinking of Kant and Lessing, among others. The effects of the new sciences (*Wissenschaften*) and scientific study of history (*Geschichtswissenschaft*) dramatically affected the course of biblical studies, reducing explanations to discrete nonnarrative forms of logical discourse.[12]

As I argued in Chapter 3, various forms of explanation operate by creating a logical conflict that heightens to a resolution that yields epistemic rest *within us*. Yet, our cultural traditioning in the West tempts us to think of narratives as mere myth, entertainment, illustration, history, art, or some combination of all these. But it might be the case that the core narratives in a collection of texts function as central arguments about the nature of humans and the cosmos.

In Christian Scripture, identifying core narratives will immediately resituate other stories as plot markers in the logic of the overarching narrative. If one takes the creation and early history sequence in Genesis 1–11 as central to the whole of Christian Scripture, then the exodus, conquests, and exiles are plot markers that lead to some grand narrative arrested within in the conflict of creation gone awry. If one takes the exodus or the exiles as central then creation becomes a backstory – a template of disobedience that leads to exile.

Paul Ricoeur alleges humans to be "incipient plotting" creatures. And because we are always plotting ourselves and everything we experience in a narrative structure, we have what he calls a "transcultural form of necessity."[13] Narrative offers a logical structure to the myriad experiences of our lives. *Like a syllogism, it gives us a formal way of processing history as considerations about the nature of things.*

Our thin understanding of logic might fool us into believing that logical devices such as syllogisms leave the realm of history, supposedly entering the abstract space of reason. If that is true, then why do the topics and content of philosophical analysis always resemble the experiences and objects of persons in history and not, say, the texture of rocks 157 miles in the earth's crust below Dallas, Texas?

12 This loss of narrative focus was famously traced in Hans W. Frei, *The Eclipse of Biblical Narrative: A Study in Eighteenth and Nineteenth Century Hermeneutics* (London: Yale University Press, 1974).

13 Paul Ricoeur, *Time and Narrative*, Vol. 1, trans. Kathleen McLaughlin (Chicago: University of Chicago Press, 1984), 52–53. I was first tipped off to this passage in Ricoeur through Craig G. Bartholomew's *Introducing Biblical Hermeneutics: A Comprehensive Framework for Hearing God in Scripture* (Grand Rapids, MI: Baker Academic, 2015).

In like kind, the chemist-turned-philosopher Michael Polanyi observed the failure to understand "significance" in naïve views of objectivity across the sciences. He understood that scientists were highly traditioned and positively biased so that they could see significance in the object of study that others could not see. As an illustration, Polanyi noted our propensity to celebrate events because they happen at round numbered intervals (e.g., a scientist's tenth anniversary).

> It would be rational for someone returning from a visit to an exhibition to relate the strange coincidence that he happened to be the 500,000th visitor. He may even have been offered, as such, a complimentary gift by the management, as was the case at the Festival of Britain in 1951. But no one would claim it as a strange coincidence that he was the 573,522nd visitor, although the chances for that are even less than those of being the 500,000th. The difference is obviously that 500,000 is a round number while 537,522 is not.[14]

Because it is significant to the narrative structure of our life stories, we favor particular types of numbers, objects, and events. We favor what we find significant, which acts as a sorting mechanism for which premises end up in our intellectual explorations. We highlight particular facts and value them over others in our philosophical reasoning *and not the bare data of sensory experience or logic of deductive arguments.* As Gary Gutting showed in the history of analytic philosophy, deductively linear arguments do not determine the favorable receptions of philosophical ideas amongst analytic philosophers.[15] Gutting showed that ideas found acceptance largely on the basis of intuitions. For Polanyi, philosophy always entails the ability to recognize significance, to hone the intuitive world of our judgments. Similarly, because we emplot our world, our emplotments will contain implications for what we view as significant (or not) in the stories we create to reason about reality.

In the following section, I review several key aspects to narrative structure that enable stories to function as a form of argument: the logical structure of a story, the rhetorical force of a story, and the authority of the narrator.

[14] Michael Polanyi, *Personal Knowledge: Towards a Post-Critical Philosophy* (Chicago: University of Chicago Press, 1962), 35.

[15] Gutting demonstrates how philosophers' intuitions and convictions, *and not deductive arguments*, have been the primary reasons why grand theories about logic and language have been accepted in the analytic philosophical community. Gary Gutting, *What Philosophers Know: Case Studies in Recent Analytic Philosophy* (New York: Cambridge University Press, 2009).

Logical Structure of Story

> For this reason, poetry [i.e., dramatic story] is more philosophical and more serious than history. Poetry tends to express universals and history the particulars.
>
> (Aristotle, *Poetics*, IX)[16]

In his *Poetics*, Aristotle explores the logic of story. For him, plots must be coherent and logical, and the good ones are surprising – but their surprising elements cannot illogically relate to the plot.[17] He discusses how good epistemic discoveries occur not only within the story but for the audience as well. Aristotle distinguishes events necessary to the plot and disdains those that have no logical connection, which he calls "episodic."[18] Good plots, then, line up events logically necessary to each other in order to create a causal chain that ends in the discovery – in other words, the resolution.

Narratives, in most cases, have a tightly structured logic that moves the reader from premises to a conclusion. The author stages the story in the setting, introduces characters, initiates the conflict, and raises the tension within the story that aims at resolution – sometimes with a climax and sometimes the climax and resolution collapse into one event. Per the logic of the narrative, akin to deductive arguments, the resolution must logically resolve the conflict. Unlike a deductive argument, narratives are not always transparent about which facets of the story act as premises. The premises are discovered in the process, so to speak.[19]

In the same vein as syllogisms and other kindred deductions, the story has to be read or heard for the logic to work. Stories and deductions alike require human effort to move from the internal tension of their premises toward their conclusions. Semioticians call this the "paratactic dimension"; where syntax is the proper ordering that Aristotle was concerned with, paratax is the logical movement through a sequence. As Esther Meek put it, "Nobody gets from point A to point B, even in a deductive syllogism, apart from human effort."[20] Logical deduction and narratives function according to our effort and the tensions created *within us*, which

[16] Aristotle, *Poetics*, trans. Malcolm Heath (New York: Penguin, 1996), 16. 1451b.

[17] Aristotle, *Poetics*, VIII–IX, 1452a.

[18] Aristotle, *Poetics*, IX.

[19] A similar sentiment about the employment of opacity and transparency in narrative can be found in Peter Lamarque's *The Opacity of Narrative* (New York: Rowman & Littlefield, 2014).

[20] Esther L. Meek, *Longing to Know: The Philosophy of Knowledge for Ordinary People* (Grand Rapids, MI: Brazos Press, 2003), 64.

aim us at the goal of resolution *for our epistemic rest* – we want the tensions to resolve. Thus, narratives and syllogisms alike could be charted this way:

Setting [outlining the frame in which conflict is discernible]
Conflict [initial tension introduced into the setting]
Climax [highest point of tension in direct logical relationship to initial conflict]
Resolution [follows from conflict created by characters in the setting]
Premise$_1$ [premise: without tension]
Premise$_2$ [premise: cognitive tension created by the relation of the premises]
Conclusion [follows from conflict created by the tension (not the syntax, symbols, etc.)]

In other words, once we know the conflict or the resolution of a story, only then we can find the corresponding premises.

Why use narrative rather than a discursive argument in a philosophical style? First, our ability to reason in the abstract with primitive propositions is demonstrably flimsy. Research into the nature of rhetorical form and argument has consistently shown that people trained in logic are often incapable of performing the most primitive operation of *modus ponens* (i.e., If P, then Q) in abstract form.

The well-known results of the Wason Selection Task (WST), a task that requires subjects to perform the simplest logic problem, revealed that the great majority of us cannot appropriately apply the rules of *modus ponens* or *modus tollens* even immediately after having been taught the rules.[21] Fewer than 10 percent could correctly select the result of $P \supset Q$ in the task, with the percentage rising to 13 percent *after having studied logic for an entire semester*. This inability to apply the most basic rules of logic further begs explanation when subjects were remarkably successful at applying *the same rule of logic* in concrete or familiar situations. In other words, the more abstract the problem – even in its most basic form of $P \supset Q$ – the more likely that subjects could not successfully solve it up to 80 percent of the time. I return to the conundrum revealed by this empirical study in Chapter 9.

[21] For a summary of this research in its various iterations, see John H. Holyoak et al., "Learning Inferential Rules," in *Naturalizing Epistemology*, 2nd ed., ed. Hilary Kornblith (Cambridge, MA: MIT Press, 1994), 359–92.

Within the style silos of regional philosophies, the now-classic dichotomy between continental and analytic styles of philosophy bears out this presumption along the lines of rigor. It is no secret that analytic philosophers often view continental style as lacking rigor and precision, and as too reliant on the lived experience. Continental philosophers view the analytic style as systematicity-obsessed, missing the forest for the trees, and detached from reality. William Wood, a philosopher with at least one foot in the analytic style, observes that the definitional difference of "rigor" does not equate to the qualitative difference of rigor in style:

> There is a certain naïve triumphalism at work here [in the analytic style]. Somehow I doubt that continental philosophers or theologians cheerfully prize writing that is vague, wordy, incoherent, rigor-free, and unclear. Moreover, what counts as clear, parsimonious, and rigorous writing will vary according to the community for which one writes .... Note, too, that someone with continental commitments might reasonably call analytic writing "thin" instead of "clear," and might reasonably call densely allusive continental writing "rich" instead of "obscure." Rhetorical virtues do not transcend disciplinary socialization. *Analytic philosophy is not the un-mediated language of thought.*[22]

Second, taking a cue from Wood, we must consider philosophical modes as thin versus thick description. The description of ornate phenomena often cannot be reduced to a propositional demonstration. The "triumphalism" noted here might apply most specifically to the undemonstrated assumption that all phenomena can be sufficiently conceptualized for the instruments of analyticity to be read like the sports section of a newspaper. Hence, selecting analytic modes in advance as the primary means of examination might exclude the central objects of study in favor of those on the periphery that fit the style. In brief, when you are carrying an analytical hammer, everything looks like an unparsed nail. The fact that biblical authors did not use analytically discursive arguments to demonstrate or explore abstract concepts cannot count against them *ceteris paribus*.

Third, biblical narratives anchor their arguments in creation and history (the creationist conviction). Even if we take stories such as Ruth or Jonah to be fictional, they still rely on Israel's covenantal presence in the Levant according to the creation, patriarchs, and exodus narratives.

[22] Italics mine. William Wood, "On the New Analytic Theology, or: The Road Less Traveled," *Journal of the American Academy of Religion* 77, no. 4 (December 2009): 949.

Returning to Aristotle's *Poetics*, Hebraic style might force us to diverge from his analysis at this creationist point. Aristotle believes that the dramatist's use of story enters the fray of universals precisely because it avoids the historical particular. However, these are not mutually exclusive and pitting poet against historian only reveals the valued modes of literature and discourse in Aristotle's thinking about literary argument.

At present, our own conceptual schemes for deductively valid arguments stem from many places, but certainly have one foot in the logical positivist movement. It was Cartesian epistemology and logical positivism that relied on deductive logic with true and false in polar opposition to each other. In our present "digital age," true and false have been further mapped over to high/low (cf. on/off, one/zero, etc.) voltage signals in our solid-state electronics. But there remains a question about how much this true/false scheme of analysis can aptly capture and analyze the pixelated arguments of Hebrew antiquity, if at all.

Biblical authors rely on a savvy Israelite audience who could glean from collections of historical narratives and ritual life as an epistemological process that fosters discernment – the biblical gold standard of knowing. This to say: *If all arguments – deductive, narratological, inductive, poetic, etc. – rely upon the cognitive-emotional tension created in the philosopher herself, a tension that seeks epistemic relief in concrete resolution, then we should question if digital engineering in the twentieth century might have funded us with inadequate metaphors for logical argument in binary terms*. As the analytic philosopher Eleonore Stump has argued, story might equal or rival such forms of analyticity in argument. And if we restrict our analyses to the instruments of reason that we prefer, we might be blind to the discourse that does not fit.[23]

Recalling the initial question – why use pixelated story and not discursive argument? – we could equally ask: Why use discursive argument and at what point are primitively reduced premises artificial to the point of becoming logically disconnected from the object of study? In other words, on which side should we err, primitive rigor or florid abduction? Scholars are now working out methods that mimic the ancient view of the philosophical ability of narratives.[24] Biblical authors tended to err on the side

[23] Eleonore Stump, *Wandering in Darkness: Narrative and the Problem of Suffering* (New York: Oxford University Press, 2010).

[24] E.g., Michael Boylan, *Fictive Narrative Philosophy: How Fiction Can Act as Philosophy* (Routledge Research in Aesthetics; New York: Routledge, 2019).

of leaving the discernment to savvy readers (transdemographic) and their discernment was maintained by ritual participation in a Torah-driven ethical society (ritualist).

Rhetorical Force of Story

Along with the logical connections, the shape and content of a story affect its ability to argue. It comes as no surprise that the best narratological arguments clearly state the conflict, demonstrate a successive string of causally connected events according to the plot, and then coherently resolve the conflict in a way that accounts for most or all of the causally connected events.

This use of narrative as an argument has been studied most closely in courtroom argumentation. In the drama of court explanation, the prosecutors and defenders have to tell the most compelling story about "the facts of the case."

James Voss et al., studied the effects of the coherence of courtroom narratives, specifically focusing on "fiction that is made to look like history."[25] These fictions are the stories that lawyers create, not knowing if they directly reflect the historical events of the crime. Rather, these stories aim laser-like at making a coherent argument. Unsurprisingly, Voss found that the most convincing cases resolved the most causal connections between the core facts of the case. However, he also manipulated the courtroom narratives to assess where compelling narratives fall apart. If the facts of the prosecutor's case are rearranged to the point that they interrupt causal coherence for the jury, jurors correspondingly found the defendant not guilty:

> Because the narratives in these three conditions contained the same facts, the results need to be attributed to how the critical information was presented. ... *Participants were quite sensitive to the disruption of chronological order and lack of coherence* ... if [the attorney] presents a somewhat incoherent narrative, the

[25] The present study supports the idea that a narrative under particular circumstances may be viewed as a component of argument; that is, a narrative can be used as a reason that supports a claim in much the same way that a reason supports a claim in an enthymeme [an argument with a hidden premise]. Further, the present study distinguishes between support for a claim coming from the facts supplied in the narrative and the story created by weaving those facts together.

James F. Voss et al., "On the Use of Narrative as Argument," in *Narrative Comprehension, Causality, and Coherence: Essays in Honor of Tom Trabasso*, ed. Susan R. Goldman et al. (New York: Routledge, 1999), 235

respect for that attorney's competence would likely be lessened … and convincingness … would be relatively low.[26]

This study left lingering questions regarding how much detail needs to be contained in a narrative to increase convincingness, *but none questioned that the narrative acted as an argument.* Narratives, depending on how they are told, have a rhetorical force that compels or stalls the hearer's sense of logical necessity toward the conclusion.

Second, the length of the story reveals its nature as an argument. Several narratological techniques can make stories more or less effective as arguments. Long and detailed stories, like those about Abraham in Genesis or David in 1–2 Samuel, can examine the character and the perdurance of God's covenant commitment despite the ramshackle human characters on display in the texts.

The brevity of the story and the absence of highly desirable details can also have the effect of focusing a reader on the story's logic. The creation of humanity in Eden, Cain's murder of Abel, Noah's generation, and the city of Babel (Gen 1–11) are all detail-anemic narratives when compared with the spectacle of Joseph's story (Gen 37–50), the nonpatriarch. We yearn for stories about the physics of creation, Moses' life in Pharaoh's house, the personalities of judges, the administrative decrees of Israel's and Judah's kings, the childhood of Jesus, and more. The absence of detail has driven many Christian and Jewish commentators to add stories or details to fill the gaps over the millennia.

But according to the house rules, we submit to the material fact that these stories are intentional in their brevity and famously "laconic" vocabulary as part of the Hebraic intellectual process.[27] Fables, unlike tragedies and comedies, also come in deliberately and deliciously small packages because the moral of the story is presumably at stake. The literary form, which includes its brevity, stems from its epistemological focus – what one is supposed to understand from the text.

Authority of the Narrator

In her astute work on narratological structures in philosophy, Sky Marsen describes the narrator's unique role concerning the reader: "All discursive constructions have a main emanating and organizing source,

[26] Italics mine. Voss, "On the Use of Narrative as Argument," 245–46.

[27] "Biblical narrative is famously laconic." Robert Alter, *The Art of Bible Translation* (Princeton, NJ: Princeton University Press, 2019), 41.

the presenter of information, or narrator, who is responsible for the amount, detail, hierarchical order and, potentially, explicit evaluation of the information presented."[28] Again, we see this exact formulation overtly stated in the narratorial comment of John's Gospel. The presenter of the gospel witnessed many accounts worth recording, "but these are written so that you trust that Jesus is the Christ, the Son of God, and so that by trusting you might have life in his name" (John 20:31).

According to Marsen, the narrator presents in two ways: logically as the utterer of the utterance, and fiduciarily as "a relationship of trust or complicity is formed between the reader and the source of enunciation."[29] Readers tend to tacitly accept that the narrator has the authority to tell the story, omitting and including details, but in command of the rhetorical sequence of events from conflict to resolution.

In a sign of possible compromise with our Enlightenment heritage, it should puzzle us that we identify narrators even if they differ from the actual author of a story, while at the same time, we ignore the question of who narrates the deductively framed argument.[30] In many ways, the story acts as a more critical tool in our culture, not only relaying a logical sequence of events but instigated by a named functionary – the narrator – who herself can be critically analyzed alongside her argument. Currently, the syllogism enjoys more blind fiducial commitments among Western intellectuals than does the story.

Similarly, Polanyi believes that the scientific enterprise is rife with fiduciary commitments and those commitments enable its basic efficacy. The "fiduciary programme" does not stop at science; it extends to the whole intellectual enterprise:

> We must now recognize belief once more as the source of all knowledge. Tacit assent and intellectual passions, the sharing of an idiom and of a cultural heritage, affiliation to a like-minded community: such are the impulses which shape our vision of the nature of things on which we rely for our mastery of things.

28 Sky Marsen, *Narrative Dimensions of Philosophy: A Semiotic Exploration in the Work of Merleau-Ponty, Kierkegaard and Austin* (London: Palgrave Macmillan, 2006), 66.

29 Marsen, *Narrative Dimensions of Philosophy*, 67–68.

30 Even the supposed father of analytic philosophy, Gottlob Frege, thinks we ought not to neglect personal assertion in logic. Frege's logical symbology included a symbol, that all propositions ought to have "⊢" implicitly preceding them, where the signpost indicates "I assert that" (i.e., ⊢P). Gottlob Frege, *Grundgesetze der Arithmetik*, in *Translations from the Philosophical: Writings of Gottlob Frege*, ed. Peter Geach and Max Black (Oxford: Blackwell, 1960), vol. 1, §5.

No intelligence, however critical or original, can operate outside such a fiduciary framework.[31]

I highlight the narrator's authority to convey what is obvious in all intellectual ventures: we must supply trust to those who narrate the arguments and evidence to us. Far from being a malingering side effect of pervasive skepticism, this trust is the grease that makes the gears of rationality turn. In a story, we tend to consider the person narrating and whether she warrants our trust. In deductive systems of reason, we tend to increase our faith in the system, even when no logical reason to support that increase in faith has been deductively demonstrated.[32]

The Logic of Law and Narratized Laws

The role of law and its interplay with the biblical narratives has been much debated by the rabbis and sages, and later, biblical scholars. However, at least two considerations can be made regarding the laws of the Torah and their role in Christian Scripture: (1) laws explore the nature of relations by working from principle to instances and (2) Hebraic legal philosophy takes a distinctly empathetic approach, employing point-of-view narrative techniques.

Joshua Berman has recently argued that our concepts of legal frameworks must be adjusted to read ancient literature in the Fertile Crescent. Because of the tort law pedigree of British and American legal systems, we approach individual laws with a statutory scheme of legislation. Berman claims these statutory concepts are anachronistic and blind the reader to how these "laws" function epistemologically in the texts and Israelite society. Rather, biblical laws "were prototypical compendia of legal and ethical norms."[33] In other words, such "laws" are not statutes as we commonly think of them today: rules that name every offense and then

31 Italics mine. Polanyi, *Personal Knowledge*, 281.

32 I am referring to Kurt Gödel's incompleteness theorems, from which he concluded: For any system of statements, it is logically impossible to prove true all the true statements within the system. In other words, in a logical universe of discourse, we know many statements are true that we cannot prove from within the system. Hence, in any set of statements believed to be logically connected, we must have faith in the truth of the statements beyond our ability to logically prove their truth-value. Kurt Gödel, "On Formally Undecided Propositions of *Principia Mathematica* and Related Systems," in *From Frege to Gödel*, ed. Jean Van Heijenoort (Cambridge, MA: Harvard University Press, 1977), 592–616.

33 Joshua Berman, *Inconsistency in the Torah: Ancient Literary Convention and the Limits of Source Criticism* (New York: Oxford University Press, 2017), 116.

are either upheld or broken. Rather, they create concepts and case studies to instruct Israel in the way that she should exist as a nation. We will see this conceptualization criterion in the interplay of legal principles and concrete instances in the Hebrew Bible and the New Testament.

Principles to Concrete Instances

First, as an example of principle-to-instance examination, consider the statement of *lex talionis* ("eye for an eye") in Exodus, which appears three times in the Torah (Exod 21:24; Lev 24:20; Deut 19:21). The variations on the statement in Leviticus and Deuteronomy directly fit into their contexts, where equity for those plotting murder or having committed murder is at stake.

Yet, applying this principle as a simple law, broken or kept, has always been difficult. Ancient rabbis quickly noticed a problem in the logic of the law.[34] What if a one-eyed man puts out the eye of a two-eyed man? The problem, you see, is that the principle of "eye for an eye" seemingly aims at parity in retaliation, restraining vengeance to only that which was harmed. But if a one-eyed man loses his eye by the rule of "eye for an eye," causing permanent blindness, then the rule is followed while the principle is simultaneously violated. Conundrums of a similar kind emerge quickly: sexual assault, causing the loss of limb, etc.

However, when viewed in its literary context, Exodus' "eye for an eye" law appears as a principle about how not to treat servants who subsist under their employer's patronage. In a stretch of teaching on slaves and relations, the text takes several asides about fights that end in murder or otherwise. This particular aside includes two men fighting, now with a pregnant woman involved (Exod 21:22–24).[35] That aside seems to have nothing to do with the treatment of slaves but speaks directly about wrongs being repaid according to the harm (Exod 21:22). And then comes the "eye for an eye" statement, but notice the ensuing statements (Exod 21:24–27):

[34] R. Shimon Bar Yochai reasons in the Mishnah that a blind man would thus be exempt from *lex talionis*. *b.Bava Qamma* 84a–b.

[35] As evidence that the quarrel with a pregnant woman comes perpendicular to the codes on slaves, Bernard S. Jackson observes that following this precise concrete example with "tooth for a tooth" instruction does not make sense, "the foetus ... can hardly lose a tooth." *Wisdom-Laws: A Study of the Mishpatim of Exodus 21:1–22:16* (New York: Oxford University Press, 2006), 185.

If any harm follows, then you shall give life for life, eye for eye, tooth for tooth, hand for hand, foot for foot, burn for burn, wound for wound, stripe for stripe.

When a slave owner strikes the eye of a male or female slave, destroying it, the owner shall let the slave go, a free person, to compensate for the eye.

If the owner knocks out a tooth of a male or female slave, the slave shall be let go, a free person, to compensate for the tooth.

Exodus states and then hones a principle – "eye for an eye" – fleshed out in the concrete illustration of striking one's slave. "Eye for an eye," according to Exodus' telling, creates protections from physical abuse for servants. Laws on property damage and loss immediately ensue these statements. Though I do not want to whitewash the regulation of servitude in these texts, the legal philosophy seemingly worked out in this section entails a principle with concrete examples that preindict any employer who might think of a slave as a beast of burden, to be whipped or hit. What's more, the Torah's stories and legal material preindicts the maltreatment of other vulnerable things, both flora and fauna, for their protection (cf. Gen 9:8–17; Exod 20:10, 23:12, 24; Deut 5:14, 20:19).

In this context, striking one's slave in the eye or tooth – and I assume a principle of extension to any part of their body – violates the principle of "eye for an eye." It also means that the aside about two men quarreling acts as an illustration of types of harm to be repaid.

The principle ambiguously discusses an aggregating claim: the notion of payback for harm. Yet, surprisingly, the examples turn the tables, instructing slave owners not to be the harming one, or they will suffer the financial loss, "for the slave is his silver" (Exod 21:21). By instructing Hebrews on how they must or cannot act toward slaves, the law in Exodus is physically shaping their concept of harm and repayment for harm – i.e., the person of privileged position might be the one who will have to repay.

In Matthew's Sermon on the Mount, Jesus also loads the onus of this principle back upon the hearer. "You have heard it said, 'an eye for an eye and tooth for a tooth,' but I say to you ... if anyone strikes you on the right cheek, to him the other cheek also" (Matt 5:38–39). If the principle in Exodus 21:24 merely focused on retribution for harm, then upon hearing it, we might create *ad extra* one of these propositional rules:

1. If someone breaks my possessions, then they will have to repay me.
2. If harm comes to me, then I am allowed to harm in kind.
3. If Condition A obtains, then the person who perpetrated Condition A becomes vulnerable with respect to me.

However, the ensuing examples in Exodus 21 reframe the ethic concretely and in principle:

4. *If it is I who harms* my slave, then my slave is repaid by freedom.
5. *If it is I who exploits* those who are vulnerable with reference to me (e.g., my slave), then I will become vulnerable to them (e.g., lose their service).

As twenty-first century Westerners, Rules 1–2 might be the first appropriations that spring to mind upon reading the "eye for an eye" passage. We cannot know if ancient Hebrews would hear such rules and position themselves as the victim of crimes or perpetrators. Admittedly, it is quite natural for us to read criminal statutes and presume that we would be the victim if those circumstances arose. Rule 3 is my attempt to abstract Rules 1–2. Rules 4–5 would probably not ever come to mind without extensive reflection, or maybe not, depending on the one reflecting.

Nevertheless, narratizing the principle, "if one of you strikes his slave ..." creates a visualized drama, with setting and characters, to illustrate the principle. Moreover, the dramatization of the principle places the one hearing the instruction in the wrongdoer's position and the slave as the victim of the wrongdoer.

The fact that Jesus follows a similar logic of principled law with a concrete illustration reconciles his corresponding claim that he "did not come to abolish the Torah or the Prophets" (Matt 5:17). He takes the interpretation according to Rules 1–3 and encourages the hearer to picture herself as the vulnerable one, whether the hearer is in the right or not. In the language of Rule 3, "If Condition A attains, then the person who perpetrated Condition A becomes vulnerable with respect to me," Jesus commends:

6. Even though you did not perpetrate Condition A upon someone who is vulnerable with reference to you, become vulnerable to the person who treats you as if you did.

Another example from Leviticus' restatement of the Decalogue (Lev 19:1–14) includes the principle – "you shall not oppress your neighbor or rob him" (Lev 19:13) – made concrete on behalf of the employee. What does it mean to rob or oppress one's neighbor? The next statement refines the principle, "The wages of a hired worker shall not remain with you all night until the morning" (Lev 19:13). Holding wages is a form of both oppression and theft, presumably because they rob the worker of the food needed from the day's work and for the morrow.

Law, like narrative and poetry, builds matrices of meaning through pixelation. If correct, relying upon here-and-there interpretations of key laws will not yield to us the philosophical content being examined by the pixelated legal literature. I only aim here to demonstrate that the logic of the legal portions themselves demands this dialectical thinking – from principle to instance and back – that narrows and sharpens the nature of the legal notion being advocated while expanding the caseload to consider.

Mary Douglas argues for an analogous approach to legal principles, where laws raise questions of principles that are then explained additively, through more examples:

> Instead of explaining why an instruction has been given, or even what it means, it adds another similar instruction, and another and another, thus producing its highly schematized effect. The series of analogies locate a particular instance in a context. They expand the meaning. Sometimes the analogies are hierarchized, one within another making inclusive sets, or sometimes they stand in opposed pairs or contrast sets. They serve in place of causal explanations. If one asks, Why this rule? The answer is that it conforms to that other rule. If one asks, Why both those rules? The answer is a larger category of rules in which they are embedded as subsets or from some of which they are distinguished as exceptions. Many law books proceed in this concentric, hierarchical way. In Leviticus, the patterning of oppositions and inclusions is generally all the explaining that we are going to get. Instead of argument, there is analogy.[36]

Although she cites this as expansion, the expansion is for the sake of creating a structure, which then narrows the range of principles undergirding laws. On the one hand, it is uncontroversial to say that both principles and circumstances become expressed in particular laws. On the other hand, espousing a particular system or principle in the legal codes becomes a task in which laws and literary contexts take priority to structure the system.

Empathetic Basis of Law

Scholars have noticed a unique empathetic basis for ethical action in the laws of the Torah, which intertwines them directly with the narratives of Israel. This empathetic pull emerges most clearly in the Levitical instructions for neighbor and stranger relations. What begins with resisting vengeance and instead loving one's neighbor (Lev 19:18) intensifies with

[36] Mary Douglas, *Leviticus as Literature* (New York: Oxford University Press, 1999), 18.

the further command to love the stranger (*gēr*) equally, "for you all were strangers (*gērim*) in the land of Egypt, I am Yahweh your all's God" (Lev 19:34).

By thinking about laws in coordination with the narratives they might presume, we can see how the storied experience of Israel creates the conditions for the treatment of native Hebrews, slaves, immigrants, animals, fields, houses, and people in vulnerable circumstances. Notably, if no actual history of Israel exists, then the ethical reasoning of Leviticus and other legal teaching struggles to find its footing.

It is often claimed that the so-called Golden Rule – do unto others as you would have them do unto you – finds its first Hebraic expression here in Leviticus. Religion scholars cite the fact that many of the world's religions have a version of the Golden Rule, from Confucianism and Hinduism to Zoroastrianism and Islam. Some have wondered if the Golden Rule finds its rationalistic expression later in Kant's categorical imperative. But the Hebraic formulation of the Rule, which might be its most ancient version, is networked to the national ethos of Israel's stranger-love (xenophilia) in Israel's personally experienced history. Because Israel has nationally experienced estrangement and exploitation, she is to empathetically extend care for strangers and be vigilant against her exploitative practices when strangers dwell with Israel (Lev 19:33–37).

Jonathan Burnside sees the narrative networks into legal instruction in the Torah's commands for asyla (e.g., cities of refuge) in the land of Israel. His claim not only depends on the connections between particular laws and the story of Israel (e.g., the exodus and Lev 19:34), but also upon the literary and rhetorical structure of the laws in their canonical form. Burnside makes the case that Israel's fleeing from a "factually incorrect" murder charge in Egypt creates the conviction to build cities of refuge where individuals charged with murder can flee and seek due process.

Regarding the positioning of law and the story with which it seems to cooperate, Burnside notes that the biblical positioning is not slapdash: "It is frequently the case that the way in which biblical law is structured and organized internally determines the meaning of its content."[37] Conversely, consider the prohibition of necrophilia in the British parliament in 2003. Burnside addresses how our statutory sensibilities today do not require logical order: "There is no reason why it has to appear at that

[37] Jonathan Burnside, *God, Justice, and Society: Aspects of Law and Legality in the Bible* (New York: Oxford University Press, 2010), 21.

particular point in the statute, and its meaning would not be affected if it appeared somewhere else." Because he considers biblical law to be inherently relational and narratologically arranged, Burnside concludes, "Behavior toward the *gēr* [stranger] is conceived as an extension of several relationships: the Israelite's relationship with their fellow citizens, their own experience of having been *gērim*, and their relationship with God."[38]

Burnside traces the peculiar aspect of asylum law in Exodus to parallel episodes in the narratives in which individuals and Israel herself needed asylum.[39] His is a rich account of multifaceted parallels, of which I can only examine partially. Of his many examples, two demonstrate most clearly what he sees in the legal teaching amongst Israel's narrative of the exodus.

Moses murders an Egyptian, which forces him to flee and seek asylum with Jethro the Midianite. Later laws will divide murders into three categories: accidental murders, "spur of the moment" murders, and those of malicious premeditation. But we do not know which category Moses' act of murder falls under. He flees and finds asylum outside of Egypt.

Israel's act of complicity with the murder of Egypt's firstborn also forces the nation to flee and eventually seek asylum from the pharaoh. In both accounts, Moses and Israel are not held accountable to the Noahide law ("Whoever sheds the blood of a man, by man shall his blood be shed." Gen 9:6), indicating to Burnside that their acts of murder are accidental to them or were justified by the heat of the moment.

This account of asylum also makes sense of the peculiarity of biblical laws about asyla, later defined as cities of refuge: that they only concern acts of murder. Asylum-seeking legal codes are not unusual in the ancient Near East, but they included "runaway slaves and artisans, runaway military and civilian captives of war, deserting soldiers and indebted

[38] Burnside, *God, Justice, and Society*, 28. Some biblical scholars have shown skepticism toward such a reading of legal texts, but largely from the position of incomplete analysis (i.e., not considering all the legal texts in the Hebrew Bible) or source criticism (i.e., the literary structure ignores the multiple sources of that literature). Given the nature of Burnside's project, the first critique appears relevant and the second probably reveals a fundamental disagreement about the nature and sources of the biblical literature. See Madhavi Nevader, "At the End Returning to Questions of Beginnings: A Response to Jonathan Burnside," *Political Theology* 14, no. 5 (2013): 619–27.

[39] Jonathan P. Burnside, "Exodus and Asylum: Uncovering the Relationship between Biblical Law and Narrative," *Journal for the Study of the Old Testament* 34, no. 3 (2010): 243–66. He also considers the horns of the altar and the need for priestly remediation in all cases of asylum.

peasants, to name a few."[40] Israel's restriction of asyla only to cases of murder fits the narrative pattern of Israel's experienced need for asylum from Egypt after its complicity in Yahweh's murder of Egypt's firstborn. The implementation of asyla, then, draws upon a national memory to create empathetic reasoning in Israel. Regarding the inevitable murders and accusations of murder to come, accused Israelites will also need adjudication and protection, just as Israel did from Egypt.[41]

As a simpler example, the prohibitive sexual teachings in Leviticus 18 seem to fund their prescriptions from the misdeeds of the patriarchs of Genesis. We could easily put names of violators next to many of the prohibited sex acts in Leviticus (18:7–18): Abraham, Lot, Lot's daughters, Reuben, and Judah. But, when we get to the end of that list, we see the oddly specific contours of a well-known narrative in the command itself: "And you shall not take a woman as a rival to her sister, uncovering her nakedness while her sister is still alive" (Lev 18:18). It is difficult to read the specificity of this instruction and not add, "here's looking at you, Jacob!"

Whether the arguments about particular laws and their narrative backgrounds are fully correct in their details, the stunning parallels between story and law mean that both are forms of arguing – the narrative is the normative disguised as descriptive and the law is normative from the principled narrative. In other words, the legal texts offer second-order analysis and advocacy of the narratives.

Narratizing Laws

In addition to the above, the particular technique within legal statements of picturing, characterization, and point of view contributes to urging an empathetic impulse. Assnat Bartor argues in *Reading Laws as Narrative* that the Torah replicates familiar tropes in ancient Near East legal code, sometimes covering the same legal principle or idea, but deploys its shared legal thinking quite uniquely as narrative.[42] In other legal codes (cf. Code

[40] Burnside, "Exodus and Asylum," 263.

[41] We can think of many more examples of like kind, such as Deuteronomy's law regarding inequitably favoring wives and children (Deut 21:15–17), which patently reflects the Jacob/Leah narrative of Genesis. "If a man has two wives, the one loved and the other unloved … and if the firstborn son belongs to the unloved …" (Deut 21:15).

[42] Assnat Bartor, *Reading Law as Narrative: A Study in the Casuistic Laws of the Pentateuch* (Ancient Israel and Its Literature 5; Atlanta: Society of Biblical Literature Press, 2010).

of Hammurabi), we find the condition and punishment most often stated in flat conditionals: "If anyone finds X, then he must return it to Y."

Addressing the matter of animals in duress, Bartor notes that neither an enemy's nor a brother's animals are to be left alone if wandering or suffering under a burden. However, the law is framed so that the audience becomes a character with a perspective and part of an unfolding drama:

> If you *see* the ass of one who hates you lying under its burden, you shall refrain from leaving him with it, you shall help him to lift it up
>
> (Exod 23:4–5)

> You shall not *see* your brother's ox ... and withhold your help from them; you shall take them back to your brother
>
> (Deut 22:1–4)

It's not that other legal codes did not deal with similar matters of justice, but that none of them narratized their legal codes as does the Hebrew Bible. Bartor claims that these animal relief codes are law, but also a scene with a protagonist and perspective:

> The description of events begins by noting the protagonist's act of seeing. The animals, so it seems, had buckled ... or gone astray in a far-off field, before this was noticed by the protagonists [*sic*]. However, the readers learn of the animals' existence and of what befell them only from the moment they are seen through the protagonist's eyes.[43]

Why narratize legal codes, especially when Hebrew laws could merely parrot some of the surrounding culture's legal codes that covered the same topics?[44] Bartor believes that form fits function – the poetics of the law and the disparate genres worked together through pixelation to "impress meanings that their addressees would understand, internalize, and act upon. These 'reading guidelines' can be discovered only by means of a narrative reading."[45]

In the New Testament, this same narratizing can be seen in Paul's prescriptive sections of his epistles. In a Torah-like fashion, Paul instructs the Corinthians to avoid meat sacrificed to idols, but only under certain circumstances (1 Cor 10:23–33). Note how he frames his instruction: setting (invited dinner party), characters (hosts and guests), conflict (knowledge of meat used in pagan worship). The rest of his instruction aims at resolving the conflict.

43 Bartor, *Reading Law as Narrative*, 165.

44 Because legal records from Mesopotamia do not engage Hammurabi's code, and because it resided in temples off limits to most people, some scholars wonder if Hammurabi's renowned laws are better known to the public today than they ever were in ancient Mesopotamia.

45 Bartor, *Reading Law as Narrative*, 184.

As Bartor observed in some Hebraic legal reasoning, narratizing the law forms the legal poetics engaging the narrative function. In this instance, Paul even visualizes the hypothetical Corinthian's perspective on the scene: "Eat whatever is *set before you*" (1 Cor 10:27). Instructing by means of a narrative prescription, the conflict demands a resolution to the drama, as opposed to the one who merely hears a law as "do this" or "don't do that." The former is emplotted into a narrative arc and the latter is not. The one who visualizes the scene of Israel's uniquely narratized laws emplots themselves in a thick conflicted matrix that only they can bring to a climax and resolution.

Because poetic function can be found in the Hebraic legal reasoning of the Torah and Paul, I now turn to poetry itself.

The Logic of Poetry and Narrative

> Since poetry is our best human model of intricately rich communication, not only solemn, weighty, and forceful but also densely woven with complex internal connections, meanings, and implications, it makes sense that divine speech should be represented as poetry.[46]

Though we often dismiss poetry as outside the field of rational analysis, our dismissiveness rarely stems from a consideration of the poetic form itself. In the long wake of Romanticism, the common caricature depicts poetry as primarily expressing an individual's feelings. Hebrew biblical poetry makes little use of rhyme and meter, the obvious poetic features for the uninitiated English-speaker. If not rhyme or meter, then what makes it poetry? The primary answer is structure. The enduring Hebraic poetic tradition features tightly logical structure, already demonstrating that poetry can function as a philosophical argument. Hebrew poetry often takes a particular form that not only has a logical structure, but is also pixelated, making it ideally suited to defining an abstract principle in light of particular instances.

Parallelism and Pixelated Logic of Poetry

> "Poetry does not simply delight and instruct; it delights in order to instruct."[47]

[46] Robert Alter, *The Art of Biblical Poetry*, new and revised ed. (Edinburgh: T & T Clark, 2011), 141.

[47] Robert Lowth quoted in Michael C. Legaspi, *The Death of Scripture and the Rise of Biblical Studies* (Oxford Studies in Historical Theology; New York: Oxford University Press, 2011), 108.

TABLE 2 *Parallelism of contrast and extension*

A: Extension	B: Contrast
When you walk, your step will not be hampered; and if you run, you will not stumble.[48]	A deceitful balance is an abomination to Yahweh, but a proper weight is his delight.[49]

The Hebraic form of parallelism functions as the simplest building block of poetic thought. Though rhythm, rhyme, onomatopoeia, alliteration, and other structural elements can play their parts (forms such as chiasm, acrostic, etc.), the parallel structure of two-line versets offers an easily scalable form of philosophical exploration.[50]

The parallel form generally works by stating a thought and then either extending the thought or contrasting it (see Table 2). In the case of extension (Example A), more than mere repetition of an idea occurs. Robert Alter distinguishes the variation in the second verset that "follows the rule of the instance of the category coming after the general term and by so doing effects an intensification or focusing of meaning."[51] This mode of intensification by extending the thought becomes more obvious in numerical examples: "How could *one* have routed a thousand, and *two* put a myriad (*rĕbābâ*) to flight" (Deut 32:30). These examples of extended parallelism, then, do not merely trade on synonyms, but often add the "how much more so" dimension to the first thought. This intensification makes the parallelism of extension ideal for focusing our attention on a coherent principle explored through restatements and clarifications of the same principle.

Parallelisms of contrast (Example B) delineate the boundaries of the principle being explored. Together, these two forms identify and distinguish en masse, making Hebrew poetry well suited to work as a *genus/differentia* mode of philosophical demonstration. A large portion of

48 Prov 4:12.

49 Prov 11:1.

50 Though light on the Hebrew Bible and seeing too much chiasm at points, John Breck's argument for chiasmus as central to Jewish thought has some merit. Beyond the simple parallelisms discussed here, Breck demonstrates how parallelisms can be piled up to achieve more complex intellectual tasks. "Chiastic parallelism … enables the biblical author to express a complex set of affirmations." *The Shape of Biblical Literature: Chiasmus in the Scriptures and Beyond* (Crestwood, NY: St. Vladimir's Seminary Press, 2008), 50.

51 Alter, *The Art of Biblical Poetry*, 24.

Proverbs and Psalms employ this parallel structure, giving repetitive examples of "kinds" with examples in theme and variation.

Because Hebrew parallelism manifests the pixelated philosophical style within the form of *genus/differentia* argument, we should consider precisely how it works. Intensification offers a focal lens, forcing a principled prism upon the object. For example, of the forty-four occurrences of the term "false" (*šeqer*) in its various forms in Psalms and Proverbs, the majority of instances split almost 50/50 between extending and contrasting thought in the parallelism. Take, for example, the following instances of extension of "falseness" (*šeqer*):

1. Acquiring treasures by a false tongue, a driven vapor and a snare of death.[52]
2. Clouds and wind without rain, a man who boasts of a false gift.[53]
3. Like a club, a sword, or a sharp arrow, a man who speaks of a friend in false witness.[54]

(In Chapter 9, I examine how "falseness" (*šeqer*) and its conceptually similar terms are not the polar opposite of "trueness" in the ways in which we are accustomed to thinking about them. I am purposefully curtailing this present treatment for the sake of illustration.)

In Examples 1 and 2, a tongue and a gift are modified with the term false (*šeqer*), which does not help us modern readers to understand what is meant by "false."[55] The parallel poetic structure focuses on the meaning of the first verset in reference to the second verset. In doing so, the verse identifies a principled "falseness." However, even this principle of falseness will require contrasting definitions to delineate what is and what is not meant by "falseness."

In Example 1, the writer does not focus on the nature of a "false tongue," but on the effects of gain by false speech, a theme that other parallelisms will develop. In this case, the falseness of the speech enables only short-term gain. Does this mean that true speech enables long-term

[52] Prov 21:6.

[53] Prov 25:14.

[54] Prov 25:18.

[55] All instances of *šeqer* in the Masoretic Text of the Hebrew Bible: Gen 21:23; Exod 5:9, 20:16, 23:7; Lev 5:22, 5:24, 19:11, 19:12; Deut 19:18; 1 Sam 15:29, 25:21; 2 Sam 18:13; 1 Kgs 22:22, 22:23; 2 Kgs 9:12; 2 Chr 18:21, 18:22; Job 13:4, 36:4; Psa 7:15, 27:12, 31:19, 33:17, 35:19, 38:20, 44:18, 52:5, 63:12, 69:5, 89:34, 101:7, 109:2, 119:29, 119:69, 119:78, 119:86, 19:104, 119:118, 119:128, 119:163, 120:2, 144:8, 144:11; Prov 6:17, 6:19, 10:18, 11:18, 12:17, 12:19, 12:22, 13:5, 14:5, 17:4, 17:7, 19:5, 19:9, 20:17, 21:6, 25:14, 25:18, 26:28, 29:12, 31:30; Isa 9:14, 28:15, 32:7, 44:20, 57:4, 59:3, 59:13, 63:8; Jer 3:10, 3:23, 5:2, 5:31, 6:13, 7:4, 7:8, 7:9, 8:8, 8:10, 9:2, 9:4, 10:14, 13:25, 14:14, 16:19, 20:6.

gain? We won't know outside of a pixelated approach, stacking up the instances to see how the idea is developed and delineated among them.

In Example 2, the promise of rain from something that can give rain – the clouds – is fleshed out by one who brags about giving a false gift:

2. Clouds and wind without rain, a man who boasts of a false gift.[56]

The sage targets the boaster in this verse, but the idea of a gift being false needs clarification. In this case, the sage gives a meteorological example, vividly tugging on an Israelite's experience of despair when sitting under an empty cloud. Something that could have given water did not. And by not giving what could have been given – a desperately needed watering of crops for survival's sake – the sage attributes falseness to the gift.

Example 3 portrays false witness as weaponized speech:

3. Like a club, a sword, or a sharp arrow, a man who speaks of a friend in false witness.[57]

Again, these presume that some form of speech about a friend could have been correct, but when he speaks falsely, it is as if he is bludgeoning, stabbing, or shooting the friend. Because wounding can also be "truthful," the sages do not consider wounding in and of itself to be fundamentally negative in this pixelated universe of meaning: "Truthful are the wounds of one who loves; profuse are the kisses of an enemy" (Prov 27:6). Wounding can be true or false depending on who is doing it and to what end.

So far, falseness appears to include shortsighted greed, wounding, and withholding what one could have (and possibly should have) been given. If we turn to two contrasting parallelisms, we will be able to notice a clearer second-order notion of falseness.

4. Rightly (*ʿal-kēn*) I esteem all of your instructions; I hate every false (*šeqer*) path.[58]
5. The wicked earn false (*šeqer*) gain; but those who sow rightly (*ṣĕdāqâ*) get true (*ʾemet*) wages.[59]

In Example 4, the sage juxtaposes one's proper esteem for God's guidance against rejecting the "false path." How can a path be false? Thinking in terms of true/false binaries, it could be the case that there is one correct metaphorical road to travel and multiple wrong roads. Hence,

56 Prov 25:14.
57 Prov 25:18.
58 Psalm 119:128.
59 Prov 11:18.

one is true and the others are all false, and somehow, favoring God's way should instill a disdain for other ways. Why? The other ways are false presumably because they do not effectively do what God's instruction does: guide one practically along the way (i.e., the path metaphor). In other words, the false path is false not in principle but because it does not work!

In Example 5, we see a similar development that now answers our question from before: "Does this mean that true speech enables long-term gain?" Here, planting rightly earns true wages. The wicked, again, are shortsighted in their gain. How are their wages false? They did not properly earn them.

Though we would have to look at more examples of falseness to complete the picture, we can already see a principle emerging through pixelation. The fuzzy edges of the principle have now been backlit:

> There exists a proper way to regard and perform our actions. Not heeding the proper way lands one in "falseness," while the sages portray heeding the proper way as "trueness."

Speaking, working, planting, giving, strategically wounding a friend, and possibly more have a proper structure to follow, discernible through the instructions of God to Israel. Hence, true and false covary concerning the proper way to act and regard all of these aspects of daily life.

The ability of Hebrew parallelism to focus (extension) and differentiate (contrast) a notion makes it a uniquely apt literary form for the philosophical task. The above discussion means to briefly demonstrate that the structure and content of Hebrew poetry advocates and practices a form of principled abstraction from pixelated examples, rooted in and constantly referencing God as creator and the prophetic instruction given through Moses and renetworked by future prophets.

Poetry Philosophically Interpreting Narrative

Not only is Hebrew poetry often used to explore the nature of concepts such as "falseness," but it also sometimes functions as a formal literary device within larger narratives, extrapolating or highlighting principles unseen in the story itself. Several instances merit explanation.

When Israel crosses into safety in Exodus 14, the narrative depicts the action: Yahweh speaks to Moses (Exod 14:15, 26), Moses performs Yahweh's instructions (Exod 14:21a, 27), and then events take place according to what Yahweh said (Exod 14:21b, 28). Within the story,

Israel fears as Egypt approaches at the seashore (Exod 14:10–12). Moses then speaks poetically[60] to explain to them what they are about to witness (Exod 14:13):

> Do not fear, stand firm, and see the deliverance
> that Yahweh will work for you today;
> for the Egyptians whom you see today
> you shall never see again.
> Yahweh will fight for you, and you have only to keep still.

Afterward, Moses opens and closes the sea with his staff at the direction of Yahweh. Yahweh splits the sea with his wind but has no involvement in the closing of the sea per the story. The story concludes with the same poetry from 14:13 now restyled in the narrator's voice (Exod 14:30–31):

> Thus Yahweh saved Israel that day from the Egyptians
> and Israel saw the Egyptians dead on the seashore.
> Israel saw the great work that Yahweh did against the Egyptians.
> So the people feared Yahweh
> and trusted in Yahweh and in his servant Moses.

Exodus then proceeds into an extended poem that describes the victory. I quote here only one portion that demonstrates the point (Exod 15:3–6, 8, 10,12):

> Yahweh is a warrior; Yahweh is his name.
> Pharaoh's chariots and his army he cast into the sea …
> Your right hand, O Yahweh, glorious in power –
> your right hand, O Yahweh, shattered the enemy …
> At the blast of your nostrils the waters piled up …
> You blew with your wind,
> the sea covered them; they sank like lead in the mighty waters …
> You stretched out your right hand, the earth swallowed them.

This poem is no mere victory song; it reinterprets the event just described in the narrative. Joshua Berman has suggested that these mutual accounts placed side by side fit the Egyptian model of history as exhortation – intentionally including different and conflicting

60 I am using this term "poetic" to delineate stylized speech with a discernible rhythm and some kind of formal structure. As Barbara Herrnstein Smith puts it, "It is simply the fact that as soon as we perceive that a verbal sequence has a sustained rhythm, that it is formally structured according to a continuously operating principle of organization, we know that we are in the presence of poetry and we respond to it accordingly." *Poetic Closure* (Chicago: University of Chicago Press, 1971), 23.

perspectives of the same account aimed at different hortatory ends.[61] Dividing the poem from the narrative as if they were two independent accounts of history commits a hermeneutical "category error." Berman surmises, "Each account conveys a different lesson to the reader or listener. ... Whereas the narrative of Exodus 14 discusses the role of human agents such as Moses and the Children of Israel, the poetic account of Exodus 15 portrays the sea event as a battle between Yahweh and the Egyptians."[62]

The story depicts Moses acting, yet the poem patently depicts Yahweh and only Yahweh fighting Egypt on behalf of Israel.[63] If the biblical authors meant for us to read the story in light of the poem and vice versa, then it seems that when Israel saw a man holding up a staff and waters being whipped about, Israel saw the breath and right hand of Yahweh at work on her behalf. Notice that this conclusion does not come from the Song of Moses alone, but the story itself presumes it.

Israel had to be preinformed that she was going to see Yahweh work against Egypt (Exod 14:13) with a concluding and symmetrically parallel comment that informs the reader that Israel correctly saw this as Yahweh's work on her behalf (Exod 14:31). The poetry in the story of the crossing (Exod 14:13, 30–31) and the Song of Moses (Exod 15:1–18) shapes our vision of what is not blatantly available by merely witnessing or considering the on-the-ground events in the story. Like Socrates attempting to get an interlocutor to see the transcendent form of horseness apart from witnessing historical instances of horses, poetry guides the reader to understand why the characters saw God as a warrior in wind and water – how they saw these events as demonstrative of the right hand of Yahweh.

The interplay between poetry and narrative, where poetry pushes the reader beyond what is depicted into the nature of the reality being described, recurs regularly in Christian Scripture. Poetry interprets narratives, from the first words uttered poetically by the man of Eden (Gen 2:23) to Deborah's praise of Yael as acting out divine intentions (Judg 5:24–31); Hannah's hymn that reveals the divine causation unseen in the narratives of messianic kings (1 Sam 2:1–10); Mary's Hannah-like Magnificat (Luke 1:47–56); and Paul's explanation of the gospel narrative as humility through a hymn (Phil 2:9–11). Poetry strategically advocates a way of

[61] Berman, *Inconsistency in the Torah*, 173–75.

[62] Berman, *Inconsistency in the Torah*, 58–59.

[63] I first heard this interpretive approach to Exodus 14–15 from Yoram Hazony.

seeing the narrative, more than merely expressing the inward feeling of the poet in florid language as we have come to think of it.[64]

Conclusions

The above discussion reveals something trite about various literary techniques, namely that in Hebrew, story, law, and poetry in the biblical texts have a rhetorical and persuasive force that makes them apt for philosophical engagement. If so, then neglecting these genres and forms in an attempt to map the philosophy of Christian Scripture essentially blinds us to its philosophical grammar. I am not claiming that every story, law, and poem is philosophy, but that they have the potential to participate in the advocacy of a particular way of reasoning through second-order intellectual matters. We ignore them, then, at our peril.

[64] When New Testament authors cite passages from the Hebrew Bible, they cite poetic passages the majority of the time in order to finish a thought or demonstrate a point (Matt 3:3, 4:4; Rom 3:10–18, etc.). Paul, both in his speeches in Acts and epistles, cites poetry – even Stoic poetry at times – within his arguments as an authoritative source (e.g., Acts 17:28) and as an instance of theological summary of divine thinking (e.g., Phil 2:9–11).

PART III

PERSISTENCE IN HELLENISTIC JUDAISM

5

The Philosophical Styles of Hellenistic Judaism

To suppose that Hellenization rushes into Judaism as if it were rational air rushing into an intellectual vacuum neglects the fact that Judaism already had its own philosophical style, now a tradition. Rather, we see hybridization, not a wholesale acquisition of the Hellenistic philosophical style. Even more than bland hybridity with Greek and Roman philosophies, Hebraic thought encounters Hellenism's philosophies to create a complex and sometimes puppeteered use of Greek tropes toward Hebraic ends.

In the chapter, I sketch out an analogy from the realm of linguistics for when two languages and cultures contact each other: pidgin and creole. I then compare Hellenistic and Hebraic philosophical styles directly to clarify their most prominent differences. The remainder and majority of this chapter then focuses on a single paradigm worked out in the Hebrew Bible, in Hellenistic Judaism, and then in the New Testament. Because of limited space, I chose Hellenistic Jewish writings that were paradigmatic of that literature – diverse as they are – and dealt with the epistemological dilemma from Deuteronomy, namely the question: Can we naturally infer a creator from the created world, or do we require divine assistance? I call this the "Deuteronomic dilemma."

Starting in Deuteronomy 4 and 29, I analyze the solutions to this dilemma posed in Wisdom of Solomon, Philo, and Paul, though I could have included Twelve Patriarchs and Ben Sira (Sirach) to extend the analysis. I end this summary chapter with the texts of the Hebraic counternarrative that valorize Torah obeisance, celebrating the Jewish heroes and heroines who refused Greek-Hebraic hybridity: Judith, 1 Maccabees, Tobit, Susanna, Prayer of Azariah, and others like them, including cultic separationist texts from Qumran.

Judaism's contact with Hellenization obliged a reaction, whether unconsciously blending, strategically appropriating, or rejecting the colonizer's theologies and philosophies. To the extent that Jewish[1] thought married the Hebraic philosophical style with the Greek, we can no longer speak purely of Hebraic thought. The case might be different for the New Testament, as I will propose in Chapter 6.

Pidgin, Creole, and Philosophical Styles

The meeting of peoples that creates pidgin and creolized languages makes an apt analog for these philosophical styles.[2] Pidgin language is often depicted as the pragmatic language of the marketplace, developed by the colonized business owner to buy and sell from the colonizer, as it were.

Pidgin versions of language consist of very small vocabularies based around mercantile necessities of interacting with the colonizing language speaker. The hallmark of pidgin versions of languages is little to no conjugation: "This good price. Give best offer please." What we might expect to see is pidgin forms of Greek philosophies developed in Jewish thought, sufficient only to do intellectual trade with their Greek colonizers for the sake of carrying out the necessities of governance, cultic duties, and the likes.

Creolization develops when the pidgin version of a language itself becomes a language with native speakers. Haitian creole is an obvious example, where a pidgin form of French became its own language. Jamaican creole also illustrates pidgin English now conjugated into a native-speaker language.

Pidgin languages always reflect economic and political power, since the colonizer or tourist does not learn the local language to communicate. Rather, those who want to do business with the occupier or contractor

[1] By "Jewish," I only mean to delineate that which derives from the Hebrew Biblical tradition (i.e., Hebraic) from that which develops amongst Second Temple Jews in the Hellenistic period (i.e., Jewish).

[2] I am thankful to Matthew Lynch for suggesting the analogy of pidgin/creole in thinking about what happens when two cultures contact each other. I am not alone in using this linguistic theory in another sphere of thought. I first saw Brent Strawn utilize the same analogy in thinking about biblical literacy. Brent A. Strawn, *The Old Testament Is Dying: A Diagnosis and Recommended Treatment* (Theological Explorations for the Church Catholic; Grand Rapids, MI: Baker Academic, 2017), 59–80. C. Kavin Rowe refers to the pidgin/creole analogy when exploring the incommensurability of rival philosophical traditions – Stoic, New Testament, and Christian. C. Kavin Rowe, *One True Life: The Stoics and Early Christians as Rival Traditions* (New Haven, CT: Yale University Press, 2016), 241.

must learn the conqueror's language. She who has more capital or political power learns fewer languages. Everyone else pidginizes.

Likewise, with philosophical styles, might it be the case that the hybridity of Greek and Hebraic philosophical styles reveals something of the internal Jewish view of the economic and political prowess of Hebraic thought? As Jewish thought turns to Greek modes and convictions of second-order reasoning, might we assume that their confidence in the Hebraic philosophical style is similarly attenuated?

But we see neither pidgin nor creolization of the Greek philosophical style amongst the Jewish intellectuals. Rather, a skillful blending of the two styles appears in Hellenistic Jewish literature that is, strangely, neither repeated nor directly cited by NT authors. Mixing the Hebraic and Hellenistic styles, texts produced in the so-called intertestamental period borrow from the Hebraic and shift the center of mass away from it, so that only a veneer remains.[3] When we examine the epistles of Paul, who is also a Hellenistic Jew, we find a more insurrectionist use of Hellenistic trends.[4] I will argue that Paul appropriates the superficial veneer of Hellenistic argument for the sake of redirecting readers to the Hebraic philosophical content.

Hellenistic versus Hebraic Philosophical Style

A Hebraic style of philosophy employs various forms of argument to advocate a method of second-order thought. In the centuries before the Jesus movement, Jews found themselves ensconced in Hellenistic thought both in the land of Israel and in the diaspora. I give examples only as paradigms, showing how different authors blended Hebraic and Hellenistic styles to deal with one particular epistemological problem: how to properly understand that created objects entail a *creator*.

Some Jewish texts from this period exhibit a particular move away from the Hebraic philosophical style to a modified Hellenist style, even if the forms of argument retain similarities. In this way, the forms of argument and literature create the outer shell of the Hellenistic Jewish intellectual world. The style (the nut in this metaphor) thus transforms from strictly Hebraic to a Hebraic/Hellenistic hybrid.

[3] Thanks to Robbie Griggs for helping me think through how to describe this Hellenistic-Jewish "hybridity."

[4] "Hellenistic" here refers to the intellectual world post-Aristotle or Roman appropriations of it, where "Hellenism" is synonymous with "Greek in origin."

TABLE 3 *Hebraic and Hellenist philosophical styles*

	Hebrew Bible	Hellenistic Tradition
Philosophical Style	**Modes of Argument:** 1. Pixelated (structure) 2. Networked (literary)	**Modes of Argument:** 1. Linear 2. Autonomist
	Convictions: 3. Mysterionist 4. Creationist 5. Transdemographic 6. Ritualist	**Convictions:** 3. Domesticationist 4. Abstractionist 5. Classist 6. Mentalist

To see the general differences in reasoning, the two styles are now worth comparing side by side (see Table 3, which is a repeat of Table 1). Again, these comparisons present caricatures only for the sake of detecting a distinct variation of philosophizing across the two traditions.

As a reminder: the Hebraic style generally consists of exemplars systematically arranged and revisited (pixelated), grounded in the notion of Yahweh as creator (creationist) by intertextual development from the Torah and prophets (networked) to be understood through a matrix of ritual participation (ritualist) in order to develop expertise in the most people possible (transdemographic) while acknowledging a logical inability to exhaustively understand (mysterionist) the nature of reality *in se*.

The Hellenistic tradition has no internally defined canon, and so this description of the Hellenistic style of reasoning will have a stronger purchase on some philosophical traditions than others. It is not my goal to define the Hellenistic philosophical style without remainder, but to describe general tendencies in the style of reasoning through second-order notions.[5]

To this end, I will discuss Hellenism's philosophical style in light of the Hebrew Bible's style. Of course, the reality of these two worlds cannot be summed so tidily. And the difference between the espoused philosophical style in the texts and the lived reality cannot be accounted for here. For instance, the Socratic dialogues describe the teacher as a midwife, helping

[5] Bertrand Russell noted that there was a sense of generalist tendencies in the ideal citizen: "Specialization characterized the age [Greece's philosophical age] in all departments, not only in the world of learning. In the self-governing Greek cities of the fifth and fourth centuries, a capable man was assumed to be capable of everything. He would be, as occasion arose, a soldier, a politician, a lawgiver, or a philosopher." *History of Western Philosophy* (New York: Routledge, 1996), 216.

the pupil to birth his preincarnate knowledge of the forms – a mentalist description of coming to know using a rich embodied metaphor (i.e., midwife). However, this process of prodding with questions, reflection, and realization is, in fact, an embodied ritualized process. Hence, it is not necessarily antithetical to ritualist concerns, but focused on the activity of the mind; whereas Hebraic ritualism overtly prescribes rituals for an epistemic effect that cannot be gained solely by mental reflection or ration.

To put the two styles in conversation, I summarize the six aspects of the styles and offer questions that could be posed to a text to discern where it best fits. Of course, such determinations require judgment calls that will vary amongst experts.

Linear – as opposed to *pixelated:* a general bent toward following an argument in a deductive fashion, as one follows the plot of a narrative. The reader is led by the argument, and is not responsible for deducing principles across disparate examples. However, linear style can operate as pixelation within Hellenism and Judaism, as we shall see. If the argument is linear, but the premises and conclusions do not follow clearly in the narrative context, other networked narratives and examples might be pertinent to complete the argument's logic. Questions to ask: Does the text require extrapolation of principles from many exemplars? If linear, does the argument exhibit features of validity and soundness? Does a linear argument still require a thick narrative background to be effective?

Autonomist – as opposed to *networked:* arguments, like ideas, are generally considered independent, standing or falling on their own merits and not textually dependent on other literature. Questions to ask: Do arguments function independently, or are they portrayed as contingently participating in a web of history and ideas? In literary terms, how much do the arguments rely on intertextuality contingent on a reader's understanding of other texts?

Domesticationist – as opposed to *mysterionist:* this is a general assumption that understanding can reveal everything that can be known, even if by mental assent. This often accompanies a related conviction that insufficient information or human finitude is problematic. This assumption presumes that if we had infinite capacity then we could, possibly, understand everything. Questions to ask: Can an individual work out all the problems posed by themselves apart from God's help/intervention? Does the writing signal skepticism toward discerning second-order notions without remainder?

Abstractionist – as opposed to *creationist:* reasoning does not rely on a discrete flow of history from creation, particular languages, or historical situatedness. Questions to ask: Does the discussion logically require, include, or entail any particular historical events? Does it seek to remove the analysis from history into the abstract space of reason without intent to renetwork its findings?

Mentalist – as opposed to *ritualist:* understanding an argument is necessarily a mental process, but not necessarily an embodied one. Questions to ask: Is the solution to problems of human understanding a ritual that incorporates the individual and social body? Or, does the resolution function individually and mentally to bring about some psychological tranquility?

Classist – as opposed to *transdemographic:* only some people can understand these second-order concepts and reasoning – namely, the philosophers and their disciples. However, most foundational ideas are not available to craftsmen, laborers, or women in most cases. This continuum of who can philosophize ranges from collectively accessible wisdom to a focus on individuals working toward spiritual tranquility. Questions to ask: Does the author indicate that this reasoning should be available to all, or just to men, elites, etc.? Does this text seek to develop insider/outsider categories or gradations of skilled thinkers?

The remainder of this chapter explores both the Hellenistic sway over Jewish thought and its rejection among styles of philosophy. Wisdom of Solomon and Philo will provide examples of unfettered influence flowing from Hellenism's style into Judaism. Sectarian documents from Qumran and other so-called apocryphal texts demonstrate a rejectionist approach to the style of Hellenistic philosophy. Yet another class of texts – hero sagas – will show minimal Hellenistic influence, but all texts from this period engage the styles that surround them.

A motley collection of Jewish literature spans the two centuries before Jesus. No generalizations of that literature will acceptably capture its breadth. But examining the reactions to various philosophical traditions will help us think about the differences between Hebraic and Hellenistic philosophy in its modes and convictions. Later, this will allow us to see the philosophical *ressourcement* movement in the New Testament. Those authors intertextually employ and redeploy deep networks of thinking from the Hebrew Bible. Those authors neither cite nor allude to the Hellenistic Jewish texts in any way similar or proportional to their use of the Hebrew biblical tradition.[6]

[6] With the singular exception of Jude 14–15.

Rather than overview the entire landscape of apocryphal and pseudepigraphal texts from the Second Temple period, I sample texts that directly interact with Deuteronomy's epistemic claim both conceptually and linguistically. Recall that I am selecting texts for examination on the three-fold criteria of presence, persistence, and relevance. Wisdom of Solomon, Philo, and Paul in Acts and Romans all demonstrably clear those three hurdles.[7]

Specifically, I see a movement from the Hebraic style to a Hellenistic-Hebraic hybridity. The following test case will show a cursory track of the style of second-order reasoning from the Hebrew Bible into Hellenistic Jewish texts and then into the New Testament. Again, I will refer to the question at hand as the Deuteronomic dilemma: *Can humans infer a creator by reflecting on created things without assistance?*[8]

Creation and Knowledge: Genesis 1 and Deuteronomy 4

The matter of creator/creation distinction is raised by a shrewd literary device in Deuteronomy, even if the distinction has been latent since Genesis 1. I want to unpack the networked conviction of the Deuteronomistic author and then show how Deuteronomy uses the conceptual cleaving of creation from creator in its epistemology to answer the dilemma that the author has created. With that analysis in hand, we will then look at how Wisdom, Philo, and Paul all address the Deuteronomistic dilemma.

Genesis 1:1–2:4 describes a cosmic creation account with a uniquely patterned placement of celestial bodies, animals, and, ultimately, humans. Most commentators see a recognizable pattern in Deuteronomy's warnings against idol-making. Its uncanny resemblance to the items created in Genesis 1 makes it a candidate for a discourse on the epistemic value of created things.

[7] For an examination of a parallel problem from Deuteronomy's view of human moral agency and divine causation that fully examines a larger array of texts (Paul, Qumran, Jubilees, 4 Ezra, and 2 Baruch) see Kyle B. Wells's dissertation "Grace, Obedience, and the Hermeneutics of Agency: Paul and His Jewish Contemporaries on the Transformation of the Heart" (PhD diss., Durham University, 2010); later published as *Grace and Agency in Paul and Second Temple Judaism: Interpreting the Transformation of the Heart* (Novum Testamentum Supplements 157; Leiden: Brill, 2014).

[8] Stoicism does not appear to have struggled with this dilemma. See Marcus Aurelius, *Meditations*, III, 11–13. Hence, it makes for a particularly apt instance of Hellenistic Jews thinking through a dilemma with a pedigree in the Hebrew Bible.

Admonishing against idolatry, Deuteronomy lists animals and celestial bodies that were forbidden to be recreated "in the likeness" as idols.[9] This prohibition comes on the basis that Israel, at the foot of Mount Sinai, "heard his voice" yet "saw no form" (4:15). In the logic of the text, Israel fails to cling to Yahweh (4:15–24) by fashioning an image from any part of creation in order to worship it. The terms used to describe the created things throughout both texts – Genesis 1 and Deuteronomy 4 – are the cognates "kind" (*lĕmînēhû*) in Genesis 1 and "likeness" (*tĕmûnâ*) in Deuteronomy 4.[10] Of specific interest, the creatures/objects on the list that were forbidden to be remade are in Table 4.

The list in Deuteronomy 4 so closely resembles the creation list of Genesis 1 that it appears to form a prescription, describing these created things as "things that Yahweh your God has allotted to all the peoples under the whole heaven" (4:19).[11] These creatures/objects were created, and, therefore, they should not be confused with the creator. Why? Created items cannot be the same as the God who rescued them from Egypt (4:20).[12] Though scholars debate how this list is related to Genesis 1, no debate exists about the fact that they are indeed related.[13]

TABLE 4 *Creature list from Genesis 1 and Deuteronomy 4*

Object Name	Genesis 1	Deuteronomy 4
Male and Female	*zākār ûnəqēbâ* (1:27)	*zākār ʾô nəqēbâ* (4:16)
Beasts	*bəhēmâ* (1:24)	*bəhēmâ* (4:17)
Winged Birds	*ʿôp kānāp* (1:21)	*kānāp ʾăšer tāʿûp* (4:17)
Creeping Things	*remeś* (1:24)	*rōmēś* (4:18)
Fish in Sea	*bidgat hayyām* (1:26)	*dāgâ ʾăšer-bammayim* (4:18)
Stars	*hakkôkābîm* (1:16)	*hakkôkābîm* (4:19)

[9] A full version of this argument can be found in Dru Johnson, *Epistemology and Biblical Theology: From the Pentateuch to Mark's Gospel* (Routledge Interdisciplinary Perspectives in Biblical Criticism 4; New York: Routledge, 2018), 91–93.

[10] Whether or not these terms would have been lexically connected in an ancient reader's mind, the notion of "similitude" is intended with items listed in both Genesis 1 and Deuteronomy 4.

[11] Seeming to draw from Paul's comment in Romans 1, Duane L. Christensen titles this section of his commentary: "Israel Is to Worship the Creator – Not Created Images," in *Deuteronomy 1–21:9*, revised, 2nd ed., Vol. 6A (Word Biblical Commentary; Nashville, TN: Thomas Nelson, 2001), 82–90.

[12] It is only here in Deuteronomy 4 where we see a special and direct appeal to creation.

[13] MacDonald notes that Fishbane is uncritical of the distinct differences between the list of Genesis 1 and Deuteronomy 4. Nathan MacDonald, *Deuteronomy and the Meaning of "Monotheism"* (Forschungen zum Alten Testament 2 Reihe; Tübingen: Mohr Siebeck,

The injunction not to make idols has a two-fold rationale based on what they have witnessed (or, what their parents have witnessed) and the order of creation that ultimately directs their focus to the creator not the creature. Or, as Nathan MacDonald frames it, the logic of this list is to avoid the ritualized error of "incorrect worship." How does one know what beings deserve ritualized worship? One must consider what one has seen in history (an imageless voice) and what one knows of their creator (maker of these created things).

After expounding the penalties for making idols in the likeness of created things, Moses directly appeals to the theophany when Yahweh spoke from the fire (4:33), which only compares to the creation event itself (4:32). This comparison to the creation event is the only direct appeal of its kind in Deuteronomy, but I suggest that it causes the reader to consider other similar appeals throughout.

Deuteronomy offers this conclusion: "To you it was shown that you might know (*lāda ͑at*) that Yahweh is God; there is no other besides him" (4:35), and then repeats, "Know therefore today ... that Yahweh is God in heaven above and on the earth beneath; there is no other" (4:39). MacDonald takes these two knowledge expressions to be constitutive of the "Shema's relational claim on Israel."[14] The knowledge they need comes through relationship, experience, and, as I have argued elsewhere, prophetic interpretation.[15]

Here in Deuteronomy 4, we read a call to listen, to remember, and to forbid idols as images of creation, and an appeal to knowledge based on what Israel has seen. Because of this theme that flourishes throughout Deuteronomy, Ryan O'Dowd concludes that Deuteronomy functions with a creationist conviction, namely that "Israel's epistemology is grounded in the ontological and ethical nexus of the creation myth,"[16] and: "Significantly, 4:32–39 appeals to both senses where Israel's 'seeing'

2003), 197; Michael A. Fishbane, *Biblical Interpretation in Ancient Israel* (Oxford: Clarendon, 1985), 321.

[14] MacDonald, *Deuteronomy and the Meaning of "Monotheism"*, 95. For a review of "knowledge" expressions, see Marc Vervenne, "The Phraseology of 'Knowing YHWH' in the Hebrew Bible: A Preliminary Study of Its Syntax and Function," in *Studies in the Book of Isaiah: Festschrift Willem A.M. Beuken*, ed. Jacques van Ruiten and Mark Vervenne (BEThL 132; Leuven: Uitgeverij Peeters, 1997), 469.

[15] This section on Deuteronomy 4 has been adapted from Johnson, *Epistemology and Biblical Theology*, 91–93.

[16] Ryan O'Dowd, *The Wisdom of Torah: Epistemology in Deuteronomy and the Wisdom in Literature* (Forschungen zur Religion und Literatur des Alten und Neuen Testaments Band 225; Göttingen: Vandenhoeck & Ruprecht, 2009), 31.

signs and 'hearing' testimony of God's works testify to his uniqueness. In verses 32–34, Israel is led to conclude that no such acts as the Horeb revelation or the Egypt deliverance have occurred since creation."[17]

Although these texts are primarily cited as proof of Israel's monotheism, MacDonald argues that these references only support a view for Yahweh's categorical uniqueness, something which Israel is meant to know from the context of this passage.[18] Whether monotheistic uniqueness or not, knowing in submission to Yahweh as a god in control of creation and human history appears to be part of Deuteronomy's precorrective to future errors.

In summary, Genesis 1 does not lead a reader to expect that the list of created things could have some epistemic function. Neither does Deuteronomy 4 offer any explicit links to creation history. Rather, the author employs the unique pattern of objects from the creation story to imply a creationist narrative network that enmeshes directly with Israel's recent exodus. The literary term for this would be metalepsis, where the writer employs enough of a known motif and then expects the reader to fill in the blanks to complete the logic of the teaching.[19] The impressive aspect of this kind of metaleptic reasoning is that neither the creation of Genesis 1 nor the idolatry of Deuteronomy 4 autonomously makes the claim. Yet, the appeal to the creationist intertextual network by Deuteronomy 4 makes a stronger claim than either text could independently.

If we read the Torah in its curated order, the logic of this passage prescribes something like the following: Israel ought to ritually serve the creator of these objects, not the objects themselves. This instruction raises the questions: What is the metaphysical relation between objects and the gods? And, how can we know?

It is now obvious that a larger literary context is networked with this particular passage. Because of the disposition toward pixelated exemplars told over the history of Israel, focusing on individual passages will suffer from a felt sense of incompleteness.

This zippering of Genesis 1 with Deuteronomy 4 to form a single prescriptive instruction reveals layers of creationism, pixelation, and networking. To understand the profundity of what is being prescribed,

[17] O'Dowd, *The Wisdom of Torah*, 41.

[18] MacDonald, *Deuteronomy and the Meaning of "Monotheism"*, 78–85.

[19] Metalepsis is distinguished by a sophisticated network to another text that requires the reader to "transume" unstated material from one referent to the other. John Hollander, *The Figure of Echo: A Mode of Allusion in Milton and After* (Berkeley: University of California Press, 1981), 133–50.

readers must adequately grasp Israel's creation in a particular textual form (i.e., the Torah) and other relevant texts.

Moses forewarns the children of Israel of impending idolatry, which appeals to the repetitive historical reasons for this warning obvious to a network-aware audience. The warning specifically aims at changing ritual behavior, which will later be examined as the culprit of Israel's epistemic dullness.[20] Moses predicates this warning with the goal of national trans-demographic wisdom: "You must observe [these statutes] diligently, for this will show your wisdom and discernment to the peoples ... who will say, 'Surely this great nation is a wise and discerning people'" (Deut 4:6).

Finally, while one might be tempted to deny mysterionist trajectories in this discourse – i.e., God's voice speaking directly from out of the fire – Deuteronomy's long-range epistemic project explicitly asserts mysterionism.

Turning to the end of Deuteronomy, mysterionist convictions appear overtly in the covenant renewal of Deuteronomy 29, another explicitly epistemological passage. Moses indicts Israel's inability to see (29:2–4 [MT 29:1–3]) and links it to her incomprehension, a rhetorical move that will reappear in the gospels. However, it makes two bold epistemic moves.

First, although Israel saw everything with her own eyes (29:2–3), God had not given her the requisite epistemological organs to know: "Yahweh has not given to you a heart to know, eyes to see, and ears to listen to this day" (29:4). And so the notion of brute and unaided seeing weakens. Israel's correct "seeing" (read: knowing) can only occur by God's action upon its epistemic organs: heart, eyes, ears. By the logic of Deuteronomy 29 (and later in ch. 30), Israelites must be made into different kinds of people in order to see.

If the philosophical style is fundamentally mysterionist, Israel's reasoning about second- and third-order matters should remain aware of the intentional hiddenness of many second-order affairs. In other words, what is not discussed or revealed is not necessarily fair game to pursue philosophically. The prescription to revere certain matters, which cannot and possibly should not be pursued intellectually, has ethical implications for the practice of philosophy in general.

Second, Deuteronomy 29 ends with an enigmatic assertion about who can know what. I will render this passage crudely from the Hebrew, but the effect is palpable: "The secret things to Yahweh our God, but the

[20] Dru Johnson, *Knowledge by Ritual: A Biblical Prolegomenon to Sacramental Theology* (Journal of Theological Interpretation Supplements 13; Winona Lake, IN: Eisenbrauns/ PennState Press, 2016), 172–78.

uncovered things to us and to our children forever, to do all the words of this *torah*" (29:29).

Taken together (Deut 4, 10, and 29), this creates what I call the "Deuteronomic dilemma": Can humans reason their way to God-as-creator by studying created order, or must God enable them to grasp creation as signaling beyond itself to a creator?[21] This dilemma has been culminating in a pixelated argument beginning in Exodus' grand epistemological narrative where plague after plague is flagged with "so that you will know" statements.[22] Deuteronomy 29 captures this lingering ambiguity about Israelite knowledge, or lack thereof: Why did so many of you (Israelites) see the signs and wonders but not understand (Deut 29:2–3)?

Deuteronomy raises this dilemma in order to land on divine intervention. God must give them a "heart to know" and circumcise the hearts (Deut 30:6), even to make proper sense of Exodus' signs and wonders. But Deuteronomy does not begin there.

In Deuteronomy 10, the author exhorts the Israelites to circumcise their own hearts out of love, because God chose their ancestors (Deut 10:15–16). In the later covenant renewal (Deut 28–29), the hope of Israel understanding and obeying fades. Maybe that covenant means to instill hope that God will step in to do what ought to have been done. Or, maybe it is purely pedagogical, bringing Israelites to understand that they could not have ever made the epistemic move on their own.

According to the Hebraic style of philosophy: God enables knowing and a discrete distribution of revealed understanding to Israel. Her rituals orient her to the program of revelation. At the same time, the text affirms a trusting mysterionism: positioning Israel's generational obligations to ritual knowing, as obliged by what has been already revealed to her. "The revealed things to us and our children forever, to do all the words of this *torah*" (Deut 29:29).

In going this far down the exegetical road, I know that many will want me to pursue these leads to their ends. I do not think passages such as Deuteronomy 4, 10, and 29 are definitive for the metaphysics and epistemology of the Hebrew Bible, but they do signify a pixelated pattern of thinking about thinking. Specifically, creation can only signal a creator when God gives a "heart to know, eyes to see, and ears to listen" (Deut 29:4).

[21] We could easily add texts that flirt with the same questions, specifically the extended discourses in Isaiah 40: 18–28; 41:18–24, 28–29; 42:18–25.

[22] For an analysis of Exodus as an epistemological discourse, see Johnson, *Epistemology and Biblical Theology*, 56–74.

With these details ready to hand, I now turn to Hellenistic Jewish texts to see the affinities and remarkable contrast with the epistemology and metaphysical discourse occurring in the Torah. My only goal is to show the hybridization of the Hebraic style when we enter Hellenistic Judaism, which contrasts with what we will find in the New Testament texts.

Wisdom of Solomon and the Deuteronomic Dilemma

Wisdom of Solomon (Wisdom hereafter) is a popular Jewish writing from around 20 BCE, read and copied in both Jewish and Christian circles. Though not fitting cleanly into any particular form of literature, its title aptly captures the content: wisdom. Some have suggested that it is "exhortatory discourse," which puts it in the category of advocacy.[23] Though superficially Hebraic in look and feel, we can easily see Hellenism's grip on the author's thinking in his admixture of Hellenistic and Hebraic philosophical styles.

Wisdom is an apt text to consider because it specifically explores the rhetoric of Deuteronomic idolatry (Deut 4:15–24) using aspects of the Hebraic philosophical style. The writer employs Deuteronomic rhetoric early on: "For the peoples saw and did not understand or take such a thing to heart" (cf. 1 Enoch 5:7; Wis 3:9b; 4:15).[24] Later, Wisdom explicitly deploys the Deuteronomic dichotomy of hidden/revealed but to up-end Deuteronomy's mysterionism: "For I learned both what is hidden and what is revealed, for wisdom the fashioner of all things taught me" (cf. Deut 29:29 [MT 29:28]; Wis 7:21). Hull argues that this refers to a Hellenistic idea called "universal sympathy": that one "perceives the nature of the mystic bonds which tie everything from the lofty stars down to the earthbound roots in one throbbing unity, he is at once saint, seer, philosopher and magus."[25]

[23] David Winston, "Wisdom of Solomon," *Anchor Bible Dictionary*, Vol. VI, ed. David N. Freedman (New York: Doubleday, 1992), 120–27; Lester L. Grabbe, "Wisdom of Solomon," in *The New Oxford Annotated Bible*, Fully Revised Fourth Edition: An Ecumenical Study Bible (New York: Oxford University Press, 2010), 1427.

[24] Scholarship has not always noticed the Deuteronomic roots of this critique. E.g., Barclay cites it as original to Wisdom 13. John M. G. Barclay, *Paul and the Gift* (Grand Rapids, MI: Eerdmans, 2015), 410n46.

[25] John M. Hull, *Hellenistic Magic and the Synoptic Tradition* (Studies in Biblical Theology 28; London: SCM Press, 1974), 34. On "universal sympathy," see: Polymnia Athanassiadi, *Mutations of Hellenism in Late Antiquity* (Variorum Collected Studies Series CS1052; New York: Routledge, 2016), 195–96.

Wisdom's description of the notion of wisdom then goes on to list twenty-one superlative attributes: "intelligent, unique, unpolluted, invulnerable, loving the good, beneficent, penetrating through all spirits that are intelligent, pure, and altogether subtle" (Wis 7:22–23). Such a list patently resembles Hellenistic ideas about divinity, specifically Pseudo-Aristotle, more than anything to be found in the Hebrew Bible.[26]

But it is this specific pairing of "hidden" (*krypton*) and "revealed" (*phaneron*) that appears in only one place in the Septuagint: Deuteronomy 29:29 (MT 29:28). However, in Deuteronomy 29, what is hidden "belongs to Yahweh," and what is revealed "belongs to us." Deuteronomy ritualistically posits them as oppositional for the sake of doing "all the words/things of this *torah*."

That particular section of Deuteronomy contains a line of reasoning showing the necessity for the covenant renewal. Namely, Israel has seen all the signs and wonders against Egypt, "before your eyes," but God did not give Israel the requisite epistemological disposition: "a heart to know, eyes to see, and ears to listen" (Deut 29:4). Reviewing their failures, this section of Deuteronomy ends by forewarning Israel about whoring after other gods, urging the future generations not to invoke the curses written in "this book": "The secret things (*ta krypta*) to Yahweh our God, but the revealed things (*ta phanera*) to us and to our children forever, to do all the words of this *torah*" (29:29).

This same hidden/revealed contrast reappears in the Gospel of Mark (4:22); notably, this pairing only occurs in contraposition in these two places in the Hebrew Bible and New Testament: Deuteronomy 29 and Mark 4.[27] The rarity and location of the hidden/revealed contrast makes them unavoidable in the present discussion.

In Mark, the author extends the Deuteronomic rhetoric into his epistemological project. He puts the hidden/revealed pairing in historical order. Formerly, things were hidden, but now, the "mystery of the kingdom of God" will be strategically revealed through Jesus, first to his disciples (Mark 4:11), and then to others through them. Jesus qualifies this epistemological journey with "for there is nothing hidden (*krypton*), but to be revealed (*phanerōthē*)" (Mark 4:22). How is the hidden revealed in Mark's gospel? The disciples come to see the "mystery of the kingdom of God" through embodied processes prescribed by Jesus to his closest

[26] See Pseudo-Aristotle, *On the Cosmos*, 397b, 400b–401b.
[27] Johnson, *Epistemology and Biblical Theology*, 120–21.

disciples (ritualism), which are then made part of the process for all who trust Jesus (transdemographic).

Just prior to Wisdom's extensive review of the history of Israel's folly and worship of other gods, the writer tugs directly on a Deuteronomic epistemology – but with a twist. Instead of two realms of knowledge – hidden to God and revealed to us – the writer of Wisdom has learned both realms apart from Torah practice. This essentially cuts off the Deuteronomic emphasis on ritually performing the Torah as a source of Israel's wisdom (Deut 29:29b).

Again, the Markan twist on this same hidden/revealed pairing posits Jesus as the prophet who reveals these hidden things to his disciples through embodied rituals of healing, exorcising demons, and miraculous feedings. However, Mark notably constrains the epistemological program in Mark 4 with the harsh words of Isaiah 6:10, the only begotten parallel passage of Deuteronomy 29:4b in the Hebrew Bible/Septuagint:

> Make the mind of this people dull, and stop their ears, and shut their eyes,
> so that they may not look with their eyes, and listen with their ears,
> and comprehend with their minds (hearts), and turn and be healed.

Jesus tells his disciples that he will give them "the mysteries of the kingdom of God," but they appear hapless and helpless throughout the Gospel, never grasping the "mystery" – not by a long shot. Though Mark's Gospel uses the Deuteronomic pairing, readers require some savvy to discern how Mark's pessimism yields signs of epistemic optimism.

Even with this emblematic use of the Deuteronomic hidden/revealed paradigm, we see the author of Wisdom diverging from Deuteronomy's constrained epistemology later revived in Mark's Gospel.[28]

Returning to Wisdom, we encounter a passage that examines the Deuteronomic warnings against idolatry. Here we find a fuller examination of what can be known by considering creation. Remember, in Deuteronomy 29:2–4, Israel could not even properly interpret the signs and wonders against Egypt on her own. Optimism about Israel's ability to discern through brute observation of creation seems Deuteronomically dubitable.

Nevertheless, Wisdom delves directly into the minds of those who were external to God's covenant. I cite this passage at length, as it is worth reading carefully (Wis 13:1–9):

[28] For an extended examination of the ritualist epistemology in Mark 4–9, see Johnson, *Epistemology and Biblical Theology*, 110–47.

1 For all people who were ignorant of God were foolish by nature;
and they were unable from the good things that are seen to know the one who exists,
nor did they recognize the artisan while paying heed to his works;
2 but they supposed that either fire or wind or swift air,
or the circle of the stars, or turbulent water,
or the luminaries of heaven were the gods that rule the world.
3 If through delight in the beauty of these things people assumed them to be gods,
let them know how much better than these is their Lord,
for the author of beauty created them.
4 And if people were amazed at their power and working,
let them perceive from them how much more powerful is the one who formed them.
5 For from the greatness and beauty of created things comes a corresponding perception of their Creator.
6 Yet these people are little to be blamed,
for perhaps they go astray while seeking God and desiring to find him.
7 For while they live among his works, they keep searching, and they trust in what they see because the things that are seen are beautiful.
8 Yet again, not even they are to be excused;
9 for if they had the power to know so much that they could investigate the world,
how did they fail to find sooner the Lord of these things?

With a *domesticationist* conviction, Wisdom 7–9 recounts how the writer himself has bedded Lady Wisdom and has come to know everything from meteorology to omenology, and beyond. But for everyone else, though they seek, they do not find. Blinded by creation's beauty or the bereavement of death (Wis 14:15), they name created things as gods. It is as if creation's ornateness should meet their intellects and lead them directly to discover the creator God, but as the Confucian saying goes, "When a wise man points at the moon, the imbecile examines the finger."

Key for Wisdom's approach to this Deuteronomic dilemma, Gentiles possess the intellectual faculties to know the creator through creation (Wis 13:9), so why do they fail in doing so? "Because they thought wrongly about God in devoting themselves to idols" (Wis 14:30b). Depending on the order of those two events – thought wrongly and devoting – Wisdom either continues *ritualist* tendencies in second-order thought or denies them.

In other words, if wrong thinking causes devotion to idols, then Wisdom cannot be read with ritualist convictions. If wrong devotion fosters wrong thinking, then ritualism remains in Wisdom's philosophical convictions.

This ambiguity eventually resolves in Wisdom's Jeremiah-like description of those who cut down a tree and carve it into an idol, naming it a god (cf. Isa 44:9–20; Jer 10:1–16; Wis 13:11–19). Did the act of making the idol distort man's thinking? Most likely not. Rather, Wisdom says, "The idea of making idols was the beginning of fornication" (Wis 14:12). Continuing the thought, Wisdom asserts: "For [idols] came into the world through the empty illusions of men" (14:14), where "empty illusions" is an Epicurean phrase.[29]

For the author of Wisdom, the idea seems to enable the action. More explicitly, Wisdom puts erroneous knowledge at the head of actions: "Then it was not enough for them to err about the knowledge of God, but though living in great strife due to ignorance, they call such great evils peace" (Wis 14:22). Because they thought wrongly, they acted wrongly.

Wisdom does not appear to hold a ritualist conviction in its philosophical style; rather, it displays a *mentalist* psychology. It is unclear where this mentalist conviction stems from if not Hellenism's proliferation into Jewish thought. What causes the Gentiles' mental errors that produce idolatry? The only answer offered by Wisdom points at predestined damnation in the line of Canaan (12:10–11) that manifests in "refusing to know" God through creation (Wis 16:16).

In reference to the Deuteronomic dilemma, in Wisdom, the author attains both hidden and revealed knowledge, but not for the sake of training others (transdemographic). Rather, the author uses the knowledge authoritatively to chastise Gentiles for their foolishness, a type of ignorance that ultimately cannot be helped. In this move, Wisdom establishes a caste system of knowledge (classist). Unlike the rites performed to dispose one to discern (ritualist) while simultaneously maintaining limits to knowledge (mysterionist), Wisdom's author appears to mentally ascend reality (mentalist) and contain his knowledge within a domain (domesticationist).

Table 5 represents a hybridization of the Hebrew and Hellenistic philosophical styles, maintaining some Hebraic style and convictions (pixelated, networked, and creationist) while abandoning others for what might be Hellenism's contribution to Jewish intellectualism (domesticationist, mentalist, and classist).

Wisdom's use of the Deuteronomic phrasing that began this line of exploration remains sufficiently vague. "I learned both what is secret and what is manifest, for wisdom, the fashioner of all things taught me" (Wis 7:21–22). How did "wisdom" teach the author the secret and

29 David Winston, *The Wisdom of Solomon: A New Translation with Introduction and Commentary* (The Anchor Bible Commentaries 43; Garden City, NY: Doubleday, 1979), 273.

TABLE 5 *Wisdom of Solomon's hybridization of Hebraic/Hellenistic philosophy*

	Hebrew Bible	Hellenist Tradition	Wisdom of Solomon
Philosophical Style	**Modes of Argument:** 1. Pixelated 2. Networked **Convictions:** 3. Mysterionist 4. Creationist 5. Transdemographic 6. Ritualist	**Modes of Argument:** 1. Linear 2. Autonomist **Convictions:** 3. Domesticationist 4. Abstractionist 5. Classist 6. Mentalist	**Modes of Argument:** 1. Pixelated 2. Networked **Convictions:** 3. Domesticationist 4. Creationist 5. Classist 6. Mentalist

manifest things? The author does not tell us. This detail deserves our attention, as will become clear in the chapters to come. The relation of embodied actions (ritualist) to understanding appears crucial throughout Christian Scripture. Where a text says or implies that one can gain understanding without action, it clearly diverges from the normative biblical style of philosophy.

Philo and the Deuteronomic Dilemma

Philo of Alexandria (ca. 20–50 BCE) contributes the most thoroughly Hellenized writings on Hebrew Scripture and Jewish thought. He makes a particularly fitting interlocutor here because of his close attention to the hybridity of Hebraic and Hellenistic thought. As David Scholer sums it, "Philo's concern to interpret Moses shows constantly his deep devotion and commitment to his Jewish Heritage beliefs, and community, and also reflects his unabashed use of [Greek] philosophical categories and traditions."[30]

Because his corpus is immense, I cannot treat his thought *in toto*, but only where he directly takes up the matter of the epistemic clues offered by creation. I consider his treatment of natural reason at the outset of *The Special Laws*, though it is difficult to know whether this was a consistent view across his writing.[31] In this section, he deals specifically with apprehending God in the natural world, quoting Deuteronomy 4:19 to connect his present line of reasoning to the Deuteronomic dilemma (III, 15).

30 David M. Scholer, ed., *The Works of Philo: Compete and Unabridged*, new updated ed., trans. C. D. Yonge (Peabody, MA: Hendrickson, 1997), xi.

31 Peder Borgen, "Philo of Alexandria," in *The Anchor Bible Dictionary*, Vol. V, ed. David N. Freedman (New York: Doubleday, 1992), 340.

Supposing that God is a kind of kings, planets then follow the laws of the cosmos as a citizen follows the kingdom's reign. "Some persons have conceived that the sun, and the moon, and the other stars are independent gods, to whom they have attributed the causes of all things that exist" (III, 13), but Moses "was well aware that the world was created." Philo sees a dividing line between the two beliefs, whether one is aware that the cosmos is created or not.

He then attributes this error to the fact that those in error have not "taken pains to travel along the straight and true road" (III, 17). The failure to travel the "true road" disposes them to a host of misunderstandings paralleling the king/kingdom analogy used at the outset of his argument. As the mind engages the senses and the intellect grapples with the objects of this world, the "straight and true road" leads one away from error.

At first blush, Philo's "straight and true road" appears to advocate a peripatetic route to understanding. Does he have a ritualist disposition in his philosophical style? No. Reading on, his case reveals a heavy-handed mentalism at work.

Philo invokes an a priori model of understanding with a mind/body simile. As an invisible and minuscule mind reigns over the organs of the body, God the King is discernibly the King-of-kings, necessitating a created view of the entire cosmos (III, 18). It seems obvious to Philo that we ought to reason from our mind/body relation to the king/King-of-kings relation, and ultimately to the King-of-kings/Creator conclusion. Our understanding of the creator comes by "transcending all visible essence by means of our reason," for God is an "invisible Being who can be comprehended and appreciated by the mind alone" (III, 20).

As for the deceived ones who name planets as gods and worship them, they have been fooled. Philo might seem to include the notion of embodied habituation in his description of deceit: by slick talk, the excesses of wealth, and the beauty of statuary (V, 29). Like the virtue ethics of Aristotle, some form of ritualized virtue seems to be in mind here. But like the Hellenistic schools, these habituated virtues aim at ordering the soul, not at achieving symbiosis between embodied knowing and reflection. The Hebraic philosophical style proposed in this present work might explain that the deceit of slick talk, wealth, and beauty inevitably leads to bad rituals. However, the view that includes and accounts for an individual's embodied education within the social body can also account best for how those deceits skew one's conceptual world.

In contrast, Philo's Moses "stamped a deep impression on the minds of men, engraving piety on them" (V, 30). Through this stamping, and the

TABLE 6 *Philo's hybridization of Hebraic and Hellenistic philosophy*

	Hebrew Bible	Hellenist Tradition	Philo's *The Special Laws*
Philosophical Style	**Modes of Argument:** 1. Pixelated (structure) 2. Networked (literary) **Convictions:** 3. Mysterionist 4. Creationist 5. Transdemographic 6. Ritualist	**Modes of Argument:** 1. Linear 2. Autonomist **Convictions:** 3. Domesticationist 4. Abstractionist 5. Classist 6. Mentalist	**Modes of Argument:** 1. Linear 2. Networked **Convictions:** 3. (skeptical) Domesticationist 4. Creationist 5. Classist 6. Mentalist

constant witness of the Torah to the cosmos as creation, "those that are attached to the living God do all live" (V, 31).

Though a ritualist disposition toward reading and knowing the Torah certainly lies in the background of this statement, Philo continues to focus on the mind and intellect as the instrumental means to understanding the nature of God (V–VII).

In the end, Philo's route through the Deuteronomic dilemma in *The Special Laws* employs the Hellenistic philosophical style, though constrained by the creationist assumptions about Israel's connections to the cosmos. He pursues the dilemma by a linear appeal to mentalist apprehension of the cosmos as created, a view available to those willing to follow the intellectual road less traveled (classist). I titled his domesticationist views "skeptical domesticationist" (Table 6) due to his advocacy of intellectually transcending this world to apprehend the real invisible qualities of the cosmos. Yet at the same time, Philo tempers his advocacy with the language of reaching and exertion funded by our love for God (*On the Creation*, I, 5). This does not appear to be naïve or triumphalist domestication of ideas, but a humble attempt to know God the creator more truly.

Now that we have briefly encountered two Hellenistic Jewish texts hashing out the Deuteronomic dilemma by mixing convictions of the Hebraic and Hellenistic philosophical styles, I turn to another Second Temple Jewish thinker wrestling with the same: Paul.

Paul and the Deuteronomic Dilemma

In at least two places, Paul directly addresses the Deuteronomic dilemma: his Athens speech at the Areopagus (Acts 17:22–34) and the opening to his letter to the Romans (Rom 1:18–27). Both explicitly engage the

Deuteronomic dilemma for the sake of making a grander point, one from a third-person speech (Acts 17) and the other from a second-person exhortation (Rom 1).

I begin with Paul's speech in Athens, which I quote here in its entirety with versification in place:

> 22 Then Paul stood in front of the Areopagus and said,
>
> "Athenians, I see how extremely religious you are in all ways. 23 For as I went
> through the city and looked carefully at the objects of your worship, I found
> among them an altar with the inscription, 'To an unknown god.'
>
> What therefore you worship unknowingly, this I proclaim to you. 24 The God who
> made the world and all things in it, he who is Lord of heaven and earth, does not live
> in shrines made by human hands, 25 nor is he served by human hands, as though he
> needed anything, since he himself gives to all mortals life and breath and all things.
>
> 26 From one ancestor he made all nations to inhabit the whole earth, and he
> appointed the times of their existence and the boundaries of the places where they
> would live, 27 so that they would search for God and perhaps grope for him and
> find him – though indeed he is not far from each one of us.
>
> 28 For 'in him we live and move and have our being'; as even some of your own
> poets have said, 'For we too are his offspring.'
>
> 29 Since we are God's offspring, we ought not to think that the deity is like gold,
> or silver, or stone, an image formed by the art and imagination of
> mortals. 30 While God has overlooked the times of human unknowing, now he
> commands all people all places to repent, 31 because he has appointed a day on
> which he will have the world judged in righteousness by a man whom he has
> appointed, and of this he has supplied trust (*pistin paraschōn*) to all by raising him
> from the dead." (Acts 17:22–31; NRSV modified)

In Acts 17, Paul's speech points the Athenians beyond the created objects and human history to the historical creator of those objects and history. Luke's storytelling indicates that the feat was only modestly persuasive: "When they heard of the resurrection of the dead, some scoffed; but others said, 'We will hear you again about this'" (Acts 17:32).

Despite the tepid outcome, the narrator simulates the Deuteronomic dilemma in this scene. Paul's speech begins with an affirmation of the Athenians' religious zeal, but noting a key gap: their "unknown god." His stated effort is to "proclaim" this "god of their ignorance" to them. His proclamation includes a transcending move from creation to creator. The mention of seasons and boundaries both call Genesis' creation and Deuteronomy's idolatry of celestial bodies to mind. For Luke's Paul, these objects and events intend to make humans grope for God and find him (17:27). The Athenians grope, but they have not found.

Paul does not argue that creation itself should dispose them to comprehend this god that he proclaims to them. Rather, their political borders, their religious practices, and the threat of judgment act epistemically upon them, initiating their pursuit of this god. The resurrection of Jesus then seals the deal rhetorically, dividing those who continue to grope for Paul's god from those who have heard enough. The narrator's turn of phrase – the "proof" statement – creates a deep ambiguity pertaining to our dilemma. To convince them of his point that God has appointed a man to come and judge all, Paul gives his evidence: "[God] has *supplied trust* (*pistin paraschōn*) to all by raising him from the dead" (Acts 17:31).

What does it mean that God "has supplied trust/conviction/proof to all"? Does this mean that the transcendent move from creation to creator requires the supplied trust? If God has supplied it "to all," then should everyone have the requisite faculties supplied by God to see?

This peculiar phrase – "supplied trust/conviction/proof to all" (*pistin paraschōn*) – cannot be found elsewhere in the New Testament. It has been translated "given assurance," "given proof," or even "furnished proof," in modern English translations.[32] But all of these evidentialist glosses on the phrase presume the same thing: that evidence – creation itself! – can be appropriately recognized *as evidence for something beyond itself*. Further, these evidentialist translations also presume that Athenians can employ this evidence rationally to deduce the correct conclusions about a creator.

But this reading of Paul renders no justice to his rhetorical goals, which begins by noting that the Athenian philosophers misinterpret all the evidence in front of them (Acts 17:22–23). The outcome of this proclamation indicates that offering reasonable evidence has little effect, which undermines the purpose of "giving proof," though perhaps not that of divinely given proof. When we turn to Romans 1, we see the epistolary Paul making a similar argument, and explicitly from a Deuteronomic perspective. But there he does not presume that the evidence can be judged correctly apart from God's revealing, or that evidence then demands a verdict.

One key to unlocking Paul's rhetoric in Athens turns on verses 30–31:

> While God has overlooked the times of human <u>unknowing</u>,
> now he commands <u>all</u> people in <u>all</u> places to repent,

[32] Cf. ESV and NRSV ("given assurance"), NIV ("given proof"), NASB ("furnished proof"). Paul does not employ the terms associated with confidence and hope (*elpidzo* and *asphileia*). ("All" – *panta* or *pas* – is used six times in this passage, so it may be more rhetorical than numerical.)

because he has appointed a day
on which he will have the world judged in righteousness
by a man whom he has appointed,
and of this he has *supplied trust* to all by raising him from the dead.

Paul began by addressing their worship of a god of *ignorance* (Acts 17:23) and referring to the creator God who *appoints* seasons, celestial paths, political boundaries, and all that happens (Acts 17:25–26). In the end, that god will cease to bear with humanity's *ignorance* and has *appointed* a particular day in which he will judge, "by a man whom he has *appointed*" (Acts 17:31).

The antidote to ignorance here is not the knowledge of God, but repentance (17:30). Unlike Philo and Wisdom, Paul does not bemoan their ignorance, but proclaims a harsh and unconvincing message, supposedly propped up by evidence that they have neither heard of nor seen (i.e., Jesus' resurrection). Nor would it be convincing if they had heard of Jesus' resurrection.

What is the point? If Paul brings a Deuteronomic perspective to this event, and we only have Luke-Acts' retelling of the speech, then "proof" in the modern sense might be off the table. I can only speculate at this point that Paul considers it God's task to *supply trust* in what he says and his task to clearly proclaim the news of Jesus to them in a way that would prod his Athenian hearers. Though he says that God has "supplied trust to all," the numerical value of "all" might be less important to Paul than its rhetorical value in the speech. "All" (*panta* or *pas*) is used six times in this short passage, emphasizing the totality of this God's powers and plans. So its use may be more rhetorical in reference to God's abilities than totalizing in reference to humanity.

Considering Paul's speech in Athens as a whole, we find him employing rhetoric to suggest an absurd argument:

> Some god they have never known rules sovereignly over all of creation, and some event of which they do not know [i.e., Jesus' resurrection] is evidence of a coming appointed judgment, a judgment which likely seemed incomprehensible to them.

Divine governance would have been a stock and trade notion in Athens, but "appointed judgment" seems to fit with Paul's "new ideas" that they were hoping to hear (Acts 17:21).

Paul then advocates the embodiment of repentance in light of his seemingly incoherent argument. Repentance would have signaled a ritual that Jews associated with either Jerusalem temple sacrifices or Jewish baptism rites now popularized by Judean disciples: baptism for the repentance of sins, the cleansing of the conscience, etc. Though this appears to be a linear style of argument, its inner logic draws upon networked narratives and logic external to the speech itself and likely unknown to his audience. Thus, this linear argument functions, if not pixelated, surreptitiously.

Though the narrator depicts the Athenians' rejection of his message at the point of resurrection and judgment, the remarkable ensuing action ensures that readers/hearers do not take this as a failure: "Some scoffed; but others said, 'We will hear you again about this'" (Acts 17:32). Though an Athenian should have found Paul's speech entirely unconvincing in theological content and rhetorical form, the narrator highlights the fact that it enticed some, possibly to subtly demonstrate God's "revealing" to some. *Most significant in this retelling of Paul's speech, we see no evidence that Paul pointed the Athenians from creation to creator.*

Of all the perplexities in this story, I only highlight how it differs from the appeals made by Wisdom and Philo. Instead of viewing the Gentiles as cursed to damnation, Paul uses judgment as a means of evoking ritual repentance. Instead of predicating his speech on their being deceived, he begins with a mutual admiration of their religious impulse, their mutual epistemological point of contact. As many have noted, Paul does not shy away from engaging their rhetoric and poets as mutual points of agreement and departure.

In other words, he does not enter the Aeropagus armed with Solomonic aphorism à la Proverbs or Wisdom as the preeminent form of philosophical discourse. He bends the mode of argument toward Athens, even if in a wonky way according to human effort. However, if he genuinely trusts that Yahweh must Deuteronomically give the Athenians hearts, eyes, and ears to know what Paul declares to them, then the formal failings of his argument do not determine its efficacy. This coheres with Paul's strong statements on philosophical practices wrapped up in "eloquent speech" that only "empties the cross of its power" (1 Cor 1:17).

In the opening appeal of Romans 1, Paul laces the Deuteronomic language and concepts into a particular form of the dilemma. Some suggest that this passage demonstrates Paul's conversance with Wisdom of Solomon 12–14, emphasizing the different tack he takes.[33] This complex

[33] James W. Thompson, *Apostle of Persuasion: Theology and Rhetoric in the Pauline Letters* (Grand Rapids, MI: Baker Academic, 2020), 43. And, "Unlike Wisdom 12–14 and the *Psalms of Solomon* (3:9–10), Romans does not distinguish between the sinners and the righteous but concludes that those who judge the unrighteous are also without excuse, for they do the same things (Rom. 2:1)" (51).

and debated passage demands a slow reading, but I merely want to observe one thing obvious within it: Paul's concern about knowing God.

> 18 For the wrath of God is revealed from heaven against all ungodliness and
> wickedness of those who by their wickedness suppress the truth. 19 For what can
> be known about God is revealed to them, because God has shown it to
> them. 20 Ever since the creation of the world his eternal power and divine nature,
> invisible though they are, have been understood [to some?] and seen through the
> things he has made.
>
> So they are without excuse; 21 for though they knew God, they did not honor him
> as God or give thanks to him, but they became futile in their thinking, and their
> senseless minds were darkened. 22 Claiming to be wise, they became fools; 23 and
> they exchanged the glory of the immortal God for images resembling a mortal
> human being or birds or four-footed animals or reptiles.
>
> 24 Therefore God gave them up in the lusts of their hearts to impurity, to the
> degrading of their bodies among themselves, 25 because they exchanged the truth
> about God for a lie and worshiped and served the creature rather than the
> Creator, who is blessed forever! Amen.
>
> (Rom 1: 18–25)

First, "the wicked suppress the truth" (Rom 1:18), which means that having eyes, they do not see creation as transcendently pointing to a creator (Rom 1:19). Second, God has shown them his invisible qualities through creation. Paul's teaching begins with the stark statement, "what can be known about God [through creation] is revealed to them, *because God has revealed it to them* (*ho theos gar autois ephanerōsen*)" (Rom 1:19).

Third, Paul aims his discourse at leaving them unexcused in the judgment to come, ultimately indicting their rituals aimed at other gods. Romans 1:21–23 then marks their downward progression: from not acknowledging God in their rituals, to becoming "futile in their thinking," to their minds being "darkened," to becoming "fools," which led to an idolatry of the Deuteronomic concern.

Most basically, God formed rational beings, "revealed Himself them," humans rejected, and God "gave them up," which led to the further darkening of their minds. Whatever epistemic mechanism Paul has in mind here, whether targeting pagan gentiles or a whoring Israel, the dynamic relationship between God's revealing and a human's understanding never reduces to simple correspondence. Further, Paul lands on what they ritually do with their bodies and possessions, which contributes to further misapprehension. Ian Scott highlights the problem of emphasis in this passage: "The vast majority of interpreters have understood that

TABLE 7 *Paul's hybridization of Hebraic and Hellenistic philosophy*

	Hebrew Bible	**Hellenist Tradition**	**Paul in Athens/Romans 1**
Philosophical Style	**Modes of Argument:** 1. Pixelated (structure) 2. Networked (literary) **Convictions:** 3. Mysterionist 4. Creationist 5. Transdemographic 6. Ritualist	**Modes of Argument:** 1. Linear 2. Autonomist **Convictions:** 3. Domesticationist 4. Abstractionist 5. Classist 6. Mentalist	**Modes of Argument:** 1. *Pixelate* (with elements of Linearity) 2. *Networked* **Convictions:** 3. *Mysterionist* 4. *Creationist* 5. *Transdemographic* 6. *Ritualist*

Paul's point in 1:18–32 is not to affirm humanity's intellectual powers, but to emphasize how much humanity has *lost*."[34]

Paul does not seem concerned for them to know God through creation *in se* or through a rationally justified process from creation as evidence. Rather, "the root problem in 1:18–32 is not an intellectual problem. It's a *moral* problem."[35] Though Israel's networked emergence from creation will feature prominently in this letter (creationist), he wants them to appropriately enact behaviors and ritual practices conducive to understanding God (ritualist) (Table 7).

Between Paul's speech in Athens and his rhetoric in Romans 1, we see two nonidentical examples of working through this question of divine epistemic agency: Must God intervene to enable understanding of the creator by means of creation? Though using narratival techniques to argue in a pseudo-linear fashion, both examples draw upon pixelated and networked stories and concepts wholly external to his argument – creation, Israel's history of idolatry, creation requiring a personal creator, and later, the Deuteronomic circumcision of the heart (Rom 2:29–30).

Paul, like Deuteronomy, seems to conclude that God must act on our epistemic abilities in order to see animals not as gods, but as creatures created by one god.[36] Regarding the blurring of moral and

34 Italics original. Ian W. Scott, *Paul's Way of Knowing: Story, Experience, and the Spirit* (Grand Rapids, MI: Baker Academic, 2009), 16.

35 Italics original. Scott, *Paul's Way of Knowing*, 19.

36 Paul's employment of Deuteronomy's rhetoric, specifically Deuteronomy 27–30 from which the Deuteronomic dilemma derives, has been demonstrated recently by the work

epistemological development in Paul's thinking (and Scripture's thinking more broadly), Kyle Wells sums Paul's interactions with Deuteronomy 30: "On Paul's reading, *in contrast to most Jews*, Scripture confirms the horrific reality that human agents are utterly incompetent. Bereft of eyes that see, ears that hear, or understanding hearts, they lack the faculties to respond to God effectively. Given this situation, resolution could not be on account of any acceptable human act."[37]

This action taken by God has both ritual inputs and outputs never reducible to a mere mental understanding of facts about God. Knowing God entails ritual practices, but bad ritual practices can hinder knowledge of God. Unlike Philo and Wisdom, the "true road" interweaves practice with understanding, where minds can comprehend the invisible features of the world, but cannot domesticate that understanding. In short, Paul maintains the Deuteronomic stance toward the Athenian gentiles and Roman Jews and Christians – that God must reveal – while Wisdom and Philo put the onus on the Gentiles' rational capacities and the lure of idolatry.

The Hebraic Counternarrative in Hellenistic Judaism

At the other end of the spectrum from Philo and Wisdom, we find a cluster of texts that seem to reject the Hellenistic trends. These texts tend to prefer the uncomplicated hero narratives akin to Daniel, Esther, and Ruth. Unlike the intricate storylines and unruly individuals throughout the Hebrew Bible (e.g., Abraham, Isaac, Jacob, Moses, Gideon, Samson, Saul, David, Solomon, etc.), the focus centers upon characters akin to Noah and Joshua. I have in mind here sections of or the entirety of Judith, 1 Maccabees, Tobit, Esther, and Daniel, with Manasseh being a notable exception.

These story-driven texts generally have a central figure situated in moral predicaments, and, unlike Daniel, the central figure acts directly in favor of the Jewish people. In the case of Judith, she must assassinate the Assyrian commander Holofernes specifically because the people did not trust in God to protect them (Jdt 8:11–12). The same goes for the Prayer of Azariah, Tobit (and Sarah), and Susanna, where texts celebrate

of David Lincicum, *Paul and the Early Jewish Encounter with Deuteronomy* (Grand Rapids, MI: Baker Academic, 2013); "Paul's Engagement with Deuteronomy: Snapshots and Signposts," *Currents in Biblical Research* 7, no. 37 (2008): 37–67.

37 Italics mine. Wells, *Grace and Agency in Paul*, 294.

personal piety and often the cunning of the main figures. These texts surrounded by Hellenistic Judaism value a certain type of instantiated Torah obeisance not found in pre- and postexilic texts. Obeying the Torah, possibly in a formalized system of practices and rules (*halakhot*), raises one to the level of righteousness.

I point out these texts for one reason only. Having made the case for narratives as arguments in a pixelated scheme of understanding, we again find a series of narratives dotting the landscape of postexilic and Hellenistic Judaism. But these stories aim at notably different targets: piety, fealty, Torah obeisance, etc. In the Torah, no developed character ever achieves such a discernibly pious status central to the story's plot. Noah and Joseph (like the later undeveloped characters, Joshua and Deborah) would constitute the closest exceptions to that rule in the Hebrew Bible. Even then, Noah and Joseph have their moments of morally dubious behavior (cf. Gen 9:21; 43:16–25).

The stories of the Torah and the so-called Deuteronomistic History present to us morally questionable characters, as complex as real-life people we know today, with whom God makes and keeps promises. Shira Weiss claims that this ethical ambiguity of protagonists in the Hebrew Bible is an intentional reasoning strategy, forcing the audience to puzzle and rethink what is good and what is detestable, even when the same character exemplifies both.[38]

By stylistically assembling pixelated arguments across law, narrative, and poetry, most of the Hebrew Bible avoids such heroic exemplarism – Daniel and Esther being possible exceptions, with Ezra-Nehemiah being a borderline case. At the end of the exile, Ezra and Nehemiah only superficially resemble unflawed characters, and Nehemiah comes across quite selfishly at the end of the book (Neh 13). The sophisticated use of repetition to explore the premise that "God makes things known" through Daniel (Dan 1–5) stands out as an extraordinary outlier among these hero sagas. Esther, Judith, Susanna/Daniel, and Tobit/Sarai provide us little ethical or epistemological girth to assess a principled account of their discernment or any normative basis for their behavior apart from Torah obeisance.

To reiterate, the presence of narratives without linear reasoning does not entail a pixelated reading that I am suggesting is distinctively Hebraic. The exemplars – stories, law, and poetry – become more complex and variegated as we come to know them. If the goal is to develop nuanced

[38] Shira Weiss, *Ethical Ambiguity in the Hebrew Bible: Philosophical Analysis of Scriptural Narrative* (New York: Cambridge University Press, 2018).

discernment, then texts profuse with complexity offer the best proving grounds for such second-order thinking. Conversely, flatly obedient or heroic figures, untested by time and circumstance and unflappable in their righteousness do not aid in the process of discerning undergirding principles.

Other Texts of Hellenistic Judaism

There exists a collection of texts that appear to hybridize the philosophical style of the Hebrew Bible with Hellenistic notions. I am thinking here of texts such as the Testament of Twelve Patriarchs[39] and Ben Sira,[40] among others. I do not want to survey all these texts or belabor the point. I only wanted to show the hybridization in the Hebraic style when we enter Hellenistic Judaism in preparation for looking at the New Testament. In the coming chapter, I will propose that the NT authors commit to an *ad fontes* movement, skipping over the rich philosophical style of Hellenism and the hybrid style of Hellenistic Judaism, to retrieve second-order notions primarily through the lens of the Hebraic style.

One last collection of texts merits brief mention: the communities that explicitly rejected Hellenism, which was likely one among several cultural influences they wanted to reject. The Community Rule from the Dead Sea Scrolls collection and the Temple Scroll can serve as other examples of this kind.

These texts do not advocate a particular philosophical style, but particular schools of Torah-obeisance in order to prepare for various eschatological events. Indeed, strict Torah adherence (according to the standards of these communities) separated the true followers from the rest. Hence, their rejections of Hellenism were secondary to the more pressing in-group/out-group maintenance.

39 I would classify the Testament of the Twelve Patriarchs accordingly as mainly Hebraic: ritualist; pixelated; networked; creationist; mysterionist; *classist* (misogynist): *T. Levi* 13:1–9 pushes to read and know Torah, where impiety and sin are the only things that can "take away wisdom." Hellenistic concepts such as proto-gnosticism and dualism appear thematically strong; cf. *T. Reu.* 1–2 and the battle of the seven-spirit anthropology (creationist, spirits from creation); but also Epicurean concerns at stake here.

40 I would classify Ben Sira accordingly as mainly Hebraic. It is "fear of the Lord" heavy (1:26ff): ritualist (7:31–36); pixelated; networked; creationist (e.g., Sirach 43, presumes, like the psalmist, that creation points to creator and 51:16ff roots itself back in traditional wisdom lingo); *domesticationist* (e.g., God is all-knowing and therefore "knows all that may be known" [Ben Sira 42:18], yet, we *can* crack the secrets [38:1–3]. Deut 29 gets decoded ("he reveals the traces of hidden things"); and *classist/misogynist* (38:24–25) even socially classist (13:1ff), though the "who can be wise" question (6:33–37) looks very much like Proverbs 1–9.

I mention these texts and the communities they represent because they exemplify writing traditions aware of the cultural slippage – such as Hellenism more generally or aristocracy in the Temple more particularly – and establish practices and concepts for the sake of actively resisting those sociopolitical structures. It would be difficult to assess their philosophical style, even though it was certainly based on the style of the Hebrew Bible, now stratified for a different end: separation and their brand of holiness.

Qumran's ritualism, creationism, networking, transdemography, and pixelation fit nicely in the philosophical circle I have advocated here as Hebraic. But these are leveraged for absolute separation from Gentiles and maintaining cleanliness at extreme ascetic costs.[41] So I would like to generalize that theirs was indeed an attempt at Hebraic thought, but a lens too distorted by their contemporary concerns for a particular eschatological event.

Conclusions

In the contact between the conquering Hellenists and the Jewish people, neither a pidgin nor creole of Greek philosophical style emerges. Rather, a variety of hybridized styles appears, sensitive to their creationist and networked convictions, but malleable to Hellenistic forms of thought. Not all reacted in rejectionist isolation from Hellenism. Yet, how aware are Hellenistic Jews of embracing, rejecting, or engaging the Hellenistic philosophical style and the conceptual vestiges of Hellenism? These texts display varying degrees of awareness of the Hellenistic influence, though hybridity remains the best analog for texts in this period. Paul, on the other hand, argues persuasively only if one maintains the Hebraic convictions of the style. Even where he appears to be linear in his style of reasoning, I will argue in Chapter 7 that his linear arguments, under scrutiny, still exhibit a pixelated style.

[41] E.g., absolute separation of gentile from Hebrew (e.g., gentile wheat not allowed in Temple; Dead Sea Scroll 4Q394 3–7, and no wine should have been in the skin of an animal not slaughtered at the Temple; Temple Scroll, XLVII).

6

Hebraic Philosophical Style in the Gospels

The New Testament displays the greatest intellectual retrieval of Hebraic thought and literature in antiquity. In this chapter, I explore the idea that the NT authors largely favor the Hebraic philosophical style and strategically engage the styles of Jewish-Hellenism and Roman philosophy. The NT texts occupy an odd space in Second Temple Jewish literature. Written largely within a Hellenistic Jewish milieu, they have predominantly Jewish authors – depending on which sources one accredits.[1] Most of the NT texts were purportedly written in or immediately after the Second Temple period.

In some ways, it would be appropriate to describe the New Testament texts as "Jewish scripture," even if not accepted as such by all Jews, then or now. Just as Qumran's Community Rule did not hold authoritative sway over all Jews in the Levant or Diaspora, neither did the teachings of Jesus or his disciples. The NT texts definitively held sway over subsections of Jews in Jerusalem and the Diaspora. Moreover, they often portrayed themselves as Jewish in source, authority, or both.

Whether we deem NT texts to be Jewish scripture or not, understanding their relationship to the literature of Second Temple Judaism is crucial for grasping the Hebraic philosophical style in this era. Even though the NT authors wrote after works such as Ben Sira, Wisdom, and 1 Maccabees had been established, they almost entirely refrain from directly engaging the circulated Hellenistic Jewish literature. Instead, the NT authors display regular and rhythmic citations, quotations, allusions,

[1] The particular authorship of the NT gospels and epistles need not be demonstrably Jewish in origins and in all facets in order for the point to hold.

echoes, and metaleptical and narratival reasoning networked from the Hebrew Bible.[2] The NT authors' near silence on Hellenistic Jewish literature deserves attention concerning their rhetorical aims.[3] It is akin to offering a history of music from the Bronze Age forward and then skipping everything from 1750 to 1980. It is difficult not to read that massive gap as a critique.

Any consideration of the philosophical style of the NT authors must reckon with the Hellenistic styles *du jour*. Hellenism's philosophies developed into sophisticated Roman rhetorical forms in the first century, forms in which some of the NT authors might have been steeped.

In this chapter, I consider which aspects of Hebraic and Hellenistic philosophical styles the gospel authors employ and possible motivations behind their employments. As with the expansive literature of Hellenistic Judaism, I cannot survey the wide variety of texts in the NT, but will focus on paradigmatic texts and topics as case studies.

My goal is to construct a series of lenses to inspect all of Second Temple literature including the New Testament. These lenses will either support my contention that the NT authors saw themselves as retrieving the Hebraic style or reveal their syncretism with Hellenistic Judaism's philosophies. To this end, I will explore Matthew's Sermon on the Mount and Markan epistemology. Paul's rhetorical logic in his letter to the Galatians will be examined in Chapter 7.

The basic questions I seek to answer here remain unchanged:

1. Is there a present, persistent, and relevant matter of second-order investigation in a given text?
2. Does the author advocate a particular method for pursuing that second-order understanding?
3. What style of philosophy best captures the pursuit?

[2] One can think of many recent works here that demonstrate the extent to which the NT authors heavily engaged the LXX. E.g., Maarten J. J. Menken and Steve Moyise, eds. *Deuteronomy in the New Testament* (Library of New Testament Studies 358; London: T&T Clark, 2007); *Isaiah in the New Testament* (London: T&T Clark, 2005); Richard B. Hays, *Echoes of Scripture in the Letters of Paul* (New Haven, CT: Yale University Press, 1989); *Echoes of Scripture in the Gospels* (Waco, TX: Baylor University Press, 2016).

[3] By "near silence," I mean that NT authors are not employing the arguments or narratives of the Hellenistic Jewish corpus. Of course, I do not mean to suggest that NT authors are not repeating concepts and terminology developed within that literature. Iain Provan also observes a conspicuous lack of rabbinic citation across Hellenistic Jewish literature: "There are no clear examples of this in Philo, Josephus, or the NT, however, nor any in Ben Sira, the authors of Maccabees, Hillel, Shammai, and all the first century Tannaim." Iain Provan, *The Reformation and the Right Reading of Scripture* (Waco, TX: Baylor University Press, 2017), 71.

Hellenist and Hebraic Style across the New Testament

Of the minefields I have trodden thus far, debates over Hellenism's reach into Christian Scripture might be the most crowded. Although many of these debates could be summarized with the token idiom "the jury is split," the debates themselves persist to this day. They will haunt the discussion as we turn to the paradigmatic passages to determine whether the Hebraic philosophical style undergirds aspects of the NT gospels and epistles.

To remind ourselves, the Hebraic philosophical style uses an array of examples (pixelated) with intertextual connections to the texts of the tradition (networked). The convictions behind this style presume that our historical connection to the creation and its creator (creationist) provide the conditions for reasoning that transcends the visible. Nevertheless, the Hebraic style holds no hope of capturing, containing, and domesticating our second-order understanding without remainder (mysterionist). Finally, the true path to understanding requires embodied participation (ritualist), which includes participation from all layers of society (transdemographic) (Table 8).

By walking through the examples below, I illustrate where the New Testament authors follow the Hebraic style of philosophizing, even when using Hellenist terms, concepts, and forms of reasoning, and even with a variety of Jewish and Roman philosophical schools available to them. It initially appears as a strategic and accommodating hybridity of styles, but reveals a commitment to the Hebraic style upon closer inspection.

Rival Traditions

What exactly is meant by the hybridity of Hebraic and Hellenistic philosophical styles? Not only does the Hebraic tradition dominate the NT

TABLE 8 *New Testament's hybridization of Hebraic and Hellenistic philosophy*

	Hebrew Bible	Hellenism	New Testament
Philosophical Style	**Modes of Argument:** 1. Pixelated 2. Networked **Convictions:** 1. Mysterionist 2. Creationist 3. Transdemographic 4. Ritualist	**Modes of Argument:** 1. Linear 2. Autonomist **Convictions:** 1. Domesticationist 2. Abstractionist 3. Classist 4. Mentalist	**Modes of Argument:** 1. *Pixelated* (with elements of Linearity) 2. Networked **Convictions:** 1. Mysterionist 2. Creationist 3. Transdemographic 4. Ritualist

author's thought (those surveyed here), but recent scholarship argues that it is actually incommensurable with some Hellenistic traditions. On this view, they are rivals. C. Kavin Rowe contends that recent analyses comparing the NT with peer Hellenistic philosophies – à la the works of Troels Engberg-Pedersen and Abraham J. Malherbe – often fund their comparisons with the wrong paradigm: an encyclopedic mindset.[4]

Citing Alasdair MacIntyre's categories – encyclopedia, genealogy, and tradition – Rowe worries about the appropriateness of "encyclopedic inquiry": the tendency to treat systems of thought as if they have "universal translatability." MacIntyre's "encyclopedic" thinking occurs where scholars believe they have the universal capacity "to make what was framed in the light of the canons of one culture intelligible to those who inhabit some other quite alien culture, provided only that the latter is our own, or one very like it."[5]

Using case studies from Stoicism on the one hand and Luke, Paul, and Justin Martyr on the other, Rowe finds that NT and Hellenistic notions are linguistically and rhetorically similar, but conceptually incommensurable. That incompatibility between systems of thought exists precisely because they are not "systems," as the encyclopedist might suppose. Rather, they emerge as traditions. Traditions cultivate skills of discernment through a community capable of maintaining those skills, developing apprenticeship, training moral habits, and facilitating long-term cooperative efforts.[6]

Key for Rowe, the basis of this schism is each tradition's ritual life. Participation in the ritualization of Stoicism or Christianity creates the conditions under which the language connects with the conceptual world within each tradition. He concludes that basic terms such as "God" and "justice" simply do not mean the same thing to Stoics as they do to Christians because they are rival traditions. Even worse for the encyclopedist, those terms are untranslatable from one tradition to the other.

[4] C. Kavin Rowe, *One True Life: The Stoics and Early Christians as Rival Traditions* (New Haven, CT: Yale University Press, 2016), 176–79. Rowe's radical critique is later reviewed by Engberg-Pedersen as "a challenge ... to the manner in which early Christianity and Stoicism have been compared since the rise of historical criticism (and even before)." This indicates that the primary threat is not the veracity or extremity of Rowe's arguments, but more ironically, their deviation from the tradition. Troels Engberg-Pedersen, review of *One True Life: The Stoics and Early Christians as Rival Traditions* by C. Kavin Rowe, *Journal of Early Christian Studies* 25, no. 2 (2017): 326.

[5] Alasdair MacIntyre, *Three Rival Versions of Moral Enquiry: Encyclopaedia, Genealogy, and Tradition* (Notre Dame, IN: University of Notre Dame Press, 1991), 171.

[6] Rowe, *One True Life*, 182–84.

Rowe believes that this opens an admittedly bizarre "possibility that different traditions can both be speaking Greek, but effectively speaking different languages."[7]

Rowe's formidable conclusion highlights an intractable problem that he sets out to examine – the logical space separating the NT's use of Stoic language from the Stoic concepts themselves. Resembling what I have described as networked literature in coordination with creationist, trans-demographic, and ritualist convictions, Rowe firmly concludes: "There is no possible way to get the Christian sense of God as 'God-as-determined-by-the-history-of-the-Jews-and-Jesus-of-Nazareth' into Stoic grammar."[8] It cannot be translated directly by a mere reemployment of the Stoic tradition's terms in a Christian context.[9]

If Rowe's analysis of these comparative philosophy/theology projects is even partially correct, and I believe it is just that, then the implications for anything I say below are crucial. However, Rowe's incommensurable translation thesis need not be correct in all its extremities as it pertains to my contentions here. I believe that some of the concepts can be translatable, but his emphasis on community, tradition, skill, and apprenticeship appreciably highlights the difficulties with any attempt to translate from Stoic to Christian intellectual worlds and vice versa.

Rival Traditions within the Hebrew Bible

Second Temple Judaism was not the first time Hebraic thought encountered rival traditions of thought. Indeed, we find rivalry in Genesis and the exile in the Joseph and Daniel stories. Dream interpretation by experts trained in scribal traditions functioned as a standard path to knowledge in the ancient Near East.[10] In those traditions, dreams aided one in understanding the invisible qualities of their waking world. Gods could be seen as reasoning with someone through dream narrative, though that is not how Egyptian or Mesopotamian scribes interpreted them. Rather, the symbology in dreams was the code sent by the gods.

7 Rowe, *One True Life*, 226.

8 Rowe, *One True Life*, 227.

9 Given his propensity to debate this topic in writing, along with his analysis of John's Gospel using Kuhnian paradigm shifts, Engberg-Pedersen's complete silence toward Rowe's argument here is remarkable. Troels Engberg-Pedersen, *John and Philosophy: A New Reading of the Fourth Gospel* (New York: Oxford University Press, 2018).

10 J. Donald Hughes, "Dream Interpretation in Ancient Civilizations," *Dreaming* 10, no. 1 (2000): 7–18.

Their texts collected the tradition's symbology of "if/then" relationships that acted as the decoder rings: "If a man sees himself eating crocodile meat, it is good, meaning that he becomes an official among his people."[11] Though all humans tell themselves stories in visualized narratives while asleep, Egyptian dream divination focused on individual elements and not the narrative structure. For Egyptian elites, ritualized nights in "sleep temples" could bring about a divinely guided dream – called "dream incubation."[12]

In a way unknown in the Hebrew Bible, dreams had a significant role to play in cult practice. In the few occasions where "dream" (*ḥălôm*) occurs in the Hebrew Bible, references vary from neutral to specious, with the notable exceptions of Joel and Solomon:[13]

dreams that speak to non-Hebrews (Gen 20:3–6; Gen 40–41; Dan 2)
dreams for prophetic deceit (Deut 13:2–6; Jer 23:25–27; 27:9; 29:8; Zech 10:2)
dreams associated with foolishness (Eccl 5:3, 7)
dreams as a metaphor for the unreal quality of an event (Psa 73:20; 126:1; Isa 29:8),
a direct report of a dream's content (Gen 31:10–11; Judg 7:13–15)
neutral references (1 Sam 28:6, 15).[14]

Skepticism about dreams occurs in Jeremiah, where he repeatedly warns those in exile against "dreamers" and prophets using the language of the Deuteronomic promise to send "dreamers" who will mislead Israel in order to test her (cf. Deut 13:2–6; Jer 23:25–27; 27:9; 29:8).

Looking at the total package of dream-talk in the Hebrew Bible, we see two things. First, when Hebrews live as foreigners within an intellectual tradition that esteems dream interpretation as skilled understanding, God speaks to non-Hebrews through dreams and uses Hebrews to interpret them (e.g., Joseph and Daniel). Second, when Israel was at her highest point of contact with an empire that highly esteemed dreams as a mode of understanding, she was strongly warned to be skeptical of such divinations. In short, apart from Genesis and Daniel, interpreted dreams are considered critically on the whole and are certainly not a normative way of bringing about understanding.[15]

11 *The Dream Book*, Plate 5, quoted in Terek Asaad, "Sleep in Ancient Egypt," in *Sleep Medicine: A Comprehensive Guide to Its Development, Clinical Milestones, and Advances in Treatment*, ed. Sudhansu Chokroverty and Michel Billiard (New York: Springer, 2015), 13–19.

12 Asaad, "Sleep in Ancient Egypt," 13–19.

13 Joel 3:1; 1 Kgs 3:5.

14 This brief list spans the variety of uses of *ḥălôm* in the Hebrew Bible, fifty-five in total by my count.

15 Numbers 12:6, "I will speak with him [a prophet] in a dream," clearly equates "vision" (*mar'â*) to "dream" (*ḥălôm*), so I am not including it here.

The Hebrew Bible nestles these twin dream accounts in exile amongst empires with a Hebrew slave: Joseph and Daniel. In Genesis, we find Jacob, Joseph, and Pharaoh having significant dreams, but only Pharaoh's dream generates an interpretive conflict needing resolution. The dreams of Jacob and Joseph fit more aptly in the category of visions (Gen 28:10–22; 37:1–11), while Pharaoh's dreams fit the dream-interpretative practices of Egypt and Mesopotamia (Gen 41:1–36). In a parallel account set in Mesopotamia, we find another king needing an interpretation of a dream, but this time irrationally demanding evidence of the interpretation's authenticity (Dan 2:8).

Daniel reveals the dream's content and his subsequent interpretation occurs in one of the most knowledge-dense sections of the Hebrew Bible (though Daniel 2 is in Aramaic, of course). The phrase "make known" occurs fourteen times in chapter two alone.[16]

Daniel affirms that the Chaldean diviners were correct in their protests (2:10–11). They were not trained to reveal dreams, only to logically apply catalogs of symbolic codes to interpret the elements of the dream. The revelation of the dream's content can only be known by the gods, who presumably sent the dream, but they do not live here with humans (2:11).

Again, Daniel affirms the diviners' protests and contradicts them only on the matter of divine communication to humans. He counters "but there is a God in heaven who reveals mysteries and he has *made known* to King Nebuchadnezzar what will be ..." (2:28). He then correctly and extemporaneously interprets the dreams, verifying that he himself did not know these things, but God revealed them.

It is not my goal to determine whether the stories of Hebrew servants interpreting kingly dreams should be considered Hebraic philosophy. In Daniel, an intentionally extended parallel of the Joseph narrative, the matter is exclusively focused on a quest for understanding and the authentic guide who can "make known" to the king "so that you may know the thoughts of your mind" (2:30).

The two rival systems of interpreting dreams are now in direct conflict. Only in the context of Hebrew servitude under empires does the Hebrew biblical tradition tell stories about dream interpretation, an otherwise taboo practice. And there was no similar practice in the Hebraic tradition (i.e., logical symbolic divination of dreams). This suggests that the

[16] This is the *haphel* form of *yādaʿ* which expresses "active causative" in Aramaic. Alger F. Johns, *A Short Grammar of Biblical Aramaic*, rev. ed. (Berien Springs, MI: Andrews University Press, 1972), 19.

Hebraic style of philosophy – how one understands – can and will adapt its method of argument to fit the setting. In Egypt and Babylon, cryptic dreams that can be skillfully interpreted were considered valid arguments for understanding the current world, its history, and maybe even the future. So God speaks to emperors in cryptic dreams but then usurps the paradigm by interjecting a Hebrew interpreter, whom God authenticates through an unambiguous confirmation to all characters in these scenes.

The idea that the Hebraic philosophical style can adapt to local modes of discourse is as ancient as Genesis. This petit leitmotif of accommodating other intellectual worlds in the Hebrew Bible then expanded in Paul's thinking (whom I will address more fully in Chapter 7). In Athens, for instance, Paul makes no overt networked appeal to the Hebraic narrative until the very end of his speech, where it does nothing but marginalize him from the Hellenistic philosophers (Acts 17: 22–32). In the synagogue and to the churches, he sculpts his epistles to the audiences and their imminent "way of life" concerns. Before we turn to Paul's similarly strategic accommodations of Hellenistic forms of appeal, we will consider the portrayal of philosophical problems in the gospels.

Jesus of the Synoptic Gospels

For reasons of space, I cannot treat much from the gospels here. My intention is only to offer some test cases from Mark and Matthew as examples that can be extended. Recall our three guiding questions:

1. Is there a present, persistent, and relevant matter of second-order investigation in a given text?
2. Does the author advocate a particular method for pursuing that second-order understanding?
3. What style of philosophy best captures the pursuit?

If correct – that above all else the NT authors employ a Hebraic philosophical style – then we should discover literary styles that compile patterns of overlapping sequences (pixelated) which are all intertextually dependent (networked) upon the history of Israel from creation forward (creationist). The aim of this style should focus on the behavior being ritualized (ritualist) and the discernment instilled in the community (transdemographic), but without any commitment to (and possibly even with skepticism of) exhaustive understanding (mysterionist).

Markan Epistemology

Mark's epistemological style manifests across a disparate collection of stories culminating in the Transfiguration (Mark 9) and then again in the crucifixion/resurrection (Mark 15–16). Spanning that patchwork of tersely told stories, we see Mark's *Leitwort* technique around epistemically loaded stories, sometimes connecting them to stories where the epistemological aspect is not obvious.

Leitwort refers to the literary style of underlining a particular emphasis across diverse narratives by repeating words, word roots, and word pairings.[17] Martin Buber described it this way: "A word or word root that is meaningfully repeated within a text or sequence of texts or complex of texts; those who attend to these repetitions will find a meaning of the text revealed or clarified, or at any rate made more emphatic."[18]

Mark's gospel is known to scholars for being an "interwoven tapestry." Though plainly written, on the surface, significant literary savvy has emerged to a recent generation of scholars.[19] To keep this examination brief and on point, I want to show how the repeated application of "hear/listen" across Mark's gospel serves an epistemic function.

But first: Is there a present, persistent, and relevant concern to deal with second-order knowledge in Mark? Yes. This quest begins in Mark 4, if not earlier, where Jesus' attention turns specifically to the disciples and their ability to understand "the mystery of the kingdom of God" (Mark 4:11). The meaning of this phrase – "the mystery of the kingdom of God" – can only be pieced together in the totality of the epistemic process rolled out across Mark. In short, it means something akin to understanding how all these disparate and perplexing events, sayings, and teachings reveal the plan of God through Jesus.

In other words, "the mystery of the kingdom of God" substantially refers to the ability to see invisible features and connections of the visible world. In this sense, it is something akin to scientific understanding.

[17] Ronald Hendel, "*Leitwort* Style and Literary Structure in the J Primeval Narrative," in *Sacred History, Sacred Literature: Essays on Ancient Israel, the Bible, and Religion in Honor of R. E. Friedman on His Sixtieth Birthday*, ed. Shawna Dolansky (Winona Lake, IN: Eisenbrauns/PennState Press, 2008), 93–110.

[18] Martin Buber, "*Leitwort* Style in Pentateuchal Narrative," in Martin Buber and Franz Rosenzweig, *Scripture and Translation*, trans. Lawrence Rosenwald (Bloomington: Indiana University Press, 1994; German original, 1936), 114.

[19] Joanna Dewey, "Mark as Interwoven Tapestry: Forecasts and Echoes for a Listening Audience," *Catholic Biblical Quarterly* 53, no. 2 (1991): 221–36.

Scientific explanation specifically does not aim at describing the visible world but at explaining the invisible features that coerce the visible world. Epistemology in Mark, like scientific communities with novices, is primarily concerned with developing the "way of seeing" and secondarily with "what is seen."

Second, does the author advocate a particular method for pursuing that second-order understanding? Yes, and this is where the *Leitwort* of "hear/listen/obey" comes to the fore. Important for understanding how the *Leitwort* pattern appears, "hear," "listen," and "obey" are the three English terms used to translate aspects of the single term used in all of these instances: *akouō*.[20]

To demonstrate this, we will need to take a quick aside through the story flow of Mark's gospel. It is a rollercoaster of a narrative, with unanticipated twists strung together by conceptual and linguistic *Leitwort*.

The disciples' epistemic journey begins in full at the Parable of the Sower (Mark 4) – a parable with noted linguistic affinities to Deuteronomy's covenant renewal.[21] Jesus opens the parable with "Listen!" (Mark 4:3) and then describes seed that was thrown on various types of soil and how it fared, ending with, "He who has ears to listen, let him listen" (Mark 4:9). All of the following occur in Mark 4 alone:

> "Listen! A sower went out to sow ..." (4:3)
> "He who has ears to listen, let him listen" (4:9)
> "... they may indeed listen but not understand ..." (4:12)

[20] Adapted from Dru Johnson, *Scripture's Knowing: A Companion to Biblical Epistemology* (Eugene, OR: Cascade, 2015), 52–59.

[21] Others have seen Deuteronomy as a background to Mark 4 for the thematic reasons given above. Gerhardsson believes that the Parable of the Sower and its explanation (Mark 4:1–9, 13–20) rely on the rhetoric of Deuteronomy's call to hear in the Shema (Deut 6:4). Birger Gerhardsson, "The Parable of the Sower and Its Interpretation," *New Testament Studies* 14, no. 2 (1968): 180.

Marcus narrows Gerhardsson's thesis into his own, evincing a specifically Deuteronomic context for Mark 4:23: "Gerhardsson is right about the relevance of the Shema for understanding Mark 4; Mark's audience could not have heard the repeated references to hearing in that passage without being reminded of the Shema. ... Rather, at least in Mark's understanding, the parable is addressed only to 'him who has ears to hear, – let him hear.'" Joel Marcus, *The Mystery of the Kingdom of God*, ed. J. J. M. Roberts and Charles Talbert (SBL Dissertation Series 90; Atlanta: Society of Biblical Literature Press, 1986), 58. Unfortunately, Marcus leaves off other possible Deuteronomic connections that would explain the very phrase he cites as Mark's narrower use of the Shema – namely, *ōta akouein* from Deuteronomy 29. Marcus later corrects this omission in his Anchor Bible Commentary. Joel Marcus, *Mark 1–8* (The Anchor Yale Bible Commentaries 27; London: Yale University Press, 2002), 513.

"... the ones who, when they listen to the word, immediately receive it ..." (4:16)
"... they are those who listen to the word ..." (4:18)
"... the ones who listen to the word and receive it ..." (4:20)
"If anyone has ears to listen, let him listen." (4:23)
"See to it with what you listen ..." (4:24)
"With many such parables he spoke ... *as they were able to listen to it.*" (4:33)

According to Jesus' explanation, the parable is solely concerned with whether people *listen*, and then whether they *do what they heard* (i.e., "accept it and bear fruit"; Mark 4:20). Pairing the parable with its interpretation, we arrive at a paradigm of advocated seeing: in order to see the mystery of the kingdom of God being shown to them, the disciples must acknowledge that Jesus is the trusted authority and then put his instruction into practice.

Mark then applies language from Deuteronomy 29 (i.e., "ears to listen") and quotes phrases from Isaiah 6:9–10.[22] Mark 4 repeatedly emphasizes "listening" yet says almost nothing about "seeing." This repeated use of the verb "listen" signals to the reader that establishing Jesus as a trusted authority is the primary goal.

Later, the disciples admit to Jesus that they do not understand the parable (Mark 4:11), to which he replies with a cryptic promise: "To you all has been given the mystery of the kingdom of God" (Mark 4:10). Then he separates the disciples from everyone else, quoting a slightly rearranged version of the Septuagint's Isaiah 6:9–10:

> But for those outside, everything is in parables so that
> "they may indeed see but not perceive,
> and may indeed listen but not understand,
> lest they should turn and be forgiven." (Mark 4:12)

Remarkably, Jesus frames his teaching with Isaiah's calling, which was meant to deafen and blind Israel. But for the disciples, he will give them "the mystery of the kingdom of God" (Mark 4:11). That is the goal, which requires the disciples to listen to Jesus as the authority and do that which he instructs them. Unsurprisingly, then, Mark concludes this passage on the subject of listening with this summary (Mark 4:33–34):

[22] The only other occurrence of *ōta akouein* ("ears to hear") is found in Isaiah 32:3 and Ezekiel 12:12. Neither is identical in form to Deuteronomy 29:3 and Mark 4:23. This does not exclude them as allusions, but I argue for Deuteronomy as the more parsimonious source of Mark in Dru Johnson, *Epistemology and Biblical Theology: From the Pentateuch to Mark's Gospel* (Routledge Interdisciplinary Perspectives on Biblical Criticism 4; New York: Routledge, 2019), 113–28.

"With many such parables he spoke the word to them, *as they were able to listen*. He did not speak to them without a parable, but privately to his own disciples he explained everything."

How do the disciples fare in their quest to know the mystery of the kingdom of God in Mark's Gospel? Not well. Essentially tasked with listening and enacting instruction, they flopped and flapped. That evening, in the story's timeline, they cross the Sea of Galilee. The storm arises and Jesus calms it (Mark 4:35–41). Notice the question the disciples rhetorically ask themselves: "Who then is this, that even the wind and sea *listen to him*" (Mark 4:41). For the reader, we cannot help but ask the same: If even the sea and wind listen to him, will the disciples?

Moving about the region of Galilee, Jesus dispossesses demons, heals, and raises the dead (Mark 5). But coming into his hometown of Nazareth, the crowds are divided between those who "listened to him" and were thus astonished by his prophetic teaching (cf. Mark 6:2, 4), and those who would not listen because he was merely the carpenter's son (Mark 6:3).

He then gives his disciples authority and sends them out, two by two, to work his same wonders. Jesus notes specifically, "If any place ... *will not listen to you* ... shake the dust off of your feet" (Mark 6:11). At this point, we have high hopes for the disciples. Jesus means to reveal the mystery of the kingdom of God to these men through enacting his instruction. They are traveling along with him, seeing the wondrous signs, and are now embodying his guidance and thus seeing the invisible kingdom of God for themselves in novel and tangible circumstances.[23]

The next turn in Mark's story brings both despair and wonderment. Upon their return to Jesus, they report their success. Jesus immediately isolates them, but crowds follow. Though his disciples want to send the hungry crowds away, Jesus instructs his disciples, "You all give them something to eat" (Mark 6:37).

What precisely Jesus had in mind by this imperative – "give them something to eat" – is difficult to discern. Whatever Jesus expected them *to do*, they do not *do anything*. The disciples flounder and quibble about how much it would cost to feed the crowds. Then, Jesus takes the existing food and feeds the five thousand. Story *seemingly* over.

[23] This connection between listen, do, and know continues in Mark. When confronted by the Pharisees about the practices of his own disciples, Jesus calls for a public audience: "Listen to me, all of you, and understand" (Mark 7:14). Jesus begins with "Hear me ... and understand" (7:14) but continues on to say that they cannot "understand" by questioning: "Do you not see ..." (7:18). Once again, the priority is placed upon hearing in order to see.

As the disciples depart by boat to the other side of the sea, Jesus catches up to their boat – walking on the water! This distresses the disciples, but Mark shows the unexpected source of their anxiety in a way sure to jolt the reader. Jesus climbs aboard and calms the disciples, who thought he was a ghost. Mark's summary of that event? "And they were utterly astounded, for *they did not understand about the loaves*, but their hearts were hardened" (Mark 6:51–52).

Mark notes that while they were distressed by his water-walking, that was not the aim of the story he tells here. Rather, their minds were still fixated upon the miraculous feeding earlier in the day – "for they did not understand about the loaves."[24] Beyond serving up brilliant narrative technique, notice that Mark's gospel describes the scene epistemologically, not ontologically. They did not understand, which presumes that the prior miraculous feeding was not merely meant to provide nutrition, but to fit into a larger pattern of knowing.

Jesus had instructed them, "You all give them something to eat." They did not enact that instruction. Later they still puzzle over the feeding. Mark sums up the epistemological condition with the harsh phrase from the Hebrew Bible, "Their hearts were hardened."[25] Hopes for the disciples seeing the mystery of the kingdom diminish here.

After more cycles of teaching and healing, Jesus and the disciples are again confronted with another hungry crowd, four thousand this time. Incredulously, his disciples hedge again about the impossibility of getting enough food for such a large crowd (Mark 8:4). And again, Jesus miraculously divides up the food to feed them all. (It is nearly impossible not to view the ensuing sequence as written to make the disciples look comically foolish.)

After this, as if to personally place the last loaf on the camel's back, the disciples discuss the fact *that they forgot to bring bread on the boat*. Jesus snaps with a tirade interlacing Deuteronomy 29 and Isaiah 6, and it is worth repeating in full (Mark 8:17–21):

> "Why are you discussing the fact that you have no bread?
> Do you not yet perceive or understand?

[24] Evans cites this as a "misplaced *gar* clause." However, Mark's comment startles the reader as an epistemological insight no matter where it was placed in the text. Craig A. Evans, "How Mark Writes," in *The Written Gospel*, ed. Markus N. A. Bockmuehl and Donald Alfred Hagner (Cambridge: Cambridge University Press, 2005), 135–38.

[25] Exodus (LXX) uses *sklērynō* to describe Pharaoh's heart where Mark uses *pōroō* to describe "hardening," a term that does not appear in the Septuagint.

Have you hardened hearts?
Having eyes do you not see, and
having ears do you not listen?
And do you not remember?
When I broke the five loaves for the five thousand, how many baskets full of broken pieces did you take up?"
They said to him, "Twelve."
"And the seven for the four thousand, how many baskets full of broken pieces did you take up?"
And they said to him, "Seven."
And he said to them, "Do you not yet understand?"

Jesus' disciple-scolding places them as the outsiders, the ones who having ears do not listen or understand. The reader's hopes for the disciples grasping the mystery of the kingdom plunges. But what is the essential problem here? We will see in the coming story of the Transfiguration that God himself diagnoses the problem, which gives us only shadows of hope for the disciples if any hope at all.

Following this chastisement, a two-stage healing of a blind man (Mark 8:22–26) leads into the Christ-question, where we find out that the disciples are still not grasping the mystery of the kingdom of God. On the way to a northern city, Jesus questions his disciples, "Who do people say that I am?" (Mark 8:27). Elijah, John the Baptist, and "other prophets" are offered. When Jesus asks, "Who do you all say that I am?" Peter instills the briefest moment of hope in the reader, saying, "You are the Christ" (Mark 8:29).

Despite the veneer of an epiphany, we quickly find out that a misinterpretation of "the Christ" pervades Peter's thinking. He simply cannot understand how the role of Christ (i.e., *māšîaḥ*) could be reconciled with Jesus' forthcoming death and resurrection. And this is precisely the kind of reckoning inherent to the mystery of the kingdom of God. Stated otherwise, Peter could not hang together both the mystery of the kingdom of God and Jesus' confidence in his own dying and rising. To ensure absolute clarity, Jesus goes further, "speaking plainly" (Mark 8:32). Not only will Jesus suffer such shame (and glory), but also everyone who follows Jesus will suffer the same (Mark 8:34–38). Peter is labeled an "adversary" (*satanas*) for opposing this plan (Mark 8:33).

This leads to the surprising climactic moment in Mark's story, apart from Jesus' death: the Transfiguration. Werner Kelber describes the scene majestically: "Structurally, its place is precisely at mid-point of the gospel. Topologically, its locale is the only 'high mountain' in the gospel ....

Dramatically, it stages God's attestation of his Son in opposition to Peter's vainglorious Christos."[26]

Only Peter, James, and John ascend the mountain with Jesus. There they see Moses and Elijah – *the* prophet of Israel and a renowned prophet, respectively. God's voice descending on a mountaintop of key prophets plainly means to paint this scene as a "new Sinai event." Jesus is transfigured and God's voice descends to say only one thing – all depicted in the language of Deuteronomy's retelling of Sinai, and not Exodus's version.[27] All of this action builds up to the hearing of God's voice. And what does God say? He quotes the Greek of Deuteronomy 18 concerning future prophets of Israel: "This is my beloved son, *to him shall you listen*" (Mark 9:7).[28] Hence, Joel Marcus sums up this scene:

> On the one hand, this divine acclamation implies Jesus' continuity with Moses and Elijah, since "listen to him" echoes Moses' own words about the arising of a prophet like himself (Deut. 18:15, 18), an oracle that by the first century was being read eschatologically.
>
> On the other hand, however, the voice designates only one of the three personages, Jesus, as God's Son, and this is a title that hints at an identity greater than that of Moses or Elijah.[29]

[26] Werner Kelber, *The Kingdom in Mark: A New Place and a New Time* (Minneapolis: Fortress Press, 1974), 85.

[27] There are similarities here to the baptism of Jesus (Mark 1:9–11), but the Deuteronomic retelling of Yahweh's presence at Horeb, and not the Exodus account, bears a more striking resemblance (Deut 4:36–37). Both the Transfiguration and Deuteronomy 4 contain an account of a voice coming from above (*egeneto hē phōnē*). Both are focused on listening to an authority, and both scenes are motivated by God's distinctly filial love (*agapaō/agapētos*). Moreover, the instruction to "listen to him" (*autou akousesthe*) in Mark 9:7 is regarded as a "virtual citation" from Deuteronomy 18:15 concerning the future prophets of Israel. Stegner argues persuasively for the Transfiguration in Mark as a combination of Exodus 34 and Deuteronomy 18. This can be maintained without conflict to my proposal that Deut 4:36–37 is a parallel of the Exodus text. William Richard Stegner, "The Use of Scripture in Two Narratives of Early Jewish Christianity (Matthew 4.1–11; Mark 9.2–8)," in *Early Christian Interpretation of the Scriptures of Israel*, ed. Craig A. Evans and James A. Sanders (Sheffield: Sheffield University Press, 1997), 98–120. See also Foster R. McCurley Jr., "'And after Six Days' (Mark 9:2): A Semitic Literary Device," *Journal of Biblical Literature* 93, no. 1 (1974): 67–81. Marcus (and D. F. Strauss, no less) cite this as an allusion to Exod 34 only. Joel Marcus, *The Way of the Lord: Christological Exegesis of the Old Testament in the Gospel of Mark*, 1st ed. (Louisville, KY: Westminster John Knox, 1992), 82–84.

[28] The instruction "to him you shall listen" in Mark 9:7 is regarded as a "virtual citation" from Deuteronomy 18:15 concerning the future prophets of Israel. See Marcus, *The Way of the Lord*, 81; Menken and Moyise, *Deuteronomy in the New Testament*, 37–38.

[29] Joel Marcus, *Mark 8–16* (The Anchor Yale Bible Commentaries 27; London: Yale University Press, 2009), 640. John Calvin takes this view as well: *Commentary on a*

By the time we reach Mark 9, we are almost to the final week of Jesus' life. The disciples have repeatedly witnessed and personally participated in the miraculous work of Jesus. *Why does God, who chooses to say just one thing, need to remind them to listen to Jesus?* The presumption appears to be that the disciples do not genuinely revere Jesus as *the* prophet of Israel enough to embody all of his prescribed actions.

Most basically, Jesus' transfiguration and God's command to "listen" only make sense if the disciples are floundering on this point. Even if they sometimes listen to his words and put them into practice, his prior chastisement – have your hearts hardened? – indicates that the matter is by no means settled.

After the Transfiguration, Mark continues to portray the disciples as dolts. In the coming chapters, the disciples argue about who is the greatest among them (Mark 9:33–37), they wrongfully rebuke children approaching Jesus (Mark 10:13–16), some blindly make power grabs for the future kingdom (Mark 11:35–45), and others betray or deny Jesus during the Passion Week (Mark 14:43–72). If we consider only the short ending of Mark,[30] one centurion (Mark 15:39) and a handful of women (Mark 16:1–8) are the only people who understand Jesus' death and resurrection.

In the end, Mark's gospel leaves the reader with only a shred of hope that the disciples will ever grasp what Jesus was trying to show them. Even that shred depends upon the conviction that because Jesus tried so hard, the apostles should somehow come to know what he was showing them. But in itself, Mark offers little insight into whether the disciples ever understood the mystery of the kingdom of God, a topic later clarified in the book of Acts. Conversely, Mark unabashedly offers a sobering depiction of people who were meant to know this mystery, yet were blind to it because they did not listen or act.

Hence, the *Leitwort* of "listening" sews a single epistemological thread throughout the pixelated stories of Mark, raising questions unanswered within. In different settings, we find the narrator returning persistently to this theme: knowing begins with listening and then doing the prescribed actions. And now that we have pulled on and followed that thread of presence, persistence, and relevance, we can identify which philosophical style is being presumed or demonstrated in Mark.

Harmony of the Evangelists, Matthew, Mark and Luke, Vol. 2 (Edinburgh: Calvin Translation Society, 1845–46), 191.

30 The "short ending" of Mark presumes that the shortest manuscripts are the oldest, which puts the ending of Mark's gospel at Mark 16:8.

Pixelated. It should be fairly obvious that Mark presents no linear account of teaching, apart from the narrative's sense of time moving the story forward. Both Hellenistic genres of *bios* and *topoi* are mixed here, together revealing a coherent epistemology, among many other goals of Mark. Only taken together, and noting the "listening" *Leitwort*, in this case, can we make sense of Mark's epistemological process.

Networked. Intra- and intertextual contexts finish the logic within Mark's gospel. Using various literary devices – allusions, echoes, metalepsis, etc. – a discernible picture of second-order knowledge emerges. Every scene is pregnant with, foreshadowed, and backlit by a conversance with the Hebrew Bible. As Joel Marcus commented, "Citations of and allusions to the Old Testament continually pop up."[31] Even more than direct references to the Hebrew Bible, Mark stitches the logic of Deuteronomy 29 and Isaiah 6 into the hems of his plot and character development.

Ritualist. There is something to be known by the disciples in Mark. Jesus is intent, as their guide, to apprentice them so that they can know it. However, their apprenticeship is not learning new ways of thinking or reasoning. Rather, Jesus gives them embodied tasks for the sake of seeing the "mystery of the kingdom of God." The narrative then follows a clear logic of outcomes: listening to Jesus and embodying his instructions ends in epistemic success (Mark 6:7–13), while not listening stunts the process – eventually requiring a Sinai-like intervention from God on a Mountain. This time, though, the tablet from heaven is a voice, and it says, "Listen to him" – putting Jesus' voice and the Torah in parallel.

Transdemographic. At first blush, Mark's gospel appears to promote classist convictions. It was only his (male) disciples who would receive the mystery. However, as we follow that storyline, it becomes paradoxically clear that, not only is the mystery becoming more and more opaque to the disciples, but it is foreigners (7:34–30; 15:39), women (cf. 5:21–34; 7:24–30), blind men (10:46–52), and children (10:13–15) who seem to grasp through embodied experience how some of these parts cohere within the mystery of the kingdom. For Jewish leaders and the disciples, hardened hearts and all sorts of idolatries underlie their inability to discern the background noise from the signal of the kingdom. The intent is for *the disciples* to discern the invisible features of the kingdom, but the narrative tells a very different story. Discernment is available to all transdemographically.

[31] Marcus, *The Way of the Lord*, 1.

Mysterionist. Again, on a surface reading, Mark appears to be classist and domesticationist. After all, the revealing of the mystery to a chosen set of disciples is at the center of Mark 4–9. However, later in the book, we find no pursuit of exhaustive knowledge. Rather, Jesus grieves at their obstinate inability to apprentice for the sake of this one general epistemic goal: the mystery of the kingdom. From the affirmations of the epistemically successful characters in Mark, we do not see a pattern of knowers who now have the whole universe of understanding opened up to them (cf. Gos Thom 1–5). Rather, we see people portrayed as confident in this one narrow sphere: Jesus is more than a prophet and seems somehow related to Yahweh's creative power and kingdom reign (e.g., Blind Bartimaeus).[32] It is precisely their minimalist epistemic grip on some aspect of the mysterious kingdom that garnered praise from Jesus.

Creationist. As I argue in *Epistemology and Biblical Theology*, deployment of Deuteronomy 29 and Isaiah 6 to structure a series of epistemically focused narratives satisfies the creationist criterion. However, other features of Mark interlock these Jesus stories with the story of the Torah. I am thinking here of small touches, such as the use of "fruitfulness" as a primary metaphor for the pragmatic epistemology of Mark 4. Though seemingly a garden-variety term, "fruit" and "fruitful" appear rarely in the Hebrew Bible as a metaphor for what we might call flourishing today – listening to God, embodying the prophets' instructions, and therefore understanding some promised state of affairs.

When "fruitfulness" is paired with "abundance" or "multiplication" – as Jesus does with his parable of the sower[33] – a traceable string of connections lines up, pointing back to the cosmic creation in Genesis 1 through Exodus and Deuteronomy.[34] In reverse order, we see

[32] Blind Bartimaeus (Mark 10:46–52) aptly captures this minimalist epistemic grip on the mystery of the kingdom. We are unsure of what exactly he knows of Jesus, but he calls out to Jesus with the Messianic signal (i.e., "son of David"), and when asked "what do you want me to do for you," he requests a return to normal physiology. We cannot know the content of his understanding, but he appears to "get it" at some level. When Jesus asked the identical question as to the sons of Zebedee in a parallel story just prior, they both quickly evince their misunderstanding of the mystery of the kingdom. Even when Jesus tries to explain, they misunderstand even further (Mark 10:35–45).

[33] Cf. Mark 4:1–9; Matt 13:1–15; Luke 8:4–10. Gerhardsson claims this parable as parsimonious support for the Deuteronomic relationship to Mark 4 between listening which leads to fruitfulness. Gerhardsson, "The Parable of the Sower," 182, 187.

[34] Cf. *karpos* in the LXX of Deut 7:12–13 and 11:17 for instances of "fruitfulness" as a positive consequence of listening in the former and the negative outcome of not listening in the latter. Also, Deuteronomy 11:9–11 makes the analogy of the "seed of Egypt" being the hard soil, while sowing seed in the Promised Land would be easy. And, Deuteronomy

fruitfulness and multiplication linguistically and conceptually paired in Deuteronomy's covenant renewal and curses (Deut 28),[35] in the myopia of Exodus' first pharaoh (Exod 1:7, 12, 20), in a recitation in Noah's commission (Genesis 9: 1–2), and finally in the earliest moments in the Hebrew Bible's history: Genesis 1:28. What at first glance appears to be an agricultural parable in fact roots the parable's logic in Israel's creationist history – both linguistically and conceptually.

Which philosophical style does Mark's epistemological focus exhibit? The Hebraic style.

Ethics and the Sermon on the Mount

Jonathan Pennington's recent study – *The Sermon on the Mount and Human Flourishing* – concluded that Jesus' discourse was, in fact, a skillful engagement with the Torah, Israel's wisdom tradition, and Aristotelian virtue ethics. For Pennington, the Sermon is "a work of wisdom literature that is born of two intersecting worlds, Second Temple Judaism and the Greco-Roman virtue tradition."[36] While correcting misunderstandings of the Torah, the Sermon also disruptively engages with the logic of Stoic ethics by strategically departing from them in order to remap them into a fear of God and a redemptive-historical narrative.[37]

To assess this claim, I ask the same questions as above: First, is there a present, persistent, and relevant matter of second-order investigation in

28:38 captures Israel's folly in agricultural metaphor, saying that they sowed much seed, but reap little specifically because they did not listen to Moses. Heil observes that fruitfulness of seed goes further, "Both G. Lohfink ... and L. Ramaroson ... independently of one another, have pointed out the importance and the scriptural background of the metaphor of the 'seed' as representative of the 'people' destined for the eschatological kingdom of God." John Paul Heil, "Reader-Response and the Narrative Context of the Parables about Growing Seed in Mark 4:1–34," *Catholic Biblical Quarterly* 54, no. 2 (1992): 278.

35 The blessings of Deuteronomy foreshadowed in 28:1–10 are now described in terms of Edenic blessing of fruitfulness. All instances of "fruit" in the Pentateuch: Gen 1:11, 12, 29; 3:2, 3, 6; 4:3; 30:2, Exod 10:15; Lev 19:23, 24, 25, 40; 25:19; 26:4, 20; 27:30; Num 13:20, 26, 27; Deut 1:25; 7:13; 26:2, 10; 28:4, 11, 18, 33, 42, 51, 53; 30:9. This particular phrase, "fruitfulness of the ground," is found in varying formulations, but only sparsely throughout the Hebrew Bible. Of its fourteen appearances, "fruit of the ground" occurs once in Genesis 4:3 to refer to Cain's offering and ten times in Deuteronomy to refer to the blessing of obeying Yahweh as the Israelites possess the land. Cf. Gen 4:3; Deut 7:13; 26:2, 10; 28:4, 11, 18, 33, 42, 51; 30:9, Ps 105:35; Jer 7:20; Mal 3:11.

36 Jonathan T. Pennington, *The Sermon on the Mount and Human Flourishing: A Theological Commentary* (Grand Rapids, MI: Baker Academic, 2017), 289.

37 Pennington, *The Sermon on the Mount*, 35.

the Sermon on the Mount (Matt 5–7)? The focus of Matthew's Jesus in this extended discourse straddles epistemology and ethics. In essence, Jesus centers his concern on the audience's understanding of the Torah, but for the sake of flourishing. Hence, corresponding to the virtue ethics tradition, the ethical life intertwines with epistemic ability: "*The Sermon is offering Jesus's answer to the great question of human flourishing, the topic at the core of both the Jewish wisdom literature and that of the Greco-Roman virtue perspective, while presenting Jesus as the true Philosopher-King.*"[38] That "Philosopher-King" then carries out a program of ritualizing his disciples into seeing the kingdom of God and then extending their discernment well beyond anything they could have understood during Jesus' life. Matthew's Jesus is more like a Hebraic Philosopher who is King, willing to play within the culture's conception of virtue formation, but using the virtue-speak to direct the social body of Israel to inhabit a Hebraic philosophical style.

Second, does the author advocate a particular method for understanding the nature of human flourishing? Yes, Jesus authoritatively calls his listeners back to a new (though old) wave of Torah practice, which fulfills the Torah. In Second Temple Judaism, "Torah obedience" entails not just a studied commitment to the letter of the law in the texts of the Torah. Torah obedience also includes devotion to a long and traditioned set of improvised and now codified ritual practices based upon the Torah.[39]

In brief, Jesus explicitly advocates understanding the Torah's logic so that some of the practices formed in Jewish traditions can be appropriately critiqued. Each section of the sermon advocates understanding the kind of human flourishing that Pennington has argued for through rituals – some familiar (Matt 5:21–26) and others counterintuitive (Matt 5:38–48). Some might be surprised to see that Jesus does not despise the ritual innovations of Jewish traditions, such as the Pharisees. Rather, he affirms them as productive but chastises them for being twisted toward personal satisfaction (Matt 23:23–28).

Pennington proposes that Matthew conceptually and linguistically maps virtue into a discourse on fulfilling the Torah – for example, using virtue language such as *telios* and *makarios*. By such moves, the gospel

[38] Italics original. Pennington, *The Sermon on the Mount*, 36.

[39] As Charry sums it, "Covenantal obedience is the rudder, the compass, the map, and the provision for one's voyage through life." Ellen T. Charry, *God and the Art of Happiness* (Grand Rapids, MI: Eerdmans, 2010), 214, also quoted in Pennington, *The Sermon on the Mount*, 44.

writer both reveals the overlap of compatible notions and redirects readers to correctly understand and practice the Torah, the source in which the overlap originates. It is the Aristotelian tradition that overlaps with the Torah and not vice versa. I will later argue that this same kind of usurpatory move becomes a *modus operandi* of Paul in his speeches and epistolary campaigns.

Third, what philosophical style does Matthew's Jesus employ? A prima facie case could be made that the sermon's style is pixelated and networked. Matthew overtly situates the sermon as such. Creationist, ritualist, and transdemographic convictions flow quite easily from the sermon. Jesus directly invokes the Torah and Jewish historical continuity with it to prescribe new rituals based on the same old Torah. I am persuaded that one goal is to understand human flourishing in its communal fullness, something only individualistically grabbed at through the Aristotelian virtue tradition. Another goal inherent to the first would be to correct the misunderstandings or thin understandings of the Torah because of a community's tradition.

"You have heard it said, . . . but I say to you" is not merely addressing gossip. Rather, "you have heard it said" appears to be metonymic for something like: "you have previously understood it this way and structured your ritual life according to this understanding." The transdemographic nature of both the audience of the Sermon and Jesus' later interactions with women, foreigners, and the disabled all signal a transdemographic approach to this human flourishing and clarity of understanding.

The mysterionist conviction is the only one that I cannot effortlessly justify from this sermon alone. Mysterionism coheres well with the apocalyptic tone of the message but is not obvious to the casual reader.[40] The only hint of mysterionism I see in the Sermon is Jesus' correctives and ensuing astonishment at his teaching authority by the audience. The mysterionist presumption behind Jesus' "you have heard it said" correctives would be this: it presumes that what some Israelites thought they clearly understood about the Torah is inaccurate at best and wrong at worst. This kind of disruptive teaching, like Socratic interrogations, seeks

[40] "The Sermon manifests a genetic relationship to the perspective of this Second Temple apocalyptic wisdom (or inaugurated, apocalyptic eschatology), providing a vision for virtue that is oriented to God's coming restorative kingdom." Pennington, *The Sermon on the Mount*, 29.

to convict the listener with a mysterionist's hesitance: I thought I knew X and now I am not so sure.

This Torah obeisance critique is sharpened by the fact that Jesus not only goes after Israel's understanding of the Torah but, by doing so, implicitly undercuts their rituals improvised in the silences of the Torah. In other words, if Jesus is authoritatively correct in his "but I say to you" understanding, it requires a reassessment of their entire ritual and ethical life. Further, by practicing these "new" rites of Torah (e.g., turn the other cheek, do not look lustfully, etc.) they will be able to comprehend the invisible kingdom of God.

In summary, Matthew's Jesus uses the Hebraic philosophical style seasoned with Hellenistic/Aristotelian language and concepts to advocate for a particular way of reasoning about the ethical good life, but also a greater epistemological grasp of the Torah.

7

Paul in Stoic Garments

The scholarly conclusions regarding Paul's relationship with Hellenistic philosophy remain divisive, to put it mildly.[1] They center around the parallels between Paul and contemporary philosophers (e.g., Seneca or Epictetus) or philosophies (e.g., Stoicism, Middle Platonism, Epicureanism, etc.), each with varying theses on Paul's uncritical consumption of such philosophies or his savvy redeployment of Hellenism.[2]

Aside from encyclopedic convictions that often fund such comparisons, noted by Rowe in the previous chapter, the *differences* between Paul and Hellenism are discussed less often.[3] What if his dispositions and diatribes could be related to his view of the prophetic office undergirding Hebraic philosophy as easily as they could to the rhetoric of the cynic or stoic?

Unfortunately, scholars sometimes resort to treating correlation as causation. Parallelomania, a bug that has bitten a few in Pauline scholarship, points up these correlations. Yet, parallels in and of themselves are

[1] The scholarly debates around Paul's relationship to Stoicism are succinctly rehearsed in this exchange between Martyn and Engberg-Pedersen: J. Louis Martyn, "De-apocalypticizing Paul: An Essay Focused on *Paul and the Stoics* by Troels Engberg-Pedersen," *Journal for the Study of the New Testament* 86 (2002): 61–102; Troels Engberg-Pedersen, "Response to Martyn," *Journal for the Study of the New Testament* 86 (2002): 103–14.

[2] There have also been fresh attempts to understand Paul by putting him in philosophical conversation with continental philosophy: Gert Jan van der Heiden et al., eds., *Saint Paul and Philosophy: The Consonance of Ancient and Modern Thought* (Berlin: De Gruyter, 2017).

[3] C. Kavin Rowe, *One True Life: The Stoics and Early Christians as Rival Traditions* (New Haven, CT: Yale University Press, 2016), 182–205.

uninteresting.[4] Demonstrating the motivations behind a witty or naïve employment of contemporary philosophies makes for a more compelling insight.

Though correlations should feature in explanations of his rhetoric, Paul's epistles do not leave us with only Hellenistic philosophical resources. James Thompson's examination of Paul's rhetoric observes modest parallels with several rhetorical forms including the letters of Plato and Aristotle. However, the evidence leads him to conclude, "While one may observe the parallels between Paul's correspondences and ancient letters, his letters do not fit into any category."[5] On most occasions, Paul openly alludes to, cites, and employs the intellectual tradition that he sees as primarily shaping his own thought – the Hebraic tradition – while simultaneously flagging up Hellenism's deficient intellectualism, which he ultimately mitigates. Hence, something else needs to clarify to which camp Paul's writings belong: Hebraic or Hellenistic.

All such studies must wrestle with the tension between the realities that, as Abraham Malherbe said in two different works, "Paul was part of all that he had met,"[6] on the one hand, and "the differences are greater than the similarities," on the other.[7]

Regarding the parallels among Paul, Cicero, Seneca, and Epictetus, N. T. Wright observes that these are to be expected: "The many parallels here would only be surprising to someone who supposed that Paul derived everything from Torah on the one hand and the teaching of Jesus on the other, and indeed that those two sources would themselves be completely discontinuous with pagan moralism."[8] I want to suggest that Paul's style of philosophy is largely Hebraic. However, because Paul's epistles are audience-centric in their formation, so, too, the style

4 E.g., Niko Huttunen's monograph displays fascinating parallels between Paul and Epictetus. But without compelling reasons to understand some kind of savvy employment by Paul of Epictetus, they remain only that – fascinating parallels. *Paul and Epictetus on Law: A Comparison* (Library of New Testaments Studies 405; New York: T&T Clark, 2009).

5 James W. Thompson, *Apostle of Persuasion: Theology and Rhetoric in the Pauline Letters* (Grand Rapids, MI: Baker Academic, 2020), 22.

6 Abraham J. Malherbe, *Paul and the Popular Philosophers* (Minneapolis: Fortress Press, 1989), 67.

7 "Yet in the final analysis, the differences are greater than the similarities, for Paul reaches his conclusions not by intellectual means but through intuition and experience." Abraham J. Malherbe, *Light from the Gentiles: Hellenistic Philosophy and Early Christianity*, Collected Essays, 1959–2012, Vol. 2 (Leiden: Brill, 2014), 729.

8 N. T. Wright, *Paul and the Faithfulness of God* (Minneapolis: Fortress Press, 2013), II, 1376.

is often garbed in Hellenistic philosophy. Nevertheless, the Hebraic style of philosophy is what drives his effort.[9]

To further complicate matters, Paul's instruments of rationality vary significantly from letter to letter – enough to warrant formal lexical examinations. Regarding his use of grammar, syntax, and rhetorical flow, Aída Bensançon Spencer's linguistic analysis of Paul's letters concludes, "It seems apparent that Paul did adapt his [rhetorical] style as he communicated with different persons and congregations."[10]

Paul had a firm second-order grasp on the notions of the new covenant, the kingdom of God, and the like. However, Paul does not appear to have a mere arsenal of stump speeches, rehearsed and repeated *ad nauseum*. Rather, because of his creationist convictions about Israel and his embodied life within these churches, his appeals are like clarifying sculptures of abstract notions hewn from materials in their local quarry. This presumably explains Spencer's stark conclusion: "Among the basic historical variables, *audience is the most important variable*, and time and place of writing the least significant variables within these three pericopes. Theme has a minor influence."[11]

I submit that Paul fits the bill as a Hebraic philosopher. However, his modes of rhetoric make his rootedness in Hebraic philosophy less obvious. What initially appears to be linear Hellenistic style can ultimately turn out to be pixelated, drawing on known narratives and hidden presumptions to complete the logic of his discourse. These are not merely sophisticated enthymemes (i.e., syllogisms with unstated premises), but entire historical narratives understood by the audience and accessed through a sometimes-specious logical flow of rhetoric. Because of this high-context rhetoric that demands what Umberto Eco has termed a deep "encyclopedic competence" from his audiences, Paul's rhetorical and grammatical style varies significantly according to the audience.[12]

[9] John Frederick makes a similar argument about Paul and the author of Colossians, that the similarities are superficial and lacking justification while a Jewish conceptuality to the ethics therein makes more sense of the grammar and language. "The Ethics of the Enactment and Reception of Cruciform Love: A Comparative Lexical, Conceptual, Exegetical/Theological Study of Colossians 3:1–17 and the Patterns of Thought Which Have Influenced It in Their Grammatical/Historical Context" (PhD diss., University of St. Andrews, 2014).

[10] Aída Bensançon Spencer, *Paul's Literary Style: A Stylistic and Historical Comparison of II Corinthians 11:16–12:13, Romans 8:9–39, and Philippians 3:2–4:13* (New York: University Press of America, 1998), 3.

[11] Italics mine. Spencer, *Paul's Literary Style*, 147.

[12] Umberto Eco, *The Limits of Interpretation* (Advances in Semiotics; Bloomington, IN: Indiana University Press, 1994), 145.

Moreover, because he saw the church as a direct product of creation history (creationist) and the Hebrew Scriptures as the authoritative guide for construing the new covenant (networked), wisdom not accessible through linear thought (pixelated) is offered to all (transdemographic) through particular practices (ritualist). This mystery has been revealed through Jesus, to Paul, and now to the church.[13]

Paul, among other NT authors, could be described most simply as critically engaging Hellenistic Judaism and Roman philosophy. He encountered its most basic premises and amended them to make the Hebrew narrative comprehensible, if not always deductively valid, to Hellenized audiences (e.g., Acts 17). Paul can then agree with pagan philosophers and Hellenistic Jewish literature insofar as these tap into a larger network of wisdom about ethics, logic, and physics.[14] Through a keen understanding of the "aspirations and expressions of the moral world of first-century paganism," Paul commits to a pattern of one-upping rather than trashing the Roman philosophies *du jour*.[15] Wright believes that this explains how Paul acts toward Wisdom of Solomon, for instance.[16] Hence, after critically disassembling the comparative project of Troels Engberg-Pedersen, Wright offers what he believes is a more explanatory option overlooked by the debate. Essentially, Wright argues that "if we take the physics, logic, and ethics of the Torah seriously, then Paul's letters will have purchase with his disparate audiences."[17]

I want to extend the logic of Wright's argument into the thesis of this book. To do that, I must again ask the same questions about second-order matters persistently pursued in Paul's letters with a Hebraic philosophical style, just as I have done with Mark and Matthew in the previous chapter.

[13] Paul cites one use of mystery: to prevent presumptions of wisdom, presumably in some kind of naïve way. Romans 11:25, "So that you may not claim to be wiser than you are, brothers and sisters, *I want you to understand this mystery*: a hardening has come upon part of Israel, until the full number of the Gentiles has come in."

[14] N. T. Wright has effectively argued that Paul tends to address this classical tripartite construction of philosophy – ethics, logic, physics – while subsuming contemporary thought into the new kingdom and cosmos awaiting a renewed creation. Wright, *Paul and the Faithfulness of God*, II, 1354–407.

[15] Wright, *Paul and the Faithfulness of God*, II, 1381.

[16] Wright, *Paul and the Faithfulness of God*, II, 1382.

[17] Wright, *Paul and the Faithfulness of God*, II, 1386–406.

Paul's Roman Garb

Before turning to my three standard questions, three preemptive questions must be set out and answered for this task:

1. Was Paul "role-playing" with Hellenistic philosophy?
2. What kind of philosophical literacies did Paul assume of his various audiences?
3. Doesn't Paul take an anti-philosophy position in his epistles?

First, was Paul role-playing with Hellenistic philosophy – displaying expected argument forms in his epistles, but strategically orienting them for an unexpected purpose? As has been argued by Mark J. Edwards concerning Justin Martyr's renowned and dogmatic Platonism, "even when he [Justin Martyr] is speaking as a Platonist, his language, impregnated as it is with the classic phrases, often turns them to a new purpose."[18] Similarly, I want to suggest that Paul evinces an impregnated understanding of Hellenism, but employs it in mode and form for a new purpose – namely, leading his audiences to the true wisdom of Hebraic philosophy.

Second, what kind of philosophical literacies did Paul assume of his various audiences? Eco's term, "encyclopedic competence," pictures a web of readers who all have cultural literacies by which words can quickly cue concepts with all their rich connotations and networks of meanings.[19] (Not to be confused with MacIntyre's critique of the encyclopedist's mode of inquiry.) Three worlds, at the least, appear in the scope of Paul's discourses: Israelite heritage as interpreted through the Hebrew Bible, Second Temple Jewish literature, and the popular consumption of the Roman philosophical schools. As we saw in Mark's Gospel and the Sermon on the Mount, Paul's allusions to the Hebrew Bible are conceptually thick, often sophisticated. They require hearers to transume entire and unspoken narratives into his current discussion in order to complete the logic of his discourses. Competence in the Hebrew Bible/LXX will be especially demanding in letters such as Galatians where the primary audience is Gentile.

The latter two Hellenistic "encyclopedias" are poked at by Paul's reformulations of their "theories, aspirations and expressions" into the

[18] Mark J. Edwards, "On the Platonic Schooling of Justin Martyr," *The Journal of Theological Studies* 42, no. 1 (April 1991): 21.
[19] Eco, *The Limits of Interpretation*, 145.

Hebraic narrative that now extends through Jesus and the coming eschaton.[20]

Third, doesn't Paul take an anti-philosophy position in his epistles (e.g., 1 Cor 1:18–31; Col 2:8)? Moreover, when Paul throws out the philosophy of this world, does he not fail to offer a philosophy to replace it? These questions fall under the explicit versus implicit goal of his rhetoric. Similarly, Paul casts Torah obeisance to the curb as a means of righteousness, and without explicitly offering a replacement for it in Galatians and Romans, for example.

Paul's pixelated conviction and Stoic garb, among other borrowings, helps to explain why "interpreters have agreed with the author of 2 Peter, however, that Paul's letters are 'hard to understand.'"[21] Over the course of an epistle, his pixelated argument clarifies his focus. As he does with Torah-obeisance Judaizers, Paul replaces the philosophies of this world with a better and notably Hebraic philosophy that must be discerned through the many and varied examples he weaves throughout his letters. In this way, the discernment fostered through participation in a community of Hebraic philosophical style matures, offering an ability to read novel circumstances presciently rather than attempt to redomesticate them in the face of conflicting information.[22]

A Case Study: Paul's Argument to the Galatians

Paul's letter to the Galatians fixes on clarifying a misunderstanding amongst a largely Gentile audience about the nature of the gospel (*euangelion*) received directly from him. Judaizers have convinced some that Torah obeisance is required of Gentiles too, a matter ultimately resolved by the apostolic council in Jerusalem (Acts 15). We must ask of Paul's letter the now-standard set of questions.

First, is there a present, persistent, and relevant matter of second-order investigation in Galatians? Many scholars agree that there is one singular focus for clarification in Galatians: the true nature of the gospel. Within a proper understanding of this gospel, Paul must clarify the nature of grace in a cultural milieu of gift-giving that could have distorted grace into a matter of qualification and reciprocation.

20 Wright, *Paul and the Faithfulness of God*, II, 1381.
21 Thompson, *Apostle of Persuasion*, 19.
22 Thanks to Michael Rhodes for pushing me to make this claim.

Paul pursues this line of clarification to the end, but what kind of logic enables him to clarify? At one time, it was common to claim that Paul's letter follows the traditional flow of Roman rhetoric. The task was to then map out the parts to the corresponding Roman rhetorical forms. However, this view has waned more recently, possibly because of the proliferation of competing maps created by the venture. If Paul constrains himself to a Roman rhetorical structure, then at least two scholars ought to agree on that structure. Further, we would expect a natural fit. But as Donald Francois Tolmie observes, "This frequently leads to an application of the model in such a way that it is 'stretched' in order to be able to describe everything that happens in the text."[23]

Even if it is too much to claim a single rhetorical form, Paul is certainly influenced by Roman rhetoric. Yet the Hebraic philosophical style might better explain why he is not compelled to follow rhetorical form closely. J. Louis Martyn's summary of Paul's rhetoric in Galatians points back to the Markan- and Torah-generated epistemology of listening to the correct authority in order to see that which invisibly works in the world:

> Fundamentally, what the Galatians need from Paul, therefore, is not a persuasive and basically hortatory argument as to what they are to do to remedy their situation. They need to be taught by God ... so that they *see* the cosmos that God is bringing into existence as his new creation. Their need of that real vision is what basically determines the nature of Paul's rhetoric.[24]

To this end, Paul follows a compelling line of persuasion, but is not constrained to make the arguments all add up to one large deductive argument. For instance, in working out the non-linear logic that leads up to the "curse of the law" statement, Bonneau concludes, "Although the argument on the curse of the law in [Gal] 3:10–14 is expressed in what appears to be a series of disconcertingly short, epigrammatic statements, it is not inscrutable to the point of eluding all logical explanation."[25]

[23] Donald Francois Tolmie, "A Rhetorical Analysis of the Letter to the Galatians" (PhD diss., University of the Free State Bloemfontein, 2004). Kern does not mince words on what he perceives as a methodological failure: "Not only does rhetorical analysis fail to produce agreement concerning the outline, but even more, the epistle does not conform to the descriptions culled from the handbooks." Phillip H. Kern, *Rhetoric and Galatians: Assessing an Approach to Paul's Epistle* (Society for New Testament Studies Monograph Series 101; New York: Cambridge University Press, 2007), 118.

[24] J. Louis Martyn, *Galatians: A New Translation with Introduction and Commentary* (Anchor Bible Commentary 33a; New York: Doubleday, 1997), 23.

[25] Normand Bonneau, "The Logic of Paul's Argument on the Curse of the Law in Galatians 3:10–14," *Novum Testamentum* 39, no. 1 (January 1997): 79.

This could also be true of the entire letter: a series of arguments not strictly bound by a single deductive logic, but "not inscrutable to the point of eluding all logical explanation." Paul cues his audience with this mix of "narrative substructure" derived from the Hebrew Bible, stories of Jesus, and linear arguments – though these all require the Galatians' cognitive participation to complete the logic of Paul's arguments with known narratives and many missing premises. This does not make Paul incoherent; it merely indicates that, even with learned and culturally acceptable rhetorical forms at his fingertips, he still favors a pixelated style when sharpening a second-order concept.

Is a second-order matter present and persistently examined throughout the letter to the Galatians? Yes, the peculiar nature of the *euangelion*, how to discern its *genus*, and correctly reject its competing *differentiae* are worked out within this letter. I address Galatians chapters three and five below to show how Paul uses linear form but loads it with overlapping examples on top of a narrative substructure. This style, by its effects, makes *genus/differentia* distinctions. What is more, this style of argument only persuades if the audience embodies the Hebraic philosophical style now being taught by Paul. I want to suggest without demonstration that this philosophical style is programmatic for Paul's epistolary campaign.

Second, does the author advocate a particular method for pursuing that second-order understanding? Because of the hortatory nature of the New Testament epistles, this question answers itself. Yes, Paul advocates a series of historical reflections meant to cohere into a particular pattern. However, his rhetorical pokes and prods can vary from an audience's personal experiences with Paul himself (e.g., 1 Cor 1:14–16; Gal 4:12–14; 1 Thess 2:5–12) to macro-structured epistle-length arguments (e.g., Galatians's argument for the "true gospel"). To understand Paul's methodological advocacy, we need to briefly fixate on what he attempts in Galatians.

Paul's concern with second-order conceptuality centers upon a stable yet complex concept of the "gospel" against false views of "gospel." As Klawans observes, in Hellenistic Jewish literature, "nothing illustrates the livelihood of a scholarly field better than disagreement."[26] Defining the nature of the "good news" gets subdivided into a discussion about "grace/ gift" through which it came and the "freedom" it engenders. The radical idea of a work of God coming to the Gentiles as "gift" has been shown by

[26] Jonathan Klawans, *Theology, Josephus, and Understandings of Ancient Judaism* (New York: Oxford University Press, 2012), 5.

John Barclay to disrupt both the Roman cultural norms of "grace" and the concepts of Torah obeisance amongst Jews.[27]

"Grace" (*charis*) hails from the linguistic turf of gift-giving in Roman culture. The term and conceptual scheme operated most commonly in an economy of exchange where strings could always be attached. We can imagine that an impoverished theology of Torah obeisance could wrongly lead Jewish practitioners to a similar view about gift-giving and God. Paul must reorient this conceptual mistake. He does not throw out the cultural notion of grace-as-gift but considers it a worthy concept in need of clarification within an entirely new conceptual order.[28]

Additionally, Paul connects this *gift* action of God on the Galatians' behalf to their freedom. Specifically, they are freed by the gift from slavery to both the Roman conceptual world and cultic practices (*stoicheia*; 4:9), but also Torah obeisance as dictated to them by Judaizers (2:11–14).[29]

Ultimately, he says that freedom itself should be enslaved to the community in love, "fulfilling the *torah*" of Christ (6:2) as "the Israel of God" (6:16). However, his rhetoric of persuasion is striking even if loosely following some canon of Roman rhetoric. Barclay notices that "Paul consciously disregards the criteria that carry persuasive force in normal human discourse .... Paul knew that 'persuasion' is effective only when it deploys the normative criteria cherished by one's audience."[30]

Does Paul advocate a particular method for reasoning through this second-order definition of the "gospel"? Yes, by using layers of overlapping metaphors, question and answer, and outlining the process in "starkly antithetical rhetoric," his method aims at their individual participation in the social body so that they could understand the notional complexity of the *euangelion*.[31] His reasoning did not merely aim at their mental conceptual world. His rhetoric, as he says in the letter (1:1, 10–12), is not persuasive by human standards and is intentionally counterintuitive at points. Here, Paul does not endorse the extreme anti-rhetorical view he

27 John M. G. Barclay, *Paul and the Gift* (Grand Rapids, MI: Eerdmans, 2015), 11–65.

28 "Paul announces the irrelevance of taxonomic systems by which society had been divided in subtly hierarchical terms: old 'antinomies' are here discounted in the wake of a new reality that has completely reordered the world." Barclay, *Paul and the Gift*, 395.

29 "That these [*stoicheia*] are apparently associated *both* with the Galatians' former pagan worship *and* with their adoption of a Jewish calendar (4:9–10) has seemed to many either impossible or nonsensical. But it is hard to deny that Paul makes these associations in both directions." Barclay, *Paul and the Gift*, 409.

30 Barclay, *Paul and the Gift*, 355.

31 Barclay, *Paul and the Gift*, 337.

asserts to the Corinthians where the "good news" was proclaimed "not with eloquent wisdom, so that the cross of Christ might not be emptied of its power" (1 Cor 1:17). Nevertheless, affinities between these two convictions – Galatians and 1 Corinthians – are apparent.

Hence, he is appealing to them by pixelated rhetoric that relies upon networked understanding while simultaneously calling them to adopt a new way of seeing the world. Using a series of dramatic binaries Paul forces the hearer to choose: "There is no place for neutrality … there are two positions, and he has moved from one to the other."[32]

The persuasiveness of Paul's letter is not only found inside the letter. He advocates a pragmatically understood view of the gospel through a new *torah*, revealed by Paul, heard by them in trust, given as a gift (*charis*) without the conventional strings attached, and seen through a new and freer *torah* obeisance. The purpose of their freedom is that they might "slave to one another (*douleuete allēlois*)," and see the evidence of the fruit of the Spirit. The true gospel is known through the *genus* of actions (e.g., "serving one another") with a range of observable outcomes (e.g., love, joy, peace, patience, etc.) and the *differentiae* of false competing gospels (e.g., immorality, impurity, idolatry, etc.). These outcomes ultimately represent the persuasiveness of Paul's argument.

Apart from tangible outcomes, the letter is just sophistry. Indeed, Paul's appeals to his prior behavior while in the presence of the Corinthians, Galatians, or Thessalonians are funded by the same logic (1 Cor 1:14–16; Gal 4:12–14; 1 Thess 2:5–12).

Third, what style of philosophy best captures Paul's pursuit of understanding the "gospel"? Paul's *pixelated* style that draws upon the *networked history* of Israel, from creation to Jesus, often forms the basis of his authority and provides the logic for his arguments. He prescribes a new *torah* obeisance ritualized for all members of the burgeoning movement of The Way, regardless of class, race, gender, or status. Though the phrase "revealed mystery" appears often in Paul, he maintains a mysterionist position, principally due to his countercultural and confusing metaphor of "gift" (*charis*) – that we cannot understand unless God reveals a mystery to us. Though this wisdom, acquired through a ritualized life in community, surpasses man's wisdom, it is never depicted as the keys that unlock all mystery.

I explore the details of Paul's Hebraic style below, but the recent volume on Roman rhetoric and the New Testament summarized the

[32] Barclay, *Paul and the Gift*, 337.

matter succinctly: "'Moses,' not 'Homer,' was the 'Bible' – the source of authority – for early Christian faith and practice, even if that faith and practice were communicated through thoroughly Hellenized rhetorical devices."[33]

Pixelated or linear? The presence of linear argument across Paul's letters has indicated to many that Paul has appropriated Roman forms of rhetoric, possibly to espouse an augmented form of Stoic philosophy.[34] However, two considerations qualify the view of Paul's philosophical style as linear: his audience-centric focus and his interweaving of narrative, metaphor, and rhetorical pixelation in his letters.

As stated above, Paul's audience-centric shaping of his texts appears to take priority: "Among the basic historical variables, audience is the most important variable."[35] Scholars' depictions of Paul's rhetoric have often focused on two aspects: the ostensible rhetorical flare of the letters and the variation in form and technique from letter to letter. Rowe is one such example:

> They do display tight arguments, thematic development, and theological profundity. Yet they make no attempt to grasp things in their entirety and to relate points on the dogmatic compass one to another for the sake of internal self-consistency. Instead ... they were written to particular communities with particular problems in mind – or a message that needed to be heard – and were delivered by a carrier as a "word on target."[36]

This implies that anything I might say about the linearity of Paul's arguments will be contingent on how he constructed it for a particular group *in situ*.

As a secondary consideration, Paul displays comfort with a diverse use of styles, including linear and pixelated approaches. One example of a linear argument is Galatians 2:16–18, where Paul juxtaposes those who

[33] Mikael C. Parsons and Michael Wade Martin, *Ancient Rhetoric and the New Testament: The Influence of Elementary Greek Composition* (Waco, TX: Baylor University Press, 2018), 9.

[34] See Malherbe, *Paul and the Popular Philosophers*; Troels Engberg-Pedersen, *Paul and the Stoics* (Philadelphia: Westminster John Knox Press, 2000).

[35] Italics mine. Spencer, *Paul's Literary Style*, 147.

[36] Italics mine. Rowe, *One True Life*, 86. Similarly, Normand Bonneau says, "Stanley's comment that Paul's concern in Galatians was not to propound 'generalized theological pronouncements that could be extracted without loss from their present argumentative contexts' expresses a growing awareness among exegetes that an adequate interpretation must remain within the specific situation addressed by the letter." Bonneau, "The Logic of Paul's Argument," 60–80.

TABLE 9 *Galatians 2:16 logical flow*

Galatians 2:16–18 (NRSV)	Logical Summary
2:16a Yet we know that a **person is justified (J)**	
not by the **[trust in] works of the law (W)**	$\sim (W \supset J)$
but through **trust in Jesus Christ (C).**	$J \supset C$
2:16b And we have come to **trust in Christ Jesus,**	C
so that we might **be justified** by **trust in Christ,**	$J \supset C$
and not by doing the **works of the law,**	$\sim C \supset \sim J$ (contraposition)
2:16c because no one will **be justified** by the **works of the law.**	$W \supset \sim J$

trust in *torah* obeisance for justification with those who live by trust in the promise given to Abraham – a group that includes Gentiles.[37]

And yet, even at this granularity of the argument, we see evidence of only some linearity. However, missing premises and predicates abound, forcing the reader/hearer to fill in the argument with narratives from the Hebrew Bible, the Gospels, and even the logical steps needed to complete it.[38] Ian Scott refers to this as arguing by "reconfigured story" using "interpretive gaps."[39] Parsons and Martin see the opening of this discourse as exemplifying the classic marks of a Roman style of *narratio* (Gal 2:1–2).[40] Even Paul's linear deductive rhetoric is thus pixelated in its details. In Table 9, I map out the logic of these two sentences that form one of the longer strings of strict linear logic in Paul. In Table 10, I have noted the missing-but-presumed elements to Paul's argument in the right column where I attempt to represent his argument's logical flow, but without quantifiers.

One clear example of *modus ponens* ($P \supset Q$; i.e., "If P, then Q.") appears here (2:16a–b), as long as we draw it inferentially from the first half of the sentence (2:16a). We can construct both a *modus ponens* and *tollens* version of the argument after supplying a conclusion in the first instance and an equivalency in the second. Notice that we must supply equivalencies from other parts of the letter:

[37] Martyn sees this trust as "a human deed" but "more than a human deed" to "trust the God who is active in the gospel." Martyn, *Galatians*, 276.

[38] Martyn refers to this pericope in Galatians 2 as "one of the most tightly concentrated theological statements in all of Paul's letters." Martyn, *Galatians*, 263.

[39] For a close analysis of Paul's argument in Galatians 2, see: Ian W. Scott, *Paul's Way of Knowing: Story, Experience, and the Spirit* (Grand Rapids, MI: Baker Academic, 2009), 179–98.

[40] The elements of *narratio* rhetorical exercise: person, action, time, place, manner, and cause. Parsons and Martin, *Ancient Rhetoric and the New Testament*, 72, 98–99.

TABLE 10 *Galatians 2:16 as* modus ponens / modus tollens

Modus Ponens	Premise 1: If "we are justified," then "we trust in Jesus Christ" (16a)	P1: J ⊃ C
	Premise 2: "We have come to trust Christ Jesus" (16b)	P2: C
	Conclusion: "We are justified"	∴ J
Modus Tollens	Premise 1: Iff[41] "we are justified," then "we trust in Jesus Christ" (16a)[42]	P1: J ⊃ C
	Premise 2: If we trust in "works of the law," then "not justified" (16c)	P2: W ⊃ ~J
	Premise 3: If we trust in "works of the law," then *no trust in Jesus* **(unstated)**	P3: W ⊃ ~C
	Premise 4: If we do *not trust in Jesus*, then we are *not justified* **(unstated)**	P4: ~C ⊃ ~J
	Premise 5: "Different gospel" (D) [1:6–7] is equivalent to "If W, then J" **(unstated)**	P5: D ≡ (W ⊃ J)
	Premise 6: "Different gospel" teachers do *not trust in Jesus* **(unstated)**	P6: D ⊃ ~C
	Conclusion: "Different gospel" teachers are *not justified* **(unstated)**	∴ D ⊃ ~J

Consider how much work Paul's logic requires of his audience. The predicates of his arguments are entire narrative frameworks with their own logic, textual histories, and prophetic layers of interpretation. Items J, C, W, and D in Tables 9 and 10 each rely on understanding of the narrative dynamics supplied by the hearer in order to realize the import of Paul's appeal. There is nothing implicitly coherent about the metaphors and analogies in and of themselves: "being justified," "trust in Christ Jesus," "works of the law," or "gospel." These all require information hauled over from narratives pixelated throughout the Hebrew literature and drawn together in the present configuration to become coherent for the audience.

I have symbolized the deductive force of Paul's terse argument above only to show its partial function. Even in this tiniest of arguments, poised to be drawn to a deductive conclusion, Paul jumps in and out of

41 "Iff" means "if and only if."

42 Because Paul sets justification up as a problem of knowledge – "we know that" – the logic of the conditional appears to flow from "justified" to observable "trust in Jesus Christ". Thanks to Joshua Blander for helping me sort out this small yet complex logical problem.

networked narratives and deductions, forcing the reader to pull together its elements, background narratives, and complete the argument to a conclusion on his behalf. An entire wing of scholarship has analyzed Paul's interweaving of incomplete narratives known to his audience as a form of argument.[43] I will not rehearse those analyses here other than to note that it further calls into question any flat claim of linear argumentation in Paul.

In many ways, Paul's strategic use of missing premises and narrative portions reminds us of the Torah's narratized legal code which Paul also parrots (see discussion in Chapter 4). The readers are enjoined to visualize the drama and complete the thoughts themselves.

As a comparison to a linear autonomous argument in Stoic philosophy, Epictetus reasons linearly and deductively on the scrutiny of logic itself:

> Since it is reason which makes all other things articulate and complete, and reason itself must be analysed and made articulate, what is it that shall effect this? Plainly, reason itself or something else. That something else either is reason or it will be something superior to reason, which is impossible. If it is reason, who again will analyse that reason? For if it analyses itself, so can the reason with which we started. If we are going to call in something else, the process will be endless and unceasing.[44]

Table 11 plots how Epictetus stated the argument quite simply and without any hidden premises given the question, "What analyzes reason: itself or something else?":

TABLE 11 *Epictetus' argument for reason analyzing everything*

P1: Reason analyzes everything, what can analyze reason? Itself (R) or something else (SE)?	P1: R v SE
	P2: SE = R v R+
P2: SE is either R or "something superior to R" (R+).	P3: ~R+
P3: It is impossible for something to be superior to R.	∴ SE ≡ R
∴ [Conclusion implied]	

[43] For a summary of that scholarship, see Bruce W. Longenecker, "The Narrative Approach to Paul: An Early Retrospective," *Currents in Biblical Research* 1, no. 1 (2002): 88–111.

[44] Epictetus, *The Discourses and Manual*, trans. Percy E. Matheson (Oxford: Oxford University Press, 1916), I, 17, 34.

In contrast to much Stoic philosophy of the day, Paul's rhetoric has elements of many styles of rhetoric that appear to be audience-dependent and extend beyond a missing premise to create a pixelated logic that requires the hearer's participation.[45]

Martyn weds this statement (Gal 2:15–21) with similar formulas in Romans and 1 Corinthians as a "rectification tradition" that might have been known to Paul.[46] So even here in Galatians, we may be reading his argument for the "rectification tradition" and not an argument *de novo*.

Though not overtly reasoned in this text, Martyn maps out nine theological convictions and phases of the "rectification" argument where Paul is "drawing heavily on traditions in the Old Testament and on strands of Jewish thinking about rectification."[47] His emerging-picture metaphor used to tease out these implications is telling of Paul's pixelated-linearity style: "While these Jewish-Christian formulas show variations, *a picture of considerable coherence does emerge from them*."[48]

In Paul's letter to the Galatians, even the linear spaces of the letter require retrieval and supply of narratives from the Hebrew Bible, the Torah's legal frameworks, and the stories of Jesus and his apostles, all delivered through a matrix of overlapping legal, agricultural, athletic, accounting, baking, social (e.g., slavery), and other embodied metaphors (e.g., eating, falling away, etc.).[49]

Additionally, Paul develops an unambiguous line of dualities to steer his audience, but Barclay notes that these too "pile up to complicate the picture."[50] Polar opposites dot the landscape of Paul's emerging picture, clearing the way for just two mutually exclusive options and forcing the reader onto one path and not the other.

45 Epictetus, *Discourses and Manual*, I, 17, 1–2.

46 Romans 3:25, 4:25; 1 Corinthians 6:11. Martyn, *Galatians*, 264–65.

47 J. Louis Martyn, *Theological Issues in the Letters of Paul* (New York: T&T Clark, 1997), 143. His nine points of the "coherent picture" are these: (1) Rectification is an act of God; (2) In that act God sets right things that have gone wrong; (3) What has made things wrong is transgressions against God's covenant committed among God's people; (4) What makes transgressing members of God's people right is God's forgiveness; (5) God's rectification is therefore God's mercy; (6) The Law is not mentioned because its continuing validity is taken for granted; (7) God has accomplished his rectifying forgiveness in Christ, specifically in Christ's death and resurrection; (8) God's messianic grace in the context of God's Law can be found; and (9) God's rectifying forgiveness in Christ is confessed without explicit reference to faith. Martyn, *Galatians*, 265–69.

48 Italics mine. Martyn, *Galatians*, 265.

49 These metaphor examples were gleaned only from a small passage of Galatians (2:1–15)!

50 Barclay, *Paul and the Gift*, 337.

Though commenting on only one portion of Galatians, Bonneau's observation seems apropos of much:

> The logic implied in 3:10–14, the unexpressed assumptions linking Paul's argument from one step to the next, are not to be sought in extrinsic theological schemes, but can be teased out of the earlier sections of the letter. … Paul hopes to persuade them that there is only one true gospel – the law-free gospel that he had preached from the outset. The diverse arguments in the letter are all calculated to achieve this end.[51]

The complexity of Paul's letters has likely been responsible for generating many scholarly maps of his rhetoric. So T. David Gordon claims, "An examination of the variety of connecting terms and particles reveals that Galatians is, essentially, a single argument. … At least by literary canons, Galatians is not a series of arguments about different matters but a series of sub-arguments about essentially one matter (which itself may, of course, have many ramifications)."[52]

Richard Hays maps the argument of Galatians historically, where the "proleptic character of the promise to Abraham" becomes the avenue for connecting ideas, even if not in deductive structures.[53] Paul's singular argument with diverse routes, onramps, and offshoots, might be a case for suggesting the following: *this is a by-product of Paul's bent toward pixelated style dressed in the Roman rhetorical garb and fueled by his mysterionist, creationist, transdemographic, and ritualist convictions of the Hebraic philosophical style.*

Networked or autonomist? Hays also delves into Paul's networked mind to reveal a Paul who freely engages the Hebrew Scriptures for present rhetorical effect, but only in the ears of a scripturally literate audience. The fact that Paul "employs citations from Deut. 27:26, Hab. 2:4, and Lev. 18:5 to drive a wedge between Law and Faith," or that Paul "take[s] the liberty of conflating Gen. 12:3 … with Gen. 22:18" in order to make claims about Gentile inheritance already betrays his networked tactics.[54]

Paul's rhetoric requires the hearer to summon and employ a host of requisite narratives. The pervasiveness of these narrative appeals along with narrative references used to complete the logic of arguments within

[51] Bonneau, "The Logic of Paul's Argument," 80.

[52] T. David Gordon, "The Problem at Galatia," *Interpretation* 41 (1987): 33, 34.

[53] For Hays, correct understanding of the "gospel" grasps it as (1) "prepreached to Abraham [the gospel] is said to be that 'all the Gentiles' (*panta ta ethne*) will be blessed in him," (2) that Scripture itself is the "quasi-personified" agent who does the prepreaching, and (3) the preproclamation to the Gentiles "must be understood retrospectively," as fulfilled by the church. Richard B. Hays, *Echoes of Scripture in the Letters of Paul* (New Haven, CT: Yale University Press, 1989), 106.

[54] Hays, *Echoes of Scripture in the Letters of Paul*, 106, 109.

Galatians leave no room for autonomous arguments that rise and fall on the internal logic of their appeals.

Though biblical narratives and Gospel stories pervade Paul's thinking and his audience's expectations, these stories do not merely haunt their cultural background as a shared memory. Rowe sees this as a significant point of departure in those who understand the use of narrative in Paul and those who do not. Therefore, I quote him at length:

> This is not at all to say, of course, that we should think of narrative as something that is only in the background of practices, normative judgments, metaphysical accounts of the world, and so forth. *Narrative, to the contrary, is present in all layers of a tradition's particularity (even if inchoate or left unarticulated).* Nor should we think of any sort of regular historical order, as if narratives must precede practice or reflective questioning. ... To put it into terms more familiar to scholars of the New Testament and early Christianity, demonstrating that Paul's letters have a "narrative substructure" simultaneously elucidates the ground of their possibility as intelligible speech.[55]

To play devil's advocate, let us say that we wanted to argue the point against Paul: the gospel requires works of the Torah. What part of Paul's argument would we engage and on what basis? Presumably, we cannot fault the logic of the argument itself that includes its unstated premises. Rather, we might find fault with Paul's interpretation of the life and death of Jesus and how it corresponds to the current traditions of *torah* obeisance. In other words, we are not attacking the logic of the argument, but, rather, Paul's understanding of history itself, and hence his authority.

Presuming Paul knows this, we can now make sense of how he uses a trope from Deuteronomy to establish his Sinai-like prophetic authority and understanding at the fore of the letter. Like Moses' instructions in Deuteronomy (Deut 4:33–40), no one, not even a "messenger from heaven" can teach a different gospel (Gal 1:8). Why not? Because of the historically unique and personally witnessed events of the first preaching, which is recalled in a Hebraism from Deuteronomy's account of Sinai: "*before your eyes* that Jesus Christ was publicly portrayed as crucified" (cf. Deut 29:2; Gal 3:1). Like Jeremiah, Paul was appointed to this prophetic task in the womb, "before I was born" (cf. Jer 1:4–5; Gal 1:15).

In brief, Paul's prophetic authority has been uniquely authenticated before the eyes of the Galatians and constitutes the context that enables his arguments to function.

[55] Italics mine. Rowe, *One True Life*, 200–201.

Creationist or abstractionist? I do not want to belabor points already made above. Only a few comments are needed here. The Hebraic tropes used to authenticate Paul's task (e.g., Gal 1) and his disdain for the misinterpreted life drawn from the Torah (i.e., "works of the law") signal that his goal is not abstraction for the sake of having mental objects to reflect upon. Below, we will see that the rituals of the new *torah* gifted to the church allow the Galatians to discern the invisible kingdom in its *genus* and *differentia*.

Even common appeals to a divine figure called "God" (*theos*) are not abstractions about *some god separate from time and space*. Paul's references to "god" are references to the storyline of the entire Hebrew Bible. "God ... is not a general term in Paul's grammar. ... The term God is quite specific and bound to a particular history. God is the God who elected Israel to be his people."[56]

Exploiting a networked method, Paul examined the Galatian church by examining Abraham, a hair's breadth away from the creation accounts. As Richard Hays has shown, "[Paul's] readings of the scriptural texts rarely seek to excavate messianic prophecies. Instead, his prevailing concern is to show how the church is prefigured and guided by Scripture," and in Galatians, it is Genesis.[57]

Ritualist or mentalist? The entire letter is about the ritual life of the early church, how the Galatians should practice it, and how their ritual practices should inform their conceptualization of second-order ideas such as "gospel," "grace," and "freedom." Rounding the last turn in the argument of the letter, Paul focuses on their habit-formation, rituals, and embodied lives (Gal 5:16–25). Just as in Romans, Ephesians, Colossians, and 1 Corinthians, the rites and practices shape and illuminate their understanding of the gospel and the contours of the kingdom of God.

Embodied life is the problem in Galatians – in other words, "works of the Law" – but it also becomes the conceptual solution that maps onto a larger framework of ritual epistemology across the biblical canon.[58] The basic logic suggests that, if what Paul argues is correct, it can be known through restraint from "the works of the flesh," crucifying "the flesh with its passions," and practicing "the fruits of the spirit" (Gal 5:19–24) – all

[56] Rowe, *One True Life*, 87.

[57] Hays, *Echoes of Scripture in the Letters of Paul*, 121.

[58] See Dru Johnson, *Knowledge by Ritual: A Biblical Prolegomenon to Sacramental Theology* (Journal of Theological Interpretation Supplements 13; Winona Lake, IN: Eisenbrauns/PennState Press, 2016), 137–250.

summed in his metaphorical commendations to "live by the Spirit" and "keep in step with the Spirit" (Gal 5:25).

If Paul carried a mentalist conviction in his philosophical style, we would expect to see a programmatic diminution of the body and constant return to seeking inner spiritual tranquility as the invisible means of intellectual grasping. On the contrary, Barclay observes that despite the "negative connotation of the term σάρξ [*sarx*] developed earlier ... [Paul] displays no negativity toward the body as such, and his conceptual map is not recognizably influenced by a bias toward the inner or the invisible."[59] Separating himself from his Hellenistic Jewish predecessors, Paul specifically targets embodied behaviors, not abstractions to be mentally maneuvered.[60]

Transdemographic or classist? This letter specifically aims at helping the audience to develop expertise in comprehending an invisible kingdom and the second-order nature of the gospel. Whether Paul brings a classist or transdemographic conviction to the task is a primary concern. Paul explicitly develops a line of argument that speaks to the natural and artificial boundaries that separate people: Jew/Gentile, slave/free, and male/female. As paradigms of these divisions that might instantiate a classist conviction, Paul creates just one separable class – "as many of you as were baptized" (Gal 3:27) – and abolishes any artificial class distinction that might be foisted upon the Galatians. In this single move, Paul establishes a case for transdemographic convictions.

Mysterionist or domesticationist? Renowned NT scholar Albert Schweitzer once tackled what he saw as the incongruence of Paul's apparent mysticism alongside his use of logic. Of the two he said: "[Paul] is a logical thinker and his mysticism is a complete system. In the interpretation and application of Scriptural passages he may proceed by the leaps and bounds of Rabbinic logic, but in his mysticism he proceeds with a logical consistency, which in its simplicity and clearness compels assent as a piece of thinking."[61]

Schweitzer suggests by a later analogy of a spider's web that Paul's thinking appears simple, but soon becomes a "hopeless tangle as soon as

[59] "We are able to appreciate in a new way how *communal practice is integral to the expression of the good news*." Not only expression, but also that any coherent understanding of the good news would have only happened in communal practice for Paul. Barclay, *Paul and the Gift*, 394. Italics original.

[60] Barclay, *Paul and the Gift*, 444.

[61] Albert Schweitzer, *The Mysticism of Paul the Apostle*, trans. William Montgomery (Baltimore: John Hopkins University Press, 1998), 139.

it is cut loose" from the tightly interwoven structure of his thought.[62] If correct, would Paul then conceive of some kind of one-to-one transfer of his whole understanding to his audience from his partial perspective? Or, would he presume that the whole is not the goal?

Galatians argues for a specifically revealed view about the gospel from God through Paul. Paul's question then becomes: Does mystery remain or resolve as a result of this teaching? To repeat Rowe's generalizing comment: "[Paul's epistles] do display tight arguments, thematic development, and theological profundity. Yet they make no attempt to grasp things in their entirety and to relate points on the dogmatic compass one to another for the sake of internal consistency."[63]

While Paul attempts to illuminate this second-order matter – of what counts as the *genus* of the necessary notions of the gospel – he hones just two facets already noted above: freedom and grace. This is suggestive, and only that, of his broader view of mystery as renderable but not domesticable. "The need was not to reach up to God a little higher in ever-clearer knowledge but for God to make himself known to them from entirely beyond what they were in principle able to know."[64]

The basic view of "mystery" from Paul's view of the gospel is not restricted to the mysterionist conviction I have referred to in this work. Rather, "mystery" for Paul is what T. J. Lang calls a "'once hidden, now revealed' mystery schema" that stems from "the social and intellectual consequences of the dual Christian commitment to apocalyptic newness and the ancient pedigree of Israel's history."[65] Paul does not use the term "mystery" to refer to the inability to exhaustively understand something. Hence, merely looking at the instances of the term "mystery" across Paul will not yield the right kind of analysis of Paul's view of knowableness.

Across Paul's corpus of letters, we do find a consistent return to a mysterionist conviction, not through the term *mystērion*, but rather in his descriptions of the *beyond-ness* of knowing.

Incomprehensible: "that which surpasses (*hyperechousa*) all understanding" (Phil 4:7),

62 Schweitzer, *The Mysticism of Paul the Apostle*, 140.
63 Rowe, *One True Life*, 86.
64 Rowe, *One True Life*, 5.
65 T. J. Lang, *Mystery and the Making of a Christian Historical Consciousness: From Paul to the Second Century* (Beihefte zur Zeitschrift für die neutestamentliche Wissenschaft 219; Boston: De Gruyter, 2015), 6.

Rendering awe: "lest you be wise ... I do not want you to be unaware of this mystery" (Rom 11:25)
Partial sufficient knowing: "Now I know in part, then [the eschaton] I shall know fully" (1 Cor 13:12)
Quality of knowledge: "surpassing greatness of revelations" (2 Cor 12:7)

Ephesians, a disputed text in the Pauline corpus, contains the most mystery language, but also the language of that which transcends our ability to domesticate knowledge:

Knowledge as partially attained: "you can perceive my insight into this mystery of Christ" (Eph 3:4)
Knowing surpassing knowledge: "to know the love of Christ that surpasses knowledge" (Eph 3:19)
Limits of imagination: "to him who is able to do far more abundantly than all that we ask or think" (Eph 3:20)

When Paul wants his audience to understand something, and to embody practices in order to understand, he qualifies their comprehension with metaphors and phrases of mysterionism, highlighting that which can be known, but not without remainder.

This case for Paul's Hebraic philosophical style is necessarily partial for the sake of being paradigmatic at best. The hope is that what I have demonstrated above can generalize to at least some of Paul's other writings in whole or in part, how Paul "'destroys arguments' (2 Cor. 2:4) in a way that was unparalleled in both Jewish and Greco-Roman letters."[66]

Conclusions about Hebraic Philosophy in the New Testament

In the New Testament literature, we see the Hebraic philosophical style encountering new cultural contexts. In this sense, the New Testament is one of the best places to see this style at work. Surrounded by Hellenistic Judaism and the literary creations of that period, the NT authors eschewed those works in favor of what they called "the Scriptures" also known as the Law, Prophets, and the Psalms.[67] The widespread silence regarding the Apocryphal and pseudepigraphal literature of Hellenistic Judaism also suggests a possible critique of that speculative tradition as well.[68]

[66] Thompson, *Apostle of Persuasion*, 267.
[67] Iain Provan, *The Reformation and the Right Reading of Scripture* (Waco, TX: Baylor University Press, 2017), 39–41.
[68] Provan, *The Reformation and the Right Reading of Scripture*, 71.

PART IV

PROTOTYPES OF HEBRAIC PHILOSOPHICAL ARGUMENTS

8

Hebraic and Scientific Epistemology

Introduction to Part IV

In these last chapters, I sketch out some examples of philosophical topics developed in the Hebraic style across the Christian Scriptures. I will begin with epistemology as a strong case, mainly because I have written on it extensively elsewhere and feel confident about my findings. I will make a tentative case for elements of truth and logic in justification across the Hebraic philosophical style.

All of these examples are meant to be illustrative, to fire up the theological and philosophical imaginations of scholars, and, chiefly, to spin up more research in this area ripe for study.

As I investigated the epistemology of the Scriptures, it became clear to me that the Hebraic account was neither primitive nor lacking. Rather, the biblical authors seemed aware of the same epistemic matters that have driven the scientific enterprise and, unlike other ancient epistemologies, avoided the logical conundrums upon which logical positivism built its house (or, the petard upon which it hoisted itself). That struck me as a remarkable feat and generated a suite of questions to put to the biblical texts.

This discovery of the deep commensurability between Hebraic epistemology that flows into the New Testament and scientific epistemology today opens the doors for other avenues of philosophical thought. For instance, Yoram Hazony, Joshua Berman, and David Novak, among others, have written on the possibilities of political philosophy in the Hebrew Bible.[1]

[1] David Novak, *Jewish Social Ethics* (New York: Oxford University Press, 1992); Joshua A. Berman, *Created Equal: How the Bible Broke with Ancient Political Thought* (New York:

If a Hebraic philosophy persists into the thinking of Jesus and the apostles, then those Jewish biblical projects could be expanded fruitfully into the New Testament texts. Similarly, the field of ethics has received much attention amongst biblical scholars, though there may be new avenues to pursue given what I have argued here.[2]

Important for my task, I view this work as handing off a heuristic to specialists and laypersons alike. Ultimately, it is up to them to assess the veracity of my generalist claims here.

In this chapter, I will lay out in short form what I have previously argued in several works: that a discernible and Hebraic epistemological process is present, relevant, and persistent across the Christian Scriptures. Moreover, when looking for present-day analogs for biblical epistemology, the scientific enterprise best fits the bill.

In the next chapter, "Biblical Truth and Human Logic," I show how the Hebraic notion of truth differs from being merely the opposite of false and reinforces its connections to scientific epistemology. Finally, in Chapter 10, "Pictures of Justification," I explore the logic of justification that convinces characters in the biblical narratives who use experiments, ouija, and witnesses.

These are proposals. All of these are open to revision upon closer inspection, but I offer them to those who still struggle to see a starting point for a Hebraic epistemology or logic, for instance, and rigorous enough method by which one could proceed.

Hebraic Epistemology

Epistemology, in the Anglo-American world, is generally concerned with the nature and justification (or, warrant) of *knowledge*.[3] Justification will be examined more closely in the following chapter.

The nature of knowledge itself will not be the primary concern of biblical accounts of epistemology, for several reasons. First, biblical

Oxford University Press, 2011); Yoram Hazony, *The Philosophy of Hebrew Scripture* (New York: Cambridge University Press, 2012); Jeremiah Unterman, *Justice for All: How the Jewish Bible Revolutionized Ethics* (Philadelphia: Jewish Publication Society, 2017).

2 Cf. John Barton, *Ethics in Ancient Israel* (New York: Oxford University Press, 2017); Christopher J. H. Wright, *Old Testament Ethics for the People of God* (Downer's Grove, IL: InterVarsity, 2004); Robertson McQuilkin and Paul Copan, *An Introduction to Biblical Ethics: Walking in the Way of Wisdom* (Downer's Grove, IL: InterVarsity, 2014).

3 Matthias Steup's article aptly captures much of what flies under the flag of epistemology in analytic philosophy departments over the last century. Matthias Steup and Ram Neta, "Epistemology," *The Stanford Encyclopedia of Philosophy*, Summer 2020 ed., ed. Edward N. Zalta, https://plato.stanford.edu/archives/sum2020/entries/epistemology/.

authors regularly appeal to second-order matters of *knowing*, but they do not typically construe knowledge-as-a-thing. Instead, they focus on the rituals, social mechanisms, and justification of knowing more than an abstract object called "knowledge."

Rather than press the biblical literature to see if analytic concepts will drip out, I pursue the knowledge-talk in the texts, beginning in the creation account and moving forward. Just as the word "mystery" could not be reconciled by a word study in Paul's epistles, merely looking at the term "know" or "knowledge" might presuppose too much, or even mislead us. The biblical authors construct an epistemological process framed around hearing and seeing, and include varying degrees of competence, also called "wisdom." Hence, word studies will not always be profitable when they stem from encyclopedist assumptions.

Does the biblical epistemology follow a Hebraic philosophical style? From Eden to the NT epistles, the biblical authors advocate that the best instances of knowing abstract matters happen through contact with the inherently pixelated world, guided by an expert who presents overlapping examples through ritualized embodied practice (ritualist). This kind of knowing is for the whole community (transdemographic), rooted in creation and Israel's formation (creationist), and has delimiting experience – bringing one to know something while simultaneously making them aware of their ignorance and the object's inexhaustible richness (mysterionist).

In the next section, I quickly survey some of the highlights of biblical epistemology and then put them in conversation with one example of twentieth-century scientific epistemology. For those who need a more detailed demonstration of both the biblical evidence and its relation to scientific knowing, please see my monographs: *Epistemology and Biblical Theology: From the Pentateuch to Mark's Gospel* (Routledge, 2018) and *Knowledge by Ritual: A Biblical Prolegomenon to Sacramental Theology* (Eisenbrauns/PennState Press, 2016).

Knowing: From Creation to New Covenant

Does the creation account care about knowing? Yes! The making of humanity includes a story of man's discovery of woman – the first act of knowing in biblical history (cf. Gen 2:20b, 23).[4] The single command

[4] This section is adapted from Dru Johnson, "A Biblical Nota Bene on Philosophical Inquiry," *Philosophia Christi* (Blog), Evangelical Philosophical Society Symposium, www.epsociety.org/library/articles.asp?pid=238.

to the man – eat from all the trees – is qualified with a caveat about a single tree conspicuously given an epistemic title: the tree of knowledge of good and evil. The ensuing story also turns on knowledge, though "knowing" is the more accurate term.[5]

Genesis

Epiphany results from a guided process in both Genesis 2 and 3. In Genesis 2, the man is guided to see that the woman, and not the animals, is his proper mate. In Genesis 3, the man comes to know "good and evil," whatever that may mean, by listening to the voice of the woman who was listening to the voice of the serpent and performing that which the serpent alone suggests.[6] Indeed, the only indictment of the humans – the only time when God identifies what went wrong in Eden – is surprisingly the error of listening; this is the cardinal diagnosis of error (Gen 3:17). "Because you *listened to the voice* of your wife and ate . . ." God identifies the man's wife as the wrong voice, though his wife was listening to the voice of the serpent with the man present (Gen 3:6).[7]

5 Knowledge is not primarily portrayed as factive or propositional across the Bible, but as a skill or adeptness. I realize that this claim pulls from longitudinal data across the biblical literature, but in general, it is more appropriate to say that the biblical authors tend to write about knowing as a skill rather than knowledge as an object. Indeed, they are keenly interested in fleshing out who knows what and how, but more concerned with the constituent factors of *how* people know than *what* they know. The two cardinal factors in how one knows in the Eden and beyond might surprise the casual reader of Scripture. The quality of knowing is contingent upon (1) acknowledging the appropriate authoritative voice, signified by the language of "listening," and then (2) doing what that authority prescribes in order to grasp what they are showing, signaled by the language of "seeing." When this process happens in the correct order, the biblical authors call it "knowing" or "seeing." When the process is habituated to refine one's knowing, biblical authors will later deem it "wisdom." I can only speak of tendencies, as the biblical authors are many and have diverse linguistic depictions of knowing gone right and gone wrong.

6 The ambiguity of the phrase "knowledge of good and evil" has not stifled speculation. I prefer to take it as a generally ambiguous term, only later clarified in Deuteronomy 1:39 to mean something akin to "those who have yet to disobey God." For a discussion of various speculations about this phrase, see: Dru Johnson, *Epistemology and Biblical Theology: From the Pentateuch to Mark's Gospel* (Routledge Interdisciplinary Perspectives on Biblical Criticism 4; New York: Routledge, 2018), 33–34, 90–91.

7 In Eden and beyond in Scripture, when that process goes awry, people still know something through their participation in the process. However, the biblical authors describe this kind of knowing as erroneous, derived from a hardened heart or stiff-necked-ness, they either refuse to acknowledge appropriate authorities (e.g., the case of Pharaoh in Exodus) or refuse to perform the instruction of the authority (e.g., wandering Israel or the disciples in the gospels). Either way, everyone comes to know something, and the biblical authors

Even when Yahweh Elohim enters the garden after the man has outed himself, God's question was not, "how did you figure this out?" or, "how did you deduce this truth?" God's only question to the man was, "who told you?" and subsequently, "have you eaten?" Both questions presume that another authoritative voice has entered Eden (Gen 3:11). This presumption is confirmed in God's indictment that parallels his questions of the man: "because you listened to the voice of [an other] and ate" (Gen 3:17).

I suggest that this passage takes primacy in the epistemological project of the Bible. In the New Testament, Luke 24 quotes Genesis 3 (LXX), but this time it is a positive instance of knowing. The disciples on the road to Emmaus are "kept from knowing" the resurrected Jesus as he explains to them the recent events through the Hebrew Bible (Luke 24:16). It is not until food enters the story that, like the man and woman in Eden, "their eyes were opened and they knew" (cf. Gen 3:6; Luke 24:31). Of course, I am only skimming the surface of these rich epistemological accounts and moving quickly for the sake of brevity.[8]

From this point on, whose voice the Israelites accredit as authoritative determines what and how they know throughout Scripture.

Exodus

In Exodus, the epistemic language manifests more directly. The first pharaoh is described simply as "a new king … who did not know Joseph" (Exod 1:8) and therefore oppresses the Hebrews with cruel slavery. Another pharaoh rises to power over the enslaved Hebrews. When Moses confronts that pharaoh for the first time, the pharaoh's response rehearses all the same language from Eden: "Who is Yahweh that I should *listen to his voice* and let Israel go? *I do not know* Yahweh and I will not let Israel go" (Exod 5:2).

"So that you will know" formulas then punctuate the plagues of Exodus, aimed specifically at Pharaoh knowing Yahweh's relationship to Israel *and Israel knowing it too*:

> "I will take you as my people, and I will be your God. <u>You shall know</u> that I am Yahweh your God, who has freed you from the burdens of the Egyptians." (6:7)

point toward knowing with discernment as the goal and knowing erroneously as the foolish path to Sheol – that is, the grave.

[8] For those who need more exegetical evidence, please consult Dru Johnson, *Biblical Knowing: A Scriptural Epistemology of Error* (Eugene, OR: Cascade, 2013) or my detailed analysis in *Epistemology and Biblical Theology*.

"By this [Pharaoh] *shall know* that I am Yahweh ... the Nile, and it shall turn into blood." (7:17)

"... so that [Pharaoh] *may know* that there is no one like Yahweh our God.'" (Exod 8:10)

"But on that day I will set apart the land of Goshen, where my people live, so that no swarms of flies shall be there, that you may know that I Yahweh am in this land." (8:22)

"For this time I will send all my plagues upon you yourself, and upon your officials, and upon your people, so that you may know that there is no one like me in all the earth." (9:14)

"The thunder will cease, and there will be no more hail, so that you may know that the earth is Yahweh's." (9:29)

"... that you may tell your children and grandchildren how I have made fools of the Egyptians and what signs I have done among them – so that you may know that I am Yahweh." (10:2)

"But not a dog shall growl at any of the Israelites ... so that you may know that Yahweh makes a distinction between Egypt and Israel." (11:7)

"I will harden Pharaoh's heart, and he will pursue them ... and the Egyptians shall know that I am Yahweh." (14:4)

"And the Egyptians shall know that I am Yahweh, when I have gained glory for myself over Pharaoh, his chariots, and his chariot drivers." (14:18)

The exodus story ends on a high note, demonstrating that Moses has been established as Israel's trusted authority, Israel has listened to Moses, and Israel has come to know Yahweh as her God through the process. But before crossing the Red Sea, we find out that bare observation does not necessarily produce understanding. Moses explains to the Israelites what is going to happen in terms of their sight, which quickly becomes understood as metaphorical for understanding as it is throughout Scripture.[9] In other words, they could all witness these events together, but they could also misunderstand them. Only after they have crossed the sea does the reader learn that Israel now knows because she listened to the voice of Moses. Merely comparing the identical language before and after the sea

[9] In her masterful survey of the Hebrew Bible, Avrahami concludes that the metaphor of sight takes primacy in epistemology: "The biblical evidences expresses this perception through sight vocabulary at least to the same – if not greater – extent as by the hearing vocabulary. Sight is a medium, a central tool for acquiring knowledge and passing it on (memory)." Yael Avrahami, *The Senses of Scripture: Sensory Perception in the Hebrew Bible* (The Library of Hebrew Bible/Old Testament Studies 545; New York: T&T Clark, 2012), 275.

crossing reveals that the event was properly interpreted, by most but not all, under Moses' guidance beforehand (Exodus 14:13–14):

Fear not, stand firm, and see the salvation of Yahweh,
which he will work for you today.
For the Egyptians whom you see today,
you shall never see again.

After crossing, the narrator relays their seeing in symmetrical style to the prior explanation. The verbs are phrased in precisely the reverse order (Exod 14:30–31):

Israel saw the Egyptians dead on the seashore.
Israel saw the great power that Yahweh worked against the Egyptians,
so the people feared Yahweh, and they trusted in Yahweh and in his servant Moses.

Israel saw correctly, trusting in Yahweh and in Moses because of it. How did the people see the dead bodies and sea-splitting power as traceable to Yahweh? They listened to the voice of Moses, embodied his instructions, and saw what Yahweh was showing them. Hence, Israel knew truly where Pharaoh did not.

Deuteronomy and Beyond

The covenant renewal of Deuteronomy is chock-full of pleas to "listen to the voice of Yahweh" in order to live long in the land and correctly know Israel's history. This includes, but is not limited to, the renowned parts of Deuteronomy:

"From heaven he made you listen to his voice to discipline you." (4:36)

"Listen, O Israel, Yahweh is our God, Yahweh alone." (6:4)

"If you listen to the voice of Yahweh your God, blessed shall you be . . ." (28:2–3)

"But if you will not listen to the voice of Yahweh your God, then all these curses shall come upon you and overtake you." (28:15)

"But if your heart turns away and you will not listen .... Therefore choose life ... listening to his voice ..." (30:17, 20)

The epistemological rhetoric of Deuteronomy is more sophisticated than this, and will eventually be reemployed in Isaiah, the wisdom literature, and the Gospels. What remains unchanged throughout those texts is the primacy of listening to the appropriate voices, avoiding pretenders, and performing what that authority prescribes in order to know.

Likewise, Proverbs 1–9 centers its epistemic efficacy on the son's attentive ear and repetitive imperatives, "listen my son" (Prov 1:5, 8, 23; 2:2; 4:1, 10, 20; 5:1, 7, 13; 15:31; 18:15; etc.). Samuel chastises Israel's first messianic king for his failure to "listen to the voice of Yahweh," which takes priority over sacrifice and signals his epistemic failure to understand the nature of the kingdom and his position within that economy (1 Sam 15:12–25).

A summary of the Hebrew Bible could be stated this way: because they listened to the wrong voices, they came to know wrongly. That accurately captures most of what happens from Eden to Exile in the Old Testament.

Epistemology: New Testament Funded from the Hebrew Bible

The pattern remains essentially the same in the New Testament, where priority is placed on (1) the correct and guiding voice and (2) the necessity of following directions in order to know. As I discussed at length in Chapter 6, the gospels depict Jesus' clear intent to reveal "the mystery of the kingdom of God" to the disciples and to blind everyone else to that mystery (Matt 13:10; Mark 4:10–12). What is the mystery? Lang sums it up well: "to be divinely empowered with a certain hermeneutical aptitude to perceive kingdom-related realities in Jesus' parabolic words."[10]

This pattern of developing skilled knowing makes sense of the inordinate amount of textual space devoted to accrediting authoritative voices who then guide Israel with specific direction. Even the directions of Israel's rituals are explicitly epistemological, from Passover to memorial stones by the Jordan River to Sukkot: "You shall dwell in sukkahs (shelters) for seven days … that your generations may know …" (Lev 23:42–43).

Public theological tests often reinforced whose voice should be heeded and were sometimes fatal for the usurper's supposed insights. For instance, Moses establishes a public experiment of Korah's theology of divine presence with the goal: "Then you all shall know that these men have despised Yahweh" (Numb 16:30). The same is true for David's unlikely deliverance from Goliath: "that this assembly may know that Yahweh saves not with sword and spear" (1 Sam 17:46). And of course, Elijah's showdown with the prophets of Ba'al evinces the same epistemic pattern: "that this people may know that you, O Yahweh, are God" (1 Kgs 18:37).

[10] T. J. Lang, *Mystery and the Making of a Christian Historical Consciousness: From Paul to the Second Century* (Beihefte zur Zeitschrift für die neutestamentliche Wissenschaft 219; Boston: De Gruyter, 2015), 17.

We are little surprised then that John the Baptist and much of the public life of Jesus focused on establishing Jesus as the authoritative prophet of Israel, *the voice to whom Israel, the storms, disciples, and demons must listen*. Noticeably, while his prophetic status is public, his messianic office is a secret. Accordingly, when Jesus later descends from the Mount of Transfiguration as a prophet and the Mount of Olives on a donkey – an unmistakably kingly act – the crowds identify him not as a king, but say, "*This is the prophet* Jesus from Nazareth of Galilee" (Matt 21:11). Titling him "the prophet" entails that Jesus is the one to whom they should listen.

The priority of Jesus' authoritative voice, and then the authoritative voice of the apostles, is the preeminent concern of the early Jesus-followers' understanding of the kingdom of God. When we see Jesus gazing over the thousands without food, the gospel narrators network this scene to the commissioning of Joshua. Just as Moses' "gives" some of his authority to Joshua so that Israelites who are like "sheep without a shepherd ... may listen," the gospels quote this unique phrase from Numbers 27 to network these two pixels for the reader (cf. Numb 27:17, 20; Matt 9:36; Mark 6:34).

The insight occurs again and again across Scripture, only after one correctly acknowledges to whom they should be listening can they then be guided to act in order to see the kingdom of God and confirm what they know to each other.

Conclusions from Hebraic Epistemology

Much more could be said about the depiction of knowing spanning the biblical literature. A minimal starting point could point out the three nodal aspects (N) of biblical epistemology, upon which good knowing is distinguished from erroneous knowing:

N1 The role of authoritative social structures in knowing. An epistemological explanation that reduces knowing to merely mental functions of an individual subject regarding a discrete proposition would be deficient if the explanation cannot recontextualize that discrete knowing within the social function of knowing without remainder.

N2 The role of embodied processes that disposes the subject to apprehend. Cognitive and physical processes directed by an accredited authority and heeded by a subject determine the subject's ability to apprehend that which they previously could not. Hence, the neglect or inability to account for embodied processes or rituals in epistemology signals a significant divergence from the interests of the biblical authors.

N3 *The role of skill in knowing.* The epistemological impetus of Scripture aims directly at wisdom as the supreme goal of knowing. Wisdom includes not just the bare ability to distinguish hits from misses (e.g., Signal Detection), but the ability to discern subtle and discrete particularities *and then lead others to do the same.* Of course, the diverse Hebrew and Greek (LXX and NT) terms for wisdom speak to skills of discernment in nautical matters, botany, zoology, meteorology, and divine action.[11] Wisdom is not a mystical or religious term; it speaks of skill, competency, and, in some cases, intelligence. Leaving out the socially fostered discussion of skill from an epistemological model renders the model myopic, blind, or hemianopic (in Eleonore Stump's language) to the very pulse of epistemological discourses in Scripture.[12]

There are and will be different methods for discerning epistemological structures in the biblical literature. However, merely considering the diverse methods biblical scholars have already applied, the findings have been remarkably consistent on these basic features of knowing.[13]

Scientific Epistemology and the Hebrew Bible

> Science will appear then as a vast system of beliefs, deeply rooted in our history and cultivated today by a specially organized part of our society. We shall see that science is not established by the acceptance of a formula, but is part of our mental life, shared out for cultivation among many thousands of specialized scientists throughout the world, and shared receptively, at second hand, by many millions.[14]

In making a general case for Hebraic philosophy absorbed by the NT authors, it is important to think about the epistemology that undergirds any philosophical style. Hence, I have roughed out a present, persistent, and relevant epistemological trajectory throughout the biblical literature. Again, I can only briefly sketch the affinities between contemporary views

[11] "[Wisdom] describes men who, in some sense and in some sphere, are 'competent,' 'skilled.' It can be used even of manual workers or sailors ... it describes a man who is an expert in the shady tricks and dodges .... Even an embryo which cannot find the way out of the womb can be described as 'unwise' (Hosea 13:13)." Gerhard Von Rad, *Wisdom in Israel*, trans. James D. Martin (Nashville, TN: Abington Press, 1986), 20.

[12] "Theories of knowledge that ignore or fail to account for whole varieties of knowledge are correspondingly incomplete." Eleonore Stump, *Wandering in the Darkness: Narrative and the Problem of Suffering* (New York: Oxford University Press, 2010), 59.

[13] For a survey of these findings that employ markedly different philological and literary techniques, see Johnson, *Biblical Knowing*, 187–201.

[14] Michael Polanyi, *Personal Knowledge: Towards a Post-Critical Philosophy* (Chicago: University of Chicago Press, 1962), 171.

of scientific epistemology and the Hebraic view pixelated across narratives and wisdom literature.[15]

Why compare Hebraic to scientific epistemology? After examining the epistemology being advocated within some biblical texts, the paucity of current epistemologies that included pragmatic evidence of epistemic success is noticeable. Pragmatic success is a marker of the Hebraic epistemology: it has to be tested and found true, in the Hebraic sense of "true."[16]

A comparative epistemology must also include an integration of the social aspects of knowing within a community and tradition of knowers, along with the hierarchical role of experts who guide others to skilled knowing (i.e., Nodes 1–3 above). In contemporary epistemology, matters of social knowing, the role of trust, and pragmatic success can be found, though still largely stuck in the analytic style of analysis.[17] Alvin Goldman glibly describes why his field of analytic thinking might falter

[15] For a more carefully argued biblical epistemology and its scientific counterpart, see Dru Johnson, *Knowledge by Ritual: A Biblical Prolegomenon to Sacramental Theology* (Journal of Theological Interpretation Supplements 13; Winona Lake, IN: Eisenbrauns/ PennState Press, 2016). This chapter borrows and adapts content from my previous book *Biblical Knowing*.

[16] See Chapter 9 for a detailed description of truth-terms in the biblical texts.

[17] There is an emerging subsection of epistemology concerned with the problem of trust and social epistemology. While these wrestle with some of the pertinent questions raised in the biblical texts, they do so within the narrower analytic modes. Trust is a "problem" for these analyses because they mostly view trust as if it is beyond deductive inferences, as something ultimately foreign to normative epistemology. Trust as a topic "departs from traditional epistemology." Alvin I. Goldman, *Pathways to Knowledge: Private and Public* (New York: Oxford University Press, 2002), 139, especially Part III. See major works: Russell Hardin, *Trust and Trustworthiness* (New York: Russell Sage Foundation, 2002), especially ch. 5; Allan Gibbard, *Wise Choices, Apt Feelings: A Theory of Normative Judgment* (Cambridge, MA: Harvard University Press, 1992), especially 233–52; Robert B. Brandom, *Making It Explicit: Reasoning, Representing, and Discursive Commitment* (Cambridge, MA: Harvard University Press, 1998), 213–21; Jennifer Lackey, *Learning from Words: Testimony as a Source of Knowledge* (New York: Oxford University Press, 2008); Richard Foley, *Intellectual Trust in Oneself and Others* (New York: Cambridge University Press, 2001), especially ch. 4; "Egoism in Epistemology," in *Socializing Epistemology: The Social Dimensions of Knowledge*, ed. Frederick F. Schmitt (Lanham, MD: Rowman & Littlefield, 1994), 53–73; Cecil A. J. Coady, *Testimony: A Philosophical Study* (New York: Oxford University Press, 1994). Also significant and helpful are: G. E. M. Anscombe, "What Is It to Believe Someone?" in *Rationality and Religious Belief*, ed. C. F. Delaney (University of Notre Dame Studies in the Philosophy of Religion 1; Notre Dame, IN: University of Notre Dame Press, 1979), 141–51; Benjamin McMyler, "Knowing at Second Hand," *Inquiry* 50, no. 5 (2007): 511–40. Kusch has an interesting attempt at bringing together a communitarian "play" of language (think early Wittgenstein) with a contextually determinate and relativist notion of truth. Martin Kusch, *Knowledge by Agreement: The Programme of Communitarian Epistemology* (Oxford: Clarendon Press, 2002).

here on the issue of how those philosophers conceptualize knowing: "Epistemic agents are often examined who have unlimited logical competence and no significant limits on their investigational resources."[18] The social economy of trust has been secondary for some in modern epistemology. Commendable steps in the biblical direction include Linda Zagzebski's *Epistemic Authority*, but even that work might struggle to fully integrate the emphases of N1–N2 above.[19]

Separate from these analytic epistemologies, the scientific enterprise made for low-hanging fruit, containing all the requisite elements of good knowing advocated across the biblical literature. This chapter turns to the unique points of affinity between the realist and pragmatically described scientific epistemology that rises from the ashes of scientific positivism in the mid-twentieth century, and the epistemological processes described, prescribed, and reified across the Christian Scriptures.

The Scientific Parallel to Hebraic Epistemology

In the remainder of this chapter, I offer a précis of Michael Polanyi's scientific epistemology as a paradigm for a collection of mid-twentieth-century thinkers challenging modernist and positivist assumptions: Marjorie Grene, Mary Hesse, Norwood Hanson, and Thomas Kuhn. I include a brief demonstration of similar epistemological sensitivities in the Pentateuch and wisdom literature of the Hebrew Bible and the New Testament. Specifically, I will focus on Polanyi's discussion of scientific epistemology in terms of:

1. skill/connoisseurship
2. reliance upon testimony
3. the role of scientific controversy
4. use of maximic language in epistemology

Further, I will address why socio-epistemological constructs, such as Thomas Kuhn's "paradigm shift," do not sufficiently grasp a Hebraic way of describing the community's knowledge and epistemological controversy when adjudicating between two competing interpretations.[20]

[18] Goldman, *Pathways to Knowledge*, 139.

[19] Linda T. Zagzebski, *Epistemic Authority: A Theory of Trust, Authority, and Autonomy in Belief* (New York: Oxford University Press, 2012).

[20] See Thomas S. Kuhn, *The Structures of Scientific Revolution*, 3rd ed. (Chicago: University of Chicago Press, 1962).

In appealing to examples from the Torah, wisdom literature, and NT epistles, I hope to demonstrate that the Hebraic sense of normative knowledge requires the accreditation akin to what we see developing in the sciences.

As a physician and chemist turned philosopher, Polanyi could not reconcile the mechanistic views of scientific positivism with the actual logic of discovery that he observed as a member of the scientific guild. In preparing for the Gifford Lectures (1951–52), he struggled to make sense of the often-ineffable sense in which facts garnered meaning for the scientist. Polanyi wrestled with describing the logic of discovery in science, so much so that he had to defer his Gifford Lectures for several years to work on what ultimately became his tome: *Personal Knowledge: Towards a Post-Critical Philosophy*.[21]

Why engage Michael Polanyi's scientific epistemology? Contemporary accounts of epistemology lacked significantly the necessary concepts and explanatory power to describe what we find in the biblical literature. In Polanyi's work, we find a rigorously argued view of knowing developed from participation within the community that accredits facets of knowledge that many epistemologists often disregarded as unanalyzable.

As an example, Polanyi takes the focused human effort and appropriation of skill to be fundamental to all acts of knowing, propositional or otherwise. This idea of epistemic skill makes knowing an act that can be coached by experts to novices. Esther Meek, an interpreter of Polanyi, echoes his belief that rationality is not best explained by reducing it to deductive inferences: "An inferential structure is not impoverished by the addition of [Polanyi's] unspecifiable features of our knowing. Rather, the inferential structure, if thought to express the act exhaustively is the thing that impoverishes our knowing." She goes on to say, "If a key kind of knowing doesn't fit our model, it's not right to discredit the knowing; it's right to discredit the model."[22] Similarly suggestive moves have also been made within analytic philosophy itself, but nothing as comprehensive and full-throated as Polanyi's view.[23]

21 See further: Martin X. Moleski and William Taussig Scott, *Michael Polanyi: Scientist and Philosopher* (New York: Oxford University Press, 2005).

22 Esther L. Meek, *Longing to Know: The Philosophy of Knowledge for Ordinary People* (Grand Rapids, MI: Brazos Press, 2003), 76–77.

23 Cf. Eleonore Stump, "The Problem of Evil: Analytic Philosophy and Narrative," in *Analytic Theology: New Essays in the Philosophy of Theology*, ed. Oliver D. Crisp and Michael C. Rea (New York: Oxford University Press, 2009), 253; Goldman, *Pathways to Knowledge*, 139; Jonathan Kvanvig, *The Intellectual Virtues and the Life of the Mind: On*

Descriptive in his approach, Polanyi tells what scientists actually do in order to know rather than how he would like knowledge to be constructed (à la logical positivism). While he tugs on embodied processes and human relationships to describe knowing, Polanyi's thought notably lacks abstract entities, as they cannot be argued for outside of describing one's own phenomenal experience of scientific practices.

Directly pertinent to what I see operative across the biblical literature, Polanyi accredits the sociological fabric of science as a community of skilled knowers. This community creates the requisite structure to all scientific knowledge: knowledge is "shared out for cultivation among many thousands of specialized scientists throughout the world, and shared receptively, at second hand, by many millions."[24] Testimony among scientists, which is built upon skilled observation, then creates a community of knowers who can move confidently toward what we call scientific knowledge.[25]

In the Torah we find community discovery (i.e., epistemology) guided by skilled seers, sometimes prophets and other times parents, who attempt to lead Israel toward skilled understanding. This knowledge gets labeled with Hebrew terms for discernment, knowledge, competence, or the more generic "wisdom" (*ḥŏkĕmâ*).[26] The epistemological model must account for the role of the human body, the social body, and analogical reasoning, which the Hebrew Bible and New Testament persistently presume.

Regarding Polanyi's structure of scientific epistemology, I first examine the skilled aspect of scientific knowing that requires apprenticeship under a specialist. Here we consider passages from the Pentateuch where

the Place of the Virtues in Epistemology (Studies in Epistemology and Cognitive Theory; Savage, MD: Rowman & Littlefield, 1992), 181–82; Linda T. Zagzebski, *Virtues of the Mind: An Inquiry into the Nature of Virtue and the Ethical Foundations of Knowledge* (New York: Cambridge University Press, 1996), 45, 66.

24 Polanyi, *Personal Knowledge*, 171.

25 Inspired by Polanyi to some degree, Thomas Kuhn would go on to describe what happens when communities of scientists strike upon an epistemological conflict: their skilled observations are not explained by the scientific theories *du jour*. However, this historical retelling of how scientific theory has been revolutionized does not actually go far enough to explain the requisite epistemological structures required for that revolution to take place. Polanyi actually describes the structures and the revolutionary process several years before Kuhn worked it out in *The Structure of Scientific Revolution*. Cf. Polanyi, *Personal Knowledge*, 150–60.

26 Of the difference between "wisdom" and "knowledge", Michael V. Fox says, "A variety of words are used for wisdom and knowledge – two concepts that are virtually identical in Proverbs." "The Epistemology of the Book of Proverbs," *Journal of Biblical Literature* 126, no. 4 (2007), 669n1.

persons submit themselves to a process to arrive at skilled knowledge of what is being shown to them (e.g., the What is it?/Manna episode of Exodus 16).

Second, to highlight discovery in definitive points of illumination, we will ask the question: What competencies are necessary to appropriate the meaning of a legal code that leads to wisdom – to discern principles that can be employed beyond an instance of a law?

Third, regarding scientific controversy, we will explore the competition between proffered explanations and the revolutionary force of the prophet's interpretation in the proverbs and prophets of Israel to overthrow less precise explanations.

Finally, to demonstrate the use of language without propositional content yet with an inferential structure, we will consider the role of aphorism in the wisdom literature (e.g., "The wise of heart will receive commandments, but a babbling fool will come to ruin," Prov. 10:8). This maximic language – as Polanyi calls it – intends to guide the knower in a particular trajectory, but its plain meaning is obscured outside of the human effort to know.[27]

The goal here is not to create a comprehensive theory of all things epistemological.[28] Rather, the goal is to redirect, pointing toward the supposition that there might be a coherent theory underlying the epistemological model that funds the various aspects of the Bible's texts. Polanyi's scientific epistemology might be ideal for this task because his model is a unifying epistemology that can accommodate Nodes 1–3 and beyond:

1. the phenomenal sense of knowing through one's body
2. the epistemological confidence maintained through testimony within a community
3. the employment of inference that is not limited to a propositional view of rationality

[27] "Maxim" is used here by Polanyi in the least Kantian sense of the word possible. A maxim is a statement that helps to guide, but only in the action being embodied and pursued. For instance, a biology professor might encourage a student to "extend their gaze" down the microscope to see some cellular phenomenon. The *maximic* language, for Polanyi, is "extend your gaze." It is not a truism, but a guide that aides the one who is intentionally trying to see biological features at the cellular granularity.

[28] Rather than presuming multiple epistemologies in the Hebrew Bible, as Michael Carasik and others have reasonably assumed, I suppose one possible account of knowledge that is robust and extends quite naturally from a non-Positivist view of scientific discovery. Michael Carasik, *Theologies of the Mind in Biblical Israel* (Studies in Biblical Literature 85; Oxford: Peter Lang, 2005).

4. the use of language that supersedes propositional content and is necessary to express what one knows[29]

Knowing, both in the sciences and the Bible, will appear as skilled, reliant on testimony, developed through controversy, and communicated through maxims.

Knowing as a Skill

> Science is operated by the skill of the scientist and it is through the exercise of his skill that he shapes his scientific knowledge. ... I shall take as my clue for this investigation the well-known fact that the aim of a skilful performance is achieved by the observance of a set of rules *which are not known as such to the person following them.*[30]

Intent on reorienting us from knowledge-as-an-object toward knowing-through-skillful-performance, Polanyi highlights a cardinal feature of scientific knowing with manifest implications. First, Polanyi believes that we know by embodied mental performance, where even our conceptual space has trajectory and movement (i.e., a from-to shape). But second, he then removes our reliance upon specifiable premises as grounds for this *performance*. In other words, knowing is an act for which the logical arguments cannot be initially specified by the one coming to know. Even after reflection, no exhaustive way exists to specify what one knows without remainder. In this way, knowing is ineffable.

He suggests that honing a skill, what he terms "connoisseurship," requires apprenticeship – a time in which the novice submits to the authority of the senior scientist who guides her to sift through a cluster of particulars, to notice what is significant, to discern a coherent pattern within a fuzzy field of observation, and so on. This resembles what I have been calling the pixelated style.

The honing of expertise develops *discernment in observation*, being able to see what one could not previously see because of such training. For instance, Spanish and Portuguese might sound like dialects of the same language to the unknowing ear, yet after learning either Spanish or Portuguese, it would be obvious that they are not dialects, but distinct languages. The ability to discern only develops through embodied apprenticeship. Acts of discernment can then be individually performed, but only

29 This more robust version of inference is what Esther Meek calls "transrational." *Longing to Know*, 76–77.

30 Italics original. Polanyi, *Personal Knowledge*, 49.

after the novice has come to know. To this end, Polanyi notes that while we are coming to know, we are trusting the instruction of our teacher, the rules of which we cannot state or question, but must follow to know the thing being shown to us.

In the realm of biology, we could observe through a microscope a blood cell shrinking as we place it in saltwater. However, mere observation does not bring us to know what we have seen. In Norwood Hanson's terms, we have "seen" but not "seen that."[31] What bridged the logical gap between "seeing" a cell shrink and the act of "seeing-that" a cell shrunk due to salinity in water was understanding the invisible biological construct of tonicity (i.e., the osmotic pressure of a cell that causes fluid to pass through a membrane due to the salinity of the water). Tonicity is a construct that gathers visible observations and concepts together, which are organized in a dynamic understanding of complex cellular relationships.

To know why a cell shrinks in saltwater, we must understand the relationship between cell construction, solutions and salinity, cellular osmosis, fluid pressure, and so on. In the nexus of all these constructs, we can make sense of what we see when we place a red blood cell in saltwater. But for Polanyi, we cannot come to know this on our own.

As we listen to the voice of our instructors who guide us and embody their prescribed actions to know the complex features of tonicity, we cannot restate all the rituals and rules by which we understand what we are seeing in the microscope. We now know why the cell shrinks because we can discern tonicity – as an invisible feature that generalizes – and can now view a particular instance of *tonicity in action* in light of that construct. Whereas we previously "saw" a red blood cell shrinking, we now see tonicity as a fuzzy organizing principle. We now have a skilled understanding of osmotic pressure and we now "see that" there is a nexus of actions that results in a shrinking cell.

Once we have grasped the impetus and structure of a formula or equation, we can embody it as a heuristic, extending ourselves into its symbols and relations as we do with physical tools. So too can we extend ourselves into constructs, such as tonicity in cells or quiescence in electrical fields. When we grasp the principle, we can employ it without

[31] As Norwood Hanson suggested, Tycho and Kepler could both recognize the sun rising if they were to watch it together, but within wholly different cognitive frameworks. "Observation," in *Theories and Observation in Science*, ed. Richard E. Grandy (Englewood Cliffs, NJ: Prentice-Hall, 1973), 146.

articulating its precise grammar and syntax. We use it transparently to the task of discovery. As a simple example, conceptually grasping how the quadratic equation functions – not just being able to solve for a particular integer in the equation – allows one to employ the equation as a heuristic. We extend our sight to see the world *quadratic-ly*, as it were, opening up quadratic vistas into everything from the braking distance required by cars to the downdraft on a ping-pong ball.[32]

Key for Polanyi is that while we are developing the skill, we are in a submitted and fiduciary relationship where we *cannot* articulate the reasons why we come to know: "To learn by example is to submit to authority. You follow your master because you trust his manner of doing things even when you cannot analyze and account in detail for its effectiveness."[33] Only after we have become skilled knowers of the particular reality of interest can we begin to name the rituals that glued together the clues that led us to understand.

Enslaved in Egypt, Israel relied on Moses' authority – which it could not vet – to come to know Yahweh and the Abrahamic promises on the distant horizon of the exodus. Knowing Yahweh as "your God" is one of the explicit motivations of the exodus account (cf. Exod 6:7; 7:17; 10:2). Neither smearing blood on a doorpost, nor leaving Egypt, nor even walking through a parted sea is sufficient for knowing Yahweh in the way intended by the distinct use of the possessive suffix on Elohim – our God (*ʾĕlōhênû*).

The golden calf event in Exodus 32 indicates that many Hebrews did not assemble the clues coherently or failed to act accordingly if they did. From the narrator's position, if Israel was to know Yahweh as her God, then the Israelites would have to pay attention to the instructions of Moses to understand why Yahweh is *her* God. While they embody those ritual instructions, they cannot vet or verify how this process is going to lead them to that knowledge. Even though this sounds fideistic, Polanyi tells us that the same goes for the scientist.

This should not be reduced to a plea for blind religious trust, or that antagonistic misnomer in the West, "faith." Rather, in both the scientist's training and the exodus of Israel, discrete, historically reliable observations are given as evidence for trusting the guidance of an

32 For more examples, see Chris Budd and Chris Sanguin, "101 Uses of the Quadratic Equation," *Plus Magazine*, May 1, 2004, https://plus.maths.org/content/101-uses-quadratic-equation-part-ii/.

33 Polanyi, *Personal Knowledge*, 53.

authority. And, the definitive goal in Israel's knowing is so *that others could know.*[34]

As we saw in Mark's epistemology, the goal of knowing is to become a skilled knower, discerning enough to direct others in developing the same skill. Even more, the level of sophistication required to discern particulars in light of the whole is elevated significantly by the time of Deuteronomy. Deuteronomy's Israelites are not only required to look for prophets authenticated by Yahweh with signs and wonders, but to be able to distinguish true from misleading prophecy from authenticated prophets. In fact, God promises to authenticate prophets with signs and wonders in order to test Israel with misleading words from their mouths (Deut 13:1–3). With Polanyi, one could argue that these texts, along with the sciences, do not promote blind or even naïve trust, but skilled knowing.

Reliance upon Testimony

> Any attempt to define the body of science more closely comes up against the fact that the knowledge comprised by science is not known to any single person. Indeed, nobody knows more than a tiny fragment of science well enough to judge its validity and value at first hand. For the rest he has to rely on views accepted at second hand on the authority of a community of people accredited as scientists. But this accrediting depends in its turn on a complex organization. For each member of the community can judge at first hand only a small number of his fellow members, and yet eventually each is accredited by all.[35]

By "testimony," I do not mean that witnesses provide data points. Rather, trust in testimony refers to the required task of trusting the interpretation of the data from another authoritative knower.

Though Polanyi's statement about the social distribution of scientific knowledge – nobody knows enough science to judge the whole – seems obvious now, it was not always so obvious in recent waves of positivism. Authority and authentication (i.e., "accreditation") enter the fray here. These must be viewed separately because the scientific controversy will be contingent on accreditation, not authority. For the social fabric of science to function, it requires that scientists know *and trust* each other.

[34] The Abrahamic covenant of Genesis 12 and Deuteronomy as a whole could be framed under that heading: knowing Yahweh so that others might know Him. After all, this is the ultimate epistemic *telos* of Jeremiah's new covenant (i.e., Jer 31:34).

[35] Polanyi, *Personal Knowledge*, 163.

The globally dispersed work done in the field or in labs cannot be verified by any one person or entity. The whole enterprise relies on a web of trust, and so its attentiveness to who is accredited as trustworthy ovaries with the fidelity of scientists likewise. Accreditation is not a badge to be worn, but the knowledge that a scientist has been trained, developing her skills as a scientist, under the supervision of other trusted scientists in a particular tradition. Trust, or faith, greases every cog and gear of science.

The implications of this description might exceed our ability to simply adjust our views of scientific inquiry. It suggests that the experimental "facts" do not speak for themselves. The scientist stands immediately behind her results, and her accreditation is what allows them to authoritatively enter the arena of scientific discourse.

Polanyi's attention will soon turn to the matter of controversy, and how the scientific community can adjudicate between competing voices. He says, "Every great scientific controversy tends therefore to turn into a dispute between the established authorities and a pretender . . ."[36] I will address controversy more in the subsection entitled "The Role of Scientific Controversy," but a central claim of Polanyi's description of science is that it necessarily rests in expansive planes of reliance upon testimony that cannot be personally verified by any one scientist.

In other words, we could imagine that for logical positivism, the logical structure of knowledge was meant to safeguard against dependence upon another person's testimony. We might have imagined that if we wanted to, we could vet the whole enterprise of science by vetting each part. However, Polanyi bypasses these possibilities and claims that working scientists cannot vet the whole by the parts, and even if they tried, it would not affirm the enterprise.

By the nature of human epistemology, science exhibits normative human knowing with strengthened systematic requirements for methodology *and accreditation*. Even today, most will point to the scientific method itself as the mainstay of scientific confidence, citing rigor or repeatability as the reason to trust our knowledge. Yet Polanyi points us back to the scientists themselves in their community as the center of the enterprise. Therefore, tradition and community standards of accreditation take priority in any scientist's epistemological confidence.

[36] Polanyi, *Personal Knowledge*, 164.

Likewise, the undisguised emphasis on authenticating Israel's authoritative voices rings loudly in the biblical literature. I offer several brief but telling instances from the Pentateuch, the Gospels, and Paul's own story of authentication.

First, authentication is pitted against authoritative knowledge in the account of Genesis 3. The story centers on coming to know, particularly through submitting to an authority. Remember that when God enters the Garden, He finds the man and woman hiding from Him. Upon questioning, God learns that the man and the woman have come to know that they are naked. Again, God does *not* ask, "Upon what premises did you reason to this knowledge which you have acquired?" God asks a question that presumes another authority to whom they have submitted has entered the scene: "Who told you that you were naked?" (Gen 3:11). As well, the sole indictment and diagnosis of error comes at the fore of the man's curses: "Because you listened to the voice of your wife ..." and by implication, to the voice of the serpent while standing with his wife (cf. Gen 3:6, 17a).

Genesis portrays the serpent as an authority in the Garden. He knows things the couple does not. And when they ritually embody his instruction in order to know, everything that the serpent forecasts comes true, and the narrator is at pains to show as much.[37] The fact that the story's narrator uses the parallel language of the serpent in the story seems to reveal an interest in showing the serpent's authoritative knowledge (cf. Gen 3:4–5, 7, 22). In the narrative, the serpent's authority is not in question, but only his accreditation to prescribe – the reason why the man and woman ought to listen to him.

Second, when Moses is made the Prophet of Israel, his jurisdiction to speak on behalf of Yahweh and circumscribe all future prophets is totalizing. The development of Moses' accreditation begins as a near-reversal of the serpent's status. Moses has no inherent authority, but is authenticated as the voice through whom Yahweh speaks. The phases of Moses' accreditation compel us to wonder if simple obedience to God is preferred over reasoning with humans:

> Moses himself must be convinced through signs (Exod 3:1–4:17),
> then Aaron is convinced to be his mouthpiece (Exod 4:27–28),

[37] Moberly makes the simple yet easily overlooked point that everything the serpent says appears to be true from within the narrative. Their eyes were opened, they did have knowledge, they did not die in the day that they ate, and they did become "like God." R. W. L. Moberly, "Did the Serpent Get It Right?" *Journal of Theological Studies* 39, no. 1 (April 1988): 1–27.

> then the Israelite leaders are convinced (Exod 4:29–31),
> then Pharaoh fails to be convinced (Exod 5–12), and
> finally, Israel is convinced as a whole (cf. Exod 14:13–13; 14:30–31).

This process of a phased and historical accreditation of Moses to all around him breaks class and power boundaries, involving lowly slaves up through geopolitical engagement at the highest layers in the ancient world. The texts of the Pentateuch in particular and Hebrew Bible as a whole are very concerned to accredit only those who can guide Israel to know the covenant relationship with Yahweh, and in a very distinct manner.

Third, Moses' authentication clarified who *was* and *was not* an authoritative knower who guides Israel (cf. Numb 12, 16). But the crisis of Moses' impending death spurs regulations concerning who *will be* the future authoritative voices to guide Israel. Specifically, Deuteronomy's teaching answers the question: How can future generations know who is accredited to guide Israel to know her covenant promises?

In view of Moses' approaching death, God will raise future prophets who will be authoritative (Deut 18:15), and he will authenticate them to Israel. But if they lead Israel away from the Torah, then they are guilty of a capital crime (Deut 13:1–5).

However, even when the question of authentication is seemingly resolved, God requires a more nuanced perceptiveness: Israel must also distinguish the authoritative from presumptuous messages of *accredited* prophets (Deut 18:15–22). The demand for the common Hebrew's discernment here is acute. But with these three terse examples before us, we can see that Polanyi's insistence on accreditation as a central to the scientific endeavor is commensurate with the Pentateuch's maximal concern for the authoritative guide to be accredited to Israel.

What about the New Testament? Given the revelation of Jesus' status to the reader, it is astonishing to note how much effort he and God (from the heavens) spend seeking authentication as the prophet of Israel. As previously discussed in Chapter 6, even the Transfiguration account focuses solely on Jesus' role as a prophet: he stands with the arch-prophet Moses and Elisha, while God's voice allusively quotes a Deuteronomic passage on future prophets whom God promised to raise within Israel. Authentication appears to be paramount for Jesus' signs and wonders campaign, and that is how the apostles construed it as well (cf. Acts 2:22; 7:36–37). So N. T. Wright contends, "The best initial model for understanding this praxis is that of a prophet; more specifically, that of a prophet bearing an urgent eschatological and indeed apocalyptic, message for Israel." And, "All the evidence so far displayed suggests that he [Jesus] was perceived as a *prophet*."[38]

In the book of Acts, an authentication conflict emerges in the apostolic circle when Saul becomes a Jesus follower.[39] In this episode of Acts, the author has already revealed to the reader both the veracity of Paul's claim to apostleship and the ignorance of the disciples (Acts 9:26–31). As a reminder, the disciples back in Jerusalem have heard about their zealous persecutor Saul, who has reportedly become a Jesus follower. However, the apostles have good reasons to be skeptical. The story in Acts 9 focused on their change of belief: from skepticism of the reports to knowing the truth about Saul.

It initially appears that if the brothers in Jerusalem only had more information, then they too, along with the reader, could know that "Saul the persecutor" is now "Paul the apostle." By not trusting Paul, are the disciples in error? The narrator reveals that this is not a lack of information, because the information is not what resolved the conflict internal to that story.[40] Rather, it was trust (*pistis*) in Barnabas' testimony that resolved the conflict.

To resolve what was deficient, the narrative itself shows us the different phases of the apostles' epistemic assent. The apostles began in fear of Saul and did not trust (Acts 9:26; *mē pisteuontes*).[41] What disposed them to move from "not believing" (Acts 9:26; *mē pisteuein*) to "learning" (Acts 9:30; *epiginontes*) that Saul had become Paul, and by implication, to believing that "Paul is an apostle"? If we assert that the apostles needed more information, then new information ought to resolve the narrative.

Rather, the Jerusalem apostles trusted Barnabas as an authoritative guide. They must not only listen to Barnabas' understanding, but also entertain the possibility that Jesus' *good news* might be more inclusive and transformative than they had previously expected, even including

[38] Though the messianic secret will eventually come out in the Gospels and Acts, it appears that accreditation as the prophet of Israel allowed that radical messianic message to be a rising signal amidst the noise of messianic expectations. N.T. Wright, *Jesus and the Victory of God* (Christian Origins and the Question of God 2; Minneapolis: Fortress Press, 1996), 150, 196.

[39] This section is adapted from Johnson, *Biblical Knowing*, 4–7.

[40] This whole scenario reveals the problem of an ahistorical, contextless, and modernist term like "information."

[41] I prefer to translate the Greek *pisteuō* as "trust" in many instances, which is an equally viable English translation. The reasons for this are given in more detail in Chapter 9.

people such as Saul the persecutor. In yielding to Barnabas' guidance, they must participate in the larger paradigm that we could call "discerning the kingdom of God." And the apostles must integrate these new events and possibilities into that paradigm, *despite the apostles' inability to gauge the veracity of Barnabas' story*. Here, knowing seemed fraught with peril.

The point here is that these apostles were disposed to know certain things about the kingdom of God and its expansiveness (e.g., Mark 4:30–34; Acts 1:6–11). But the apostles were not disposed to discern that Saul could become Paul under that same rubric. Only in their commitment to know by trusting the guidance of Barnabas could these indiscernible particularities of Saul's life become discernible to resonate with knowing the expansiveness of the kingdom of God.

The disciples' initial skepticism toward Paul appears to be an error on their part only if we remove the story from its larger epistemological context. But if we plot this account in a more comprehensive "path to knowing," which we could title "the disciples coming to know that the kingdom of God expands to all humanity," then we see this episode as disposing the disciples to know the kingdom of God. We could also include episodes such as Peter and the Gentiles (Acts 10), and the apostolic council (Acts 15), along with many similar instances in the Gospels themselves where the disciples couldn't comprehend the expansiveness of the kingdom.[42]

The biblical emphasis on trusting in order to understand broad principles and discrete realities resonates with the kind of authentication that makes the scientific enterprise functionally efficacious.

The Role of Scientific Controversy

The dispersion and diversity of knowers also creates the opportunity to see the same data differently – parting with traditions, starting new traditions, or reinvesting in former ways: "To the extent to which a discoverer has committed himself to a new vision of reality, he has

[42] See Jeffrey B. Gibson, "The Rebuke of the Disciples in Mark 8:14–21," *Journal for the Study of the New Testament* 27 (1986): 31–47; Kelley R. Iverson, *Gentiles in the Gospel of Mark: "Even the Dogs under the Table Eat the Children's Crumbs"* (Library of New Testament Studies 339; London: T&T Clark, 2007). As Blakely summarizes: "the harshness of Jesus' rebuke in Mark 8:14–21 is occasioned not by the disciples' lack of faith or incomprehension but by their active resistance to his Gentile mission." J. Ted Blakley, "Incomprehension or Resistance?: The Markan Disciples and the Narrative Logic of Mark 4:1–8:30" (PhD diss., University of St. Andrews, 2008), vii.

separated himself from others who still think on the old lines. His persuasive passion spurs him now to cross this gap by converting everybody to his way of seeing things."[43]

In a section titled "Scientific Controversy," Polanyi narrates what actually happens when competing interpretive frameworks must be adjudicated within a scientific community. He writes: "The two conflicting systems of thought are separated by a logical gap, in the same sense as a problem is separated from the discovery which solves the problem."[44] He then goes on to describe how advocates of each system begin trying to persuade others in their community to appropriate this new framework for observing the data: "Those who listen sympathetically will discover for themselves what they would otherwise never have understood. Such an acceptance is a heuristic process, a self-modifying act, and to this extent a conversion."[45]

Here, the matter is not of accreditation, something that would have easily disqualified a competing view. Rather, the matter turns on how to discern between two incommensurable views, both from accredited scientists. Again, he describes how scientific communities arbitrate conflicting paradigms against the view that the preponderance of data alone determines the correct view.

The reader will be forgiven if she thought that I was describing Thomas Kuhn's 1962 work *The Structure of Scientific Revolutions*, published ten years after Polanyi's Gifford Lectures. Kuhn's reliance on Polanyi in developing the seminal ideas in *Scientific Revolutions* has already been meted out.[46] As a consequence of the ubiquitous attention that Kuhn has received compared with Polanyi, Kuhn's thinner version of paradigms became renowned in the humanities. This is unfortunate for at least one reason: Polanyi more roundly situates controversy within an extensive epistemological description of discovery. Struan Jacobs summarizes the differences in Polanyi's and Kuhn's approaches to scientific discovery this way:

> Kuhn sees most scientific research ("normal science") as assuming, and extending, currently received knowledge which exists in the form of a "paradigm." Kuhn's paradigms in effect *present* normal scientists with "puzzles," whereas Polanyian scientists draw from personal knowledge in order to *choose*

[43] Polanyi, *Personal Knowledge*, 150.

[44] Polanyi, *Personal Knowledge*, 151.

[45] Polanyi, *Personal Knowledge*, 151.

[46] See further: Struan Jacobs, "Michael Polanyi and Thomas Kuhn: Priority and Credit," *Tradition & Discovery* 33, no. 2 (2006–7): 25–36.

> problems. "In choosing a problem," Polanyi argues, "the investigator takes a decision fraught with risks." . . . Polanyian problem-solving discovery looks to be a less structured affair, calling for acumen and audacity on the part of the individual scientist.[47]

Fortuitously, the popular reception of Kuhn's work (and that of Gadamer, among others) has abated the naïve view of "bare evidence," even among scientists. It had to be acknowledged that the paradigm – what Polanyi calls "heuristic passion" – controls the scientist's view of the evidence. Consequently, scientific controversy is not resolved by a mere return to the facts, but is resolved within the same socio-epistemological layers with which Polanyi has always described science itself: "Deeply rooted in our history and cultivated today by a specially organized part of our society."[48]

The Hebrew Bible has elicited a similar history of theological controversies at key junctures. Ultimately, Israel's theology is contingent upon listening to the accredited voice of a prophet and then following their instructions to the degree required. Some are wary of Polanyi's suggestions about scientific discovery and controversy because they appear to locate truth or reality in the minds of interpretive communities accredited as scientists implying that there is no ultimate ground for truth in an objectively real world. This neglects the fact that both Polanyi and the Hebrew Bible directly address the relativity of our frameworks.

First, Polanyi posits a world where reality intrudes upon and reforms our knowing. Additionally, the goal of Polanyi's description of knowing is to "make contact" with reality, not to attain knowledge for which he has to seek abstract epistemic guarantors or foundations.[49] In the preface of *Personal Knowledge* he contends: "Such knowing is indeed *objective* in the sense of establishing contact with a hidden reality; a contact that is defined as the condition for anticipating an indeterminate range of yet unknown (and perhaps yet inconceivable) true implications. It seems reasonable to describe this fusion of the personal and the objective as Personal Knowledge."[50]

47 Jacobs, "Michael Polanyi and Thomas Kuhn," 25.

48 Polanyi, *Personal Knowledge*, 171.

49 Esther L. Meek, "'Recalled to Life': Contact with Reality," *Tradition and Discovery* 26, no. 3 (1999–2000): 72–83. See also: *Contact with Reality: Michael Polanyi's Realism and Why It Matters* (Eugene, OR: Cascade, 2017).

50 Italics original. Polanyi, *Personal Knowledge*, vii–viii.

Second, the biblical literature argues for knowing by means of accredited authorities and resolves the question of theological controversy by bringing Israel into contact with objective historical reality as well, if I can use such terms here without qualification.

Theological controversy, like scientific controversies, clarifies through historic and experimental means. For instance, Numbers 16 focuses on two conflicting paradigms of holiness: Korah with his band of men and Yahweh with his prophet Moses. Korah claims that all are holy and Yahweh is among all. This claim questions the paradigm that only the Levites are holy and can serve in the Tabernacle and raises even more questions about the nature of holiness (*qōdeš*).

An equally substantial claim emerges in the story's literary symmetry. Korah begins his revolutionary theology with the charge that Moses has gone "too far" (Numb 16:3). Moses' rejoinder to Korah and these Levites states, "*You* have gone too far sons of Levi" (Numb 16:7). Yahweh's instruction then emphasizes the physical separation of Korah's band and their incense offerings. There is a visible, spatial, objectively historical resolution to this controversy offered to us by the narrator. The narrator frames it as an experiment for the sake of knowing.

The ensuing scene shows that the paradigm offered by Korah is not only in conflict and incommensurable with Moses' paradigm, but that Yahweh clearly distinguishes the appropriate view of holiness by a definitive act, an objectively real and physical removal of the wrong framework.

The narrator ensures that we see this by constructing the entire scene of Korah's rebellion in epistemological terms. The purpose of the objective and brutal judgment of Korah, et al., is stated clearly within the narrative: "Then you shall know that these men have despised Yahweh." Similar comments could be made about Miriam and Aaron (Numb 12), David and Goliath (1 Sam 17), or Elijah and the prophets of Ba'al (1 Kgs 18).

In the New Testament, we find similar structuring around events meant to demonstrate a principle. Jesus forgave a lame man's sins before healing him "that you may know (*hina de eidēte*) that the son of man has authority" (cf. Matt 9:6; Mark 2:10; Luke 5:24). Jesus identifies the epistemic effect that should result from his crucifixion in John's Gospel: "When you have lifted up the Son of Man, then you will know that I am he (*tote gnōsesthe hoti egō*)" (John 8:28). The same goes for his resurrection: "in that day you will know (*en ekeinē tē hēmera gnōsesthe hy*)" (John 14:19).

Two factors then help us to see the connections between Polanyi and the biblical literature. First, experimental outcomes resolve conflicting paradigms by determinable actions in the real world. These actions give sufficient epistemological justification to the correct paradigm. In the above cases, the normative theology of Israel must begin within a framework that identifies Moses as Yahweh's unique prophet (Numb 12), the priesthood as the uniquely holy mediators of Israel (Numb 16), and Yahweh as a unique god of Israel who answers by one name: Yahweh (1 Kings 18).

Second, these are not bare theological points. They require specific actions by Yahweh who frames the controversy to highlight the incommensurability between the normative and faulty paradigms. But the Torah as a work of literature has prepared the reader for these controversies. What is clear to the reader of the Torah, with the aid of the narrator, is that any claim or action that is not rooted in the instruction of Moses will be framed as leading Israel to false or erroneous knowledge of her covenant with Yahweh.

The point remains that each party encounters the same data, the same events, and the same words spoken. Each advocate in the controversy interprets the evidence differently. Yahweh sometimes acts within these narratives right at the point where the epistemological interest of the community is at stake. The community needs to understand which paradigm will allow them to know truly, and Yahweh acts "so that [they] will know."

Many theologians interpret Jesus' incarnation as the historical act of God par excellence, as historically definitive clarification of the new covenant theology and simultaneously as the prophetic guide in that task. The speeches of Peter and Stephen in Acts certainly portray Jesus' life that way (cf. Acts 2:14–40; 7:2–53). Jesus is pictured as explaining himself under this paradigm in Luke's gospel (Luke 24:25–27). I have already demonstrated in Paul's letter to the Galatians that the purpose of the entire letter was to settle the controversy over which paradigm of the gospel correctly interprets the historical experiences of the audience.

Because the biblical texts are epistemically focused, when compared with their peer intellectual traditions, controversy will naturally take a central role in developing a nuanced second-order understanding within a community.

Maximic Language

Finally, Polanyi proposes a specific way in which language is employed to aid in knowing – from connoisseur to novice. He calls this pedagogical use of language a "maxim." "Maxims are rules, the correct application of which is part of the art which they govern . . . . Maxims cannot be understood, still less applied by anyone not already possessing a good practical knowledge of the art."[51] For Polanyi, knowing is "ineffable" in a general sense. It is because we know that we can then articulate what we know, but our speech never approaches or exhausts our knowledge.[52]

If we know more than we can say, then we encounter an obstacle to fostering knowledge in others.[53] How do we bring others to know *that which we know* if we cannot articulate *what we know* in language? This is where the maxim as a speech-act comes to the fore in the ritualized process of scientific discovery.

Maxims are peculiar statements that have no substantive meaning unless they are heard within the context of ritual performance, prescribed by the accredited authority. If we have ever played tennis, cricket, baseball, or golf, we can imagine that a coach might advise us: "Tighten up your swing" or "choke up on the bat."[54] That sentence, as directive language, is indiscernible *in se*. The only way in which that sentence becomes meaningful is if we have a bat or club in our hands and are actively swinging it while analogically applying the instructions. In the context of listening to the authoritative voice of our coach and doing that

[51] Polanyi, *Personal Knowledge*, 31.

[52] These observations show that strictly speaking nothing that we know can be said precisely; and so what I call "ineffable" may simply mean something that I know and can describe even less precisely than usual, or even only very vaguely. . . . Although the expert diagnostician, taxonomist and cotton-classer can indicate their clues and formulate their maxims, they know many more things than they can tell, knowing them only in practice, as instrumental particulars, and not explicitly, as objects. The knowledge of such particulars is therefore ineffable, and the pondering of a judgment in terms of such particulars is an ineffable process of thought. This applies equally to connoisseurship as the art of knowing and to skills as the art of doing, wherefore both can be taught only by aid of practical example and never solely by precept.

To his detractors, Polanyi warns: "It is not difficult to recall such ineffable experiences, and philosophic objections to doing so invoke quixotic standards of valid meaning which, if rigorously practised, would reduce us all to voluntary imbecility." *Personal Knowledge*, 87–88.

[53] "To speak . . . is therefore a performance based on knowledge, and it is indeed only one of an indefinite range of conceivable performances by which such knowledge can be manifested. We grope for words to tell what we know and our words hang together by these roots." Polanyi, *Personal Knowledge*, 102.

[54] In order to proceed, we must set aside the analogical use of "tighten" as well.

which they prescribe, the maxim guides us to know not just the general category "what it is like to hit a ball," but also "what it is like to drive a ball *so that it hooks at the end*" or something similar.

Polanyi wants us to understand that this is not only true of sports but also of the scientist's ability to know:

> The true maxims of golfing or of poetry increase our insight into golfing or poetry and may even give valuable guidance to golfers and poets; but these maxims would instantly condemn themselves to absurdity if they tried to replace the golfer's skill or the poet's art. Maxims cannot be understood, still less applied by anyone not already possessing a good practical knowledge of the art. ... Another person may use my scientific maxims for the guidance of his inductive inference and yet come to quite different conclusions. It is owing to this manifest ambiguity that maxims can function only – as I have said – within a framework of personal judgment. Once we have accepted our commitment to personal knowledge, we can also face up to the fact that there exist rules which are useful only within the operation of our personal knowing, and can realize also how useful they can be as part of such acts.[55]

It is difficult to resist the notion that Israel's wisdom literature exhibits Polanyi's maximic ideal. To see this, we will have to ignore other prevalent features of wisdom. For instance, we must temporarily suspend the poetic aspects of wisdom literature. Although it could be argued that the poetic and parallel literary forms of wisdom sayings contribute significantly to knowing, I will not integrate those here. Instead, I focus on a single aspect of meaning in the book of Proverbs: how aphorism is meant to act maximic-ly on knowers.

First, a brief discussion of the terms associated with wisdom reveals that wisdom most closely resembles the idea of a "developed skill." Second, Proverbs and New Testament epistles alike frame wisdom in light of accredited authorities. Third, aphoristic wisdom then acts as a maxim, shaping the knowledge of the one who is performing the prescribed actions.

First, the connotative range of terms used to describe wisdom in the Hebrew Bible is exceptionally broad, especially considering how commonly "wisdom" is employed outside of Proverbs. The semantic range of overlapping terms includes: discern (*bîn*), wisdom/skill (*ḥŏkĕmâ*), instruction (*mûsār*), knowledge (*da'at*), understanding (*tābûn*), discretion

[55] Polanyi, *Personal Knowledge*, 31.

(*mĕzimmâ*), clever/prudent (*'arum*), and the antonyms of wisdom: folly (*nĕbālâ/'ĕwîl*) and fool (*kĕsîl*).[56]

The most common term for "wisdom" (*ḥŏkĕmâ*) also appears in unexpected contexts. In Exodus, the requisite qualifications for the tabernacle craftsmen are given by Yahweh to Bezalel: wisdom (*ḥŏkĕmâ*), understanding (*tābûn*), and knowledge (*da'at*).[57] Within Proverbs, wisdom is not only attainable (e.g., Prov 3:13), but attained specifically by apprenticeship (e.g., Prov 4:10f; 9:9–10: 13:1). Accordingly, in the English-speaking world, wisdom should be conceived of as skill rather than its more sagacious and mystical connotations that it has earned in the West. Von Rad describes wisdom's connotations from the Hebrew Bible:

> [*ḥŏkĕmâ*] describes men who, in some sense and in some sphere, are "competent." "skilled." It can be used even of manual workers or sailors ... it describes a man who is an expert in the shady tricks and dodges. ... Even an embryo which cannot find the way out of the womb can be described as "unwise"
> (Hosea 13:13).[58]

The Septuagint often papers over the diversity of the Hebrew wisdom language with the single term *sophia*.

Second, Proverbs emphasizes accredited authority within the epistemological process. On the whole, wisdom is not a commodity that can be attained, but begins by submission to an authority. Proverbs 1–9 is regularly concerned with "to whom one listens." One cannot miss the conversational tone of the opening chapters in which parents and the female personification of wisdom are coaching the sons of Israel. This entire conversation is premised upon the call to listen to authority, one of several competing authorities at that (e.g., Prov 7–8). Proverbs contains twenty-five individual calls to "listen" (not including all of the "incline your ear" directives), fourteen of which are in the first nine chapters:

> "Let the wise listen ..." (Prov 1:5)
> "Listen, my son, to your father's instruction ..." (Prov 1:8)
> "Whoever listens to me will dwell secure." (Prov 1:33)

[56] The dizzying field of semantically overlapping terms causes Gerhard von Rad to comment (re. Prov 1:1–5): "How can an exegesis which takes words seriously deal adequately with this series of statements?" *Wisdom in Israel*, 13.

[57] Cf. Exodus 31:3; 35:31; 36:1.

[58] "In the majority of instances, the wise man is not the representative of a position, but simply the wise man who is contrasted as a type, with the fool." Von Rad, *Wisdom in Israel*, 20.

"My son, if you receive my words ... making your ear attentive ..." (Prov 2:1–2)
"My son, do not forget my teaching ..." (Prov 3:1)
"Listen, O sons, to a father's instructions ..." (Prov 4:1)
"Listen, my son, and accept my word ..." (Prov 4:10)
"And now, O sons, listen to me ..." (Prov 5:7)
"I did not listen to the voice of my teachers or incline my ear to my instructors." (Prov 5:13)
"And now, O sons, listen to me and be attentive ..." (Prov 7:24)
"Listen, for I will speak noble things ..." (Prov 8:6)
"And now, O sons, listen to me ..." (Prov 8:32)
"Listen to instruction and be wise ..." (Prov 8:33)
"Blessed is the one who listens to me ..." (Prov 8:34)[59]

In Proverbs 1–9, Yahweh, the father, the mother, and wisdom herself are lauded to sons as the rightful possessors of skilled discernment, and the sons are cautioned against the seduction of folly. Hence, the only viable route to wisdom requires submitting to instruction under a skilled knower.

Third, maxims participate in this epistemological process at the point of apprenticeship and human action. Again, I am not considering wisdom to be knowledge-content that can then be practically applied. Rather, the aphoristic language of wisdom instructs us while we are performing the coached actions. We come to know as we listen, act, and thus see how the proverb is true in ways we could not have understood apart from performing it.

The "didactic poem" was valued for its role in fostering Israelite wisdom, not as the content of knowledge that can be transferred from one generation to the next, as if the knowledge existed within the literature itself. Wisdom is honed by doing while listening. Von Rad views this didactic expression as particularly precious: "Indeed, it requires an art to see objectively things which have always been there and to give them expression. ... for every sentence and every didactic poem is pregnant with meaning and is unmistakably self-contained, so that, notwithstanding the many features common to them all, they strike us as being peculiarly inflexible."[60] That is, the ability to discern is embedded in the act.

Consider the adage "youth is wasted on the young." Although my great uncle regularly reminded me of this poem in my twenties, it is not

[59] Eleven more similar instances of "listen" act as the bases for wisdom in Proverbs 10–31: Prov. 12:15; 13:1; 15:31–32; 19:20; 19:27; 21:28; 22:17; 23:19; 23:22; 25:12; and 28:9.
[60] Von Rad, *Wisdom in Israel*, 5–6.

until my forties that the sentence began to make sense to me. This is not necessarily a didactic poem, but the truth of the statement gains meaning as we perform life and our bodies begin to underperform life.

For a more direct version of a maxim in the Polanyian sense, consider the pair of aphorisms in Proverbs 13:2–3, which are introduced with "a wise son listens to his father's instruction, but a scoffer does not listen to rebuke" (Prov 13:1):

> From the fruits of a man's mouth, he relishes good.
> But the desire of the treacherous is violence.
> The one who guards his mouth keeps his life.
> The one who opens wide his lips, ruin is his.

Those who have mentored others or been mentored themselves recognize the truth in this pair of sayings because we have experienced it in action. But as maxims, they function differently for those who are coming to know the truth of these statements. Von Rad notices, "In Ecclesiastes the effectiveness of the wise men's words is compared to that of ox-goads" (Eccl 12:10).[61] The aphorism firmly smacks us, correcting and guiding us as we go.

If Polanyi is correct, then we should be able to see that the sentences *in se* do not convey any propositional content, for lack of a better term. In reality, fruits do not grow out of the mouths of men, nor can one "guard" or "keep watch" over one's own mouth. The proverb advocates something that we know to be physically impossible. But we are not arguing against the deep and rich metaphors of "relishing," "wide lips," or the analogical use of "ruin." And we certainly should not neglect the fact that Hebrew wisdom found its expression in rich metaphors such as "the fruits of a man's mouth." I want to suppose that this metaphoric language only attains meaning in praxis.

Let me attempt a description in which these maxims play a role in the epistemological process described above. The lacuna in knowing addressed in this proverb appears to be the idea that "what we say burgeons from within us and can bring good or ill," or something to that effect. Hence, we ought to attend to our spoken words. But this proverb does not seem to instruct us about the mere act of speech, but speech in the context of relationship to others.

The lesson many of us young men and women learned the hard way was that our speech often betrayed more than the content that we

[61] Von Rad, *Wisdom in Israel*, 21.

presumed we were delivering to others. Our statements conveyed arrogance, carelessness, or insecurities of which we were not even aware. According to this aphorism, there is some correlation between the content (what we say) and the performance (how we say it) on which we need to focus in order to understand.

When we attend to those dimensions of our speech while we are speaking, these proverbs then act as a coach, highlighting to us aspects of how others perceive us, or how we want to be perceived, that were previously unknown to us. Or as Michael V. Fox tells us: "[A] proverb must meet a particular need, and this imbues it with ever fresh 'performance-meaning.' A proverb receives its full meaning only in application, when it is spoken to a particular end."[62]

As for the New Testament texts, the trend continues. Let us consider just one series of maximic sayings in Ephesians and attempt to understand how they fit the epistemological pattern proposed thus far.[63] Paul states in Ephesians:

> And you were dead in the trespasses and sins in which you once walked, following the course of this world, following the prince of the power of the air, the spirit that is now at work in the sons of disobedience – among whom we all once lived in the passions of our flesh, carrying out the desires of the body and the mind, and were by nature children of wrath, like the rest of mankind. But God, being rich in mercy, because of the great love with which he loved us, even when we were dead in our trespasses, made us alive together with Christ – by grace you have been saved – and raised us up with him and seated us with him in the heavenly places in Christ Jesus, so that in the coming ages he might show the immeasurable riches of his grace in kindness toward us in Christ Jesus. For by grace you have been saved through faith. And this is not your own doing; it is the gift of God, not a result of works, so that no one may boast. For we are his workmanship, created in Christ Jesus for good works, which God prepared beforehand, that we should walk in them. (Eph 2:1–10)

To consider how deeply analogical this instruction to the Ephesians is, it might help if we pretend that we are a child attempting to understand the meaning of the above passage.[64] We would have to ask basic questions, such as:

> How can we be dead in our trespasses?
> How do we walk in sin? Is sin a substance to be stepped in?

62 Michael V. Fox, *Proverbs 10–31* (Anchor Yale Bible; New Haven, CT: Yale University Press, 2009), 484.

63 This section on Ephesians is adapted from Johnson, *Biblical Knowing*, 143–47.

64 Paul presumes a spiritual transformation that backlights his theological metaphors with meaning.

How does flesh have passion?
How do "rich" and "mercy" correlate?
From what have we been saved?

These statements found in Ephesians make little, if any, sense in and of themselves beyond them being metaphors and analogies. There is not a logical way to build a bridge from the grammar, syntax, or literalistic meaning of the words to the presumed intention of the communication. In the same way that we cannot understand the sentence "choke up on the bat" unless we understand (1) the physical act of choking someone or something with two hands, (2) that the bat stands in for the neck of the thing that we are choking, and (3) what direction "up" refers to in our hand-hold on the bat. Although the sentence necessarily requires imaginative participation to make sense, when we are physically participating (i.e., maneuvering our grip on the bat), the sentence can be fully coherent and guiding to us. Our ability to combine our analogical reasoning with our current embodied situation makes the instructions like wisdom to us – maximic language that guides us in the act of doing.

Similarly, the writer of Ephesians employs a string of cryptic phrases to bring the reader to know something. If the epistle contains this maximic language, then there is no way to understand the meaning – or at least, understand it well – apart from embodied participation. The description "by grace you have been saved through faith" can only make sense to us if we have had prior experiences that can be aptly represented by concepts like "trust" (*pistis*) and "rescue" (*sōzō*), both embodied constructs.

Paul's rhetorical employment of "walking" throughout Ephesians could become slippery here, so let me clarify. A summarized version of the letter's teaching is something akin to "since we have been rescued from death in judgment, then live ethically as if we have been rescued." Walking in wisdom refers to discerning between the foolishness of the world (cf. 2:1b; 5:17a) and the will of God (cf. 2:10b; 5:17b). This type of "walking in wisdom" is a skilled discernment that requires certain experiences and actions based on what Paul is teaching. As an analogical metaphor, "walking" must be imaginatively employed in order to make any sense because Paul is not referring to actual walking.

We cannot understand the analogical reasoning behind maxims such as "polish up your finish" without actually swinging a club. The meaning is not only logically separated from us, but it also comes from another human activity entirely (i.e., polishing silver to a shiny finish, where "finish" itself is a metaphor). Similarly, the audience can miss much of what Paul advocates without prior experiential knowledge of something analogous to physical salvation.

Being saved, a conceptual metaphor from the Hebrew Bible, depends for its meaning on a time when we were in physical peril but were rescued from it. If we know Paul's salvation and then live (or "walk") according to what Paul is instructing us, then we should come to know well the veracity of his other claims as we participate. This does not mean that we must have a near-death experience to understand salvation, but that the Scriptures tug on the analogical concept of physical salvation from death to relate to us the broader concept. The point is that the physical experience precedes the concept.

This didactic aspect of the wisdom literature, of which I have only scraped the surface here, shows signs of following the same epistemological priorities staked out above. It begins with an intent to focus on listening to accredited authorities. More than listening, knowing results from doing and seeing as a consequence.

The proverbs linguistically extend the epistemological process into the embodiment of the authority's instruction and their maximic coaching along the way. We are not handed instructions and left to our own, as with some horrendous piece of build-it-yourself furniture. Rather, those accredited to us guide us to see by the use of maximic language. We find these maxims meaningful only to the extent to which we submit, listen, and adjust according to them. Hence, we will always be logically separated from the meaning of "tighten up your swing" or "notice the cell evacuating water" until we commit to the act and the instruction.

Conclusions

It should now be obvious that a much larger thesis lurks behind this attempt to show parallel structures between the Hebraic epistemological style and Polanyi's scientific epistemology. However, I have restricted my observations to these four central points as tropes to consider in developing views about the philosophical elements of the Bible. Polanyi and the biblical literature share primary concerns regarding:

1. coming to skilled knowledge
2. the knower's reliance upon testimony-as-guidance that demands accreditation
3. the role of controversy in knowing
4. the use of maximic language to guide knowers

Given the above, the reasons for the epistemological affinities between the Hebraic philosophical style and scientific epistemology can now be seen in rough form. Scientific pursuits deal with an indeterminate field of data, in which some structural coherence is perceived (pixelated). All understanding has to fit the scientific storyline (networked) grounded in an understanding of its relationship to a creation event and all current explanations (e.g., Big Bang creationist). Failure to reconcile data to a context or storyline in science is considered a profound problem (e.g., the failure to reconcile Einstein's general relativity with quantum mechanics).

Novice scientists enter the tradition through rituals aimed at fostering their understanding, and then they go on to practice experimental science in the community (ritualist). Scientists perform experiments as embodied rituals that closely follow scripts to understand a phenomenon and share that understanding trustingly amongst colleagues – fellow scientists who hail from all demographics and lend their mutually enriching expertise to the enterprise (transdemographic). The practice of this scientific grammar both yields epistemic confidence through embodied and community experience and sharpens one's awareness of what is unknown from that which is unknowable (mysterionist).

9

Biblical Truth and Human Logic

> To be able to rely on something, to be able to count on it – this seems to be the heart of the truth of the Bible.[1]

If the scientific epistemology parallels Hebraic epistemology in any significant way, then the conceptual paradigms of truth and the mechanics of justification could – or, perhaps, *should* – follow suit. The Hebraic model of "truth" that emerges differs at key points from some, but not all, of our folk notions of truth today. Specifically, the true/false binary that funds current and popular models of justification appears to be too rigid a model for the Hebraic style.

Biblical authors work with a notion of truth not restricted to a true/false binary. Their sensibilities here do not preclude such a notion; it just does not appear as a concern when they depict matters of truth against falsity. Their sense of "true" requires a framework of knowing aimed primarily at the goal of skilled discernment. Justification, therefore, involves experimentation, a basic scheme of logic, and personal agency.

Any realist depiction of "true knowing" requires a coherent account of truth and its logic of justification. A key component of justifying what is true, as we will see, is the test of "time and circumstance." What is true can only be evinced over time and across circumstances. And if "time and circumstance" factor natively in the biblical authors' conception of truth, then justification must be able to track *truly* over both.

[1] Yoram Hazony, *The Philosophy of Hebrew Scripture* (New York: Cambridge University Press, 2012), 200.

In this chapter and the next, I examine a Hebraic notion of truth and justification in the Hebrew Bible and the New Testament. Although I will put both truth and the logic of justification in conversation with contemporary ideas, I do so only to show both the kinship we share with biblical notions, and the critique offered from the biblical texts. By the end of the next chapter, we will have seen truth, logic, and justification depicted as central to the rationality depicted in scenes pixelated across Scripture by biblical characters and teaching.

The Nature of Truth

If we believe the claim "the sky is blue" is true, we must consider the reasons for espousing its truth before discussing how biblical literature develops ways of discovering *truly*. The reasons a three-year-old and a meteorologist believe the sky is blue derive from two different mechanisms: trusting relationships and skilled understanding built through trusting instruction. Both mechanisms are required, but biblical authors focus on the development of skilled discernment as the natural route of epistemology.

Though these same concepts of truth, validity, and justification populate our intellectual world today, we often lean into another conceptual scheme for truth: that something is either true or false and none other. And, even more unhelpful for the biblical discourse, popular speech reaches to modify truth as "absolute" or "subjective." Specifically, we need to consider if our own presumptions about truth might be running interference, blocking us from the biblical conception of truth.[2]

Several philosophical theories of truth attempt to give the most reasonable view of whether a proposition, such as "the sky is blue," is true or false. The most popular truth-theory amongst English-speaking philosophers, the correspondence theory of truth, maintains that a proposition is

[2] The section on logic and nonbinary truth is a rewritten argument from Dru Johnson, *Knowledge by Ritual: A Biblical Prolegomenon to Sacramental Theology* (Journal of Theological Interpretation Supplements 13; Winona Lake, IN: Eisenbrauns/PennState Press, 2016), 72–78. When I teach undergraduate classes that the biblical authors cannot conceive of a simple notion of "absolute truth," some students immediately go into epistemic arrest. Many of them have been taught their whole lives that absolute truth – sometimes known as "capital-T Truth" – is the ideal and everything else is "small-t truth." Not only does this idea of truth risk importing very dangerous notions into the biblical world, but it also does not make sense of the epistemological task. I will eventually show that this view does not make sense in *any* epistemological structure that can account for religious and scientific knowledge without reducing them both to mere caricatures.

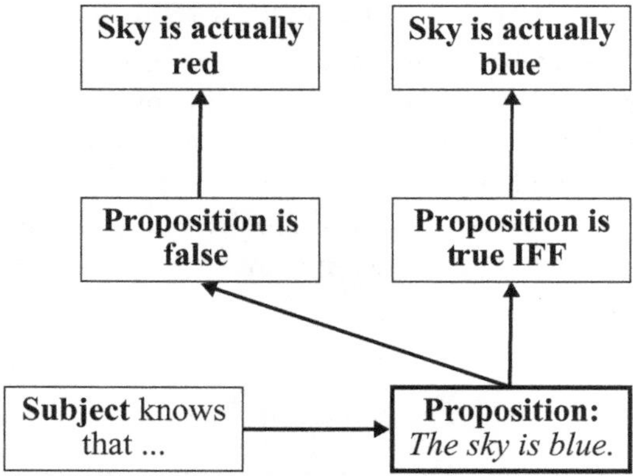

FIGURE 2 "The sky is blue" correspondence
Source: Created by Dru Johnson

true when the reality to which it refers actually is the case (Figure 2).[3] The proposition represented by the sentence "the sky is blue" is true *if and only if* (*iff*) the sky is actually blue in some way.

Other theories of truth work out the same problem using a different metric for truth from correspondence. Coherence theories seek to situate the truth of a proposition in a larger, logically connected scheme, within which "the sky is blue" is coherent. Truth, then, means making sense within a given web of knowledge.[4]

Pragmatic views of truth (i.e., it is true if it works) have the admirable quality of being inextricably tied to reality, but they also bring some ethical baggage. The ethical notions needed to define what "it works" means has a slippery history.[5] Medical experiments in Nazi-occupied Poland and in Tuskegee "worked," but they are not the kind of truth most of us seek. Moreover, in the Christian tradition, the cosmos is not the way that it is supposed to be metaphysically or epistemologically.

[3] According to a recent survey, approximately 62 percent of philosophers, largely from the Anglo-American tradition, believe in some kind of correspondence theory of truth ("The overall list included 62 departments in the US, 18 in the UK, 10 in Europe outside the UK, 7 in Canada, and 5 in Australasia."). David Bourget and David J. Chalmers, "What Do Philosophers Believe?" *Philosophical Studies* 170, no. 3 (September 2014): 468.

[4] For coherence theory, "a true proposition is one that coheres appropriately with certain other propositions." Robert Audi, *Epistemology: A Contemporary Introduction to the Theory of Knowledge*, 3rd ed. (New York: Routledge, 2011), 288.

[5] See discussion on Naturalized Epistemology in Dru Johnson, *Biblical Knowing: A Scriptural Epistemology of Error* (Eugene, OR: Cascade, 2013), 169–71.

Hence, something "working" might make it pragmatically true, but lacks the imagination to conceive of the cosmos any other way in which it presently exists.

The Christian imagination, if not also the Hebraic, requires such imaginative hesitations about raw pragmatism. If for no other reason, the metaphysical claims at the head of Genesis and the tail of Revelation make clear that this world is not the way it is supposed to be and will ultimately be metaphysically reordered. Hence, whether something is pragmatically true is contingent upon one's definition of operational success (i.e., "it works") and for the biblical philosophy, on the future reorientation of a disordered cosmos, even if we do not know what that reorientation entails.

What must be observed in these approaches to truth is that the proposition – the thing to be believed – functions as the centerpiece of truth or falsity. True and false are posited as opposite ends in a binary relationship, and are applied to an idea or state of affairs *disembodied and independent of the knowing subject*.

My two goals are: (1) to reorient us toward the biblical notion of "truth" and (2) to propose a process of knowing in which rituals move the knower toward recognizing and discerning through the body. After seeing how biblical authors used truth conceptually, we are left without recourse to a merely binary notion, where something must be either true or false and nothing in between. Rather, we always and constantly know something more *truly* or less so. Truth, then, is fidelity to a purpose or function.

Discussions such as this cause many readers epistemological duress, especially if they have habituated various and popular definitions of truth from recent philosophical thinking. Even more, this can make for an uncomfortable conversation for those who have simply mapped those contemporary views of truth directly onto their reading of Scripture. However, any view of truth that hopes to accurately reflect the biblical construct must wrestle with the fact that the term for truth (*ʾemet*) in the Hebrew Bible modifies many unusual actions, statements, and objects:

Actions: Treatment of a servant (Gen 32:10); Anointing (Judg 9:15); Walking (1 Kgs 2:4)

Statements: Reports (Deut 17:4); Accusations (Deut 13:14); Pledges (Josh 2:12); Words of God (2 Sam 7:28)

Objects: Tent pegs (Isa 22:23); Roads (Gen 24:48); Seeds (Jer 2:21); Men (Exod 18:21)

Similarly, in the New Testament, "truth" (*alēthēs*) describes people,[6] actions,[7] statements,[8] realizations,[9] and itself becomes nominalized as a metaphor for the faithful instruction of God: "the truth."[10] Truthfulness becomes a supreme quality of important statements according to Jesus himself: "Truly (*ʾamen*) I say to you." This describes his speech, using the transliterated Hebrew term *ʾamen*, as truly guiding, not necessarily as statements of truth in the binary scheme.[11]

How is a tent peg true in the same way that reports or actions are true? We must begin by frankly admitting the semantic distance between the modern English "true" and the ancient Hebrew *ʾemet*/*ʾaman*. Yoram Hazony explores this problem in *The Philosophy of Hebrew Scripture*, and I will closely follow his conclusion about true speech:

> [W]e could say that *emet* and truth are simply two different things. What prevents us from reaching this conclusion is not only the traditional translation of *emet* as truth ... it is also the fact that *emet* is the only term available to describe the truth of speech in the Bible. Thus if we were to dispense with the term *emet* as referring to the truth of speech, we would be left without any way in which biblical Hebrew could express the idea that something that someone said or thought was true![12]

The transliterated Hebrew term in the dozens of Jesus sayings – "truly (*ʾamen*) I say to you" – indicates that the NT authors felt similarly about the unique role and conception of "true" appropriate to Jesus' assertions.

True, in Scripture, does not refer to the tradition of truth in which true propositions exist independently of our knowledge of them. For instance, Scripture does not seem to contain a persistently developed notion that it is true that "Jesus is the messianic king" independent of whether or not anyone knows this to be the case. Hazony incisively shows what many philologists and biblical scholars have observed for some time – that Scripture develops a notion of truth as a function of reliability. Whatever denotations and connotations we have packed into the word "true," should not the *emic* meaning of "truth" in the vernacular of the biblical authors have some sway in our thinking about a Hebraic philosophical style?[13]

[6] E.g., Jesus, Matt 22:16; teacher, Mark 12:14; worshipers, John 4:23.

[7] E.g., practicing truth, John 3:21; standing in truth, John 8:44; sanctifying in truth, John 17:17.

[8] Mark 5:53; Luke 4:25; Acts 26:25.

[9] Matt 27:54; Mark 14:17.

[10] Romans 1:25; 2:8.

[11] E.g., Matt 5:18; passim in the synoptic Gospels.

[12] Hazony, *The Philosophy of Hebrew Scripture*, 338n36.

[13] James Barr pursues the problematic insistence by theologians Herbert and Torrance that there is a "fundamental meaning" of a Hebrew word root (e.g., *ʾaman*). Their debate then

Without rehearsing his entire argument here, Hazony's critique of the slip and grip between our notion of truth and Scriptural vocabulary is worth considering in detail. Scripture employs *ʾemet* similarly to the narrower sense in which "true" is used in carpentry today.[14] A true cut (or maintaining a true course in a ship) is one that reliably "is what it ought to be": "In the Hebrew Bible, that which is true is that which proves, in the face of time and circumstance, to be what it ought; whereas that which is false is that which fails ... to be what it ought."[15]

Unlike the correspondence theory of truth, this view does not hold that a truth obtains at one time-slice, or independently of the knower. According to the correspondence theory, knowledge of the proposition "Jesus is the Christ" and the proposition itself "Jesus is the Christ" are equally true because the proposition is made true by the objective fact that Jesus actually is the Christ.

In contrast, Hazony contends, "We find, therefore, that to adopt the biblical account of truth and falsity has the following consequence: that the truth and falsity of speech is found to be dependent on the truth and falsity of the object [or person] to which this speech refers."[16] An object or person being true to their purpose over time and circumstance is a way

proceeds by arguing for this fundamental meaning, and according to Barr, commits several hermeneutical fallacies in the process. See "'Faith' and 'Truth,'" in James Barr, *The Semantics of Biblical Language* (Eugene, OR: Wipf & Stock, 1961), 161–205. See also: Arthur G. Hebert, "'Faithfulness' and 'Faith,'" *Reformed Theological Review* 14, no. 2 (June 1955): 33–40; Thomas F. Torrance, "One Aspect of the Biblical Conception of Faith," *Expository Times* 68, no. 4 (January 1957): 111–14. To be sensitive to Barr's critique, this analysis must proceed with an affinity to sentences bearing theological meaning within larger contexts, both narratival and rhetorical. This means that support for a theological position cannot be asserted solely based on individual terms (e.g., *yādaʿ*, *rāʾâ*, *šāmaʿ*, etc.). Rather, support must be demonstrated from the linguistic context from which those terms gain their meaning. It might be further argued that the larger narrative structures often bear the ultimate theological meaning, as pithy truisms do not occur in a narratival vacuum. The conflict, narratival tension, characters, and plot movement toward resolution can all play on the words and meaning to such a degree that the story becomes the ultimate context for the lexical stock, thereby nullifying the notion of "lexical stock" itself. Something similar has been argued in "The Narrative Approach to Paul" where *dianoia* (i.e., interpretive framework) applied to the Hebrew Bible and Gospel narratives constrain the rhetorical meaning of Paul's letters. Bruce W. Longenecker, "The Narrative Approach to Paul: An Early Retrospective," *Currents in Biblical Research* 1, no. 1 (October 2002): 88–111.

[14] Because I can appeal to the carpenter's sense of "true," we do maintain one sense of the biblical denotation in the semantic range of the English word "true."

[15] Hazony, *The Philosophy of Hebrew Scripture*, 201.

[16] Hazony, *The Philosophy of Hebrew Scripture*, 205.

of saying "it works." Thus, a peculiarly pragmatic function of truth emerges across the biblical accounts.

The cognate word-groups now coalesce around this meaning of truth. If something is what it ought to be over time and circumstance (*ʾemet*), then it is considered faithful (*ʾāman*) and can, therefore, be trusted (*ʾĕmûnâ*).

Two factors then become central for biblical truth: proving fidelity over time and proper interpretation. First, Hazony uses the phrase "proves, in the face of time and circumstance" to mean that truth, by its very nature, cannot be determined in a singular instance. Truth can only be interpreted through a process of attending to someone or something's veracity – its reliability. In addressing the question of how a tent peg and speech can both be considered diachronically true, the matter of interpretation becomes primary. The faithfulness of the peg to do what it ought to do – to hold down the tent in sun and storm – is the hallmark of its *ʾemet*. So it goes with speech; its veracity, fidelity, or faithfulness to interpret that to which it speaks is its truth, like the carpenter's true cut or the ship's true course (see Figure 3).

This analogical notion of truth has linguistic support in the Hebrew – that truth captures the fidelity between what is and what ought to make sense of the cognate terms of *ʾemet*. One of the few Hebraisms to persist

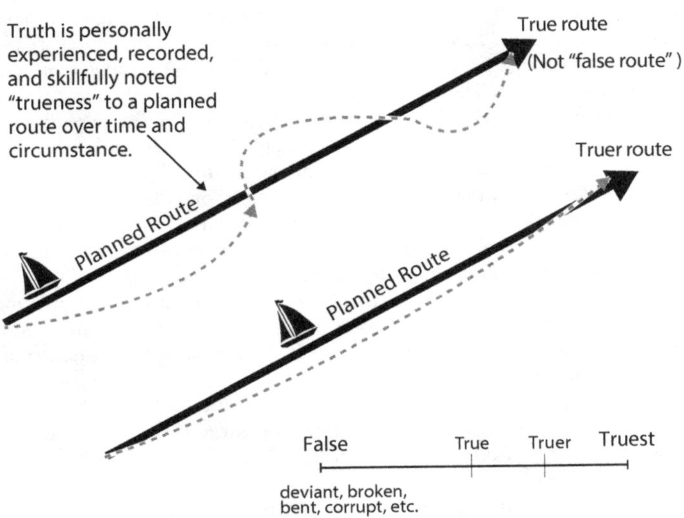

FIGURE 3 True course of boats
Source: Created by Dru Johnson

into English, "amen" derives from the root term *ʾemet*, as well as *ʾĕmûnâ*, often translated both from the verb and adjective as "faithful." To propose that truth is more like veracity or faithfulness does have currency in modern English. However, it is the conceptual barrier that truth-is-a-thing-in-and-of-itself that often distances us from the biblical meaning.

Second, although Hazony does not explore the matter of speech as interpretation, true interpretations appear to be resident in his thinking of truth-talk and fit his description well. When speech is referred to as "true," this indicates that it reliably interprets actual events or objects. Many statements can be offered, but the true one interprets best according to need. Notice that in this last statement, "the true one interprets best," "true" does not refer to the statement by itself, but the interpretation of the one who offers the statement. Just as with maps, the truest map serves its purpose best (e.g., to guide tourists to landmarks, to reveal water systems, to navigate highways, etc.). However, *the map itself is not true* in the biblical sense. Rather, the instruction of the cartographer by instrumental means of the map is true. Hence, truth-talk speaks to the relationship between knowers and the referents of what they are interpreting – that which they recognize and discern.

To extend this example, we do not consider a water table map false merely because it does not lead tourists to local landmarks. Water table maps are not true to the aims of local tourism as tourist maps are not true to aquifer locations. Yet, that does not make those maps fundamentally true or false. Again, the biblical sense of truth generally accounts for a thing doing what it ought to do per the context and *in situ*.[17]

In this sense, a tent peg cannot be true/false *in and of itself* any more than a proposition can be true/false *in se*.[18] Much like Aristotle's view of artificial production, we could say that a tent peg can be true to its maker's intention.[19] The biblical sense of truth has the advantage of parsimony over the propositionally dependent views of truth, not requiring the existence of *ad extra* abstract objects such as propositions to evince truth.

For instance, Deuteronomy discusses the possibility of a true report of adultery in the land. Specifically, in discussing how to deal with adultery, Deuteronomy raises the matter of a report of adultery first and then its veracity. "If it is told" (*nāgad* in the *hophal*) is followed by "and if the

[17] I am not suggesting that there is no correspondence between reality and the guidance that disposes us to see it truly. Rather, I am arguing that traditional correspondence theory does not do justice to what biblical authors seem to be doing with truth as a term and concept.

[18] Johnson, *Biblical Knowing*, 154–66.

[19] Aristotle, *Physics*, 2.8.

truth was established" (Deut 17:4). The relationship between that which was told and that which is true is not resolved by an extra and intervening proposition "Mr. X was adulterous," which is then determined to be true or false. The truth of the report is established by how well the reporter has interpreted the actions of the one being reported. This veracity, the establishment of the truth of the matter, necessarily unfolds over time, unable to be true in an instant. On this theme, Hazony summarizes: "It would seem that the truth or falsity of the spoken word [i.e., interpretation] cannot be known until it has proved itself reliable in the course of an investigation, which is to say, over the course of time."[20] As a term and concept, "true" primarily functions epistemically and diachronically.

Essentially, Hazony argues for situating truth between the dialectic of persons and things – interpretation of events by persons over time. This requires a process of knowing robust enough to distinguish a nonbinary version of truth from falsity – discerning the truest. We arrive at true statements, such as "the sky is blue," through diachronic knowing, embodied experiences over time and circumstances (Figure 4). Just as a carpenter's cut can be more or less true to the penciled line on the wood, our understanding can be corrected to matters great and small. In the Hebrew Bible and New Testament, a correct understanding conforms to the way Yahweh intends Israel to know.

However, if a truth is absolute – "X is true without reference to anyone's understanding of it, even God's understanding" – then what can we say about such a truth? What would an absolute truth even look like that could be reasonably discussed without appeals to our active interpretation of it?[21] Though they had language for doing so, the biblical authors

[20] Hazony, *The Philosophy of Hebrew Scripture*, 205.

[21] Philosophically speaking, absolute here means "without reference to," in contrast to the idea of being relative to other truths. Regarding the problem of modifying truth with "absolute," Max Black demonstrated something analogous with the notion of absolute position in space (i.e., that there is a position in space independent of everything else). Black offered a thought experiment presuming that there were two spheres in absolute space, meaning that they existed completely independent of anything. Any attempt to describe one sphere will inevitably refer to either the other sphere or some location relative to the spheres. Without discussing the relative positions between the two spheres, they are indiscernible, possibly even the same sphere when described absolutely. Though not his primary goal, Black succeeds in showing the absurdity of our attempt to have any meaningful discussion about those two spheres, despite whether or not they exist in an absolute position in space. Merely trying to discriminate one from the other becomes an impossible task. A thin notion of absolute truth may turn out to be equally indiscernible and therefore inconsequential to a biblical view of understanding. Max Black, "The Identity of Indiscernibles," *Mind* 61 (April 1952): 153–64.

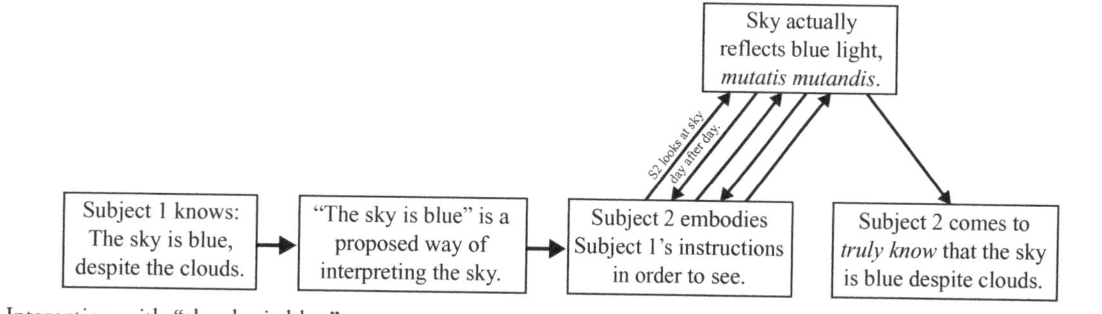

FIGURE 4 Interaction with "the sky is blue"
Source: Created by Dru Johnson

did not modify truth in this way. Instead, they describe and employ truth-talk as if it were in the ken of wisdom and discernment.

To discuss without discernment a supposedly true thing apart from its context invites either talk of nonsense or the need to contextualize. But discussing the context defeats the purposes of designating it absolute. Or, "absolute" becomes an ad hoc fideist position about the thing being discussed. For instance, I might speculate that every speck of reality is haunted by an equal and opposite nonbeing (something akin to a Taoist metaphysic). The only way I can describe nonbeing is by saying it is everywhere that being exists as the nonexistent mirror of being. Though there might be such realities, they appear to us as wholly uninteresting at the very least, and more likely, indiscernible from other realities.[22] And as I have attempted to show, discernment is the very ideal of biblical philosophy.

Another advantage of discussing truth in terms of biblical vocabulary is that ethics and knowing are no longer separable. To know, and to know truly, we must hear another person's interpretation. We must indwell their vision of the thing, their lens for looking at the same reality, to see how true their interpretation is. Scientists call this repeatability. Hence, biblical knowing is fundamentally ethical, dictating what we ought to do to discern finer and finer particularities.

Logic

Since true and false do not operate under a strictly binary opposition – although the binary view can still be coherent within the biblical understanding – what kind of reasoning do biblical authors generally employ?[23] Before we discuss their use of logic, we must first consider our novel conception of logic and rationality, and particularly how humans actually use logic in daily life. This will require a wide-ranging discussion, not of logic per se, but human reasoning and the formation of concepts of logic *within the human body*.

Anyone who has studied analytic philosophy in the past generation might be tempted to tune out the following section; I must deal with the problems of practically employing logic and the implications for

[22] For a summary of why such "truths" are not helpful, or even accurate understandings of said truths, see Johnson, "Broad Reality and Contemporary Epistemology," in *Biblical Knowing*, 149–80.

[23] This section was adapted from sections within Johnson, *Knowledge by Ritual*, 99–116.

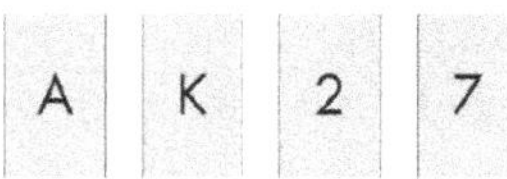

FIGURE 5 Wason Selection Task cards
Source: Created by Dru Johnson

phenomenological understanding of applied logic. However, I ask you to resist the temptation because it will be difficult to understand the biblical authors and their sense of logical relations if we do not grasp the connection of the body to logic in their minds.

Some Problems with Reasoning in the Mind

Even after they have studied logic, humans are not as logically capable as we might presume. The boxes in Figure 5 represent four cards, each with a letter on one side of the card and a number on the other. Suppose you were told, "If there is a 'vowel' on one side of a card, then there is an 'odd number' on the other side." Which card or cards must be turned over to sufficiently confirm what you have been told?

Essentially, this task requires participants to apply the basic logical formulation: *modus ponens* (i.e., "If P, then Q," or P ⊃ Q) and *modus tollens* (i.e., "If not Q, then not P," or ~Q ⊃ ~P).

The well-known results of this simple test of applied logic undermine the notion that humans reason apart from the sphere of experience. This experiment, the Wason Selection Task, has revealed that the great majority of us cannot appropriately apply the rules of *modus ponens* or *modus tollens* even immediately after having been taught the rules.[24] Fewer than 10 percent could correctly select the correct two cards (i.e., "A" and "2") according to the most primitive rules of logic in the above task. The success rate only rose to 13 percent if a person had studied logic *for an entire semester.*

Even more puzzling, this inability to apply the most basic rules of logic further begs explanation after different iterations of the test expanded the problem. Many subjects were successful at applying the exact same rules of logic, even with no training in logic, but in a variation of the original test where they were given a familiar situation (e.g., "In order to drink alcohol, you must be 21 years old). In other words, the more abstract the

[24] For a summary of this research in its various iterations, see: John H. Holyoak et al., "Learning Inferential Rules," in *Naturalizing Epistemology*, 2nd ed., ed. Hilary Kornblith (Cambridge, MA: MIT Press, 1994), 359–92.

problem – even in its most basic form of $P \supset Q$ – the more likely that subjects could not successfully solve it.

> The near-total ineffectiveness of purely abstract training in logic contrasts starkly with the ready ease with which people seem able to apply a naturally acquired pragmatic reasoning schema. For example, after one semester's training in standard logic, students solved only 11 percent of the arbitrary problems correctly, whereas the same students solved 62 percent of the permission problems [e.g., alcohol to age permission] correctly before receiving any formal training.[25]

How do we explain this? Some seek to root our ability to reason within the larger framework of evolutionary success – the most rational creatures win in natural selection.[26] Regardless of its origins in hominins, there are other ways that the rules of inference can be formed into human thinking: embodied experience. This explains why undergraduates without training in logic fare remarkably better in logic tasks that resemble their experience in the world. In fact, the closer the task is to their experiences (e.g., whether or not they can legally drink alcohol), the better they performed.

To argue that reason might have its roots in the body, I will first suggest that schemata formation and analogical reasoning may provide a basis for the embodiment of logic. Second, I will review examples of critical and rigorous analysis that is embodied before it can be articulated. This rattles the distinction between "know-how" and "know-that" as two different forms of knowledge. These will be important for considering models of biblical reasoning and justification in Chapter 10.

Analogical Reasoning

Returning to a brief discussion in Chapter 2, George Lakoff and Mark Johnson began the analogical revolution with their book *Metaphors We Live By*.[27] They argued that all of the images and schemas required to understand the world around us are conveyed through layers of metaphor. These metaphors are ultimately rooted, however, in our embodied experience of the reality to which they refer. In other words, the basic concepts that we take for granted, even logical deduction itself, are

[25] Holyoak et al., "Learning Inferential Rules," 385.

[26] Thus Stephen P. Stich writes, "Natural selection will favor rational inferential strategies." "Could Man Be an Irrational Animal? Some Notes on the Epistemology of Rationality," in *Naturalizing Epistemology*, 2nd ed., ed. Hilary Kornblith (Cambridge, MA: MIT Press, 1994), 345.

[27] George Lakoff and Mark Johnson, *Metaphors We Live By* (Chicago: University of Chicago Press, 1980).

derived from our experience. The embeddedness of metaphor in experience is clear from the example "theories are buildings." We speak of theories regarding their *foundation*, their *support*, a theory is *shaky*, we must *construct* an argument, our argument *stands* or *falls*, our *framework*, etc. Or, the "ideas are plants" metaphor reasons about ideas in terms of *fruition*, *budding*, *offshoot*, *fertility*, *ripening*, *branching*, *flowering*, etc.

Lakoff and Johnson's ensuing work, which developed into a theory of analogical reasoning, is of specific interest for Hebraic philosophy. Analogical reasoning is the form of reasoning that necessarily involves our embodied discernment for certain ideas to be logical to us.

As with most philosophically rigorous works, the real test of the description is mathematics. George Lakoff and Mark Johnson both go on to produce separate works arguing that even the operations of logic and mathematics derive from the same source: our bodies.

Johnson develops the concept of image-schema, which are not images, but patterns of action or shape, or both. For instance, the "compulsion schema" is derived from the experience of physical force in the world – compelling an object or being compelled. That image-schema can be analogically mapped onto many other dimensions, including deductive logic itself: "In the epistemic realm this movement *just is* an inferential pattern, for, if something *must* be true, then we are forced to infer that it *is* [true] – no other conclusion will do."[28] Physical pushing provides the necessary image-schema to understand the notion of "logical necessity." Likewise, the balance image-schema can only derive from our embodied experience of balance, and is then analogically mapped onto other ideas, such as mathematic equations. Combine the compulsion schema with balance and you can make logical sense of otherwise abstruse statements such as this: the two sides of an equation must balance by logical necessity.[29] Johnson is worth reading at length:

> In sum, we are now in a position to begin to explain how our notion of abstract (purely logical) rationality might be based on concrete reasoning that makes use of image-schematic patterns and metaphorical extensions of them. Our acts of reasoning and deliberation are not wholly independent of the nonpropositional dimension of our bodily experience. We can, and do, abstract away from this experiential basis, so that it sometimes looks as though we are operating only with

[28] Italics original. Mark Johnson, *The Body in the Mind: The Bodily Basis of Meaning, Imagination, and Reason* (Chicago: University of Chicago Press, 1987), 63.

[29] George Lakoff, *Women, Fire, and Dangerous Things: What Categories Reveal about the Mind* (Chicago: University of Chicago Press, 1989), 363.

a priori structures of pure reason; however, the extent to which we are able to make sense of these extremely abstract structures is the extent to which we can relate them to such schematic structures as connect up our meaningful experiences.[30]

Hence, we are not locked permanently into our narrow field experience, but our conceptual world starts there and expands outward from it.

Johnson offers a much richer account and defense of his position than I can rehearse here. However, his work should be considered in detail by anyone advancing an embodied epistemology or antagonistic to it. Johnson demonstrates in *The Body in the Mind* that the nature of inference itself should be considered as logically rooted in our embodied engagement of reality.[31]

By the end of Johnson's treatise, it is genuinely difficult to imagine anything that does not somehow find its origins in a core set of image-schematic patterns built and applied analogically from human experience. Conversely, it also helps to explain our difficulties grasping quantum mechanics, for instance (something Johnson does not address). Humans encounter profound conceptual barriers to understanding those things for which we have no experience-based schemas. Quantum mechanics flirts with having empirically verifiable results that simultaneously defy our concepts of reality. We only describe them in ways that sound like nonsense to the average observer and physicist alike (e.g., indeterminacy, superposition, and quantum entanglement, which Einstein officially called *spukhafte Fernwirkung* or, "spooky action at a distance"[32]).

30 Johnson, *The Body in the Mind*, 64.

31 I mean "logical" here in the sense that there is an internal logic to the embodied experience. As Lakoff says elsewhere,

> Each of these schemas is understood in terms of direct experience. Each of them has an internal structure, that is, there is a "logic" of each schema. Entailment is characterized in terms of truth, which is, in turn, characterized in terms of understanding. When made fully explicit, the result would be a cognitive semantics that covers the subject matter of predicate calculus. The resulting logic would apply to any subject matter that can be understood in terms of these schemas. Such a logic would cover pretty much the same subject matter as classical logic, but it would have an experientialist rather than an objectivist interpretation.
>
> (Lakoff, *Women, Fire, and Dangerous Things*, 366)

32 Albert Einstein, "To Max Born," 3 March 1947, Letter 84 in *The Born-Einstein Letters: Friendship, Politics, and Physics in Uncertain Times*, ed. Diana Buchwald and Kip S. Thorne, trans. Irene Born (Hampshire: Macmillan, 2005), 155.

This lack of sensical (in both senses) conceptions of quantum phenomena has even led to some backlash from physicists. The title of a recent essay in *The New York Times* sums up the problem. As a theoretical physicist recently lamented the attrition of explanation in his field: "Even Physicists Don't Understand Quantum Mechanics: Worse, They Don't Seem to Want to Understand It."[33] These Schrodinger-esque "explanations" all come across as logically nonsensical when described to us because, given that quantum theory is relevantly true, we do not have image-schemata for these from which we can analogically reason about them. Our experiences give us no conceptual buckets within which we can imagine our way to indeterminacy, quantum entanglement, or simultaneous super-positions.[34]

Beyond concepts and logical necessity, George Lakoff clarifies how the mathematics of calculus can be derivable from embodied image-schemata. Relying partially on previous work from the philosopher of mathematics Saunders Mac Lane, Lakoff begins by tackling the presumption that mathematics as a field must *uniquely* deal with *transcendental truth*, whether Platonic or something else. First, using the Zermelo-Franklin axiom of choice, Gödel's incompleteness theorem, and Hilary Putnam's critique of sets in mathematics, Lakoff concludes, "It follows that there can be no unique body of truths that we can correctly call 'mathematics.' That result is itself a truth of mathematics, *whatever* plausible referent that term has."[35] Hence, math is functionally plural (mathematics, not mathematic), not "subsumed in any one big model or by any one grand system of axioms."[36]

Third, and following Mac Lane, Lakoff argues that the grand question of mathematics dealing with transcendental truth is stymied by one simple "nontrivial" question: "Why does mathematics have the branches it has?"[37] Basically, of the various matters dealt with (e.g., real numbers,

33 Sean Carroll, "Even Physicists Don't Understand Quantum Mechanics: Worse, They Don't Seem to Want to Understand It," *The New York Times* (*The Opinion Pages*), September 7, 2019, www.nytimes.com/2019/09/07/opinion/sunday/quantum-physics.html.

34 A similar view is hinted at in Richard Healey's recent volume, *The Quantum Revolution in Philosophy* (New York: Oxford University Press, 2017), 1–12. The lack of ability to visualize the microscopic world is the philosophical impediment for thinking about it correctly.

35 Italics original. Lakoff, *Women, Fire, and Dangerous Things*, 360.

36 Saunders Mac Lane, "Mathematical Models: A Sketch for the Philosophy of Mathematics," *The American Mathematical Monthly* 88, no. 7 (1981): 470.

37 Lakoff, *Women, Fire, and Dangerous Things*, 361.

Euclidean geometry, linear space, etc.), nothing internal to the discourse of mathematics itself can decide or explain which one of these fields should be dominant, or at times, when to employ one over the other. Hence, Saunders Mac Lane reverts to embodied activity itself for the explanation:

> In our view, such a Platonic world is speculative. It cannot be clearly explained as a matter of fact (ontologically) or as an object of human knowledge (epistemologically). Moreover, such ideal worlds rapidly become too elaborate; they must display not only the sets but all the other separate structures which mathematicians have described or will discover. The real nature of these structures does not lie in their often artificial construction from set theory, but in their relation to simple mathematical ideas or to basic human activities. Hence, we hold that mathematics is not the study of intangible Platonic worlds, but of tangible formal systems which have arisen from real human activities.[38]

Mathematics has the body for its foundation, both the individual and social body.

Lakoff takes Mac Lane's suggested areas of human activities and connects them to the image-schemata on which he and Johnson have written prolifically.[39] Lakoff lists over a dozen mathematical operations where there is a commensurate image-schema to the mathematical concepts and functions required to do calculus (e.g., math function-IMAGE-SCHEMA) such as correspondence-LINK, equality-BALANCE, operator-AGENT, prime-PART-WITH-NO-OTHER-PARTS, etc. He concludes, "What this list is intended to show ... is that basic ideas in mathematics are understood in terms of basic concepts in cognition, as revealed by empirical studies in cognitive semantics."[40]

In the end, mathematics appears as a collection of models because it does not deal with an underlying Platonic reality, but with the cognitively encountered reality of human experiences and activities. Mathematics is not reducible to one grand scheme, and for any given experience, there are various mathematical ways to model that discrete event. Mathematics itself is a pixelated plurality of methods and concepts. It is not my present concern to convince us of the Lakoff/Mac Lane thesis of mathematics. However, I am concerned to show a grand sweep of scholarship that argues persuasively for the centrality and priority of the body in knowing reality, even mathematically. That scholarship does not reside in just one

[38] Mac Lane, "Mathematical Models," 470.
[39] Lakoff, *Women, Fire, and Dangerous Things*, 363.
[40] Lakoff, *Women, Fire, and Dangerous Things*, 363.

field, but everywhere the body is a natural object of study, now including the philosophy of mathematics.

The Hebraic style of philosophy also roots knowing in the body, both the individual's body and the social body in which she is traditioned. Ritualized epistemology, by the nature of its emphasis, develops skilled discernment in the body that can then be conceptualized and extended in the mind. Michael Polanyi's scientific epistemology follows the same track.

And because the Hebraic anthropology asserts that all human bodies are made in the image of God Himself – male and female, slave and free – there are no humans excluded from this intellectual tradition.

Embodied Judgment and Critical Appraisal

Lastly, I want to address the stumbling block that arises for many when articulation is separated from logic. In other words, can we make incisive logical judgments prior to our ability to articulate them? I will survey various pieces of evidence for precise judgments that are made apart from a discursive verbal argument. In short, we can and do judge precisely and rigorously using nonpropositional logic once we habitually embody practices prescribed to us. As Polanyi noted, "This ineffable domain of skilful knowing is continuous in its inarticulateness with the knowledge possessed by animals and infants, who, as we have seen, also possess the capacity for reorganizing their inarticulate knowledge and using it as an interpretative framework."[41]

We know through our bodies both internally and externally, a dichotomy that is quickly losing its utility. We grasp concepts through analogical employment of experience. We can extend our cognition into tools in order to better explore and understand.[42] Yet there are other things we come to know that are much less articulable, possibly ineffable, but certainly critical, nonetheless.

Thomas Nagel claimed in his renowned essay that there is something that it is like to be a bat. And if there is *something*, even if we cannot say exactly what that *something* is, then that *something* cannot be reduced to a mere mechanism of chemicals in the human brain.[43] But, that *something* is not necessarily an amorphous blob in our consciousness. There may be

[41] Polanyi, *Personal Knowledge*, 90.

[42] Andy Clark and David Chalmers, "The Extended Mind," *Analysis* 58, no. 1 (1998): 7–19.

[43] Thomas Nagel, "What Is It Like to Be a Bat?" in *The Mind's I: Fantasies and Reflections on Self and Soul*, ed. Douglas R. Hofstadter and Daniel C. Dennett (Toronto: Bantam Books, 1982), 391–402.

an epistemic structure to these *somethings*. Even our ability to conceptualize and reason mathematically may be a collection of these *somethings*.

Similarly, there is something that it is like to discern that a family conflict has been resolved, a good golf swing, an incorrect waveform on an oscilloscope, or that an argument has tenuous logical backing and is about to fall apart. In the same vein, a now popular anonymous article on Quora.com, commended to me by several mathematicians, lists sixteen *somethings* in response to the question, "What is it like to understand advanced mathematics?" These include being "comfortable with imprecision," "aesthetic preference," "comfort with feeling like you have no deep understanding of the problem," and being "confident that something is true long before you have an airtight proof for it."[44]

These *somethings*, whatever they might be, are a type of knowing that we have because we have habitually practiced, recognized, and can now discern patterns of complex realities even if we cannot say them. They are muscle and habituated brain attentiveness that dispose us to discern those *somethings*. We are no longer concentrating on the particulars of our formulae. We do not have to get caught up in every little argument in a book-long thesis. We can now see how those particulars take part in a focal pattern, discernible only through habituation that has disposed us to see.

Because we can discern the developing pattern, we can then say something about what we know. However, our speech will not exhaust that which we know. Polanyi's notable example concerns the common practice of riding a bike – something known only by habituated practice trained into the body. Polanyi reminds us that knowing the articulation of bicycle balance is entirely unhelpful in riding a bike:

> A simple analysis shows that for a given angle of unbalance the curvature of each winding is inversely proportional to the square of the speed at which the cyclist is proceeding. But does this tell us exactly how to ride a bicycle? No. You obviously cannot adjust the curvature of your bicycle's path in proportion to the ratio of your unbalance over the square of your speed; and if you could you would fall off the machine, for there are a number of other factors to be taken into account in practice which are left out in the formulation of this rule.[45]

[44] Anonymous, "What Is It Like to Understand Advanced Mathematics?" (www.quora.com/What-is-it-like-to-understand-advanced-mathematics-Does-it-feel-analogous-to-having-mastery-of-another-language-like-in-programming-or-linguistics). See also William P. Thurston, "On Proof and Progress in Mathematics," *Bulletin of the American Mathematical Society* 30, no. 2 (April 1994): 161–77.

[45] Polanyi, *Personal Knowledge*, 50.

Knowing the articulated formulation of balance is useless to the person balancing a bike, and that only pertains to balance. Many other activities occurring in one's body while riding a bike would create a cacophony of formulations if articulated in order to describe "riding a bike." But this point is uncontroversial.

What Polanyi goes on to suggest is that all appraisals, either within our bodies (e.g., balance) or of events external to us, are equally dependent upon our bodies knowing before and apart from articulation. The articulation of that which we know is a *post hoc* affair.

For instance, much of experimental science relies upon observation as the primary tool of discovery. A central question in experiment design is always: What will be measured and how will that measurement be made? Polanyi, a research chemist himself, reminds us repeatedly that the scientist *herself* brings a habituated body to the act of observation. The critical judgments and identification of what is significant in an observation depend upon the scientist *herself*, who has been trained and habituated to see what is before her. The nonhabituated scientist cannot discern enough to make a scientific observation. Or, as Polanyi says, "Any process of enquiry unguided by intellectual passions would inevitably spread out into a desert of trivialities."[46]

As one example among many, those trained in the tradition can "read" normally inscrutable data and critically evaluate it apart from the articulation of evaluations. In studies of data interpretation, raters assess and critically appraise electroencephalography (EEG) results (Figure 6). These raters were then asked to articulate their appraisals verbally, but the verbal articulation entered the process as a tool postjudgment.

In the Japanese study of EEG interpretation, all the participants were given the same data and were required to evaluate complex patterns on an EEG readout. The raters' initial disagreements concerning interpretation were only realized as they attempted to agree on a statement that captured their complex nonverbal analysis of the EEG readouts. Through refining

[46] Polanyi, *Personal Knowledge*, 135.

> I want to show that scientific passions are no mere psychological by-product, but have a logical function which contributes an indispensable element to science. They respond to an essential quality in a scientific statement and may accordingly be said to be right or wrong, depending on whether we acknowledge or deny the presence of that quality in it .... The excitement of the scientist making a discovery is an intellectual passion, telling that something is intellectually precious and, more particularly, that it is precious to science. And this affirmation forms part of science.
>
> (134)

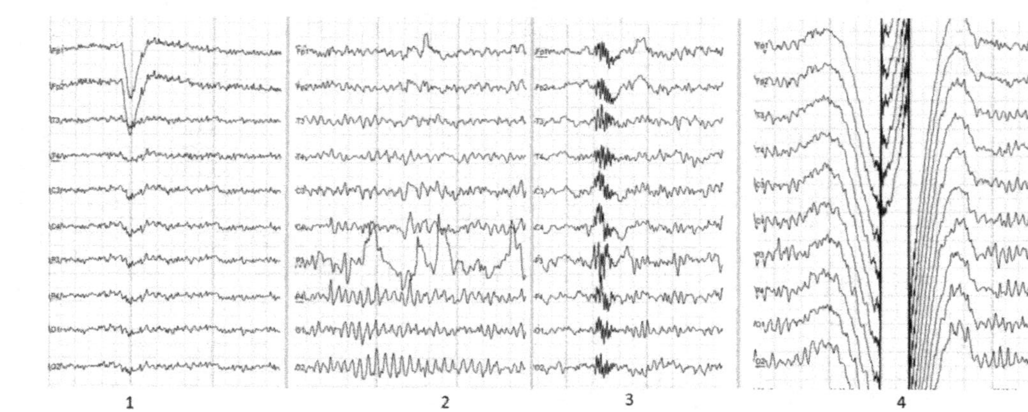

FIGURE 6 A typical EEG readout

the definition and normalizing their language of articulation, they were able to improve their interpretations over time. Nevertheless, they made their critical and exacting analyses prior to the articulation of their judgment or utterance of their evaluations.

The question confronts us now. What epistemically differentiates the inarticulable observations from the verbal statements about observations? The articulation of what the raters know is necessary to communicate with each other about what they critically appraised, to confirm results, to aid in recall, and to arrive at clear summaries. The objection to knowledge being ineffable might presume that such knowing lacks rigor, analysis, and precision in critique, yet these rigorous analyses of EEG data all happened at the embodied phase of observation before the raters could articulate what they have judged.[47]

In these experiments, the observer-rater must learn to critically judge and analyze minute actions before she is allowed to articulate what she observed. Importantly, the raters are then statistically scrutinized against each other for interrater reliability. The rigor, calculus, critique, and rater's skill are all honed before the rater becomes skilled at organizing the observable behavior into something that looks to us like articulated knowledge.[48]

Though there is a wealth of research that supports the critical judgment involved in nonpropositional rating, one experiment in particular highlights what I am contending. A head trauma assessment (TEMPA) relies on raters who make qualitative decisions based on watching patients' limb movements.[49] These assessments are compared with those of other raters once the observation is articulated by a metric. Again, the statistically measurable reliability between raters speaks to the quality of critique and analysis without the use of articulation. It is not until they articulate what has already been skillfully known that raters can confirm their own experiences.[50]

[47] In psychological research, experimenters are sensing, storing, and critiquing nonverbal stimuli that are prior to a propositional judgment concerning the nonpropositional analysis.

[48] Hideki Azuma et al., "An Intervention to Improve the Interrater Reliability of Clinical EEG Interpretations," *Psychiatry and Clinical Neurosciences* 57, no. 5 (October 2003): 485–89.

[49] TEMPA is a French acronym (*Test Evaluant la performance des Membres superieurs des Personnes Agees*) that translates in English to: Upper Extremity Performance Evaluation Test for the Elderly.

[50] Anne M. Moseley and M. C. Yap, "Interrater Reliability of the TEMPA for the Measurement of Upper Limb Function in Adults with Traumatic Brain Injury," *The Journal of Head Trauma Rehabilitation* 18, no. 6 (2003): 526–31.

Those who observe and rate nonverbal behavior must be fluent in understanding stimuli such as eye-tracking while observing certain spatial movements. The rater of the head trauma assessment must be fluent in the "quality of limb movement." Claiming that critical evaluation of experience as a skill (so-called know-how knowledge) that is annexed to knowledge proper (so-called know-that knowledge) does not sufficiently appreciate the reality of the critique. Some interpenetration of skill and articulate knowing in a community must be accounted for in all instances of knowing. The biblical authors take precisely this tack on epistemology.

Semantic Logic

Arthur Gibson's *Biblical Semantic Logic* remains the gold standard for thinking about the linguistic analysis of logic in the biblical texts, especially in his James-Barr-like linguistic warnings about "scholarly intuitions" and use of evidence.[51] Gibson spends most of his time imagining what the semantics of biblical language could do logically and then how we could discern it. Like others before and after him, Gibson recognizes that biblical logic need not be explicit or formulated as Gottlob Frege might have wanted it for it to be legitimately "logical." "The absence of an explicit use of logic does not entail inability to apply logic to assess presence or absence of consistency."[52]

He also warns that a pixelated use of a single instance among scattered others can have a logic to them, but strict systematization might distort the logical connections:

> This is a warning to those who, by imagination or misuse of reason, would regiment biblical language into permissible forms by imposing a belief or attitude as criterion of meaning, although there may be a possibility of constructing an adequate system at a certain level; but candidates scanned in the preceding sections generate law-like collision of presupposition with data and consistency. Nor ought one to acquiesce in subjective response to individual cases.[53]

The twin errors Gibson highlights are overreading current standards from the linguistic turn in logic on the one hand, and only considering one-off examples on the other. This has been my goal above: rather than attempting to find a system of logic, I have attended to what kinds of logic

[51] Arthur Gibson, *Biblical Semantic Logic: A Preliminary Analysis* (Oxford: Basil Blackwell, 1981).

[52] Gibson, *Biblical Semantic Logic*, 82.

[53] Gibson, *Biblical Semantic Logic*, 207–8.

are employed toward justification in order to see if that is what we find in Scripture.

Summary of Truth and Logic

I have only scraped the surface of the linguistic and conceptual cosmos of Hebraic philosophy here. My only goal has been to show how a Hebraic concept of truth might not fit cleanly into a true/false binary that is commonly presumed today. Truth is personal, but not in a way that makes it just another form of relativism. Truth requires attention over time and is carved up according to its purpose (e.g., the true tent peg).

My discussion of human logic has not been rooted in the biblical forms of logic, but rather has been preparatory for what we will see in episodes of epistemic justification to follow in Chapter 10.

10

Pictures of Justification

In *The Art of Biblical Narrative*, Robert Alter proposes type-scenes as one way of exposing the literary artistry of the biblical authors. The use of type-scenes across biblical literature explains why a particular story gets told and retold with different characters in different places. Even more, Alter suggests that this literary method has an epistemological edge to it.[1] The biblical authors explore a topic by retelling a new story with a "fixed constellation" from the known story. "Fiction fundamentally serves the biblical writers as an instrument of fine insight into these abiding perplexities ..."[2]

Concerning consistent epistemological views within the Christian Scriptures, I want to examine a collection of texts to answer the question: Is there a recurring scene of epistemic justification? If so, is it a binary resolution, true or false justification? Or, is justification more akin to degrees of confidence in the sciences? I will contend that it is more like the latter, and that the extreme instances of signs and wonders highlight the peculiarities of justification – that it simultaneously creates second-person knowledge and validates the thing to be known or trusted. This makes the scenes of justification in the biblical literature more like scientific confidence and less like some of the epistemologies popular today.

When a character in the premonarchical texts of the Hebrew Bible is unsure of whether she understands something (states of affairs, promises

[1] "All these formal means have an ultimately representational purpose ... the biblical writers seek to know through their art ..." Robert Alter, *The Art of Biblical Narrative*, revised and expanded ed. (New York: Basic Books, 2011), 219.

[2] Alter, *The Art of Biblical Narrative*, 220.

being kept, facts of the matter, etc.), tests for justification often ease their wariness. For example, Yahweh tests Abraham through a sacrificial ritual in order to know something. The climactic outcome, "Now I know that you fear God ..." (Gen 22:12), resolves the initial tension of the opening line: "After these things, God tested Abraham" (22:1). Likewise, after Moses' recurring skepticism toward Yahweh's planned exodus, Moses himself is finally swayed by signs and wonders to carry out God's plan (Exod 4:1–9, 27–31).

Gideon also challenges Yahweh to authenticate Himself and His plan with a sign. Even then, Gideon persists to ask for another sign in reverse, presumably to test the first sign against the possibility that it happened by chance (Judg 6). In these episodes, and more like them, there is no evidence of blind obedience to a divine being. People want assurance of what they *believe they have understood* and seek it through historically enacted experiments.

All of these acts appear to be part of a pixelated regime of type-scenes, where the texts portray justification being provided for the very thing meant to be known or trusted in each circumstance. I will review the above instances, and others of their ilk, to explore the disparate ways in which justification is established and maintained using tests, ouija, and witnesses as means of justification. Attention will be given to how these stories reflect or diverge from scenes of justification in classical logic (e.g., *modus ponens/modus tollens*) and offer some implications for the study of the rationality schemes of the biblical authors.

What Is Justification for Philosophers?

Forgive my overly simple caricature below, but the recent history of logic and justification provides a sobering context for what we should expect of the biblical texts. Classically construed, justification falls into the philosophical domains of logic and epistemology. To reach confidence in our knowing, we prefer deductive justifications for our beliefs. Our conclusions logically *must be the case* by necessity, given the premises. Syllogisms nicely capture *this kind of logical necessity*:

> My pet is a cat
> All cats are misanthropes.
> THEREFORE, [by deductive necessity] My pet is a misanthrope.

The assurance of the conclusion is as secure as our mathematical sense of justification – as sure as "3" is precisely the number of times "9" can divide "27." Of course, the paradoxes of deductive logic and its inability to deductively justify itself to the expected degrees of completeness consumed discussions of logical justification in the twentieth century. Despite the persistent gaps in explaining how deductive justification itself is *justified*, we need not toss deduction out as a means of reasonable explanation. As the naturalized epistemologists have pointed out, classical deductive logic works in the world of empirical sciences and engineering, even if we can no longer explain exactly how or why it can overcome the problems and paradoxes now associated with it.[3]

Inductive logic, on the other hand, justifies conclusions by the accumulation of evidence, which raises their probability. Of course, the inner workings of inductive inferences are just as cryptic as those of deductive inferences. David Hume loudly rang the alarm bell on this front. The classic argument for the belief that "the sun will rise tomorrow" is based on all previous risings of the sun (so to speak).[4] But there is no deductive-logical connection between previous sun-risings and future ones, if by "logical" we mean that it must be the case given the premises.

As it turns out, my only justification for believing that the sun will rise tomorrow is based on a mixture of habit and the hope that the future will resemble the past. Hume merely pointed out that this habituated hope is not strictly logical in the deductive sense of the term, but more of an eschatological hope. All scientific experimentation operates on this same hope, that events in the world outside of the laboratory will resemble events of a much smaller sample size inside the laboratory.

The way that these kinds of probability calculations manage to correspond to the actual events has a tendentious explanation at best. As Kurt Gödel, Carl Hempel, Nelson Goodman, and others showed us from within math and logic, advances in logic, math, and technology have not alleviated that tendentiousness.[5] And so W. V. O. Quine reminded

[3] W. V. O. Quine, "Epistemology Naturalized," in *Naturalizing Epistemology*, 2nd ed., ed. Hilary Kornblith (Cambridge, MA: MIT Press, 1997), 15–32; "Natural Kinds," in *Ontological Relativity and Other Essays* (New York: Columbia University Press, 1969), 114–38.

[4] See David Hume, *An Enquiry Concerning Human Understanding, and Other Writings*, ed. Stephen Buckle (Cambridge Texts in the History of Philosophy; Cambridge: Cambridge University Press, 2007), 28–53.

[5] Kurt Gödel, "On Formally Undecided Propositions of *Principia Mathematica* and Related Systems," in Jean Van Heijenoort, *From Frege to Gödel* (Cambridge, MA: Harvard University Press, 1977), 592–616; Charles Parsons, "Platonism and Mathematical Intuition in Kurt Gödel's Thought," *The Bulletin of Symbolic Logic* 1, no. 1 (1995): 44–74; Carl G. Hempel, "Studies in the Logic of Confirmation (I)," *Mind* 54, no. 213

his contemporaries *two centuries after Hume*: "The Humean predicament is the human predicament."[6] In the sciences, inductive reasoning is often connected to "generalizability." But, justifying our convictions (or beliefs) by inductive hope that future events will resemble past events – or that far away events will resemble events that we have witnessed locally – does not seem to meet expectations associated with classical logic.

Some degree of hope undergirds those probabilities when employing inductive justification for our predictions. Quine goes on to argue that it's hard to not conceive of all logic as ultimately trapped in the Humean predicament: inductive justifications that cannot ever be completely and deductively satisfied by logical necessity. On such hopes a whole wave of positivism rose and subsequently fell in the mid-twentieth century.

But also, whatever is true here of deduction and induction applies to other attempts to secure knowledge by probability or inference to the best explanation (abduction). Hume and Quine remind us that all epistemologies presuppose or employ hope. I want to suggest that such hopes are not improper. The attempts to eradicate intuitions, hope, trust, and ineffable knowledge from the equation do not escape the above critiques of Hume and Quine. In fact, philosophers have recently attempted to deal social facets of knowing back into the equation (Coady, Zagzebski, Stump, etc.).

However, as long as an epistemology defines epistemic success as knowing a discrete articulable proposition, it remains trapped in the above critique. There are, of course, those who do not constrain epistemologies to propositional knowledge. This move is often yoked with the epistemic division of labor: know-that, know-how, and know-who, where know-how has been subsumed by some to know-that knowledge. What we find in most (if not all) of popular epistemologies differs in structure and process from whatever epistemology is operative in the biblical texts explored here. The biblical authors seem to have skilled observation at the center of their epistemic world, which requires community, tradition, and the individual and social body acting in coordination in order to know. The biblical components of knowing look less like current epistemological models and more like the scientific epistemology proposed by folks like Marjorie Grene, Michael Polanyi, Thomas Kuhn, Norwood Hanson, Mary Hesse, and so on.

(1945): 1–26; Nelson Goodman, "Reply to an Adverse Ally," *The Journal of Philosophy* 54, no. 17 (August 1957): 531–35.

[6] Quine, "Epistemology Naturalized," 17.

I offer this study of the problems inherent to logic and justification for the following purpose: When we turn to ancient Hebraic texts, we should not hold them to some standard of logic and justification that philosophers and others do not trust in today. In league with much current analytic philosophy, these Hebraic justification stories eschew a rationalist mental game of logic in which one can calculate propositions as premises toward a logical conclusion in advance. Instead, they favor historical verifiability, and in doing so, they are not acting irrationally or without a desire for veracious justification.

I suggest that the rational type-scene of justification culminating in Joshua-Judges most closely resembles a scientist in a lab. Like the biologist, biblical authors often portray justification as a matter of historically observed events, contrived through experiment, and meant to justify a conviction or defeat it. Unlike the biologist of scientific positivism's fictions, these scenes often concern themselves with second-person knowledge of those involved.

What Logic Counts toward Justification?

When assessing justification in the biblical narratives, we must consider how much the author reveals about justification in the text itself, and, only then, what types of justification appear to be employed by the characters. (Note: I am including God as one of the biblical characters.) There are at least three possible type-scenes used across these texts to justify a conclusion: tests, ouija, and witnesses. Following this, I will review how the NT authors employ the same means of justification.

Some Test Cases

Deuteronomy 8 makes a startling claim about Yahweh: that forty years of wandering in the Sinai was a test "to know what was in your heart" (8:2). In this sense, testing (*nāsâ*) features someone who does not know something and finds it out by setting up an experiment *in order to know*. The historically observed event then acts as the justification for a subsequent belief, at least tentatively. In this passage, as with some others, testing-in-order-to-know also connotes "proving true" in the sense of "being trued to a purpose over time and circumstance."[7] These kinds of tests go back

[7] Yoram Hazony, *The Philosophy of Hebrew Scripture* (New York: Cambridge University Press, 2012), 201; Dru Johnson, *Knowledge by Ritual: A Biblical Prolegomenon to*

to Genesis, sometimes with Yahweh as the one who needs to know something.

Yahweh tests Abraham (Gen 22) by asking him to sacrifice his son with the result that "now I know that you fear God seeing you have not withheld your son, your only son, from me" (Gen 22:12). Notice that the ritualized experiment was devised for Elohim to know something, and only after "seeing" it does he conclude with the justified conviction of Abraham's intentions. It is akin to scientists trading on the justification of invisible laws and ideas: only after devising an experiment and observing a physical manifestation of what was previously invisible do scientists claim some justification for their hypothesis. In Genesis 22, Robert Alter would also want us to notice the narrator's immoderate repetition of the "relational epithet," twelve occurrences over fifteen verses ("his father," "his son," "my father," etc.) as if the reader needed to be constantly reminded how Abraham and Isaac were related to each other.[8]

Similarly, Yahweh's two messengers go down into Sodom and Gomorrah "to see" whether or not the "outcry that has come to [God]" is true. Presumably, the content of that outcry is something like public violence against vulnerable sojourners. And only after seeing it for themselves, by being the human lures meant to evince the invisible intentions of the Sodomites, does Yahweh assess judgment against the city (Gen 19).

After the exodus from Egypt, Yahweh tests (*nāsâ*) the Israelites with *manna* to know whether they "walk in my *torah* or not" (Exod 16:4). To sum up the long story of Israel: They do until they really do not.

After sentencing that generation to death in the wilderness, Yahweh again claims to be testing (*nāsâ*) their children with the promise of authenticated prophets speaking untruly (Deut 13:3). Of particular interest to the prior discussion of "true," Yahweh does not promise either true or false prophets as two binary categories. Rather, he promises them that he will send prophets who *will be authenticated by signs and wonders*, who will then guide Israel either to act according to the Torah or to deviate from it. Specifically, this is a test of their devotion to Yahweh, invisible to the naked eye apart from such testing. From the average Israelite's perspective, this also requires a level of *torah*-savvy to discern which *authenticated* prophets are speaking truly to or deviating from Moses' instruction.

Sacramental Theology (Journal of Theological Interpretation Supplements 13; Winona Lake, IN: Eisenbrauns/PennState Press, 2016), 71–89.

[8] Alter, *The Art of Biblical Narrative*, 224.

After conquering and settling the land of Canaan, the book of Judges opens with Yahweh testing (*nāsâ*) Israel by not driving out the nations who would lead them to Ba'al worship (Judg 2:22; 3:4). Leaving some nations in the land was explicitly "for testing Israel to know whether Israel would listen to the commandments of Yahweh" (Judg 3:4).

These tests run both ways. Humans are not afraid to test Yahweh and Yahweh mostly acquiesces to sincere tests of his intentions. Abraham tests Yahweh (Gen 15) after a promise of land, which turns out to span the entire Fertile Crescent. When Yahweh promises possession of this land, Abram responds by balking, "How am I to know that I shall possess it?" (Gen 15:8). Yahweh and Abram then perform a cryptic covenant ceremony. Whatever might be happening in that scene between the animals and the firepots, it is clear that this ceremony was meant to justify trust in the promise when Yahweh punctuates it with, "Knowingly you shall know (*yādōa' tēda'*) ..." (Gen 15:13).[9]

In Exodus 3–4, Moses' recurring skepticism toward Yahweh's rescue is ultimately settled by Yahweh's use of three unnatural events meant to convince Moses first (4:1–9), then to convince Aaron (4:27–28), then the elders of Israel (4:29–30), and then the Hebrew people more generally (4:31).

Notice that the initial pushback from Moses ends with signs that convince Moses but are ineffective on Pharaoh. Moreover, the story unfurls a sequential demonstration of the signs/wonders that starts with Moses and ends with the Israelite people, who affirm the efficacy of the signs as justification: "And [Moses] did the signs in the sight of the people and the people trusted (*wayya'ămēn*) ..." (Exod 4:30–31). This sequential justification was initiated by Moses' demand for justified reasons, and it sets up a stark contrast to Pharaoh's obstinate response to Yahweh's signs through Moses. The narrator highlights Pharaoh's obstinacy to the signs that eventually convince Israel, the Egyptians more generally (Exod 9:20; 11:3), and Pharaoh's courtiers specifically (Exod 10:7), but not Pharaoh.

In Numbers 5, the jealousy of husbands can be resolved with a binary test: guilty or innocent. If their wives were indeed adulterous, then the cultic beverage will rot their thigh and womb (5:11–31). Conversely, if the wife is innocent, the husband's jealousy is now *justifiably unjustified*. (I will return to this in the Conclusions section at the end of this chapter.)

[9] See also Genesis 24:14.

Later in Numbers 16, there are multiple tests of Moses and Aaron. Most dramatically, Korah's group of renowned men tests Moses and Aaron, which Yahweh resolves through a binary historical act. As previously discussed, Moses separates Korah and his fellows from the rest of Israel and spells out the experiment clearly (Numb 16:28–30):

> Hereby you all shall know that Yahweh has sent me to do all these works, and that it has not been of my own accord. If these men die as all men die, or if they are visited by the fate of all mankind, then Yahweh has not sent me. But if Yahweh creates something new, and the ground opens its mouth and swallows them up with all that belongs to them, and they go down alive into Sheol, then you all shall know that these men have despised Yahweh.

Yahweh then opens the earth and swallows them alive, and their fire-pans were hammered out and used to plate the altar "as *a sign* (*l'ôt*) to the people of Israel" (Numb 16:38 [17:3]).

These all lead up to the conquest of the land and create the epistemic palette in which the authors of Joshua and Judges dab their brushes. In Joshua's initial conquests, the people need to know that God will drive out the Canaanites from the land. "In this *you all shall know* ... the waters of the Jordan shall be cut off from flowing and the waters coming down from above shall stand in one heap" (Joshua 3:7, 10, 13). Indeed, many have noticed that Joshua's entry into Cana'an resembles the exodus from Egypt:

1. Like Moses before him, Israelite trust is established "in Joshua" (3:7; 4:14).
2. Israel's leader has a personal encounter with a messenger of Yahweh, including the removal of sandals because of a holy place (5:13f).
3. Passover is related to a water crossing, including the crossing on "dry ground" (5:10f).
4. Protection is offered from divine judgment by sheltering in a faithful household (6:17, 22).

These unprovoked signs and wonders, the lack of which Gideon will later complain about, have the effect of establishing and maintaining justifiable trust in Joshua and Yahweh, and in the same pattern used to patently establish Moses: "When Israel saw the great power which Yahweh had used against the Egyptians, the people feared Yahweh, and they *trusted* in Yahweh and in His servant Moses" (Exod 14:31). Joshua appeals to this same rhetoric in an inclusion (cf. 3:7; 4:14): "This day I will begin to exalt you in the sight of all Israel, so that they may know that I will be with you as I was with Moses."

Turning to Judges, Gideon famously tests Yahweh to determine the authenticity of Yahweh's intention to "save Israel by [Gideon's] hand" (Judg 6:36). When the divine messenger of Yahweh greets Gideon with "Yahweh is with you," Gideon's skeptical realism questions the premise with his own experience: Then why has this Midianite oppression happened to us and "where are all His wonderful deeds that our fathers recounted to us?" (Judg 6:13).

Yahweh commissions Gideon to save Israel, and the scene then begins to resemble that of Moses at the burning bush. This resemblance forces the question of whether this scene is what Robert Alter would call a type-scene. Moses-like, Gideon shies away with excuses of weakness and lesser tribal membership. Yahweh again promises his presence in this audacious plan, and Gideon, again like Moses, needs to be convinced of this promise by a sign or three. Yahweh obliges by burning up a meal with a mere touch of a staff. In a scene reminiscent of Jacob in Genesis, Gideon acknowledges the divine encounter: "For now I have seen the messenger of Yahweh face to face" (Judg 6:22). He builds an altar there and names the place.

Yahweh then tasks Gideon with tearing down an altar to Ba'al, and he obeys, which leads to the Spirit of Yahweh clothing Gideon (Judg 6:34) and enabling him to amass followers from the tribes of Asher, Zebulun, and Naphtali. Now having veracious historical reasons to trust Yahweh, Gideon revisits the plan to save Israel with a rightful skepticism. Gideon asks for another sign to confirm the ambitious plan to save Israel by his hand.

He proposes the following test to yield the result that "I shall know . . .":

> Test 1: "If there is dew on the fleece only and it is dry on all the ground" (6:36)

The first experiment was meant to justify Gideon's trust in the plan. For reasons unknown to us, Gideon then pushes Yahweh for another sign to justify his trust in the first sign, through a reversal of the first sign as a "test" (*nāsâ*).

> Test 2: "Let it be dry on the fleece only and on all the ground let there be dew," (implied) "I shall know . . ." (6:39)

Both experiments contain the assumption that Yahweh caused both of these instances to happen, but the second test confirms this premise – God caused this – by creating an implausibly reversed demonstration of the first sign. The first sign could have been a meteorological fluke. Indeed, using a fleece to gather moisture overnight is a common Bedouin practice in the region. The second sign, in particular, required actions upon a natural environment that could only be solved by a personal agent with power over meteorology.

This seemingly settles the matter, though more signs and wonders are yet to come that convince Gideon to undertake what would otherwise be a suicide mission. Yahweh then informs Gideon that his force of 32,000 men is too large and whittles it down to 300. Yahweh offers a sign that Gideon can spy on the Midianite camp and hear for himself the evidence of future success. Gideon heard a fear-inducing dream from the Midianite soldier that was interpreted as such, which the narrator reports as Gideon's reason for worship (Judg 7:15).

The question of a type-scene explanation that spans the burning bush and Gideon's commissioning is now unavoidable. Gideon and Moses are both confronted by a "messenger of Yahweh," are both commissioned to perform an infeasible feat, both shy away from the task, and both ask to be convinced. Finally, both scenes then focus on extraordinary means of justification for trusting Yahweh to bring about the inconceivable outcome. This appears to meet what Alter refers to as "the manipulation of a fixed constellation of predetermined motifs."[10]

In all of these examples of God testing persons and Israelites testing God, the construct requires an experimental design with determinable parameters. Or, in the language of signal detection theory, the sign/wonder or the response from humans functions as a "hit" distinguishable from "misses" and provides room for "correct rejections." In the cases of Moses and Gideon, who demand definitive evidence, God uses multiple instances of signs to justify the conviction at hand.

Israel's Use of Ouija

Israel has access to other types of contrived experimentation with more discrete parameters for epistemic justification. Ouija – a neologism of French and German meaning "yes-yes" – is a physical technology employed to evince something invisible and often unknown among the characters in the narrative. In Leviticus, lots are cast to determine which goat is for sacrifice and which is for wandering on Yom Kippur, a seemingly benign revelation unless you are a goat. Casting lots will also

[10] Alter, *The Art of Biblical Narrative*, 60.

be used to apportion the land of Canaan to the tribes after the conquests of Joshua (Josh 18).

In Joshua 7, Achan steals precious metals from Jericho in direct violation of God's instructions beforehand. He is found out by the casting of lots, where some physical device is employed to determine God's direction on a matter. In this case, God fingers Achan through the lots (Josh 7:13–15, 18). Though these instances appear to merely reveal something hidden, in the only other scene in the Hebrew Bible where Israel is gathered together to reveal someone by casting of lots, lots do not merely reveal Yahweh's choice *to the reader*.

In the books of Samuel, the prophet, Saul, *and the reader* already know that Saul is the first messianic king of Israel. The lots serve to confirm to them – the prophet, Saul, and Israel – within the logic of the story that this choice is from Yahweh. Every time Samuel casts the lots before now-gathered Israel, Yahweh must make them sequentially land on Saul's tribe, Saul's clan, Saul's family, and then Saul himself. Hence, the casting of lots in the Achan narrative was setting us up for yet another physically demonstrated experiment where Yahweh must act in history and within discrete parameters to reveal what the omniscient narrator has already told us: that Achan was guilty. When Yahweh does so, the historical action properly displayed acts as a form of justification. The sequential nature in the call of Moses and here with Saul adds an emphatic exclamation to the justification through its sequential improbability.

But how does this justify the belief that Achan is guilty? By acting as a physical manifestation of divine witness. Thus, the use of ouija by David or the high priest in Yom Kippur is definitively different from its role in the revealing of Saul as king or Achan as *ḥērem* violator.

In the use of ouija, there are discrete outcomes, but in the casting of lots upon Achan and Saul, the improbability of landing on a single tribe, clan, family, and individual seems to work because it rules out chance. In both cases, the reader knows in advance who the single individual is supposed to be, meaning that there is authorial intent to show a particular outcome given its improbable occurrence against chance.

Rule of Witnesses

In using ouija as a witness, we now see the third aspect of epistemic justification come to the fore. Because it is ripe for exploitation, the role of witnesses is also legally constrained with stories that warn of the downfall of false witness.

The biblical term for witness (Hebrew: *ʿēd*) itself reinforces the logic of truth in biblical Hebrew. The Greek *martyrion* generally describes persons testifying to something, but the Hebrew – *ʿēd* – includes connotations of perpetuity. Covenants, permanent structures like stones, memorized songs, the heavens, or Yahweh himself served as "witnesses" to the promises being made. The sense that the stone monument, for instance, will not vary *over time and circumstance* makes it ideal for covenants in perpetuity.[11] Its fidelity to mark the promises *over time and circumstance* also makes it ideal in matters of epistemic uncertainty and justification – putting it in lexical league with the *ʾemet/ʾāman/ʾĕmûnâ* word-group: truth, true, and trustworthy respectively.

For the sake of justice, the Torah requires a minimum of two witnesses to prosecute a capital crime, and this rule plays out in various ways over the biblical storyline. In the case of an unlawful action that is unwitnessed or only witnessed by one person, the situation must be ruled legally ambiguous (Numb 35:30). Conversely, only by the witness of two or more can someone be legally condemned (Deut 17:6). But even then, there are warnings not to use one's witness power to favor the masses (Exod 23:2).

Witnesses also have a legally binding obligation to testify if they know something and to testify faithfully (Lev 5:1). With so much power in the hands of a few, lying in order to falsely indict someone has a steep cost. Intentionally false witnesses, if found out, will suffer the same fate as those they sought to accuse (Deut 19:16–19). It is no surprise then that offering true witness in legal proceedings (i.e., not bearing false witness) also appears in the Ten Commandments. "True" here means an account with high fidelity to what happened in history.

And so, in the biblical narratives of wrong- and right-doing, we find the proper and injurious use of a witness's power to offer epistemic justification for what one is to believe – *for what has been found to be true.* The pluperfect passive voice in this last statement is crucial for understanding truth-talk and the conceptualization of truth across much of the biblical literature. Notice that I did not say that witnesses confirm *that which is true.* Though colloquial and harmless enough, the Hebraic logic of truth is assessed over time and circumstance – i.e., across multiple and disparate perspectives of noncolluding witnesses. The truth is not a state of a proposition's conformity or correspondence to affairs, but something discerned over time by persons, including God (cf. Gen 11:5; 18:21).

[11] E.g., Genesis 31:44–46, 52; Deuteronomy 4:26, 30:19, 31:19; Joshua 22:26–28.

How do witnesses function in the narratives? The Edenic "crime" highlights the fact that the primeval man and woman acted as their own two witnesses against themselves (Gen 3:12–13). Skipping ahead to Achan's crimes in Joshua, Achan was one of the witnesses against himself, and the cast lots acted as the other witness (Josh 7:20–21). Yahweh Himself bore witness through the lots.

Witness narratives reach a zenith in frequency and subtlety in 1–2 Kings illustrating the warnings from the Torah – for good and for ill. In 1 Kings 1, David is coerced into anointing Solomon as King by the witness of two strategically staggered testimonies choreographed by the prophet Nathan (1 Kgs 1:11–14). Nathan suggests that Bathsheba approach the dying king and remind him of his promise to install Solomon as a successor. Coming out of the books of Samuel, readers have not heard of this promise prior to Nathan's suggestion of it.[12] The motivation is stated plainly: "Let me give you advice, so that you may save your own life and the life of your son Solomon" (1 Kgs 1:12). Without using too much imagination, we might suppose that Nathan was also plotting to save his own life through this political arrangement.

Nathan arranges to enter the scene in order to independently affirm the promise to David: "Then while you are still speaking with the king, I also will come in after you and confirm your words" (1 Kgs 1:14). This strongly resembles the constellation of a type-scene where Rebekah coerces a dying Isaac to gain an advantage for her favored son Jacob (Gen 27). David then selects Solomon, violating one of Deuteronomy's few criteria for future kings: "You may indeed set a king over you whom Yahweh your God will choose" (Deut 17:15a).

This royal appointment scene prepares the reader for future problems with Solomon, but it is only part of a theme of corrupt witnesses, a theme starkly contrasted with at least one proper instance of witness.

Later on, in the divided kingdom, the wife of King Ahab uses two witnesses in a devious form anticipated and warned against in the Torah. To secure Naboth's vineyard, she arranged two "sons of worthlessness" to witness against Naboth and formally condemn him to death (1 Kgs 21:8–16).[13] However, Yahweh carries out the Torah's principled

[12] This promise to install Solomon as successor does show up in 1 Chronicles 28:9–29:1.

[13] Wells notes that this see, though devoid of a courtroom, does appear to be a legal proceeding, especially in light of the ancient Near East background of legal witnesses. Bruce Wells, *The Law of Testimony in the Pentateuchal Codes* (Wiesbaden: Harrassowitz Verlag, 2004), 26.

punishment against false witnesses – that they suffer the fate they prescribed against others – not against the two "worthless" men, but King Ahab and Jezebel (1 Kgs 21:17–24).

These two instances of fraudulent witnessing are then juxtaposed against another woman in the royal court asking for a favor. This time, it is not a woman wrongly seeking gain for her son, but a foreign widow who gained a son but lost her land in a famine. This widow was the same one who welcomed Elisha, bore a son through Elisha's promise (cf., Gen 18:14; 1 Kgs 4:16), lost a son to an unnatural death (1 Kgs 4:18–20), and regained a son through unnatural resuscitation by Elisha (1 Kgs 4:32–37).

In a near-reenactment of Bathsheba's coercion of David, a genuine and independent confirmation of Elisha's divine power occurs, with this Shunammite widow playing an unwitting role in the king's epistemic confidence. The narrator tells the story with attention to the timing of the events. An anonymous king asks Elisha's servant to recount these miraculous deeds of the renowned prophet (1 Kgs 8:4): "And while he was telling the king how Elisha had restored the dead to life, behold, the woman whose son he had restored to life appealed to the king for her house and her land." Gehazi, Elisha's servant, had to point out, "Here is the woman and here is her son whom Elisha restored to life" (1 Kgs 8:5).

The epistemic effect can only be inferred from the narration. The story centers on the efficaciousness not just of her witness, but also that it came independent of other stories and with a living artifact of Elisha's powers *standing in front of this king*. There appears, then, a preference for an independent witness who can bolster epistemic justification *for* and confidence *in* reports one has heard – something Nathan and Bathsheba twist to their advantage to install Solomon as king.

In short: *Witnesses true reports*, where "true" is most aptly a verb in Hebraic justification. To this end, we find commands in the legal material to the same effect. If idolatry is reported in one of their villages, then Deuteronomy demands, "*You shall inquire and make a thorough investigation*, and if the truth (*ʾemet*) is established, then ..." (Deut 13:14; HB 13:15). The NRSV translation is struggling to translate the three different terms for "inquire" used in succession in this command: *dāraš*, *ḥāqar*, and *šāʾal* (cf. Deut 13:14; 17:4). The connection between the divine demand for a "thorough investigation" and truth is now unmissable. Witnesses true-up reports, where "true" is a verb.

In the Hebrew Bible's narratives and legal code, witnesses play a key role in epistemic justification. Though Yoram Hazony labeled witnessing as the distinctly *juridic* function of the NT texts, we see that personal and ethically bound witness is baked into the logic of Hebraic epistemology from the outset.[14]

A similar logic of witness abounds in the Gospels and epistles, where Jesus prescribes the rule of two or more witnesses (e.g., Matt 18:16), warns against false witness (e.g., Mark 10:19), and assigns the disciples roles as witnesses (e.g., Luke 21:13). However, the NT authors do not pioneer this role as witnesses, but assume the task in a continuation of Israel's witness to Sinai, exile, and return. Parents were ritually commanded to witness to their children about what they had experienced in Egypt (Exod 13:8–9), at the Jordan River (Josh 4:21–24), and their failure to practice this ritualized witnessing is cited as the reason for the calamitous horror show of Israelite behavior in the book of Judges, Kings, and Nehemiah (Judg 2:10; 2 Kgs 23:22; Neh 8:17).

Jesus' witness-talk presumes an auspicious connection to Deuteronomy's instructions about reports of idolatry. He presumes that reports from the villages of him being a "misleading prophet" and his divine-power campaign will circulate and be properly and improperly investigated: "And you will be dragged before governors and kings because of me, as a testimony to them and the Gentiles" (cf. Deut 13; Matt 10:18).

When Jesus declares, "you all will be my witnesses ... to the ends of the earth," the purpose of the witness-talk that he uses throughout the Gospels is not merely to encourage spreading the news, but also the profoundly Hebraic and ritualized truing of the reports, even to the children.

Tests and Ouija in the New Testament

In the New Testament, the Hebraic concept for "test" (*nāsâ*) acquires a connotation of temptation (*peirazō*). But temptation also has a truing function in many of these scenes. First and most obvious, the Holy Spirit drives Jesus into the wilderness where he was "tested" (*peirazō*) by the "adversary" (*satanas/diabolos*).[15] This testing of by the "adversary" focuses then on whether Jesus will be true, over forty days of duress,

[14] By "juridic," Hazony means that the texts primarily serve to witness to the events in Jesus life and making them, therefore, distinct from the overall aims of Hebrew Scripture. Hazony, *The Philosophy of Hebrew Scripture*, 48–55.

[15] Matthew 4:3; Mark 1:13; Luke 4:2.

to his father's plan. In this Hebraic use of "true," temptation arrests both the time and circumstance features of testing.

Second, the Pharisees and others "test" Jesus by seeking a sign or seeking to entrap him in his words. Jesus refuses both kinds of tests in various and unexpected ways.[16] Their requests for a sign/wonder would presumably shortcut the process of discerning truth over time and circumstance. Though the demand for a sign does not seem unfair in itself, the requester's disposition delineates appropriate from inappropriate ouija in the Hebrew Bible and now the New Testament. Previous instances from the Hebrew Bible show the same kinds of requests for signs (Abraham, Moses, Korah, etc.), yet some are portrayed as negative. The problem regularly presented in divination and wonder narratives concerns the disposition of the ones who request.

Though not a striking resemblance, Israel's forcing the Ark into battle (1 Sam 4:1–11), Saul's raising Samuel up from Sheol (1 Sam 28:15–20), and even the Pharaoh's sign/wonder viewing in Exodus all share in a pattern: the person(s) needing to be convinced has an insatiable demand that dictates how God's actions will be viewed and used in that instance. The story of Pharaoh – though not his servants and household – and Israel – though not all of Israel – includes a recalcitrant witnessing of wonders that do not work to convince them. In these instances, biblical authors depict God's response in signs and wonders as if it were a wasted epistemic effort. However, the psychological profiling of the Gospel-writers clues us in to one particular aspect of these requests that reveal their illegitimacy: they are disingenuous from the outset.

The Jonah narrative displays these two dispositions in direct contrast. Jonah cannot be convinced that God should have mercy on Nineveh, even at the very end when God is directly attempting to convince him. Yet, the sailors who had no other means of calming the tormented sea cast lots, fully intent on letting the lots discern the angry god's intent and acting immediately upon the lots' outcome. It is not surprising to find Jesus refusing such signification through signs and wonders, and only offering the perplexing "sign of Jonah" as a playfully frustrating move.

The epistemology pixelated across the Hebrew Bible now networks into these gospel scenes. The argument that seeing does not equate to proper interpretation effectively prepares readers for more signs and wonders that are erroneously interpreted in order to reject Jesus'

[16] E.g., Matthew 16:1; Mark 8:11; Luke 11:16; John 8:6.

authority. Such was the case with the pharaoh of Exodus, the golden calf worshippers, and countless others in the Hebrew Bible. Miraculous signs and wonders are neither self-interpreting nor efficacious as proof to those who are already disposed to distrust the one performing the wonders. Indeed, the Pharisees and others never question the unnatural acts associated with Jesus' miracles, but only the source of the power behind them or the day of the week on which they were done. The attempts to trip up Jesus superficially appear to be testing his orthodoxy against the theological-ritual traditions as they have understood them. These are not genuine tests, in the sense seen throughout the Hebrew Bible, because the Gospel writers tip us off that the outcome was already determined before the test was posed to Jesus.

Jesus also tests his disciples at several points, but most overtly when he sends them out.[17] Demons must be dispossessed and the sick healed, over time and circumstance, or Jesus would lose credibility within his inner circle, even more so than he did in Mark's Gospel. Jesus tests his disciples when they encounter logistically impossible circumstances. When the crowds follow too far from home and need food, Jesus tells his disciples: "You all give them something to eat" (Mark 6:37). John's Gospel portrays a more cunning Jesus, who asks Philip how they will feed the crowds: "He said this to test (*peirazō*) him, for he himself knew what he would do" (John 6:6).

The epistles' use of "testing" mostly has the temptation connotation; Paul's instruction to the Corinthians to "test (*peirazō*) yourselves to see if you are in the faith" appears to share the goal of truing oneself over time and circumstance (2 Cor 13:5).

At least one use of ouija appears in an unusually prominent position in the New Testament texts. With only eleven disciples left, the apostles feel that the number of twelve disciples was significant enough to warrant appointing a replacement for Judas. The problem: they have two equally qualified men – Justus and Matthais – and no way to adjudicate between them. Without commentary from the narrator, they "cast lots for them and the lot fell on Matthias" (Acts 1:26).

Unlike the stories of Saul and Achan, and more akin to David's use of ouija to "inquire of Yahweh," we do not know which man the lots were supposed to fall on, as it were.[18] We only know which one it did fall on, displaying the apostles' trust in God and in ouija to reveal God's preference here.

[17] Matthew 10:9–15; Mark 6:8–11; Luke 9:2–5.
[18] E.g., 1 Samuel 30:7–8.

Conclusions

The distance between classical epistemology and Hebraic epistemic justification now seems wider. In the former, the answer to "how do you know that" consists of deductively or inductively connected ideas that flow from some collection of premises toward a conclusion. In the latter, the answer consists of experimental data observed and interpreted by small groups, sometimes with repeatability. Like arguments in the biblical literature, we must be tuned into reality itself over pixelated time and circumstance to see the truing of our conceptual maps and ideas.

In order to know, persons must perform experiments and pay attention to outcomes – including when Yahweh needs to know something. When a question is posed, the answer cannot be logically justified by mental operations alone. Rather, justification derives from a historically justified memory of the experiment's outcomes – sometimes an individual's memory and other times a community's.

This is the logic of scientific experimentation, where an observed instance justifies the experimental question. However, scientific experimentation seeks to make pixelated groups of events (e.g., disparate instances of viral infections) coherent without reference to a *personal cause*. The observed events in the biblical accounts are not impersonal occurrences reducible to data. Rather, because the experimental outcomes in the Hebrew Bible occur through personal agency in history, the justification is personalized to the ones interacting in the story. Hence, justification simultaneously involves both second-person knowing and epistemic confidence in what is meant to be known.

Returning to the logic that undergirds the test for adultery in Numbers 5: a wife's thigh *not* rotting away might personally convince an ancient Israelite husband of his wife's fidelity, but the justificatory power of that particular nonrotting thigh is locally and historically understood (i.e., they aren't designed to convince you or me or even other Israelites who are not aware of the particular accusation and experiment). In other words, even an Iron Age Israelite could not justify a lack of adultery in a village merely because it was full of healthy-thighed women. That thesis has to be put to the test. It is the experimental ritual predicated on the accusation that justifies the claim "I know that she did not commit adultery because her thigh is healthy." Likewise, a wet fleece over dry ground is not a self-interpreting justification of God's intentions for Gideon *to anyone but Gideon*, the designer of the experiment. And so too with raw experimental data of any scientist today.

In the end, what we find in the premonarchical texts of the Hebrew Bible is a type-scene of justification, nestled in a matrix of epistemic scenes and language, where classically deductive experiments employ persons acting in history. These tests, ouija, and witnesses contain an implicit or explicit conditional design: If P, then Q (if ~Q, then ~P), where P is a historical event caused by a person and Q is the justification of a belief or state of affairs predicated on the caused event. These are often stated in variations of the phrase translated as "then I shall know," "in order for you all to know," "knowingly you shall know," etc.

Rationality in these instances of the biblical literature is just that: rational. However, this kind of Hebraic rationality is also personal, enacted by agents who then additionally come to know the other person through the experiment. And because these are thoroughly personal signs meant to justify, thinking of them as analogous to rationality schemes such as classical logic or the scientific enterprise cannot encapsulate their logic without remainder.

Stories of epistemic justification through tests, ouija, or witness reveal a sense of the Hebraic rationality through "instruments of fine insight" integrated through a narrative in a way that linear models of justification might not be able to replicate. This form of justification spans not just personal confirmation of divine plans, but also resembles the logic of scientific experimentation and extends in the biblical texts to principled matters of justice. This means that their sense of justification in these type-scenes is not relegated or restricted to what Christian theologians have called "special revelation." Rather, divine communication might just participate in a broadly normative scheme of justification available to all.

In the ancient Near East more broadly, things were different. Notably, this Hebraic use of *modus ponens* contrasts sharply with that of the largest scholarly community in the period of the Israelite kingdoms: Babylon. The Babylonians practiced divination sciences rigorously and according to a long tradition of divination. The basic presumption of Mesopotamian divination also relies on "if P, then Q" reasoning. As Francesca Rochberg illustrates, "Thus, 'if Jupiter becomes steady in the morning: enemy kings will be reconciled' ... Jupiter is steady in the morning. Therefore, enemy kings reconcile."[19]

[19] Francesca Rochberg, "'If P, Then Q': Form and Reasoning in Babylonian Divination," in *Divination and Interpretation of Signs in the Ancient World* (Oriental Institute Seminar 6; Chicago: University of Chicago Press, 2010), 19.

In this example, and thousands like it in Babylon, the inputs are constrained, so that there is no justification of a prior idea (or ensuing confidence) because the diviner did not create the experiment in order to know. Rather, it is code-work. The goal is to discern what the gods are saying in a textualized world conceived of as a tapestry of portents to be read. Besides the production of the endless lists of portents, personal agency is not strictly required in the basic reasoning needed to understand the cosmos of Babylon. The gods might be talking, but they are not generally talking *to them* – at least, not in a form that requires their input.

Babylon's translation of events in the real world does not lack in rigor, systematicity, or logic. Unlike the Hebraic use of tests to establish justification, these aspects of Mesopotamian thought do not make it scientistic. Again, Rochberg notes: "Despite its logical and systematic nature Mesopotamian divination does not conform to (modern) scientific standards of causality or knowledge."[20] Not so with Hebraic philosophy.

In the NT, the trend continues, where Jesus uses unnatural control over creation to signal his role in history, though he is aware that the signs inevitably fall on the blind eyes of the defiant as much as on those willing to trust.

[20] Rochberg, "'If P, Then Q'," 23.

Ending with a Beginning

> Why did I find this disturbing? Because, in my morals and ethics, I was not a Spartan or a Roman at all .... Assumptions that I had grown up with ... *were not bred of classical antiquity, still less of "human nature," but very distinctively of that civilisation's Christian past.*[1]

Tom Holland, the Oxford historian, surprises himself by concluding that the more he knew of Greco-Roman culture and literature, the more foreign and uncivilized they appeared to him. Though not a religious person, he had to also concede that his own world and intellectual traditions had been infused with "Christian" concepts and schemes of morality, politics, education, and more. Holland correctly questions the story of the West's Greek intellectual pedigree, which is more myth than fact. His sober conclusions, even if reached reluctantly, fan the flames of the fire I seek to kindle here.

Unfortunately, Holland commits a simple yet fundamental error in his reflections. Along with most of the Western tradition, he confuses the adjective "Christian" for "Hebraic." The conceptual structures and shaping influences he labels as "Christian" actually descend from a rich intellectual heritage begun in the Hebrew Bible and later continued in the New Testament.

Throughout this book I have trained my attention on one goal: to sketch a consistent philosophical style persistent across the biblical literature. Tracing these pixelated networks of discourse reveals a distinct intellectual tradition, a tradition that should enrich a conversation on

[1] Italics mine. Tom Holland, *Dominion: How the Christian Revolution Remade the World* (New York: Basic Books, 2019), 17.

TABLE 12 *The Hebraic philosophical style*

	Hebrew Bible and New Testament
Philosophical Style	**Modes of Argument:** 1. Pixelated (with elements of Linearity) 2. Networked **Convictions:** 3. Mysterionist 4. Creationist 5. Transdemographic 6. Ritualist

all other ancient philosophies more generally. What is more, this Hebraic style (Table 12) exhibits genetic markers that distinguish it from other scholarly, speculative, and philosophical enterprises in the empires that surrounded and invaded ancient Israel. Its creation-rooted and transdemographic intellectualism advocates a ritualized society of knowers who seek to understand the real world around them with a mysterionist humility.

I end by surveying the roles Hebraic philosophy might play in wider philosophy today, how we might reexamine our intellectual history in light of it, and see how this philosophical tradition generates a different series of practical and theological questions. On this final point, I will briefly compare the Hebraic emphases in epistemology to one popular religious epistemology broadly influential in theology today: Alvin Plantinga's Reformed Epistemology.

Biblical Philosophy in World Philosophy and Intellectual History

A recent movement in comparative philosophy has sought to bring non-Western works of literature back into the philosophy curricula of the West. To varying degrees, Southeast Asian, Central Asian, and African philosophies have all been invited into the study of ancient philosophies. Yet ancient Southwest Asian philosophies have been noticeably absent from the calls to include other Asian philosophies.

One can only speculate as to why this gap exists. Ancient philosophies entangled in their respective religions (e.g., Hinduism, Buddhism, Confucianism, Taoism, and more) still have native practitioners to this day. Not so with the religions or speculative worlds of Egypt and Mesopotamia.

Unlike her Mesopotamian peers, Hebraic philosophy not only has current practitioners of both Jewish and Christian stripes, but has had an outsized impact on our political, ethical, and scientific philosophies in the West to this day. Hence, the neglect of Hebraic philosophy causes us to overlook or misinterpret the intellectual genealogies of our own inherited philosophical traditions.

There is, after all, an open research question about whether Greek philosophy helped or hindered the West: Was our conceptual world too long unhelpfully shackled to Hellenist theologies? Did modern mathematics and scientism represent a return, of sorts, to Hebraic "critical intellectualism" and could that have contributed to the proliferating success of our mathematics and sciences over the past few centuries?

> Here is the seeming paradox that a people, freely recognized as supremely *the* religious people of the ancient world, at the same time were without a peer in the power and scope of their critical intellectualism. But indeed it is not paradoxical, for religion that is not criticized quickly deteriorates into mere superstition .... Hebrew thinkers were able to attain a view of the world that still shapes our outlook.[2]

Did Israel's creature-creator distinction, monotheism, divinely given law, divinely enacted covenants, and more form the conceptual foundation bequeathed to the West that enabled realist scientific work in these last centuries? That is a project of another sort, but this question is now approachable through the present thesis.

To repeat an insight from the scholars of the mid-twentieth century, the Greco-Roman intellectual tradition does not adequately explain the modern West:

> The boundary between the ancient world and the modern is to be traced, *not in the Aegean or the middle Mediterranean, but in the pages of the Old Testament*, where we find revealed Israel's attainments in the realms of thought, her facility in literary expression, her profound religious insights, and her standards of individual and social ethics.[3]

Or, as the same historian cited at the fore of this chapter summed it: "To live in a Western country is to live in a society still utterly saturated by Christian [read: Hebraic] concepts and assumptions."[4]

Mine is not merely a descriptive work, but a proposition that the Hebraic philosophical style and the intellectual world that issues from practicing it might have prescriptive value for us today.

[2] Italics original. Henri Frankfort et al., *The Intellectual Adventure of Ancient Man: An Essay on Speculative Thought in the Ancient Near East* (Chicago: University of Chicago Press, 1946), 234.

[3] Italics mine. Frankfort et al., *The Intellectual Adventure of Ancient Man*, 224.

[4] Holland, *Dominion*, 13.

As one example, the shackles of Hellenist theology arrested the debates about planetary orbits in the early seventeenth century. Neither Galileo nor Kepler could shake their Aristotelian and Neo-Platonic theologies, respectively. Because of their dogged theological commitments to Hellenist versions of geometry – the perfect form of circularity, Platonic solids, or perfect ratio of ellipses – they never skeptically engaged their own Hellenized assertions to reconcile them with the real cosmos above their heads every night.[5]

Might there be other ways in which a realist conceptual world could be found in the "skeptical" Hebraic tradition? At what point should we have cast out Greek theology in order for us to grow in our understanding? Currently, the Hellenistic models are often naïvely held up as the very devices that freed us from obtuse superstitious religiosity. Returning to Frankfort's insight about uniquely Hebraic skepticism, "*It was only by virtue of their skeptical mood* that the Hebrew thinkers were able to attain a view of the world that still shapes our outlook."[6]

And so we should continue to question both the enabling and disabling features of the Hellenist conceptual world.

Is Hebraic Epistemology Compatible with Reformed Epistemology?[7]

How does this Biblical style of philosophy comport with the philosophies of religion today? Again, that is another project in need of an author. As a brief example from the school of analytic philosophy of religion, we can highlight the continuity and sticking points between the styles and substance of biblical epistemology.

Returning to the story at the beginning of this book, the reader might remember the philosophers at that conference asking why I was using the Bible to make a philosophical argument. Now I ask Christian philosophers and theologians alike two questions:

1. In light of the biblical philosophy explored here, can we make arguments about the nature of knowing, logic, God, and so on,

5 Cf. William R. Shea and Mariano Artigas, *Galileo in Rome: The Rise and Fall of a Troublesome Genius* (New York: Oxford University Press, 2003), 26; Wade Rowland, *Galileo's Mistake: A New Look at the Epic Confrontation between Galileo and the Church* (New York: Arcade, 2003), 35.

6 Italics mine. Frankfort et al., *The Intellectual Adventure of Ancient Man*, 234.

7 This section was adapted from Dru Johnson, *Biblical Knowing: A Scriptural Epistemology of Error* (Eugene, OR: Cascade, 2013), 173–79.

without considering in detail the style and content of biblical philosophy (i.e., not jabs at proof-texting)?

2. At what point does our work turn so far away from Scripture's conceptual world and the real world to which Scripture forces our focus as to become disconnected rhetoric?

A concrete example might help clarify the benefits and deficits of answering "no" to question 1 above. Alvin Plantinga and his renowned brand of Reformed Epistemology (RE) represents an example of working apart from the content, convictions, and mode of Hebraic philosophy. Although Plantinga works aloof from the biblical texts – aside from citations that graze the surface of biblical literature – could he still end up dovetailing his epistemology with that of the biblical authors? The answer is a complicated "sort of, but not really." To be fair to Plantinga's task, it might not be his goal to produce an epistemology that biblical authors could appreciate.

Of course, this kind of critique could be carried out for all the different appropriations and positions within religious epistemologies. I will engage Plantinga's work as represented in *Warranted Christian Belief* by how I imagine the biblical authors might respond to him.

Reformed Epistemology offers ample ground for comparing the findings of this present study with a theologically minded analytic epistemology.[8] Alvin Plantinga's RE is as robust and well-defended as any of several analytic categories of epistemology.[9]

Unlike most, Plantinga puts a kind of classically *unjustifiable* belief at the center of knowing. His notion of a *properly basic belief* contains within it beliefs that we cannot justify but which we must hold in order to navigate the world epistemically. Because our most fundamental beliefs (i.e., properly basic beliefs) cannot be justified, we must decide if our beliefs are warranted. Does one have strict means of justification for believing that there are other minds in the world apart from one's own mind? This turns out to be a very difficult belief to justify – for all

[8] Moser's recent work would be the notable exception to this statement. Although he is still utilizing the vernacular of analytic epistemology, he often comes close to espousing a kindred epistemology to the present study. See Paul K. Moser, *The Elusive God: Reorienting Religious Epistemology* (New York: Cambridge University Press, 2008).

[9] E.g., Nicolas Wolterstorff, *Reason within the Bounds of Religion*, 2nd ed. (Grand Rapids, MI: Eerdmans, 1976); William P. Alston, *Perceiving God: The Epistemology of Religious Experience* (Ithaca, NY: Cornell University Press, 1991).

philosophers – in a rigorously logical way.[10] The goal, then, is to consider the conditions that create warrant for our beliefs.

Plantinga and others, such as William Alston and Nicholas Wolterstorff, describe something unique among current epistemologies in that their theories of knowing include a belief about God and also require a theological conviction about sin.[11] They all take the biblical metanarrative seriously in their thinking. In *Warranted Christian Belief*, Plantinga goes further to argue that *properly basic beliefs* can correspond to theologically necessary concepts.

Additionally, Plantinga takes Calvin's "sense of the divine" (*sensus divinitatis*) as a theological tenet of RE. This *sense of the divine* has been implanted in all humans and is offered by Plantinga as a *properly basic belief* from which other beliefs can be related and sustained. Because we believe that there are other minds, for example, we can believe that others have intentions. Beliefs about intentions are not properly basic but contingent on belief in other minds existing in other people.

Plantinga also incorporates sin and sinfulness as modes that corrupt proper epistemic function.[12] Beyond sin, Plantinga also provides a provisional case for epistemological error: if our cognitive processes functioned properly, then error could largely be avoided.[13] Because our cognitive faculties are affected by sin, the rest of our epistemological problems ensue. This provides an eloquent panacea to the problem of error: if our epistemic faculties functioned correctly (e.g., before the Fall of humanity), then we would not err. Plantinga and company have staked out an epistemology that goes a long way toward explaining what the biblical authors might have taken for granted: belief in God, other minds, faulty cognitive faculties, proper functioning, etc.

But Plantinga's analysis of error and knowing might be too narrow to explain what we have discovered in the biblical texts. Even within analytic philosophy, Plantinga's work may be too narrow because it does not take into account the ritualism and social complexities of the Hebraic philosophical style.

Jonathan Kvanvig, a virtue epistemologist, critiques Plantinga and others of the analytic tradition exactly because of their myopic "focus

[10] Plantinga might answer that no justification can be given in a foundationalist scheme of knowledge, but the belief in other minds is warranted. Alvin Plantinga, *Warranted Christian Belief* (New York: Oxford University Press, 2000).

[11] See also Alston, *Perceiving God*; Wolterstorff, *Reason within the Bounds of Religion.*

[12] Plantinga, *Warranted Christian Belief*, 199.

[13] Plantinga, *Warranted Christian Belief*, 146.

on a single belief of a single person at a single time and also to the fact that the object of a belief is presumed to be a discrete proposition."[14] Or, as another analytic epistemologist laments, "[Epistemology] typically consider[s] the prospects for knowledge acquisition in 'ideal' situations."[15] For Kvanvig, propositional-focused epistemologies reverse the actual order of knowing, diminishing our rich experience of reality: "Experience conveys information only en masse, and the individuation into propositional form often imposes structure rather than conforming to it."[16] Kvanvig does not want to argue that propositions have no use in epistemology, but rather that they may atomize content that is meant to be understood as a whole and is only interpretable as a whole because that is the way our minds are structured.[17] This seems to come closer to the biblical philosophy's focus on discernment and skilled integration.

This critique especially targets the examples Plantinga uses to illustrate his epistemology. For instance, Plantinga poses the problem of mistaking one twin brother for another or the happenstance of a broken clock being correct once a day. Such examples of error exemplify Kvanvig's singularity critique against the narrow epistemological approach of Plantinga and others.[18] All of these thought experiments invent problems due to ignorance of a wider context and historical setting.[19]

These Gettier-type errors are uninteresting because they turn on time-slice happenstance: "a single belief of a single person at a single time." How would one ever be able to determine that Peter (Paul's twin) was mistaken for Paul without appealing to the broader context of the situation?

14 This pithy quote from Zagzebski is a summary of Kvanvig's position. Linda T. Zagzebski, *Virtues of the Mind: An Inquiry into the Nature of Virtue and the Ethical Foundations of Knowledge* (New York: Cambridge University Press, 1996), 44; Jonathan L. Kvanvig, *The Intellectual Virtues and the Life of the Mind: On the Place of the Virtues in Epistemology* (Studies in Epistemology and Cognitive Theory; Savage, MD: Rowman & Littlefield, 1992), 181–82.

15 For this and other reasons, Goldman actually believes that testimony "departs from traditional epistemology and philosophy of science." Alvin I. Goldman, *Pathways to Knowledge: Private and Public* (New York: Oxford University Press, 2002), 139.

16 I do not adhere to the totality of Kvanvig's argument for information as "chunks." This quote is Zagzebski's summary of Kvanvig's critique. Kvanvig, *The Intellectual Virtues*, 182.

17 Kvanvig, *The Intellectual Virtues*, 183.

18 Plantinga, *Warranted Christian Belief*, 157–58.

19 See "Contextualism and Communitarianism" in Martin Kusch, *Knowledge by Agreement: The Programme of Communitarian Epistemology* (Oxford: Clarendon Press, 2002), 131–68.

The inimitable Miss Anscombe deconstructed such formulations as "material, but not formal" examples when the intentions, social setting, and broader contexts are considered.[20] They run the risk of trivializing the reality of what was known *and how*. Interesting errors occur over time and circumstance, not merely in one time-slice. The biblical authors are intensely interested in epistemic confidence and error, but they explore these through pixelated stories of social interactions that remedy errors or yield confidence. Notably absent: singular reasoning upon singular propositional beliefs within a single knower's mind at a single moment in time.

Having given a terse description and critique of Reformed Epistemology, two questions emerge: How does RE account for the social epistemic role of authority so central to biblical epistemology? And, is RE commensurable with what we have found in Scripture?

First, to the matter of authority, Plantinga neglects the communal nature of knowing as foundational. In his section titled "How Does Faith Work?" Plantinga sidelines testimony or authentication of testimony as a subpar and nonnormative route to knowledge.[21] Cornelis Van der Kooi comments on this move:

> Plantinga too characterizes testimony as a *de iure* [*sic*] second-class citizen in the republic of epistemology. ... We must keep well in mind that there is a difference between uncertainty with regard to a specific item of testimony, and a skepticism which in principle finds little to go on in the witness of others in general. ... He does certainly suggest that knowledge which is obtained through one's own perception is superior to knowledge which people have based on the testimony of others.[22]

In other words, Plantinga elevates the testimony of Scripture as authoritative while simultaneously devaluing testimony today. He does this without making an adequate distinction between testimony offered by Scripture and other kinds of testimony.[23] As we saw in Chapter 10, testimony and guidance are central to discernment.

[20] Plantinga, *Warranted Christian Belief*, 155–58; Anscombe and Morgenbesser expose these problematic aspects of "mistakes" as lack of broader historical context in their 1963 essay: G. E. M. Anscombe and Sidney Morgenbesser, "The Two Kinds of Error in Action," *Journal of Philosophy* 60, no. 14 (July 1963): 393–401.

[21] Plantinga, *Warranted Christian Belief*, 249–52.

[22] Cornelis Van der Kooi, "The Assurance of Faith: A Theme in Reformed Dogmatics in Light of Alvin Plantinga's Epistemology," *Neue Zeitschrift für systematische Theologie und Religionsphilosophie* 40, no. 1 (1998): 102–3.

[23] This suspicion of testimony prompts Helm to criticize Plantinga regarding his "quick" move from Scripture (i.e., testimony) to inferred belief:

Second, Plantinga's epistemological account of sin and sinfulness has been weighed and found wanting. This aspect of his work is important for my analysis because of the central significance of the first epistemic error in Genesis 2–3. Merold Westphal faulted Plantinga for inadequate treatment of sin in Plantinga's earlier work, especially for an epistemology claiming the "Reformed" banner.[24] Plantinga remedies this lacuna regarding sin in *Warranted Christian Belief*, although some of his critics remain unsatisfied.[25]

Despite the time-slice view of knowing in Plantinga's RE and some other analytic theologies, a more problematic silence looms in their scholarship that may hinder theological work: the nature of trust and the prophetic voice.[26] I have shown that the epistemological process pixelated and

> What decides what inferences are elementary or obvious or quick? To illustrate, Plantinga says that "what I know in faith, is the main lines of specifically Christian teaching – together, we might say with its universal instantiation with respect to me. Christ died for my sins" (pp. 248–9). But the proposition that Christ died for my sins is certainly a momentous inference from the Scriptures, not a good candidate for an inference which is quick and easy and obvious.

In Helm's mind, this move seems too rash. Paul Helm, review of *Warranted Christian Belief* by Alvin Plantinga, *Mind* New Series 110, no. 440 (October 2001) 1110–15.

[24] I am referring here to Westphal's critique of Plantinga:

> Sin as an epistemological category cannot be, as Fichte and Plantinga, Marx and Freud seem to want it to be, merely a device for discrediting one's opponents. To take Paul [the apostle] seriously is to take seriously the universality of sin. ... Isn't this in fact Calvin's own conclusion, his critique of natural theology being but a subordinate moment in a larger argument denying that we can have any trustworthy knowledge of God, direct or inferential, apart from the divine gift of the Word and the Spirit?
>
> (Merold Westphal, "Taking St Paul Seriously: Sin as an Epistemological Category," in *Christian Philosophy*, ed. Thomas P. Flint [Notre Dame: University of Notre Dame Press, 1990], 216–17)

See also Paul Helm, "John Calvin, the *Sensus Divinitatis*, and the Noetic Effects of Sin," *International Journal for Philosophy of Religion* 43 (1998): 87–107.

[25] We cannot actually settle the matter here of the "Reformed" value of Plantinga's Reformed Epistemology other than to say it is not entirely clear that Plantinga is using Calvin in a way that expresses Calvin's Humanistic tendencies toward the biblical texts. Or perhaps this simply raises the question as to whether Plantinga is appropriating the Neo-Calvinian Protestant scholasticism rather than Calvin himself. The *Institutes* are exclusively cited in Plantinga without reflection upon the biblical texts to which those sections reflect. But Plantinga has not necessarily attempted to be faithful to historical theology and biblical scholarship as his central task. And we also have acknowledged in our introductory chapter that there can be theological accounts that comport with biblical epistemology, yet do not make specifically exegetical arguments (e.g., Kierkegaard's epistemology).

[26] Although we have not explored it here, there is an emerging subsection of epistemology concerned with the problem of trust and social epistemology. While these wrestle with

networked across the biblical literature centers upon two facets: knowing whom to trust based on external authentication, and participating in a process prescribed by the prophetic voice to know what is being shown.[27]

To the former, Plantinga's discussion of sin is most revealing of his view of the significance of trust. Plantinga asserts that sin not only makes one imperceptive, dull, or stupid, but also keeps one from loving one's neighbor as oneself (i.e., participating in the prophetic injunctions of Scripture).[28] There is a case to be made for this from across Scripture and Calvin makes it consistently in his commentaries. But absent from Plantinga's discussion is why one would ever believe that they ought to love their neighbor in the first place. Because Plantinga sets aside the authentication of the prophetic authority of Scripture, the question is: Why should one trust the witness of Scripture at all?

Further, sin keeps us from trusting God, which Plantinga roots in the primeval story of Adam and Eve.[29] At this point, Plantinga explores the germ of sin, and the epistemology at the center of a story featuring two key aspects we have observed in Scripture: Why should we trust the prophetic voice of Scripture and how does sin keep us from enacting the prophetic directives? These two could be reconciled in a discussion of Genesis 2–3, but Plantinga chooses another route.

To the latter issue of the authoritative voice, Plantinga comes close to exploring the serpent's voice as it relates to the error in the Garden. But he ends his discussion of the error by simply concluding that it lay in man's self-deception because he believed he could be both autonomous and like God. This is not, as we saw, how the biblical philosophy portrays the matter in the Eden narrative or other pixelated reiterations of it. In other words, Plantinga believes the error to be autonomy, a common but

some of the pertinent questions raised in the biblical texts, they do so within the narrower analytic modes. Trust is a "problem" for these analyses because they mostly view trust as if it is beyond deductive inferences, as something ultimately foreign to normative epistemology. Trust as a topic "departs from traditional epistemology." Goldman, *Pathways to Knowledge*, 139. See major works cited in Chapter 8, fn. 17.

[27] Plantinga has inexplicably chosen to pick up Calvin's argument for the *sensus divinitatis* in Book I, chapter 3 of the *Institutes of the Christian Religion*, while largely ignoring Calvin's foundation for proper epistemology in I, 2. In this move, Plantinga appears to shift Calvin's epistemology from fundamentally social to semiautonomous. Calvin begins with the knower in a subjected relationship to his Creator who cannot think of such a being without realizing his own utter dependence upon and service due to that Creator (I, 2).

[28] Plantinga, *Warranted Christian Belief*, 208.

[29] Plantinga, *Warranted Christian Belief*, 212.

off-kilter reading, achieved solely through the epistemic faculties of the man without any necessarily communal roots.[30] The failure to enact God's commands ensues as a consequence of man's turn to the voice of the woman and serpent.

For Plantinga's version of error, the man is "self-deceived" and "contemptuous of truth." And so, on the cusp of addressing the role of the serpent's prophetic voice, Plantinga instead identifies the mystery of free will and the man's envy as the ultimate error in the Fall:

> Of course the final mystery remains: where does this sneaking desire to be equal with God come from in the first place? How could the very idea so much as enter Adam's soul? ... I can take pleasure in my [the man's] condition, which is wonderfully good, or I can give in to envy.[31]

He offers no discussion of how exactly humanity went from being in truth to being in error, to borrow Kierkegaard's formulation. If the centerpiece of Plantinga's epistemology is proper functioning based on the biblical account of Eden, then a substantive analysis of that biblical account seems required to demonstrate how the first properly functioning humans erred – the most properly functioning humans of all time!

Plantinga has provided what no other contemporary philosopher has: a comprehensive analytic epistemology that attempts to represent the Christian tradition in epistemology. Notwithstanding the merits of his work, how might the biblical philosophical tradition critique Reformed Epistemologies of which Plantinga's is one type?

The focus of Plantinga's RE appears to miss the aims of the biblical style because of its singular concern with knowing a proposition at a time-slice. RE's precision might still suffer from what the analytic philosopher Eleonore Stump calls *hemianopia*:

> It is therefore misleadingly imprecise, I think, to diagnose the weakness of analytic philosophy as its narrowness. Its cognitive hemianopia is its problem. Its intellectual vision is occluded or obscured for the right half of the cognitive field, especially for the part of reality that includes the complex, nuanced thought, behavior, and relations of persons.[32]

[30] See Chapter 8 of this book, or for a detailed analysis: Dru Johnson, *Epistemology and Biblical Theology: From the Pentateuch to Mark's Gospel* (Routledge Interdisciplinary Perspectives on Biblical Criticism 4; New York: Routledge, 2018), 17–55.

[31] Plantinga, *Warranted Christian Belief*, 212.

[32] Eleonore Stump, *Wandering in Darkness: Narrative and the Problem of Suffering* (New York: Oxford University Press, 2010), 25.

These blind spots to a broad reality might be large enough to render RE unsuitable for fully capturing the epistemological process found in the biblical texts.[33]

Plantinga and others like him do not seek to clarify the social-prophetic role in epistemology because such a role does not fit under RE's emphases. His treatment of the Eden error as a matter of self-deception overlooks the problem diagnosed by Yahweh himself: "Because you listened to the voice of your wife ..." (Gen 3:17a). Though a Hebraic style of epistemology need not be properly "Reformed," it must correctly diagnose the error that it takes to be the universal human error. Biblical authors would surely affirm the broad contours of Plantinga's Reformed Epistemology (i.e., broken epistemic faculties, proper function, properly basic beliefs, etc.), but due to the deficiencies noted above, Plantinga's RE can only function as a truncated theological tool without demonstrable and developed roots in the biblical literature.

Paths for Future Research

I end this venture knowing that it will be frustratingly incomplete for most of us. More work must be done on every front studied here. Political philosophy, metaphysics, ethics, logic, existentialism, aesthetics, and more could be pursued in similar veins to my suggestions here. Of course, scholars have worked on these topics in fits and starts. Nevertheless, I suggest here a new beginning, a wide movement of retrieval from the biblical philosophy that forms and shapes our conceptual world, our philosophies, our theologies, and, thus, our practices.

This proposal requires scrutiny from those in the relevant disciplines. I recognize that my descriptions, generalizations, and inability to integrate every facet of a complex intellectual heritage need more attention. My only hope is that I have given enough skeletal framing to continue a meaningful conversation beyond the Hebrew Bible that will proliferate, sharpen, and *necessarily include the texts of the New Testament.* With that humbling thought in mind, the need for more research emerges in several trajectories.

In ancient Near Eastern scholarship, the fields are ripe for those who want to work in the intellectual world of Israel's neighbors, especially those outside the empires of the great rivers: Egypt, Neo-Assyria, and

[33] Van der Kooi, "The Assurance of Faith," 100.

Babylon. Building upon the work in Assyriology and Egyptology discussed in Chapter 2, comparative work with the Hebrew Bible would be a delightfully natural outcome.

In biblical studies, fresh research is needed to carefully build upon the anthropological and philological debates of the last century, while being wary of their progressivist and encyclopedist assumptions. There has been a general sentiment, even among religiously convicted scholars, that the biblical literature can teach us about things in the ken of religion and political power, but not about the nature of reality as such. The anthropologist Franz Boaz and his diverse group of successors overcame this progressivist and evolutionist hubris – "the West and the rest" – that allowed us to take other traditions seriously, even if they didn't appear "civilized" by our lights. To recognize a biblical philosophical tradition is to admit that we might need to learn from this particular group of ancient Semites about the nature of our world according to *their* lights of reason and *their* ritualized methods of reasoning.

No small amount of research agendas could be generated on the Hebrew Bible and New Testament, both within and between its texts. Given the philosophical conviction of creationism and ritualism, the connections between the material and conceptual worlds of biblical authors need the most attention. Hence, archaeology, anthropology, and biblical scholars all have contributions that will bear on Israel's intellectual world in the Bronze, Iron, and so-called Axial Ages and the philosophically attuned texts she produced.

In the New Testament world, much good work has thrown the Jewishness of Jesus and his disciples into sharp relief. But that result has also made Second Temple Judaism the lens of all first-century Jewish thought, including the New Testament texts. Unintentionally, this much-needed pendulum swing might have become a myopic lens through which we now view the largely Jewish texts of the New Testament.

Does the Hebraic philosophical style persist into the New Testament texts? I have demonstrated that it appears in two Gospels, speeches of Acts, and some of Paul's corpus if not all. The remaining question is to what extent the thesis can generalize to the other texts and beyond into the Patristic material. That will have to be taken up by NT scholars and early church historians alike.

And there are conceptual questions that need to be answered that will inevitably bear on our scholarly pursuits today:

1. Is Hebraic philosophy prescriptive or descriptive of good philosophy more generally?

2. Are we all practicing a Hebraic philosophy unaware, just poorly or excellently?
3. Is Hebraic philosophy fundamentally better than other forms? Is it a niche philosophy for a certain culture and place? Is it truer to the outputs of science, possessing more explanatory power?
4. Is biblical philosophy incommensurable with other philosophical styles? Is the epistemological process or metaphysics in Scripture incompatible with any present or historical possibilities?

These questions could multiply, but I leave it to my colleagues in these fields to generate their own lists and agendas.

To my colleagues in philosophy and theology I would throw down this gauntlet:

> IF the Hebraic philosophical tradition is as robust and rigorous as anything found in Hellenism,
> AND IF this biblical philosophy explains the real world more adequately to embodied humans,
> AND IF we no longer need to accommodate the Scripture to the theological philosophies of Hellenism,
> THEN should we not think, to some extent, about the work of theology and philosophy as a retrieval of biblical philosophy?

Should we not attempt to resituate our thinking in the conceptual schemes of the biblical authors to check if we have become blind, myopic, or hemianopic to the rigorous philosophical structures and convictions of Scripture?

Can we work entirely aloof from the biblical philosophical tradition? In the end, we might find our theology to be largely commensurable with the philosophical convictions of the biblical authors. However, if we have not done the actual work of socially embodying the biblical philosophy, then can we properly assert our theological conclusions? As Christian theologians and philosophers, are we satisfied to have *accidentally* paralleled a biblically rigorous notion, or should we be compelled to demonstrate the *necessary* and *thick* connections to pixelated networks of ritualized biblical thinking?

For the sake of both biblical studies and philosophy/theology, more interdisciplinary work needs to include apprenticing with each other, collegial skybridges between the silos, and broader explorations into the material worlds of Scripture.

The philosopher might read this and think to herself, "Am I supposed to learn Hebrew and Greek to become literate in biblical philosophy?"

An elementary understanding of biblical languages and basic literacy in Scripture would not hurt anyone working in theology. However, it is fairly easy to make a friend in other disciplines from whom we can learn and who can save us from novice errors. The same holds of biblical scholars with philosophy.

As an anonymized example of how it could go wrong: A particularly shrewd philosopher was presenting at a conference mixed with biblical scholars. In the questions, she answered someone by saying what she thought were uncontroversial claims about the biblical god, something like this: "Of course, God cannot be evil, do evil, or be associated with evil in any way." At this, murmurs swelled to a ruckus. The biblical scholars were politely throwing a fit because they knew something the philosopher did not: there are many uncontroversial instances in the Hebrew Bible of God planning and executing evil upon Israel and others (cf. Gen 6:5, 8:21; Exod 32:11–14; Deut 32:23; 1 Kgs 21:20–21, etc.). In the New Testament, there is also at least one example of Jesus planning to do evil (*ra'*) in the Hebraic sense of the term (i.e., the Judgment).

In modern English translations, the term "evil" – *ra'* – is usually translated away to "calamity," "misfortunes," or "disaster" when God is the one doing evil. When humans do *ra'*, it's translated as "evil." What this skilled philosopher took for granted – the concept of evil as monolithic and separate from God's character and being – did not fully comport with the biblical conception of either good or evil. The thicker concepts worked out in biblical philosophy have been thinned. Ironically, this thinning might be partly due to Christian theology that descended from Hellenism which conceptualized evil differently – such as, evil is the privation of good. Running through her philosophical assumptions with a biblical scholar (or theological wordbook or dictionary) would have inevitably redirected her thinking, truing it to the pixelated Hebraic discourse on good and evil that Jesus, Peter, and Paul conceptually develop in the New Testament. The same is true for biblical scholars using and abusing premises or philosophical programs. We all stand to learn from each other.

Lastly, I genuinely wonder, with the scholars cited at the start of this chapter, how much the biblical philosophical content and style have constructed Western thought more generally. While we may be romantically fond of the philosophies from the Aegean, when viewed as an entire system of thought, Hellenism does not feel like the intellectual nest out of which modernity has hatched and flown. How deeply can you cut into our intellectual world and find the sinews and arterial flow of Hebraic thought?

And so, I end with what I hope to be another bellow-blast of air on the fire of biblical philosophy – so that the grand intellectual tradition built and maintained in the individual and social bodies of Israel, Christianity, and their texts will be given its deserved credence under the lights of comparative traditions. The Hebraic approach to philosophy matches and possibly outstrips other philosophical traditions that we have tacitly accepted as the ancestors of our own intellectual heritage. I hope to have handed readers and my colleagues a tool with which we can return again, to one significant source of our intellectual world and try it out for true.

Bibliography

Alston, William P. *Perceiving God: The Epistemology of Religious Experience* (Ithaca, NY: Cornell University Press, 1991).

Alter, Robert. *The Art of Bible Translation* (Princeton, NJ: Princeton University Press, 2019).

The Art of Biblical Narrative, revised and expanded ed. (New York: Basic Books, 2011).

The Art of Biblical Poetry, new and revised ed. (Edinburgh: T&T Clark, 2011).

Anderson, Hugh. "The Old Testament in Mark's Gospel," in *The Use of the Old Testament in the New and Other Essays: Studies in Honor of William Franklin Stinespring*, ed. James M. Efird (Durham, NC: Duke University Press, 1972), 280–306.

Annus, Amar. "On the Beginnings and Continuities of Omen Sciences in the Ancient World," in *Divination and Interpretation of Signs in the Ancient World*, ed. Amar Annus (Oriental Institute Seminars 6; Chicago: University of Chicago Press, 2010), 1–18.

Anonymous. "What Is It Like to Understand Advanced Mathematics?," *Quora*, May 14, 2015, www.quora.com/What-is-it-like-to-understand-advanced-mathematics-Does-it-feel-analogous-to-having-mastery-of-another-language-like-in-programming-or-linguistics.

Anscombe, G. E. M. "What Is It to Believe Someone?" in *Rationality and Religious Belief*, ed. C. F. Delaney (University of Notre Dame Studies in the Philosophy of Religion 1; Notre Dame, IN: University of Notre Dame Press, 1979), 141–51.

Anscombe, G. E. M. and Sidney Morgenbesser. "The Two Kinds of Error in Action," *Journal of Philosophy* 60, no. 14 (July 1963): 393–401.

Aristotle. *Poetics*, trans. Malcolm Heath (New York: Penguin, 1996).

Arvan, Marc. "What Counts as Philosophy? On the Normative Disguised as Descriptive," *The Philosophers Cocoon*, http://philosopherscocoon.typepad.com.

Asaad, Terek. "Sleep in Ancient Egypt," in *Sleep Medicine: A Comprehensive Guide to Its Development, Clinical Milestones, and Advances in Treatment*, ed. Sudhansu Chokroverty and Michel Billiard (New York: Springer, 2015), 13–19.

Assmann, Jan. *Death and Salvation in Ancient Egypt*, trans. David Lorton (Ithaca, NY: Cornell University Press, 2005).

God and Gods: Egypt, Israel, and the Rise of Monotheism (Madison: University of Wisconsin Press, 2008).

The Mind of Egypt: History and Meaning in the Time of the Pharaohs, trans. Andrew Jenkins (New York: Metropolitan Books, 1996).

Athanassiadi, Polymnia. *Mutations of Hellenism in Late Antiquity* (Variorum Collected Studies Series CS1052; New York: Routledge, 2016).

Audi, Robert. *Epistemology: A Contemporary Introduction to the Theory of Knowledge*, 3rd ed. (New York: Routledge, 2011).

Avrahami, Yael. *The Senses of Scripture: Sensory Perception in the Hebrew Bible* (The Library of Hebrew Bible/Old Testament Studies 545; New York: T&T Clark, 2012).

Azuma, Hideki et al. "An Intervention to Improve the Interrater Reliability of Clinical EEG Interpretations," *Psychiatry and Clinical Neurosciences* 57, no. 5 (October 2003): 485–89.

Barclay, John M. G. *Paul and the Gift* (Grand Rapids, MI: Eerdmans, 2015).

Barfield, Owen. *Poetic Diction: A Study in Meaning* (Middletown, CT: Wesleyan University Press, 1974).

Barr, James. *The Semantics of Biblical Language* (Eugene, OR: Wipf & Stock, 1961).

Bartholomew, Craig G. *Introducing Biblical Hermeneutics: A Comprehensive Framework for Hearing God in Scripture* (Grand Rapids, MI: Baker Academic, 2015).

Where Mortals Dwell: A Christian View of Place for Today (Grand Rapids, MI: Baker Academic, 2012).

Barton, John. *Ethics in Ancient Israel* (New York: Oxford University Press, 2017).

Bartor, Assnat. *Reading Law as Narrative: A Study in the Casuistic Laws of the Pentateuch* (Ancient Israel and Its Literature 5; Atlanta: Society of Biblical Literature Press, 2010).

Bates, Matthew W. *Salvation by Allegiance Alone: Rethinking Faith, Works, and the Gospel of Jesus the King* (Grand Rapids, MI: Baker Academic, 2017).

Benson, Hugh H. "Socratic Method," in *The Cambridge Companion to Socrates*, ed. Donald R. Morrison (Cambridge Companions to Philosophy; New York: Cambridge University Press, 2010), 179–200.

Berman, Joshua A. *Ani Maamin: Biblical Criticism, Historical Truth, and the Thirteen Principles of Faith* (Jerusalem: Magid, 2020).

Created Equal: How the Bible Broke with Ancient Political Thought (New York: Oxford University Press, 2011).

Inconsistency in the Torah: Ancient Literary Convention and the Limits of Source Criticism (New York: Oxford University Press, 2017).

Black, Max. "The Identity of Indiscernibles," *Mind* 61 (April 1952): 153–64.

Blakley, J. Ted. "Incomprehension or Resistance?: The Markan Disciples and the Narrative Logic of Mark 4:1–8:30" (PhD diss., University of St. Andrews, 2008).

Bobzien, Susanne. "Ancient Logic," *Stanford Encyclopedia of Philosophy*, Summer 2020 ed., ed. Edward N. Zalta, https://plato.stanford.edu/archives/sum2020/entries/logic-ancient.

Boman, Thorlief. *Hebrew Thought Compared with Greek*, trans. Jules L. Moreau (Library of History and Doctrine 1; London: SCM, 1960).

Bonneau, Normand. "The Logic of Paul's Argument on the Curse of the Law in Galatians 3:10–14," *Novum Testamentum* 39, no. 1 (January 1997): 60–80.

Borgen, Peder. "Philo of Alexandria," in *Anchor Bible Dictionary*, Vol. V, ed. David N. Freedman (New York: Doubleday, 1992), 333–42.

Bourget, David and David J. Chalmers. "What Do Philosophers Believe?" *Philosophical Studies* 170, no. 3 (September 2014): 465–500.

Bouxsein, Hilary. Review of Mortal and Divine in Early Greek Epistemology: A Study of Hesiod, Xenophanes, and Parmenides by Shaul Tor, *Bryn Mawr Classical Review*, April 8, 2020, https://bmcr.brynmawr.edu/2020/2020.04.08.

Boylan, Michael. *Fictive Narrative Philosophy: How Fiction Can Act as Philosophy* (Routledge Research in Aesthetics; New York: Routledge, 2019).

Bradatan, Costica. "Philosophy Needs a New Definition," *Los Angeles Review of Books*, December 17, 2017, https://lareviewofbooks.org/article/philosophy-needs-a-new-definition/.

Brandom, Robert B. *Making It Explicit: Reasoning, Representing, and Discursive Commitment* (Cambridge, MA: Harvard University Press, 1998).

Breck, John. *The Shape of Biblical Literature: Chiasmus in the Scriptures and Beyond* (Crestwood, NY: St. Vladimir's Seminary Press, 2008).

Brinks, C. L. et al. "Symposium on *The Philosophy of Hebrew Scripture*," *Journal of Analytic Theology* 2 (2014): 238–81.

Buber, Martin. "*Leitwort* Style in Pentateuchal Narrative," in Martin Buber and Franz Rosenzweig, *Scripture and Translation*, trans. Lawrence Rosenwald (Bloomington, IN: Indiana University Press, 1994; German original, 1936), 90–98.

Budd, Chris and Chris Sanguin. "101 Uses of the Quadratic Equation," *Plus Magazine*, May 1, 2004, https://plus.maths.org/content/101-uses-quadratic-equation-part-ii.

Burnside, Jonathan P. "Exodus and Asylum: Uncovering the Relationship between Biblical Law and Narrative," *Journal for the Study of the Old Testament* 34, no. 3 (2010): 243–66.

God, Justice, and Society: Aspects of Law and Legality in the Bible (New York: Oxford University Press, 2010).

Calvin, John. *Commentary on a Harmony of the Evangelists, Matthew, Mark and Luke*, 3 vols., trans. William Pringle (Edinburgh: Calvin Translation Society, 1845–46).

Carasik, Michael. *Theologies of the Mind in Biblical Israel* (Studies in Biblical Literature 85; Oxford: Peter Lang, 2005).

Carmy, Shalom and David Shatz. "The Bible as a Source for Philosophical Reflection," in *History of Jewish Philosophy*, ed. Daniel H. Frank and Oliver Leaman (New York: Routledge, 1997), 13–37.

Carroll, Sean. "Even Physicists Don't Understand Quantum Mechanics: Worse, They Don't Seem to Want to Understand It," *The New York Times* (*The Opinion Pages*), September 7, 2019, www.nytimes.com/2019/09/07/opinion/sunday/quantum-physics.html.

Cassuto, Umberto. *A Commentary on the Book of Genesis* (Jerusalem: Magnes Press, 1961).

Chakrabarti, Arindam and Ralph Weber, eds. *Comparative Philosophy without Borders* (New York: Bloomsbury, 2016).

Charry, Ellen T. *God and the Art of Happiness* (Grand Rapids, MI: Eerdmans, 2010).

Christensen, Duane L. *Deuteronomy 1–21:9*, revised, 2nd ed., Vol. 6A (Word Biblical Commentary; Nashville, TN: Thomas Nelson, 2001).

Clark, Andy and David Chalmers. "The Extended Mind," *Analysis* 58, no. 1 (1998): 7–19.

Coady, Cecil A. J. *Testimony: A Philosophical Study* (New York: Oxford University Press, 1994).

De Cruz, Helen, Johan De Smedt, and Eric Schwitzgebel, eds. *Philosophy through Science Fiction Stories* (New York: Bloomsbury, 2021).

Dewey, Joanna. "Mark as Interwoven Tapestry: Forecasts and Echoes for a Listening Audience," *Catholic Biblical Quarterly* 53, no. 2 (1991): 221–36.

Diamond, James A. *Jewish Theology Unbound* (New York: Oxford University Press, 2018).

Diodorus Siculus. *Library of History*, Vol. 1, trans. C. H. Oldfather (Cambridge, MA: Loeb Classical Library, 1933).

Douglas, Mary. *Leviticus as Literature* (New York: Oxford University Press, 1999).

Eco, Umberto. *The Limits of Interpretation* (Advances in Semiotics; Bloomington, IN: Indiana University Press, 1994).

Edmonds, David and Nigel Warburton, hosts. "What Is Philosophy?" *Philosophy Bites*, http://philosophybites.com/2010/11/what-is-philosophy.html.

Edwards, Mark J. "On the Platonic Schooling of Justin Martyr," *The Journal of Theological Studies* 42, no. 1 (April 1991): 17–34.

Einstein, Albert. "To Max Born," March 3, 1947, Letter 84 in *The Born-Einstein Letters: Friendship, Politics, and Physics in Uncertain Times*, ed. Diana Buchwald and Kip S. Thorne, trans. Irene Born (Hampshire: Macmillan, 2005), 156–59.

Elkanna, Yehuda. "The Emergence of Second-Order Thinking in Classical Greece," in *The Origins and Diversity of Axial Age Civilizations*, ed. Shmuel Noah Eisenstadt (Albany: State University of New York Press, 1986), 40–64.

Engberg-Pedersen, Troels. *John and Philosophy: A New Reading of the Fourth Gospel* (New York: Oxford University Press, 2018).

Paul and the Stoics (Philadelphia: Westminster John Knox Press, 2000).

"Response to Martyn," *Journal for the Study of the New Testament* 86 (2002): 103–14.

Review of *One True Life: The Stoics and Early Christians as Rival Traditions* by C. Kavin Rowe, *Journal of Early Christian Studies* 25, no. 2 (2017): 326–28.

Epictetus. *The Discourses and Manual*, Vol. I, trans. Percy E. Matheson (Oxford: Oxford University Press, 1916).

Discourses and Selected Writings, trans. Robert Dobbin (New York: Penguin Books, 2008).

Evans, Craig A. "How Mark Writes," in *The Written Gospel*, ed. Markus N. A. Bockmuehl and Donald Alfred Hagner (Cambridge: Cambridge University Press, 2005), 135–38.

Fishbane, Michael A. *Biblical Interpretation in Ancient Israel* (Oxford: Clarendon, 1985).

Biblical Myth and Rabbinic Mythmaking (New York: Oxford University Press, 2003).

Flynn, Shawn. *Children in Ancient Israel: The Hebrew Bible and Mesopotamia in Comparative Perspective* (New York: Oxford University Press, 2018).

Foley, Richard. "Egoism in Epistemology," in *Socializing Epistemology: The Social Dimensions of Knowledge*, ed. Frederick F. Schmitt (Lanham, MD: Rowman & Littlefield, 1994), 53–73.

Intellectual Trust in Oneself and Others (New York: Cambridge University Press, 2001).

Foster, Benjamin R. "Transmission of Knowledge," in *A Companion to the Ancient Near East*, ed. Daniel C. Snell (New York: Wiley-Blackwell, 2004), 245–52.

Fox, Michael V. "Egyptian Onomastica and Biblical Wisdom," *Vetus Testamentum* 36, no. 3 (1986): 302–10.

"The Epistemology of the Book of Proverbs," *Journal of Biblical Literature* 126, no. 4 (2007): 669–84.

Proverbs 10–31 (Anchor Yale Bible; New Haven, CT: Yale University Press, 2009).

Frankfort, Henri. *Ancient Egyptian Religion: An Interpretation* (New York: Columbia University Press, 1948).

Kingship and Gods: A Study of Ancient Near Eastern Religion as the Integration of Society and Nature (Chicago: University of Chicago Press, 1948).

et al. *The Intellectual Adventure of Ancient Man: An Essay on Speculative Thought in the Ancient Near East* (Chicago: University of Chicago Press, 1946).

Frederick, John. "The Ethics of the Enactment and Reception of Cruciform Love: A Comparative Lexical, Conceptual, Exegetical/Theological Study of Colossians 3:1–17 and the Patterns of Thought Which Have Influenced It in Their Grammatical/Historical Context" (PhD diss., University of St. Andrews, 2014).

Frege, Gottlob. *Grundgesetze der Arithmetik*, in *Translations from the Philosophical: Writings of Gottlob Frege*, ed. Peter Geach and Max Black (Oxford: Blackwell, 1960), 137–58.

Frei, Hans W. *The Eclipse of Biblical Narrative: A Study in Eighteenth and Nineteenth Century Hermeneutics* (London: Yale University Press, 1974).

Garfield, Jay L. and William Edelglass, eds. *The Oxford Handbook of World Philosophy* (New York: Oxford University Press, 2013).

Garfield, Jay L. and Bryan W. Van Norden. "If Philosophy Won't Diversify, Let's Call It What It Really Is," *The New York Times* (*The Opinion Pages*), May 11, 2016, www.nytimes.com/2016/05/11/opinion/if-philosophy-wont-diversify-lets-call-it-what-it-really-is.html.

Gerhardsson, Birger. "The Parable of the Sower and Its Interpretation," *New Testament Studies* 14 (1968): 165–93.

Gericke, Jaco. *The Hebrew Bible and Philosophy of Religion* (Society of Biblical Literature Resources for Biblical Study 70; Atlanta: Society of Biblical Literature Press, 2012).

A Philosophical Theology of the Old Testament: A Historical, Experimental, Comparative and Analytic Perspective (Routledge Interdisciplinary Perspectives on Biblical Criticism; New York: Routledge, 2020).

"When Historical Minimalism Becomes Philosophical Maximalism," *Old Testament Essays* 27, no. 2 (2014): 412–27.

Gibbard, Allan. *Wise Choices, Apt Feelings: A Theory of Normative Judgment* (Cambridge, MA: Harvard University Press, 1992).

Gibbs, Raymond W. Jr. "Metaphor Interpretation as Embodied Simulation," *Mind & Language* 21 (2006): 434–58.

Gibbs, Raymond W. Jr. and Teenie Matlock. "Metaphor, Imagination, and Simulation: Psycholinguistic Evidence," in *The Cambridge Handbook of Metaphor and Thought*, ed. Raymond W. Gibbs Jr. (New York: Cambridge University Press, 2008), 161–76.

Gibson, Arthur. *Biblical Semantic Logic: A Preliminary Analysis* (Oxford: Basil Blackwell, 1981).

Gibson, Jeffrey B. "The Rebuke of the Disciples in Mark 8:14–21," *Journal for the Study of the New Testament* 27 (1986): 31–47.

Giles, Harry. "Visa Wedding," in *Tonguit* (Glasgow: Freight Books, 2016).

Gödel, Kurt. *On Formally Undecidable Propositions of Principia Mathematica and Related Systems*, trans. B. Meltzer (New York: Dover, 1962).

"On Formally Undecided Propositions of Principia Mathematica and Related Systems," in *From Frege to Gödel*, ed. Jean Van Heijenoort (Cambridge, MA: Harvard University Press, 1977), 592–616.

Goldman, Alvin I. *Pathways to Knowledge: Private and Public* (New York: Oxford University Press, 2002).

Goodman, Nelson. "Reply to an Adverse Ally," *The Journal of Philosophy* 54, no. 17 (August 1957): 531–35.

Goppelt, Leonhard. *Typos: The Typological Interpretation of the Old Testament in the New*, trans. Donald H. Madvig (Grand Rapids, MI: Eerdmans, 1982).

Gordon, T. David. "The Problem at Galatia," *Interpretation* 41 (1987): 32–43.

Grabbe, Lester L. "Wisdom of Solomon," in *The New Oxford Annotated Bible* (Fully Revised Fourth Edition: An Ecumenical Study Bible, 1427; New York: Oxford University Press, 2010).

Green, Joel B. *Body, Soul, and Human Life: The Nature of Humanity in the Bible* (Grand Rapids, MI: Baker, 2008).

Gunton, Colin E. *The Triune Creator: A Historical and Systematic Study* (Grand Rapids, MI: Eerdmans, 1998).

Gutting, Gary. *What Philosophers Know: Case Studies in Recent Analytic Philosophy* (New York: Cambridge University Press, 2009).

Hadot, Pierre. *Philosophy as a Way of Life: Spiritual Exercises from Socrates to Foucault*, trans. Michael Chase (Oxford: Blackwell, 1995).

What Is Ancient Philosophy?, trans. Michael Chase (Cambridge, MA: Harvard University Press, 2002).

Hagberg, Garry L., ed. *Fictional Characters, Real Problems: The Search for Ethical Content in Literature* (New York: Oxford University Press, 2016).

Hajek, Peter. "Fuzzy Logic," in *The Stanford Encyclopedia of Philosophy*, Summer 2010 ed., ed. Edward N. Zalta, http://plato.stanford.edu/archives/fall2010/entries/logic-fuzzy.

Hall, David L. and Roger T. Ames. *Thinking through Confucius* (Albany, NY: State University of New York Press, 1987).

Hanson, Norwood. "Observation," in *Theories and Observation in Science*, ed. Richard E. Grandy (Englewood Cliffs, NJ: Prentice-Hall, 1973), 129–46.

Hardin, Russell. *Trust and Trustworthiness* (New York: Russell Sage Foundation, 2002).

Hays, Richard B. *Echoes of Scripture in the Gospels* (Waco, TX: Baylor University Press, 2016).

Echoes of Scripture in the Letters of Paul (New Haven, CT: Yale University Press, 1989).

Hazony, Yoram. *The Philosophy of Hebrew Scripture* (New York: Cambridge University Press, 2012).

Healey, Richard. *The Quantum Revolution in Philosophy* (New York: Oxford University Press, 2017).

Hebert, Arthur G. "'Faithfulness' and 'Faith,'" *Reformed Theological Review* 14, no. 2 (June 1955): 33–40.

Heil, John Paul. "Reader-Response and the Narrative Context of the Parables about Growing Seed in Mark 4:1–34," *Catholic Biblical Quarterly* 54, no. 2 (1992): 271–86.

Heim, Erin M. *Adoption in Galatians and Romans: Contemporary Metaphor Theories and the Pauline Huiothesia Metaphors* (Biblical Interpretation Series 153; Leiden: Brill, 2017).

Helm, Paul. "John Calvin, the *Sensus Divinitatis*, and the Noetic Effects of Sin," *International Journal for Philosophy of Religion* 43 (1998): 87–107.

Review of *Warranted Christian Belief* by Alvin Plantinga, *Mind* New Series 110, no. 440 (October 2001): 1110–15.

Hempel, Carl Gustav. "Studies in the Logic of Confirmation (I)," *Mind* 54 (1945): 1–26.

Hendel, Ronald. "*Leitwort* Style and Literary Structure in the J Primeval Narrative," in *Sacred History, Sacred Literature: Essays on Ancient Israel, the Bible, and Religion in Honor of R. E. Friedman on His Sixtieth Birthday*, ed. Shawna Dolansky (Winona Lake, IN: Eisenbrauns/PennState Press, 2008), 93–110.

Hesse, Mary. *Revolutions and Reconstructions in the Philosophy of Science* (Brighton: The Harvester Press, 1980).

The Structure of Scientific Inference (London: Macmillan Press, 1974).

Hill, David. *New Testament Prophecy* (Marshalls Theological Library; London: Marshall, Morgan & Scott, 1979).

Hoffmeier, James K. "Some Thoughts on Genesis 1 & 2 and Egyptian Cosmology," *Journal of the Ancient Near Eastern Society* 15 (1983): 39–49.

Holland, Tom. *Dominion: How the Christian Revolution Remade the World* (New York: Basic Books, 2019).

Hollander, John. *The Figure of Echo: A Mode of Allusion in Milton and After* (Berkeley: University of California Press, 1981).

Holyoak, John H. et al. "Learning Inferential Rules," in *Naturalizing Epistemology*, 2nd ed., ed. Hilary Kornblith (Cambridge, MA: MIT Press, 1994), 359–92.

Hughes, J. Donald. "Dream Interpretation in Ancient Civilizations," *Dreaming* 10, no. 1 (2000): 7–18.

Hull, John M. *Hellenistic Magic and the Synoptic Tradition* (Studies in Biblical Theology 28; London: SCM Press, 1974).

Hume, David. *An Enquiry Concerning Human Understanding, and Other Writings*, ed. Stephen Buckle (Cambridge Texts in the History of Philosophy; Cambridge: Cambridge University Press, 2007).

Huttunen, Niko. *Paul and Epictetus on Law: A Comparison* (Library of New Testaments Studies 405; New York: T&T Clark, 2009).

Inglis-Arkell, Esther. "Why Don't Electrons Just Fall into the Nucleus of an Atom?" *io9/Gizmodo* (Blog), http://io9.gizmodo.com/why-dont-electrons-just-fall-into-the-nucleus-of-an-ato-1597851164.

Iverson, Kelley R. *Gentiles in the Gospel of Mark: "Even the Dogs under the Table Eat the Children's Crumbs"* (Library of New Testaments Studies 339; London: T&T Clark, 2007).

Jackson, Bernard S. *Wisdom-Laws: A Study of the Mishpatim of Exodus 21:1–22:16* (New York: Oxford University Press, 2006).

Jacobs, Struan. "Michael Polanyi and Thomas Kuhn: Priority and Credit," *Tradition & Discovery* 33, no. 2 (2006–7): 25–36.

Jamrozik, Anja et al. "Metaphor: Bridging Embodiment to Abstraction," *Psychonomic Bulletin and Review* 23, no. 4 (2016): 1080–89.

Jaynes, Julian. *The Origin of Consciousness in the Breakdown of the Bicameral Mind* (Toronto: University of Toronto Press, 1976).

Johns, Alger F. *A Short Grammar of Biblical Aramaic*, rev. ed. (Berien Springs, MI: Andrews University Press, 1972).

Johnson, Dru. *Biblical Knowing: A Scriptural Epistemology of Error* (Eugene, OR: Cascade, 2013).

"A Biblical Nota Bene on Philosophical Inquiry," *Philosophia Christi* (Blog), Evangelical Philosophical Society Symposium, www.epsociety.org/library/articles.asp?pid=238.

Epistemology and Biblical Theology: From the Pentateuch to Mark's Gospel (Routledge Interdisciplinary Perspectives in Biblical Criticism 4; New York: Routledge, 2018).

Knowledge by Ritual: A Biblical Prolegomenon to Sacramental Theology (Journal of Theological Interpretation Supplements 13; Winona Lake, IN: Eisenbrauns/PennState Press, 2016).

Review of *The Hebrew Bible and Philosophy of Religion* by Jaco Gericke, *Journal of Analytic Theology* 4 (2016): 428–33.

Scripture's Knowing: A Companion to Biblical Epistemology (Eugene, OR: Cascade, 2015).

Johnson, Mark. *The Body in the Mind: The Bodily Basis of Meaning, Imagination, and Reason* (Chicago: University of Chicago Press, 1987).

Kelber, Werner H. *The Kingdom in Mark: A New Place and a New Time* (Minneapolis: Fortress Press, 1974).

Kern, Phillip H. *Rhetoric and Galatians: Assessing an Approach to Paul's Epistle* (Society for New Testament Studies Monograph Series 101; New York: Cambridge University Press, 2007).

King, Richard. *Indian Philosophy: An Introduction to Hindu and Buddhist Thought* (Washington, DC: Georgetown University Press, 1999).

Kivy, Peter. *Once upon a Time: Essays in the Philosophy of Literature* (New York: Rowman & Littlefield, 2019).

Klawans, Jonathan. *Theology, Josephus, and Understandings of Ancient Judaism* (New York: Oxford University Press, 2012).

Knierim, Rolf. "Science in the Bible," *Word and World* 13, no. 3 (1993): 242–55.

Koch-Westenholz, Ulla. *Mesopotamian Astrology: An Introduction to Babylonian and Assyrian Celestial Divination* (Carsten Niebuhr Institute Publication 19; Copenhagen: Museum Tusculanum Press, 1995).

Kuhn, Thomas S. *The Structures of Scientific Revolution*, 3rd ed. (Chicago: University of Chicago Press, 1962).

Kusch, Martin. *Knowledge by Agreement: The Programme of Communitarian Epistemology* (Oxford: Clarendon Press, 2002).

Kvanvig, Jonathan. *The Intellectual Virtues and the Life of the Mind: On the Place of the Virtues in Epistemology* (Studies in Epistemology and Cognitive Theory; Savage, MD: Rowman & Littlefield, 1992).

Kynes, Will. *An Obituary for "Wisdom Literature": The Birth, Death, and Intertextual Reintegration of a Biblical Corpus* (New York: Oxford University Press, 2019).

Lackey, Jennifer. *Learning from Words: Testimony as a Source of Knowledge* (New York: Oxford University Press, 2008).

Lakoff, George. *Women, Fire, and Dangerous Things: What Categories Reveal about the Mind* (Chicago: University of Chicago Press, 1989).

Lakoff, George and Mark Johnson. *Metaphors We Live By* (Chicago: University of Chicago Press, 1980).

Lamarque, Peter. *The Opacity of Narrative* (New York: Rowman & Littlefield, 2014).

Lambert, David A. *How Repentance Became Biblical: Judaism, Christianity, and the Interpretation of Scripture* (New York: Oxford University Press, 2016).

"Refreshing Philology: James Barr, Supersessionism, and the State of Biblical Words," *Biblical Interpretation* 24, no. 3 (2016): 332–56.

Lang, T. J. *Mystery and the Making of a Christian Historical Consciousness: From Paul to the Second Century* (Beihefte zur Zeitschrift für die neutestamentliche Wissenschaft 219; Boston: De Gruyter, 2015).

Langer, Susanne K. *Philosophy in a New Key: A Study in the Symbolism of Reason, Rite, and Art* (New York: New American Library, 1948).

Legaspi, Michael C. *The Death of Scripture and the Rise of Biblical Studies* (Oxford Studies in Historical Theology; New York: Oxford University Press, 2011).

Lenzi, Alan. *Secrecy and the Gods: Secret Knowledge in Ancient Mesopotamia and Biblical Israel* (State Archives of Assyria Studies XIX; Helsinki: Neo-Assyrian Text Corpus Project, 2008).

Levenson, Jon D. *Resurrection and the Restoration of Israel: The Ultimate Victory of the God of Life* (New Haven, CT: Yale University Press, 2006).

Lewis, C. S. *Surprised by Joy: The Shape of My Early Life* (San Francisco: HarperOne, 2017).

Lichtheim, Miriam. *Ancient Egyptian Literature: The Old and Middle Kingdoms* (Berkeley: University of California Press, 1973).

Lincicum, David. *Paul and the Early Jewish Encounter with Deuteronomy* (Grand Rapids, MI: Baker Academic, 2013).

"Paul's Engagement with Deuteronomy: Snapshots and Signposts," *Currents in Biblical Research* 7, no. 37 (2008): 37–67.

Longenecker, Bruce W. "The Narrative Approach to Paul: An Early Retrospective," *Currents in Biblical Research* 1, no. 1 (October 2002): 88–111.

Lycan, William G. *On Evidence in Philosophy* (New York: Oxford University Press, 2019).

Mac Lane, Saunders. "Mathematical Models: A Sketch for the Philosophy of Mathematics," *The American Mathematical Monthly* 88, no. 7 (1981): 462–72.

MacDonald, Nathan. *Deuteronomy and the Meaning of "Monotheism"* (Forschungen zum Alten Testament 2 Reihe; Tübingen: Mohr Siebeck, 2003).

Machinist, Peter. "The Question of Distinctiveness in Ancient Israel: An Essay," in *Ah Assyria . . .: Studies in Assyrian History and Ancient Near Eastern Historiography Presented to Hayim Tadmor*, ed. Mordechai Cogan and Israel Eph'al (Scripta Hierosolymitana 33; Jerusalem: Magnes Press, 1991), 196–212.

MacIntyre, Alasdair. *Three Rival Versions of Moral Enquiry: Encyclopaedia, Genealogy, and Tradition* (Notre Dame, IN: University of Notre Dame Press, 1991).

Malherbe, Abraham J. *Light from the Gentiles: Hellenistic Philosophy and Early Christianity*, Collected Essays, 1959–2012, Vol. 2 (Leiden: Brill, 2014).

Paul and the Popular Philosophers (Minneapolis: Fortress Press, 1989).

Marcus, Joel. *Mark 1–8* (The Anchor Yale Bible Commentaries 27; London: Yale University Press, 2002).

Mark 8–16 (The Anchor Yale Bible Commentaries 27; London: Yale University Press, 2009).

The Mystery of the Kingdom of God (SBL Dissertation Series 90; Atlanta: Society of Biblical Literature Press, 1986).

The Way of the Lord: Christological Exegesis of the Old Testament in the Gospel of Mark, 1st ed. (Louisville, KY: Westminster John Knox, 1992).

Marsen, Sky. *Narrative Dimensions of Philosophy: A Semiotic Exploration in the Work of Merleau-Ponty, Kierkegaard and Austin* (London: Palgrave Macmillan, 2006).

Martyn, J. Louis. "De-apocalypticizing Paul: An Essay Focused on *Paul and the Stoics* by Troels Engberg-Pedersen," *Journal for the Study of the New Testament* 86 (2002): 61–102.

Galatians: A New Translation with Introduction and Commentary (Anchor Bible Commentary 33a; New York: Doubleday, 1997).

Theological Issues in the Letters of Paul (New York: T&T Clark, 1997).

Mbiti, John S. *African Religions and Philosophy* (London: Heinemann, 1969).

McCurley, Jr., Foster R. "'And after Six Days' (Mark 9:2): A Semitic Literary Device," *Journal of Biblical Literature* 93, no. 1 (1974): 67–81.

McGuinn, Colin. "Philosophy by Any Other Name," *The New York Times* (*The Opinion Pages*), March 4, 2012, https://opinionator.blogs.nytimes.com/2012/03/04/philosophy-by-another-name.

The Problem of Consciousness (Oxford: Blackwell, 1991).

McMyler, Benjamin. "Knowing at Second Hand," *Inquiry* 50, no. 5 (2007): 511–40.

McQuilkin, Robertson and Paul Copan. *An Introduction to Biblical Ethics: Walking in the Way of Wisdom* (Downer's Grove, IL: InterVarsity, 2014).

Meek, Esther L. *Contact with Reality: Michael Polanyi's Realism and Why It Matters* (Eugene, OR: Cascade, 2017).

Longing to Know: The Philosophy of Knowledge for Ordinary People (Grand Rapids, MI: Brazos Press, 2003).

"'Recalled to Life': Contact with Reality," *Tradition and Discovery* 26, no. 3 (1999–2000): 72–83.

Menken, Maarten J. J. and Steve Moyise, eds. *Deuteronomy in the New Testament* (Library of New Testament Studies 358; London: T&T Clark, 2007).

Isaiah in the New Testament (London: T&T Clark, 2005).

Midgley, Mary. *Evolution as a Religion: Strange Hopes and Strange Fears*, revised ed. (New York: Routledge, 2002).

Moberly, R. W. L. "Did the Serpent Get It Right?," *Journal of Theological Studies* 39, no. 1 (April 1988): 1–27.

Moleski, Martin X. and William Taussig Scott. *Michael Polanyi: Scientist and Philosopher* (New York: Oxford University Press, 2005).

Moseley, Anne M. and M. C. Yap. "Interrater Reliability of the TEMPA for the Measurement of Upper Limb Function in Adults with Traumatic Brain Injury," *The Journal of Head Trauma Rehabilitation* 18, no. 6 (2003): 526–31.

Moser, Paul K. *The Elusive God: Reorienting Religious Epistemology* (New York: Cambridge University Press, 2008).

Müller-Wille, Staffan and Isabelle Charmantier. "Lists as Research Technologies," *Isis* 103, no. 4 (2012): 743–52.

Nagel, Thomas. "What Is It Like to Be a Bat?" in *The Mind's I: Fantasies and Reflections on Self and Soul*, ed. Douglas R. Hofstadter and Daniel C. Dennett (Toronto: Bantam Books, 1982), 391–402.

Neusner, Jacob. "The Mishnah's Generative Mode of Thought: *Listenwissenschaft* and Analogical Contrastive Reasoning," *Journal of the American Oriental Society* 110, no. 2 (1990): 317–21.

Nevader, Madhavi. "At the End Returning to Questions of Beginnings: A Response to Jonathan Burnside," *Political Theology* 14, no. 5 (2013): 619–27.

Nietzsche, Friedrich. *The Birth of Tragedy and Other Writings*, ed. Raymond Geuss and Ronald Speirs, trans. Ronald Speirs (Cambridge Texts in the History of Philosophy; New York: Cambridge University Press, 1999).

Novak, David. *Athens and Jerusalem: God, Humans, and Nature* (The Gifford Lectures 2017; Toronto: University of Toronto Press, 1992).

Jewish Social Ethics (New York: Oxford University Press, 1992).

O'Dowd, Ryan P. *Proverbs* (The Story of God Bible Commentary; Grand Rapids, MI: Zondervan, 2017).

The Wisdom of Torah: Epistemology in Deuteronomy and the Wisdom in Literature (Forschungen zur Religion und Literatur des Alten und Neuen Testaments Band 225; Göttingen: Vandenhoeck & Ruprecht, 2009).

Ohaneson, Heather C. "Turning from the Perfection of God to the Wondrousness of God: Redirecting Philosophical-Theological Attention in Order to Preserve Humility," in *The Question of God's Perfection: Jewish and Christian Essays on the God of the Bible and Talmud*, ed. Yoram Hazony and Dru Johnson (Philosophy of Religion – World Religions 8; Leiden: Brill, 2018), 211–30.

Parsons, Charles. "Platonism and Mathematical Intuition in Kurt Gödel's Thought," *The Bulletin of Symbolic Logic* 1, no. 1 (1995): 44–74.

Parsons, Mikael C. and Michael Wade Martin. *Ancient Rhetoric and the New Testament: The Influence of Elementary Greek Composition* (Waco, TX: Baylor University Press, 2018).

Pedersen, Johannes. *Israel, Its Life and Culture*, 2 vols. (Oxford: Geoffrey Cumberlege, 1959).

Pennington, Jonathan T. *The Sermon on the Mount and Human Flourishing: A Theological Commentary* (Grand Rapids, MI: Baker Academic, 2017).

Plantinga, Alvin. *Warranted Christian Belief* (New York: Oxford University Press, 2000).

Polanyi, Michael. *Personal Knowledge: Towards a Post-Critical Philosophy* (Chicago: University of Chicago Press, 1962).

Provan, Iain. *The Reformation and the Right Reading of Scripture* (Waco, TX: Baylor University Press, 2017).

Quine, W. V. O. "Epistemology Naturalized," in *Naturalizing Epistemology*, 2nd ed., ed. Hilary Kornblith (Cambridge, MA: MIT Press, 1997), 15–32.

"Natural Kinds," in *Ontological Relativity and Other Essays* (New York: Columbia University Press, 1969), 114–38.

Ricoeur, Paul. *Time and Narrative*, Vol. 1. 3 vols., trans. Kathleen McLaughlin (Chicago: University of Chicago Press, 1984).

Rochberg, Francesca. "A Critique of the Cognitive-Historical Thesis of the Intellectual Adventure," in *The Adventure of the Human Intellect: Self, Society, and the Divine in Ancient World Cultures*, ed. Kurt A. Raaflaub (Ancient World: Comparative Histories; Hoboken, NJ: Wiley-Blackwell, 2016), 16–28.

The Heavenly Writing: Divination, Horoscopy, and Astronomy in Mesopotamian Culture (New York: Cambridge University Press, 2004).

"'If P, Then Q': Form and Reasoning in Babylonian Divination," in *Divination and Interpretation of Signs in the Ancient World*, ed. Amar Annus (Oriental Institute Seminar 6; Chicago: University of Chicago Press, 2010), 19–28.

Rowe, C. Kavin. *One True Life: The Stoics and Early Christians as Rival Traditions* (New Haven, CT: Yale University Press, 2016).

Rowland, Wade. *Galileo's Mistake: A New Look at the Epic Confrontation between Galileo and the Church* (New York: Arcade, 2003).

Russell, Bertrand. *History of Western Philosophy* (New York: Routledge, 1996).

Rutledge, David, host. "Thinking the Country," *The Philosopher's Zone*, July 7, 2019, www.abc.net.au/radionational/programs/philosopherszone/thinking-the-country/11278558.

"Three Things You Should Know about Time," *The Philosopher's Zone*, August 27, 2017, www.abc.net.au/radionational/programs/philosophers zone/the-three-things-you-should-know-about-time/8817626.

Schaefer, David Lewis, ed. "Symposium on Yoram Hazony's *The Philosophy of Hebrew Scripture*," *Perspectives on Political Science* 45, no. 3 (2016): 173–207.

Scholer, David M., ed. *The Works of Philo: Compete and Unabridged*, new updated ed., trans. C. D. Yonge (Peabody, MA: Hendrickson, 1997).

Schweitzer, Albert. *The Mysticism of Paul the Apostle*, trans. William Montgomery (Baltimore: John Hopkins University Press, 1998).

Schwitzgebel, Eric. "What Philosophical Work Could Be," *The Splintered Mind* (Blog), June 11, 2015, http://schwitzsplinters.blogspot.co.uk/2015/06/what-philosophical-work-could-be.html.

Scott, Ian W. *Paul's Way of Knowing: Story, Experience, and the Spirit* (Grand Rapids, MI: Baker Academic, 2009).

Shea, William R. and Mariano Artigas. *Galileo in Rome: The Rise and Fall of a Troublesome Genius* (New York: Oxford University Press, 2003).

Shetter, Tony L. "Genesis 1–2 in Light of Ancient Egyptian Creation Myths," April 22, 2005, https://bible.org/article/genesis-1-2-light-ancient-egyptian-creation-myths.

"The Implications of Egyptian Cosmology for the Genesis Creation Accounts" (PhD diss., Asbury Theological Seminary, 2005).

Smith, Barbara Herrnstein. *Poetic Closure* (Chicago: University of Chicago Press, 1971).

Smith, Eric. "The Sumerian Mythographic Tradition and Its Implications for Genesis 1–11" (PhD diss., University of Bristol, 2012).

Sommer, Benjamin D. *Revelation and Authority: Sinai in Jewish Scripture and Tradition* (New Haven, CT: Yale University Press, 2015).

Spencer, Aída Bensançon. *Paul's Literary Style: A Stylistic and Historical Comparison of II Corinthians 11:16–12:13, Romans 8:9–39, and Philippians 3:2–4:13* (New York: University Press of America, 1998).

Stegner, William Richard. "The Use of Scripture in Two Narratives of Early Jewish Christianity (Matthew 4.1–11; Mark 9.2–8)," in *Early Christian Interpretation of the Scriptures of Israel*, ed. Craig A. Evans and James A. Sanders (Sheffield: Sheffield University Press, 1997), 98–120.

Steup, Matthias and Ram Neta. "Epistemology," in *The Stanford Encyclopedia of Philosophy*, Summer 2010 ed., ed. Edward N. Zalta, https://plato.stanford .edu/archives/sum2020/entries/epistemology.

Stich, Stephen P. "Could Man Be an Irrational Animal? Some Notes on the Epistemology of Rationality," in *Naturalizing Epistemology*, 2nd ed., ed. Hilary Kornblith (Cambridge, MA: MIT Press, 1994), 337–58.

Strawn, Brent A. *The Old Testament Is Dying: A Diagnosis and Recommended Treatment* (Theological Explorations for the Church Catholic; Grand Rapids, MI: Baker Academic, 2017).

Stump, Eleonore. "The Problem of Evil: Analytic Philosophy and Narrative," in *Analytic Theology: New Essays in the Philosophy of Theology*, ed. Oliver D. Crisp and Michael C. Rea (New York: Oxford University Press, 2009), 251–64.

Wandering in Darkness: Narrative and the Problem of Suffering (New York: Oxford University Press, 2010).

Tall, David. *How Humans Learn to Think Mathematically: Exploring the Three Worlds of Mathematics* (New York: Cambridge University Press, 2013).

Thompson, James W. *Apostle of Persuasion: Theology and Rhetoric in the Pauline Letters* (Grand Rapids, MI: Baker Academic, 2020).

Thurston, William P. "On Proof and Progress in Mathematics," *Bulletin of the American Mathematical Society* 30, no. 2 (April 1994): 161–77.

Tolmie, Donald Francois. "A Rhetorical Analysis of the Letter to the Galatians" (PhD diss., University of the Free State Bloemfontein, 2004).

Tor, Shaul. *Mortal and Divine in Early Greek Epistemology: A Study of Hesiod, Xenophanes, and Parmenides* (Cambridge Classical Studies; New York: Cambridge University Press, 2017).

Torrance, Thomas F. "One Aspect of the Biblical Conception of Faith," *Expository Times* 68, no. 4 (1957): 111–14.

Tresmontant, Claude. *A Study of Hebrew Thought*, trans. Michael Francis Gibson (New York: Desclee, 1960).

Unterman, Jeremiah. *Justice for All: How the Jewish Bible Revolutionized Ethics* (Philadelphia: Jewish Publication Society, 2017).

Van De Mieroop, Marc. *Philosophy before the Greeks: The Pursuit of Truth in Ancient Babylonia* (Princeton, NJ: Princeton University Press, 2017).

Van der Heiden, Gert Jan et al., eds. *Saint Paul and Philosophy: The Consonance of Ancient and Modern Thought* (Berlin: De Gruyter, 2017).

Van der Kooi, Cornelis. "The Assurance of Faith: A Theme in Reformed Dogmatics in Light of Alvin Plantinga's Epistemology," *Neue Zeitschrift für systematische Theologie und Religionsphilosophie* 40, no. 1 (1998): 91–106.

Van Norden, Bryan W. *Taking Back Philosophy: A Multicultural Manifesto* (New York: Columbia University Press, 2017).

Veldhuis, Niek. "The Theory of Knowledge and the Practice of Celestial Divination," in *Divination and Interpretation of Signs in the Ancient World*, ed. Amar Annus (Oriental Institute Seminars 6; Chicago: University of Chicago Press, 2010), 77–91.

Vervenne, Mark. "The Phraseology of 'Knowing YHWH' in the Hebrew Bible: A Preliminary Study of Its Syntax and Function," in *Studies in the Book of Isaiah: Festschrift Willem A.M. Beuken*, ed. Jacques van Ruiten and Mark Vervenne (BEThL 132; Leuven: Uitgeverij Peeters, 1997).

Voegelin, Eric. *Order and History: Israel and Revelation*, ed. Maurice P. Hogan (The Collected Works of Eric Voegelin; Columbia, MO: University of Missouri Press, 2001).

Von Rad, Gerhard. *Wisdom in Israel*, trans. James D. Martin (Nashville, TN: Abington Press, 1986).

Voss, James F. et al. "On the Use of Narrative as Argument," in *Narrative Comprehension, Causality, and Coherence: Essays in Honor of Tom Trabasso*, ed. Susan R. Goldman et al. (New York: Routledge, 1999), 235–52.

Warren, James. "Hellenistic Philosophy: Places, Institutions, Character," in *The Routledge Companion to Ancient Philosophy*, ed. James Warren and Frisbee Sheffield (New York: Routledge, 2014), 393–98.

"Introduction," in *The Routledge Companion to Ancient Philosophy*, ed. James Warren and Frisbee Sheffield (New York: Routledge, 2014), xxvii–xxx.

"The World of Early Greek Philosophy," in *The Routledge Companion to Ancient Philosophy*, ed. James Warren and Frisbee Sheffield (New York: Routledge, 2014), 3–17.

Weinberg, Justin. "What Kinds of Things Count as Philosophy?" *Daily Nous* (Blog), June 11, 2015, http://dailynous.com/2015/06/11/what-kinds-of-things-count-as-philosophy.

Weiss, Shira. *Ethical Ambiguity in the Hebrew Bible: Philosophical Analysis of Scriptural Narrative* (New York: Cambridge University Press, 2018).

Wells, Bruce. *The Law of Testimony in the Pentateuchal Codes* (Wiesbaden: Harrassowitz Verlag, 2004).

Wells, Kyle B. *Grace and Agency in Paul and Second Temple Judaism: Interpreting the Transformation of the Heart* (Novum Testamentum Supplements 157; Leiden: Brill, 2014).

Wenham, Gordon J. *Story as Torah: Reading Old Testament Narrative Ethically* (Grand Rapids, MI: Baker Academic, 2000).

Westphal, Merold. "Taking Plantinga Seriously: Advice to Christian Philosophers," *Faith and Philosophy* 16, no. 2 (1999): 173–81.

"Taking St Paul Seriously: Sin as an Epistemological Category," in *Christian Philosophy*, ed. Thomas P. Flint (Notre Dame: University of Notre Dame Press, 1990), 200–26.

Whitehead, Alfred North. *Process and Reality* (New York: The Free Press, 1978).
Whitehead, Alfred North and Bertrand Russell. *Principia Mathematica*, 2nd ed. 2 vols. (New York: Cambridge University Press, 1963).
Whybray, Roger N. *The Intellectual Tradition in the Old Testament* (Beiheft zur Zeitschrift für die alttestamentliche Wissenschaft 135; Berlin: De Gruyter, 1974).
Winston, David. "Wisdom of Solomon," in *Anchor Bible Dictionary*, Vol. VI, ed. David N. Freedman (New York: Doubleday, 1992), 120–27.
The Wisdom of Solomon: A New Translation with Introduction and Commentary (The Anchor Bible Commentaries 43; Garden City, NY: Doubleday, 1979).
Wolterstorff, Nicolas. *Reason within the Bounds of Religion*, 2nd ed. (Grand Rapids, MI: Eerdmans, 1976).
Wood, William. "Analytic Theology as a Way of Life," *Journal of Analytic Theology* 2 (May 2014): 43–60.
"On the New Analytic Theology, or: The Road Less Traveled," *Journal of the American Academy of Religion* 77, no. 4 (December 2009): 941–60.
Woods, John. *Truth in Fiction: Rethinking Its Logic* (New York: Springer, 2018).
Wright, Christopher J. H. *Old Testament Ethics for the People of God* (Downer's Grove, IL: InterVarsity, 2004).
Wright, N. T. *Jesus and the Victory of God* (Christian Origins and the Question of God 2; Minneapolis: Fortress Press, 1996).
Paul and the Faithfulness of God, 2 vols. (Minneapolis: Fortress Press, 2013).
The Resurrection of the Son of God (Christian Origins and the Question of God 3; Minneapolis: Fortress Press, 2003).
Zagzebski, Linda T. *Epistemic Authority: A Theory of Trust, Authority, and Autonomy in Belief* (New York: Oxford University Press, 2012).
Virtues of the Mind: An Inquiry into the Nature of Virtue and the Ethical Foundations of Knowledge (New York: Cambridge University Press, 1996).

Index

CPSIA information can be obtained
at www.ICGtesting.com
Printed in the USA
LVHW110936180721
693008LV00004B/244